October 4-7, 2017
Rochester, NY, USA

**Association for
Computing Machinery**

Advancing Computing as a Science & Profession

SIGITE'17

Proceedings of the 18th Annual Conference on
Information Technology Education

Sponsored by:

ACM SIGITE

Supported by:

Dell EMC, Oracle Academy, TuringsCraft, Illinois Institute of Technology, Rochester Institute of Technology, & Wentworth Institute of Technology

**Association for
Computing Machinery**

Advancing Computing as a Science & Profession

The Association for Computing Machinery
2 Penn Plaza, Suite 701
New York, New York 10121-0701

ISBN: 978-1-4503-5100-3 (Digital)

ISBN: 978-1-4503-5605-3 (Print)

Additional copies may be ordered prepaid from:

ACM Order Department
PO Box 30777
New York, NY 10087-0777, USA

Phone: 1-800-342-6626 (USA and Canada)
+1-212-626-0500 (Global)
Fax: +1-212-944-1318
E-mail: acmhelp@acm.org
Hours of Operation: 8:30 am – 4:30 pm ET

Printed in the USA

SIGITE 2017 Conference Chair's Welcome

It is with great pleasure that I welcome you to Rochester, NY, site of the 18th Annual Conference on Information Technology Education (SIGITE 2017) and the 6th Annual Conference on Research in Information Technology (RIIT 2017). The Information Sciences and Technologies Department of Rochester Institute of Technology is proud to once again serve as the host for this premier set of conferences. Our Program Chairs, Tom Ayers and Dan Bogaard, have put together a great program, and I thank them for all of their work putting the program together. I also want to thank our Sponsorship Chairs, Bryan Goda and Hollis Greenburg for their work as well. And certainly, a huge thank you to the sponsors themselves.

The BS Information Technology program at RIT, established in 1991, was one of the very first IT programs in the country. Thursday evening you'll be able to have a tour of the facilities—I hope you take advantage of it. Our dinner Thursday evening will also feature a selection of local Rochester foods—you'll get to try red and white hots, the famous Garbage Plate, and many other unique foods. I also hope you have time to visit Rochester while you are here. In addition to the George Eastman Museum, the Strong Museum of Play, and many other special venues, we are home to many craft breweries and close by to New York's wine region. You can sample some of these by taking part in our excursions on Wednesday evening and Saturday afternoon.

The conference will be at the Hyatt Regency in downtown Rochester, not far from the Genesee River and the waterfalls that were responsible for Rochester's early claim to fame as a milling town and its original moniker, "Flour City". Today Rochester is known as the "Flower City" with numerous parks throughout the city featuring many species of flowers, but none as famous as the Highland Park lilacs that are featured every May. In addition to touring the Upper Falls and the parks, you can also visit nearby museums and other dedications commemorating the work of abolitionists and activists such as Frederick Douglas and Susan B. Anthony.

I hope you enjoy the conference and get to know Rochester during your stay. Please, let me know if you have any questions.

Steve Zilora
SIGITE/RIIT 2017 Conference Chair
Rochester Institute of Technology, USA

Program Chairs' Welcome

It is our great pleasure to welcome you to the 18th Annual Conference on Information Technology Education (SIGITE 2017) and the 6th Annual Conference on Research in Information Technology (RIIT 2017). The theme this year is "Enabling the Future", with a focus on the need for preparing Information Technology students for a future that includes defining the Internet of Things (IoT). Rochester is a fitting place for this theme, as it has long been a city that has leveraged the technological innovations of the day. The Erie Canal allowed Rochester millers to ship their flour across the state to Albany (earning it the nickname, "Flour City"), and flexible photographic film allowed George Eastman to grow his Kodak empire. The canal, and the flexible film are enablers, but with the Internet of Things, ubiquitous computing, and smart communities; information technology is the enabler.

This year, 90 reviewers conducted a total of 384 reviews of 94 submissions of papers, panels, posters, lightning talks, and workshops. For RIIT, 6 of 11 papers were accepted for a 54% acceptance rate; for SIGITE, 23 of 58 papers were accepted for a 39% acceptance rate. A great deal of thanks goes to both the reviewers and, of course, the authors for their excellent work. Not surprisingly, both RIIT and SIGITE papers have a preponderance of topics such as IoT, ubiquitous computing, and dealing with interconnectivity. While many of the papers relate to this year's theme, you will also find papers on curriculum development, capstone ideas, and innovative lab and classroom approaches among a variety of other IT education topics.

SIGITE/RIIT 2017 runs from Thursday to Saturday and is preceded by the annual Chairs and Program Directors Meeting, and vendor workshops on Thursday morning. The formal program begins on Thursday at noon. The program offers a combination of papers, and lightning talks on research in progress, and concludes with a dinner reception for networking with colleagues old and new. Friday features additional paper sessions and lightning talks for SIGITE and RIIT, a poster session in the afternoon, and concludes with a reception for Community College educators. Those not attending the community college reception can find dinner at one of the many nearby restaurants. On Saturday morning, the conference continues with additional papers and an author-submitted workshop. The conference concludes Saturday at 11a.m. Rochester, friends, and lots of opportunities to share—all the necessary ingredients for a great experience. We hope to see you at SIGITE/RIIT 2017 where we can not only discuss "Enabling Our Future", but we can also build new alliances for the future. Thank you!

Dan Bogaard
SIGITE/RIIT 2017 Program Co-Chair
Rochester Institute of Technology, Rochester NY, USA

Tom Ayers
SIGITE/RIIT 2017 Program Co-Chair
Broward College, Fort Lauderdale FL, USA

Table of Contents

3B: Panel Session

Session Chair: Russell McMahon *(University of Cincinnati)*

3C: Lightning Talk Session

Session Chair: Rick Homkes *(Purdue University)*

4A: Paper Session

Session Chair: Karen Patten *(University of South Carolina)*

4B: Panel Session

Session Chair: Hollis Greenberg *(Wentworth Institute of Technology)*

4C: Paper Session

Session Chair: Amos Olagunju *(St. Cloud State University)*

Poster Session

SIGITE 2017 Conference

Conference Chair: Stephen Zilora *(Rochester Institute of Technology, USA)*

Program Chairs: Thomas Ayers *(Broward College, USA)*
Daniel Bogaard *(Rochester Institute of Technology, USA)*

Sponsorship Chairs: Bryan Goda *(University of Washington Tacoma, USA)*
Hollis Greenburg *(Wentworth Institute of Technology, USA)*

Reviewers: Shereef Abu Al-Maati *(American University of Kuwait, Kuwait)*
Vangel Ajanovski *(Saints Cyril and Methodius University, Macedonia)*
Zahra Alqubaiti *(Kennesaw State University, USA)*
Frank Appunn *(Northcentral University, USA)*
Victor Arenas *(Broward College, USA)*
William Armitage *(University of South Florida, USA)*
Prateek Basavaraj *(University of Central Florida, USA)*
Angela Berardinelli *(Mercyhurst University, USA)*
Larry Booth *(Clayton State University, USA)*
Reinhardt Botha *(Nelson Mandela Metropolitan University, South Africa)*
Redjem Bouhenguel *(Broward College, USA)*
Yu Cai *(Michigan Technological University, USA)*
Brian Canada *(University of South Carolina Beaufort, USA)*
Ankur Chattopadhyay *(University of Wisconsin Green Bay, USA)*
Sam Chung *(Southern Illinois University, USA)*
Bill Dafnis *(Capella University, USA)*
Joan E. DeBello *(St. John's University, USA)*
Maxime Descos *(Illinois Institute of Technology, USA)*
Ronald Erdei *(University of South Carolina Beaufort, USA)*
Stephanie Etter *(Broward College, USA)*
Pedro Guillermo Feijóo García *(Universidad El Bosque, Columbia)*
Alan Flaten *(Broward College, USA)*
Bryan French *(Rochester Institute of Technology, USA)*
Rob Friedman *(Montclair State University, USA)*
Ilenia Fronza *(Free University of Bolzano, Italy)*
Chunming Gao *(University of Washington Tacoma, USA)*
Sandra Gorka *(Pennsylvania College of Technology, USA)*
Hollis Greenberg *(Wentworth Institute of Technology, USA)*
Meng Han *(Kennesaw State University, USA)*
Eiji Hayashiguchi *(Informatiom Technology Promotion Agency, Japan)*
Richard Helps *(Brigham Young University, USA)*
Larry Hill *(Rochester Institute of Technology, USA)*
Edward Holden *(Rochester Institute of Technology, USA)*
Rick Homkes *(Purdue University, USA)*

SIGITE 2017 Sponsor & Supporters

Sponsor:

Supporters:

A Holistic Capstone Experience: Beyond Technical Ability

Andrew Scott
Math and Computer Science
Western Carolina University
Cullowhee, NC, USA
Telephone 828-227-3950
andrewscott@email.wcu.edu

William Kreahling
Math and Computer Science
Western Carolina University
Cullowhee, NC, USA
Telephone 828-227-3944
wkreahling@email.wcu.edu

Mark Holliday
Math and Computer Science
Western Carolina University
Cullowhee, NC, USA
Telephone 828-227-3941
holliday@email.wcu.edu

Scott Barlowe
Math and Computer Science
Western Carolina University
Cullowhee, NC, USA
Telephone 828-227-3948
sabarlowe@email.wcu.edu

ABSTRACT

This paper presents a two-semester capstone experience successfully employed over three years within a CS department of just four faculty members faced with growing enrollment. This year long capstone experience is a significant overhaul of an earlier capstone implementation that increases the breadth and depth of project topics. This restructuring facilitates a greater emphasis on research, planning, and soft skills that are typically not emphasized in computer science courses, while allowing enrollment growth. Assessment is based on the product and the software development process including research, planning, coding and communication to various audiences in written, visual and verbal forms. This new model more closely aligns the students' capstone experiences with skills necessary for a career in computer science while aligning with student outcomes laid out in our program design.

INTRODUCTION

Our CS program is small with a moderate but growing enrollment and four CS faculty with a 3-3 teaching workload. Despite this, for several years we have run a capstone experience and place great importance on it. Previously, our capstone had one instructor supervising all student projects. The amount of time instructors spent familiarizing themselves with a wide variety of topics, meeting with groups, monitoring progress, and grading the projects of every student team was burdensome. With growing enrollments, instructor workload of our capstone model had become unsustainable.

This experience paper discusses how we have improved the capstone experience for both the students and faculty. The experience greatly enhances the project scope, duration and skills coverage of the capstone, while at the same time reducing the burden for any single instructor, despite a growing student enrollment. We anticipate our experience to be of interest to small to medium institutions considering starting their first capstone course or making amendments to an existing one.

SIGITE'17, October 4-7, 2017, Rochester, NY, USA
©2017 Association for Computing Machinery.
ACM ISBN 978-1-4503-5100-3/17/10...$15.00.
DOI: http://dx.doi.org/10.1145/3125659.3125680

BACKGROUND

The capstone is an important part of CS curricula. In the field of computer science (CS) the ability to work self-sufficiently with peers on the research and development of non-trivial software projects is a sought after skill central to the success of graduates. The ACM/IEEE joint task force on computing curricula has defined the capstone as a significant software engineering task, with a real world basis, that spans a full academic year and goes beyond concept implementation [1]. Although the task force outlines the main features of the capstone well, they do not provide guidance on how the capstone should be structured or delivered. However, there is a significant quantity of academic literature on these topics.

Clear, et al. establishes several principles in the delivery and design of a capstone experience [3]. While valuable, Clear et al. did not prescribe or evaluate a particular capstone model. Capstones can be implemented over one [12] or two [11] semesters. Two semesters facilitate greater depth and skills coverage but increase instructor workload. Within capstones, there are no conventions on team size. This varies from institution to institution, from solo experiences [6] to team based endeavors of around four [12] or more students [2, 17]. With teams come problems such as free-riding and "taking over" [4]. A lack of self-confidence can also impact engagement [10]. Teamwork assessment techniques have emerged to monitor individual contribution in teams [14,18]. In teams, students will commonly divide the work so each student has a narrowed focus on one or two aspects of the implementation. Consequently, a student will exercise some skills to the exclusion of others, narrowing what they learn.

Some capstones have commercial partners [18, 8, 12], others do not [6, 19], and some do both [17]. While our department does, on occasion, work with external clients, primarily our projects are defined by the instructors who perform the role of a client. Our institution's wish to own the intellectual property developed, puts off potential clients. Also, as a small program in a rural institution, finding external clients has proven difficult. When an external client is involved, the commitment to a completed and polished project can easily compete with educational objectives [18].

OUR HOLISTIC CAPSTONE EXPERIENCE

This section outlines the structure of our capstone and then the underpinnings and rationale for the capstone experience.

The Capstone Structure

The capstone structure (summarized in Table 1) has a workflow reflective of iterative agile development practices such as Scrum

[15] that are now common in the software industry. The students pass through this twice, once per semester. In semester one they are expected to produce a basic proof of concept, or develop the underlying framework and knowledge for their eventual product. In semester two they expand their work into a finished project. Our experience is that having two semesters is essential since we previously had a one semester capstone and found it inadequate in skill coverage and depth.

Table 1. Capstone Structure

Week	Project Phase	Sem1	Sem2	Skill focus
prior	Project Assignment & Supervisor Allocation	X		
1,2	Project Proposal Report	X	X	Written communication, Research.
2 -14	Iterative Development • *Research,* • *Plan & Design,* • *Implement & adapt* • *Bi-weekly meetings & progress reports*	X	X	Research, Professional Practices, Written & oral communication, Interpersonal Skills.
12(spring only)	Poster Presentation		X	Research, Written, Oral & Visual communication.
Due 16	Final Presentation	X	X	Research, Written, oral & visual communication.
Due 16	Final Report	X	X	Research, written & Visual Communication.
Due 16	Product Delivery	X	X	Professional practices.

Before semester one, the faculty decide on a list of project descriptions from which students rank their top choices. This is used to divide students into pairs who are assigned a faculty supervisor with relevant expertise to support their project. The pairings are chosen to match ability and maximize collaboration.

In the first two weeks of the pairs are expected to develop a project proposal report of approximately 800 to 1500 words featuring a problem statement, requirements specification, the proposed solution, a plan for testing, and a schedule of completion. Students should back up key decisions with scholarly citations and other investigative research activities. The pairs prioritize feature development using the MoSCoW method [5].

After proposal submission the capstone moves into the iterative development phase. Guided by their schedule of completion, the pairs iteratively: research, design, implement, and test their software product, piece by piece, starting with the most important. Each iteration lasts two weeks and culminates in a 30-40 minute review and planning meeting with the pair's supervisor. Prior to the meeting, the students are expected to outline their progress by submitting a 200 word (minimum) progress report. In the meeting the pairs demonstrate and defend their ideas and progress and adapt plans for the next iteration. This exercises technical, communication, and interpersonal skills. The meetings are graded and the progress, quantity and quality of work are critically reviewed and feedback given.

In the Spring, the students are expected to produce and present a research poster to technical and non-technical peers and faculty members. The poster session, realistically simulates a professional conference. The students are graded both on the quality and oral presentation of their poster.

The end of the semester culminates with a 20 minute project presentation to a technical audience consisting of peers, at least three faculty, and other project stakeholders, such as clients. Each pair is expected to describe the problem they are addressing, the solution they propose, achievements, challenges, test results, and future plans. They also give a live demonstration of the software product they have built. Each presentation is graded on the content of the talk, quality of slides, speaking skill, timing, and demeanor.

In the last week of the semester, the teams submit a compiled program, source code, documentation, and their final report. In assessing the quality of the program, the faculty concentrate on fulfillment of stated goals and plans, quality of the code (i.e. modularization, programming style, efficiency, use of design patterns, appropriate use of programming paradigms), effectiveness of documentation, and the quality of the user experience. The final report documents the project in a reflective capacity. Like the proposal, the final report begins with the problem definition. It provides details of the solution and the underpinning research, rational and problem definition. It also serves to evaluate the project and present test results, problems encountered, deviations from the timeline, and critical reflection. The report is graded based on the quality of writing, accuracy of the information and detail of research presented.

Utilizing Pairs

Our literature search found no evidence of a CS or technology capstone program utilizing pairs. However, we felt that by utilizing pairs we could provide the experience of interdependence while maximizing accountability. With pairs, each student has to be involved in multiple facets of the project and thus cannot narrow their focus and skills to a small subset of the solution domain.

When assigning pairs, care is taken to ensure there is a good match in ability. Because we are a small department we are able to assess characteristics and compatibility of our students with detailed insight. Larger departments might consider software tools help with this [14]. We match students based on technical proficiency, work ethic, personality, and prior interactions with peers. We are mindful that where mismatches occur, serious issues often arise, such as one student taking over, friction, or low self-esteem, which can result in decreased engagement in one or both of the pair [10].

Research Focus

When the capstone became a two semester experience, it was possible for it to be more research oriented than the previous one semester capstone. It is designed to emphasize student ownership of the project and key implementation decisions though informed scholarly research and experimentation. Throughout the experience, students are expected to read scholarly materials and use this to justify key decisions and communicate the results in bi-weekly meetings, formal reports and presentations. For the same reason, the students are also expected to learn, experiment with, and assess different implementation techniques and frameworks. Commonly, we expect teams to employ implementation technologies they are unfamiliar with. Thus, students gain significant practice and confidence in self-guided skill acquisition. Occasionally, with the benefit of hindsight, students realize they could have made better choices. Sometimes students are able to redesign and implement alternate solutions; just as often, students must live with their decisions due to time constraints. The fact that students think about their choices and the ramifications of those choices with regard to their project is a positive outcome.

Soft Skills Development

Our Industrial Advisory Board (IAB), indicated that CS graduates appear to have a distinct weakness in their "soft skills." The IAB felt providing students with a greater opportunity to express their work through written, oral, and visual communication to technical and non-technical audiences would help. For the purposes of our capstone we defined soft skills as communication (oral, written, and visual) along with interpersonal skills. In revising the capstone our goal was to place a greater emphasis on soft skills development. Therefore, the students' soft skills are exercised at every stage of the revised capstone experience.

Written Communication

Written communication is important because in industry, most developers will have to write reports and documentation for a wide range of technical and non-technical stakeholders.

Project Proposal:
- *Proposal report (Technical Audience)*
Iterative Development
- *Bi-weekly Progress Reports (Technical Audience)*
- *Poster Presentation (Non-Technical Audience)*
- *Code Documentation (Technical Audience)'*
Final Report
- *Final Report (Technical Audience)*

Each written deliverable presents unique challenges to the students' ability to communicate in written form. The proposal focuses on the "big picture" centering on problem definition, the identification of solution technologies and planning. The progress reports focus on accountability, defense of decisions, and the development of individual features. The poster exercises the skills of brevity and clarity as students have to condense their project into a single sheet. In producing code documentation, the students must communicate clearly and concisely to other developers. The final report represents the largest, most in-depth document that students produce during the capstone. It is a technically oriented, research focused paper which reflectively documents the project, its design, rationale, and progress.

Visual Communication

Visual communication is an important career focused skill that goes hand in hand with written communication. Visually focused deliverables are required at each project stage.

- *Project Proposal*
- *Wireframes and Storyboards (Technical Audience)*
- *UML and/or ERD Diagrams (Technical Audience)*
- *Iterative Development*
- *The maintenance of existing diagrams*
- *The development of visual elements for the UI*
- *Poster (Non-Technical Audience)*
- *Final Presentation*
- *Development of presentation slides*

As part of the proposal and iterative planning process, students must develop UML diagrams, Entity Relationship diagrams, and storyboards (as appropriate). Use of these visual communications typically evolves over the course of the semester and is a useful way, during progress reports and presentations, to show clearly the system design. In producing storyboards, wireframes, and designing UI elements, the students focus on the usability and attractiveness of their product from a visual and tactile perspective. The poster and presentation slides focus on the ability to use color, font, layout and imagery to articulate ideas succinctly and effectively.

Oral Communication

Oral communication is as important as written and visual communication. For every written assignment there is a corresponding oral communication component.

Planning stage
- *Progress report discussion (Audience: Supervisor/Client)*
Iterative Development
- *Bi-weekly meetings (Audience: Supervisor/Client)*
- *Presentation of poster (Audience: Non-Technical)*
Project Delivery
- *Final presentation (Audience: Technical, Non-Technical)*

Once a pair has submitted their draft proposal, they walk their instructor through the document, defending why they feel the project meets the expectations of a capstone project. During each bi-weekly meeting, students orally summarize their progress and defend their decisions with well-considered and researched rationales. Pairs must also present any work products and research. They must also deliver a code walk-through and/or code demonstration as they would in their profession.

In both the poster presentation and final presentation, students gain practice in presenting their work to a wider audience. In the poster presentation the pairs are required to explain their work and its motivation to a non-technical audience. The final presentation is treated as a professional presentation that one might give in a work environment.

Interpersonal Skills

One benefit of the capstone process that cannot be ignored is the development of interpersonal skills. These skills include: collaboration, learning together, negotiation and compromise (conflict management), and demeanor. Students get to exercise these skills throughout the capstone through the interdependency of a pair and by interaction with their peers, their instructors, stakeholders, and the general public.

Professional Practices

To prepare students for academic or industrial careers in software development, the course is structured so that supervisors can emphasize professional software practices.

Agile Development

The structure of the capstone aligns well with the principles of agile development and in particular Scrum[15]. The bi-weekly meetings and the development that happens in between function very much like a sprint. Planning is done upfront to define the direction, scope and general shape of the solution, but it is not exhaustive. Throughout development, all capstone projects deviate from the initial plans. Therefore, much of the effort put in to produce detailed upfront plans eventually becomes redundant.

Instead, like agile, we favor an evolutionary approach to software development and design. Starting with the most important features, software and its design artifacts are grown organically, with design and function being developed iteratively over a number of two week sprints. Each sprint ends with a bi-weekly meeting in which the progress is reviewed (and graded), plans are adapted and the tasks for the next sprint decided. This has four key benefits. Firstly, it results in a bi-weekly delivery schedule of completed features, i.e continuous delivery [11]. This promotes steady progress throughout the capstone rather than a frantic rush at the end. Secondly, it also allows the development task to scale more responsively to issues that may impact the speed of task completion such as student ability, or overcoming technical hurdles. Thirdly, the review results in a greater level of accountability and feedback during the development process rather than after it. Finally, engagement with this workflow prepares them for a career employing twenty-first century software development practices.

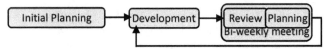

Figure 1 - Development and Bi-Weekly Meetings

Task Prioritization

Before any coding takes place, we believe it is important to focus the students on the skills of estimation and scheduling. For this we require the students to think deeply about the priority of the requirements using techniques such as the MoSCoW method [5]. The initial scheduling is conducted at the end of the planning phase. However, students are expected to adapt their plans throughout the capstone to re-evaluate the scope of the project in light of their productivity and the results of their research.

Version Control

As the pairs develop source code concurrently and often remotely, they are expected to select and utilize version control systems (VCS) such as *Git* and *Subversion* and source code repositories such as *GitHib* and *BitBucket*. Not only does this develop professional skills, a VCS will limit the risks of 'lost work' and the impact of mistakes as changes can be reversed. It also streamlines the review process, as the instructor can quickly assess contribution from the quality and quantity of commits [4].

Documentation

In developing their project, students are expected to exercise skill in producing high quality code that is readable, efficient, and well documented. To aid readability, the pairs are expected to adopt a project wide coding style such as Google Java Style guide [7]. The pairs will produce fully documented code, not as an afterthought, but as the code is written. The pairs will apply code documentation frameworks such as JavaDoc and Doxygen for generating documentation from code comments. Prior to the capstone students will not have maintained such a large code base over a sustained period. In our experience, students start to appreciate good documentation and code style during the second semester of capstone when they start to revisit some of their earlier code.

Testing

Students are expected to approach the implementation phase with a clear plan on testing, as laid out in their proposal. The term testing defines three activities that include acceptance testing, unit testing of code, and end user testing. Although completing all three activities within the time constraints of the course is nearly impossible, that does not preclude the pairs from gaining worthwhile experience in testing activities. Acceptance tests in their fullest extent are, in general, not required. Instead, the prioritized list of requirements is used to assess the extent of completion. The students are also expected to demonstrate competency in constructing unit tests. However, they are not expected to unit test each and every class.

GUIDING TEAMS AND WORKLOAD

Our capstone class is not the typical lecture/homework class; students have a much broader range of freedom. While that is one of the biggest positives of the capstone experience, we feel that mentoring the students plays a crucial role in student success.

At our institution, our students present us with a diverse range of abilities. Just as there are students who are self-motivated and conscientious, there are also students, who without mentoring, lack the skills or motivation they need to succeed in the course. Therefore, we adapt the scope and complexity of the solution domain and/or level of guidance to suit each team. In this section we discuss the matter of team guidance and issue resolution.

Level of Challenge and Advising

Because there is a disparity of ability between teams, we adapt the level of challenge accordingly. To describe how we tailor the capstone experience support to the abilities of each team, we have categorized them into high, mid, and low tiers. Some teams fall in between these categories; therefore we may utilize techniques from multiple categories as necessary.

High Tier Teams

For teams at this level, we give general guidelines, but the teams are responsible for all choices made in the research, design, and implementation of their project; they are expected to explain and defend their ideas in the bi-weekly meetings. These teams tend to be self-sufficient and need little guidance in most aspects of the capstone experience. Our general approach to supervising high-tier students is as follows:

- *Introduce technological themes or professional sources of information such as books, conference proceedings or journals.*
- *Few to no suggestions on implementation techniques or technologies,*
- *Challenge assumptions and decisions more rigorously than mid or low tier students to promote critical thinking and communication skills.*
- *Final reports target journals or conferences.*

Mid Tier Teams

Students of this level are competent with a good level of self-sufficiently. They are capable of producing work to a high standard, but often need external motivation and support to reach their potential. Our general approach to supervising mid-tier students is as follows:

- *Suggest technologies and concepts to investigate*
- *Provide help in making choices, but let students live with the consequences of the choice they make.*
- *Offer more hands on motivation to ensure the quality and quantity of work is maintained throughout the capstone.*
- *Monitor the quantity and quality of the work by more frequent student-led code reviews and demonstrations*
- *Taking corrective action by adjusting goals or making shorter term objectives to keep the team on track. For example, teams may be expected to learn a new technique to demonstrate understanding or its utilization at the next meeting.*

Low Tier Teams

Students of this level are generally competent but lack motivation. They are capable of producing good work, but need more guidance and support than mid-tier students to achieve a successful outcome. Our general approach to supervising low-tier students is as follows:

- *Limit the scope of their design and implementation choices so they are not overwhelmed.*
- *Give help making choices and overrule poor decisions.*
- *Provide specific instruction on solution techniques and tools.*
- *Develop more clearly defined and structured goals that are not as open ended as mid and high tier teams.*
- *Use frequent benchmarks to identify delays and stumbling blocks, monitor motivation, and maintain steady progress.*

Workload Impact

In restructuring the course and sharing the supervisory duties, the faculty has noticed a significant improvement in the number of instructional hours required to support the capstone experience. Typically, each of our four CS faculty members takes between two to four teams each per semester. Each instructor banks partial credit for each team supervised, eventually gaining enough for a course release. The new model has increased the capacity of our capstone without negatively impacting other aspects of the CS program. Table two breaks down the instructional hours required to supervise and grade a two person team over a 15 week semester.

Table 2. Instructional Hours (hrs) Per Team

	Attend time (aprox)	Grade time (aprox)
Bi-weekly meetings	8 x 45 min = 6 hrs	10 min
Poster presentation	15 min	10 min
End of semester presentation	25 min	10min
Proposal report		1 hrs
Final report & deliverables		2 hrs
Support of the capstone expr	3 hrs	
Hours per semester	13.10 hrs per team (52:40 for four)	
Hours per week	0:52 hrs per team (3:31 for four)	

Addressing Teamwork Problems

A common problem is lack of communication between the students in a pair. By encouraging regular and well documented communication, this issue is often alleviated. This is where collaboration tools, such as Trello [16], can help. Personality conflicts can be a tricky problem to solve. During the two years we have been teaching capstone with this model, there have been times when the tension within pairs got to a point that it was negatively affecting the work and grade of one or both students. On more than one occasion, collaboration between team members has suffered for a variety of issues, for example: self-esteem issues,

one student taking over, one student not fulfilling their responsibilities, or differences in ability surfacing during the capstone. In extreme cases, the quality of a student's work was so poor that it is unusable. In these cases, the instructor can reduce the co-dependent impact on grading by assigning specific responsibilities to each student of the pair. However, there are times when student work is too tightly coupled to separate effectively. In such cases, a last resort has been to split the students and make them work alone, essentially doubling the instructor's workload for that pair.

FEEDBACK FROM STUDENTS

A small, nine statement open response questionnaire was developed for students who had completed the new capstone and had graduated. To gain the feedback, the questionnaire was emailed to all graduates for whom we had or could obtain contact information. In all, the questionnaire was emailed to 76% of the alumni who had taken the new capstone. Responses were gained from 38% of the total enrollment. All the respondents are working in the field of computing.

In reviewing the students' feedback, we conducted a process of thematic analysis [9]. We noticed several recurring themes in the responses we obtained, which we categorized under three headings: Gaining Employment, Development and Technical Skills, and Soft Skills. These are discussed below and illustrated with quotes from students.

Gaining Employment

One of the most apparent themes in the responses, mentioned by all but one alumni, was the positive benefits the capstone had in seeking employment, particularly in the job interview process

"Mostly it [capstone] impressed upon me the importance of a development methodology; and how poor communication can lead to unnecessary pitfalls and rework." [Respondent H]

A number of respondents also remarked on how the presentation and communication skills they practiced during the capstone helped during the interview process.

"I feel like the presentation part of the capstone greatly helped me in landing my job and was a skill I had to use straight away." [Respondent G]

One of the respondents indicated that the capstone was not helpful in interviews. This graduate became an embedded software engineer, but his capstone project was a web app. However, the alumnus later acknowledged benefits once employed.

Development Skills

A theme appearing in the vast majority of the alumni's feedback was a general belief that the capstone was beneficial to their career readiness or skills.

"The process, from start to finish, is the closest thing to industry that you can get within an academic setting." [Respondent I]

Others commented on the software development life cycle and agile methodologies they practiced during the capstone as giving them a useful insight into the development process.

"While my career does not directly involve the software development process, the general idea of planning, implementing, and supporting any type of project or process has proved beneficial. If anything, this process works well because it teaches time management, problem-solving, and customer support." [Respondent D]

However, the most commented-on aspect of development skills by respondents was the concept of learning to learn. Many responses remarked on the fact that during capstone they had to "figure things out on their own".

"The capstone overall gave me the confidence in learning new languages and frameworks by myself... without the fear of 'I won't be able to figure it out'." [Respondent C]

There were a number of students who felt the capstone course could be improved in regards to development skills. Some respondents felt the coverage of testing was not sufficient. Several felt that we did not go far enough in our coverage of agile methodologies.

"I think that focusing more on the agile process would be VERY beneficial because, in my eyes, the content of your capstone project is much less important to employers, than your experience and the time it takes you to get up to speed with their procedures." [Respondent L]

Soft Skills

It was quite heartening to see that almost all the respondents appreciated the benefits they received from having to communicate in written and oral form during their capstone. Most responses indicated the importance of effective communication in the workplace.

"We have to write a proposal for every new project as well as any change to an existing project. The writing process is more important in the CS field than some people may think." [Respondent I]

A number of respondents also noted that they had to communicate with both technical and non-technical audiences and that capstone helped prepare them for that eventuality.

"Being able to articulate yourself is imperative. Many times I have had to deal with non-technical peers, customers, and executives." [Respondent H]

CONCLUSIONS

The focus of this research was to present our two semester holistic capstone experience and show how it has benefits the faculty and students. The course evolved from a technically focused program managed by one faculty member, to one distributed among all departmental faculty. This enabled the program to better cope with a growing enrollment and instructor workload imbalance while greatly broadening the skills focus the capstone encompassed.

Our next step is to work towards a greater emphasis on testing while minimizing the impact on other skills and the development time available. While we use components of agile development at all stages of the capstone and a Scrum influenced methodology during the development, in line with our feedback we want to do more. We plan to further integrate agile methodologies into the capstone process in order to further familiarize students with the nomenclature and techniques of agile development. However, we do want to acknowledge other development methodologies and

will aim to contrast agile techniques with alternatives, even if only in discussion.

We believe our feedback demonstrates the effectiveness of the changes made to the capstone model. The broadened focus of our amended capstone to include research lead planning, iterative development, and soft skills is benefiting our graduates significantly. Furthermore, despite growing enrollments, the amended capstone has balanced the teaching load, for which the benefits are many. We believe the approach is repeatable, and hope others find our experience beneficial.

REFERENCES

[1] ACM/IEEE-CS Joint Task Force on Computing Curricula. 2015. Curricula 2013. ACM Press and IEEE Computer Society Press, New York, NY, USA.

[2] L. Alperowitz, D. Dzvonyar, B. Bruegge, 2016, Metrics in Agile Project Courses, In proc of of the 38th International Conference on Software Engineering Companion, Austin TX, USA, ACM, New York – NY, USA, pp. 323-326.

[3] T. Clear, M. Goldweber, F. Young, P. Ledig, K. Scott, 2001, Resources for Instructors of Capstone Courses in Computing, ACM SIGCSE Bulletin, Volume 33, Issue 4, ACM, New York – NY, USA, pp. 93-113.

[4] Chamilard and K Braun, 2002, The Software Engineering Capstone: Structure and Tradeoffs, In proc of the 33rd SIGCSE Technical Symposium on Computer Science Education, ACM Press, New York - NY, USA, PP 227-231.

[5] S. Hatton, 2007m, Early Prioritization of Goals, In proc of the 2007 Conference on Advances in Conceptual Modelling: Foundations and Applications, Springer-Verlag, Berlin, pp. 235-224.

[6] A. Fedoruk, M. Gong, M. McCarthy, 2014, Student Initiated Capstone Projects, In proc of the 15th Annual Conference on Information technology education, ACM Press, New York – NY, USA, pp. 65-70.

[7] Google Inc, 2009,Google Java Style Guide, <Online: Accessed 3/4/2017> https://google.github.io/styleguide/javaguide.html

[8] A. Goold , 2003 Providing Process for Projects in Capstone Courses, In proc of the 8th annual conference on Innovation and technology in computer science education: Volume 35 Issue 3, ACM Press, New Work – NY, USA, pp. 26-29.

[9] G. Guest, Greg, (2012, Applied thematic analysis, Sage Publications, Thousand Oaks – CA, USA, ISBN: 1412971675

[10] D. Hall and S. Buzwell, 2012, "The Problem of Free-Riding in Group Projects: Looking Beyond Social Loafing As Reason for Non-Contribution," Journal of Active Learning in Higher Education, vol. 14, no. 1, pp. 37-49.

[11] C. Lianping, 2015, Continuous Delivery: Huge Benefits but Challenges Too, IEEE Software, Volume 32, Issue 2, IEEE Press, New York – NY, USA, pp. 50-54.

[12] S. Mohan, S. Chenowth and S. Bhohner, 2012, Towards a Better Capstone Experience, in proc of the 43rd ACM technical symposium on Computer Science Education, ACM Press, New York – NY, USA, pp. 111-116.

[13] A. Neyem, J. I. Benedetto and A. F. Chacon, 2014, Improving Software Engineering Education through an Empirical Approach: Lessons Learned from Capstone Teaching Experiences, Proceedings of the 45th ACM technical symposium on Computer science education, ACM Press, New York – NY, USA, pp. 391-396.

[14] M. Ohland, D. Giurintano, B. Novoselich, P. Brackin and S. Sangelkar, 2015, "Supporting Capstone Teams: Lessons from Research on Motivation," International Journal of Engineering Education, vol. 31, no. 6, pp. 1748-1759

[15] K Rubin, 2013, Essential Scrum, Addison Wesley, Upper Saddle River, NJ, ISBN: 0-23-704329-5

[16] J. Spolsky ad M. Pryor, 2011, Trello, Trello Inc, New York - NY, USA <Online accessed 8/4/2016> https://trello.com

[17] D. Wilkins and P Lawhead, 2000, Evaluating Individuals in Team Projects, Proceedings of the thirty-first SIGCSE technical symposium on Computer science education, ACM New York, NY, USA, pp. 172-175.

[18] J. Williams, B. Blair, J. Börstler, T.Lethbridge and K Surendran, 2003, Client Sponsored Projects in Software Engineering Courses, ACM SIGCSE Bulletin, Volume 35, Issue 1, ACM, New York, pp. 401-402.3

[19] S. Zilora, 2015, Industry Emulated Projects in the Classroom, In proc of the 16th Annual Conference on Information Technology Education, ACM Press, New York – NY, USA, pp. 115-119

Engaged IT Experience Course to Enable the Future Workforce

Rajesh Prasad
Saint Anselm College
Manchester, NH 03102
rprasad@anselm.edu

Carol Traynor
Saint Anselm College
Manchester, NH 03102
ctraynor@anselm.edu

Adam Albina
Saint Anselm College
Manchester, NH 03102
aalbina@anselm.edu

ABSTRACT

Computer Science (CS) and Information Technology (IT) education needs to find new ways to boost students' interest in selecting and completing undergraduate degrees in these disciplines. In addition to retaining them in the major, we need to equip them with the right skills and knowledge so they are workforce ready when they graduate. In this paper, the authors present a novel learning model in IT, *The IT Experience Course*. Through a unique partnership with the IT department, the course leverages both traditional classroom teaching methodology and internships to form a new style of engaged learning. Engaged learning allows students to participate in real-life activities through collaboration, exploration, and discovery with peers. The course has three components, learning, shadowing/training, and a real world IT experiential project. The three components give the students a better understanding of the diversity of the field of IT, an insight into different career paths, and the confidence to see themselves working in the field through mentorship. *The IT Experience Course*, can be replicated at institutions across the country since most institutes of higher learning have an IT department, potentially increasing the future IT-capable workforce.

CCS CONCEPTS

Social & Professional Topics → Professional Topics • **Computing Education** → Computing Education Programs → Information Technology Education.

KEYWORDS

Engaged learning; Hybrid teaching; Information Technology; Mentoring and shadowing

SIGITE'17, October 4-7, 2017, Rochester, NY, USA
© 2017 Association for Computing Machinery.
ACM ISBN 978-1-4503-5100-3/17/10...$15.00
https://doi.org/10.1145/3125659.3125694

1 INTRODUCTION AND MOTIVATION

The United States has led the world in scientific and technological advancements. With just five percent of the world's population, the United States employs nearly one-third of the world's scientific and engineering researchers [1]. Vast improvements in computer and information technologies have played a significant role in changing the way people live their lives, and the demand for CS/IT capable workers has increased across all occupational fields. In a knowledge-based economy, innovation and technology contribute significantly to the competitive position United States industries hold in an increasingly global market [1]. Yet, despite this growing need, there is a lack of adequate, well-trained CS/IT-capable workers in the United States [2].

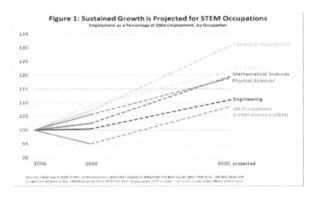

Figure 1: All STEM jobs are projected to grow significantly, with computer occupations growing the most rapidly [4].

Between 2014 and 2024 the US Department of Labor predicts job growth of 18.8% for software and application development positions and 20.9% for computer system analyst positions. The actual job growth in these two sectors alone equates to 253,900 jobs [3]. The growth in jobs for all STEM fields [4] is also evident from Figure 1, and computer skills are increasingly indispensable across STEM fields [5][6]. Moreover, the ubiquitous use of technology has led to a demand for STEM-literate workers even in non-STEM occupations [7].

Research has shown that the intensity of first-year coursework and students' individual performance in that coursework may play an important role in students' decisions to leave STEM fields and switch to other majors. For example, about one-quarter of high-performing students (defined as students with a college GPA of 3.5 or higher) who began pursuing a bachelor's degree between

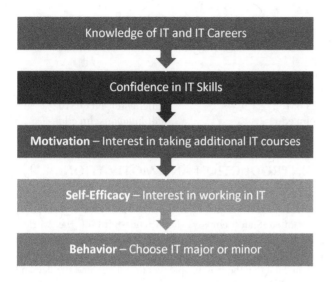

Figure 2: As shown in the logic model above, the authors hope that IT Experience course would improve students' knowledge, confidence, motivation, self-efficacy, and behavior.

2003 and 2009 declared a STEM major [8]. However, nearly one-third of these students had transferred out of STEM fields by spring 2009. Analysis of the regression suggests that intensity of first-year STEM coursework and individual performance in STEM courses may have played an important role in students' decisions to leave STEM fields and switch to other majors [8]. The same study found that low-level performers (defined as students with a college GPA of less than 2.5) who had declared a STEM major were more likely to drop out. The literature shows that students do not consider CS/IT as a potential major because they often do not know what professionals in these areas do [9]. In regard to our own experience of teaching CS/IT courses, informal feedback from students has supported the findings in [8][9].

In most colleges and universities current IT courses employ a more traditional and theoretical model of learning. The learning model is based on traditional classroom teaching methods and/or working in a laboratory. While the curriculum has been effective in producing numerous graduates who are now members of the workforce, this model lacks the engaged learning experience (theory, mentorship and real life practice) to build confidence, keep them motivated and retain them in IT.

The authors hypothesize low recruitment and retention rates in CS/IT are the result of the following factors:
1. lack of understanding of what the CS/IT field entails,
2. lack of understanding of careers in CS/IT, and
3. lack of confidence in their ability to succeed.

In this research the authors have collaborated with the Office of Information Technology at their college to test their hypothesis by creating a hybrid IT course that uses engaged learning. This research work consists of an engaged learning course, henceforth

termed, *The IT Experience Course*, that is neither a traditional classroom course nor an internship, but rather a hybrid that leverages both of these teaching styles to form a new style of engaged learning. Engaged learning is defined as the process in which students actively participate in their learning, are involved in the decision making of their course study, and make discoveries based on their choices. Engaged learning allows students to participate in real-life activities through collaboration, exploration, and discovery with peers [10]. This learning improves understanding, retention of concepts and information, and helps students identify as scientists. Additionally, participation in scientific thinking with peers promotes early identification with the scientific community.

This hybrid IT course is constructed using a building block approach. In the early weeks of the term students spend time in the classroom learning the basic principles of IT, organizational structures, and business support requirements. Next they shadow a mentor from the IT department to learn the implementation of the fundamental principles they learned in class. Finally they work on a real world IT project in an area of IT that interests them.

In a more traditional approach, students are often discouraged by the amount of theoretical knowledge they have to absorb without fully understanding its practical purpose. In contrast, this course gives students an overview of the field of IT and quickly engages them in practical application of that knowledge. Follow on class time introduces new concepts such as IT project management and technology return on investment through a lens which is appropriately colored by practical experience.

Through hands-on learning and working in an actual IT department, students are immersed in the field early on. The practical work that they do is "real" work and contributes to the running of the IT department at the college. This real-world experience may inspire them to see themselves as contributing members of a future workforce, even at this early stage. This real-world experience and shadowing professionals from IT will give the student confidence. Confidence, or self-efficacy, is a requirement for students to persist in a chosen field of study [11]. Learning and professional identification increase confidence, and consequently, motivation, which in turn spurs academic success and the likelihood a student will feel like a scientist, thus creating mutually reinforcing experiences.

The authors hope to meet the following objectives through the course:
1. Increase participants' IT knowledge and experience.
2. Increase participants' knowledge and experience of IT careers.
3. Increase participants' confidence in their own IT abilities.
4. Increase participants' motivation to take additional IT courses.
5. Increase participants' ability to see themselves using IT in their career.

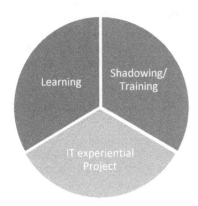

Figure 3: The IT Experience Course.

2 COURSE DESIGN

As a broad field, IT is pervasive in business, nonprofits, and government. The design of *The IT Experience Course* ensures that students gain an understanding and are able to demonstrate practical knowledge in the following topic areas:

1. IT in the enterprise
2. Components of IT: people, process, technology,
3. IT organizational models
4. Computer systems with a focus on desktop computer systems and customer support
5. Networks and network systems in the enterprise
6. Information systems development and maintenance
7. IT project management

Students taking this course are exposed to different areas of IT within an institution of higher education (IHE) and see first-hand each area's role and function. Students gain an understanding of the role of IT in the enterprise and the different aspects of IT as an organization.

The IT Experience course is composed of three components as shown in Figure 3:

1. learning,
2. shadowing/training, and
3. IT experiential project.

We have successfully implemented this course as a pilot study. In the following sections we describe the different components of the course and relate them to our experiences in the pilot study.

2.1 Learning

The introduction to the course is active learning in the classroom where students learn about the concepts, content, and methodology related to IT that has a direct application in the field. The instructor and mentors from the IT department provide classroom instruction. Students are assessed on the classroom-based learning with content knowledge in tests developed by

course instructor and mentors. After a brief lecture on the pertinent topic, students engage in practical application of the topic. The rationale for active learning is that it improves understanding and longer retention of the concepts. This style of learning helps students develop a strong correlation between what they have learned conceptually and its real-world application [12].

2.2 Shadowing/Training

Data suggests that "Computing Identity Mentoring" contributes to students' self-efficacy regarding computing and leadership and solidifies students' commitment to a career in computing [13]. In our research students were assigned to small groups, which had a personal mentor from the IT department who provided training and exposure to different areas within the IT field. Students were able to see how the knowledge they have learned in the classroom is applied in the field. The direct link between classroom learning and practical application helped students envision themselves as productive members of a future workforce, potentially motivating them to continue in the field. The rationale for this component is that it helps foster a highly collaborative and dynamic relationship between the instructor, student, and mentor. It also reduces isolation since students were in small groups while shadowing mentors, encouraging student-to-student interaction. This component included interviews and focus groups between the students and mentor.

2.3 IT Experiential Project

Students gain first-hand experience in working in real-world IT careers. They work on various projects within the IT department as if they were already members of the workforce. They fill out time cards, keep logs, and write weekly reflections about their experience. The project component validates the students' perception of careers in IT and ultimately allow them to see themselves pursuing a career in this field. The rationale for this component is that it fosters a collaborative learning environment where students work together to solve problems as a team. This in turn helps sharpen their individual skill sets, preparing them to become members of the future workforce. Hands-on projects engage the students and they are able to easily relate their classroom experience to real life, which serves to cultivate purposeful problem-solving skills and enhance the process of translating theory into practice.

3 IMPLEMENTATION

A critical component of the pilot study is the integration of the IT department with experiential learning. In our implementation the instructor of the course was a member of the IT department who is also an adjunct faculty member in the CS department but this is not a requirement of the implementation. Certainly, he/she needs to be qualified to teach an IT course. In either case, a unique relationship between the academic department and the IT department needs to already exist or be fostered to create the mentoring/shadowing and implementation components. However, this type of partnership provides advantages and benefits to both parties (CS/IT academic department and IT [non-academic] department). The participating IT department benefits from the real-world work carried out by the students taking the course. These students may even be future support staff or full-time employees at the institution.

A regular semester at our institution is usually 15 to 16 weeks long. The first four weeks of class consisted of regular class meetings, hands-on labs, and reading/video assignments. After 4 weeks of traditional classroom meeting, the next four weeks of class consisted of shadowing and training with mentors in IT. The shadowing component provided students with an overview of a particular IT organization. Students met in small groups with the head of the different IT divisions to get a broad overview about the work being done in that division. This was time consuming as it required the head of the division to present to several groups over a period of time. Student reflections where graded and they had reading assignments during the shadowing rotations. Students rotated through four areas in the IT department and spent one week in each of the following areas:

1. Computer Support and Customer Service,
2. Information Systems,
3. Network Service and Systems Administration, and
4. Instructional Design and Support.

After shadowing for four weeks, students were assigned to one of the four areas listed above for the rest of the semester. Students did indicate a preference but the instructor conducted the assignments based on where he/she felt the student were best suited as well as needed in collaboration with the IT mentors. Students worked on a project in their assigned area. Parameters for each project were different. However, projects were equitable across functional areas in scope and effort.

Students maintained a portfolio with required items for the course. Required items in the portfolios included time cards to be signed by their site instructor/mentor weekly. Students submitted (keeping copies for themselves) all time cards to the instructor for the duration of the course. Failure to secure appropriate signatures or submit time cards resulted in time being ignored. Students also were required to submit weekly reflection journal entries during the rotation as well as during the project phases of the course. Portfolios were turned in and graded at mid-term and end-of-term. The college Learning Management System (LMS) provided the instructor and students a forum for sharing materials and documents, participate in blog/discussion and view their grades.

4 STUDENT PROJECTS

For the experiential project in the pilot study students were split between four areas in IT. A number of students in the pilot course applied for and were accepted to participate in the Customer Service Experience. Students conducted hands-on personal computer preparation for the institution's Computer Replacement Program (CRP). In a supervised environment, students removed hard drives from computers, imaged hard drives, installed specialized software, and delivered computers to staff and faculty. Students moved personal files from old computers to new computers and reviewed with the customer any environmental changes. They also experienced supervised shifts at the Help Desk assisting students, faculty, and staff with standard Help Desk requests. Students gained experience with standard problem solving skills, troubleshooting techniques, and standard enterprise Tier 1, Tier 2, and Tier 3 trouble ticket processing. Students logged and recorded tickets through the enterprise Help Desk software.

Another group of students engaged in research for Instructional Technology, conducting technical writing through the development of faculty training materials for the new version of the Learning Management System. Students translated technical material into user-friendly documentation.

Some of the students actively developed production software for the institution. Projects included developing a set of C++ and ESQL programs to implement a randomization algorithm for assignment of student registration groups and updating the enterprise DBMS with the results of the algorithm. This program is in production at the institution. One student developed a major interface to our digital medical records hosting service using C++ and ESQL to provide demographic information for the interface and automatically SFTP the data to our cloud based medical records partner; this program is also in production. Another student developed a C#.NET application that is part of the telephone billing system integrated into the institution's enterprise portal; this system is in production.

A student conducted a supervised site survey for wireless access coverage on campus and mapped the coverage gaps using specialized software for zone generation and coverage. This student made recommendations for the addition of access points based on the analysis across campus. These recommendations have been implemented and have resulted in a decrease of Help Desk tickets to remedy wireless coverage issues.

The students had to write a self-reflection about their experience during the course. The students' responses were generally positive. Below are several selected quotes from the respondents.

"I also know this code will serve a real purpose compared to the games and exercises I do in class. That gives me lots of motivation to make my codes as simple and efficient as possible. This program will be in use at the college for many years, and it has the potential to make many people's lives easier or harder."

"This week the concept of communication was the largest takeaway."

"I have the opportunity to improve people's lives through the work I do in this project. This is what pushed me to work hard, and gave me a real purpose to my coding that has not existed before."

"The project needs to be easily scalable in the future."

"It is about people, and no matter what my code says, unless it is able to be understood by people my code will ultimately be useless"

"The execution is the most important part by far, but most of the work comes in the planning and revising phases. This echoes the idea that IT isn't just about computers. After this week I feel far more confident going forward."

"I found out that the quickest way of doing things was not necessarily always the best way of doing things. While the way that I was writing the different functions used by this project wasn't always the fastest way to accomplish my goals, I understood that in the long run, it would save future developers time in reusing and understanding what exactly my application was trying to accomplish.""

5 DISCUSSION

The IT Experience course tried to address the following research questions:

1. does the IT Experience program lead to increased understanding of the IT field and careers in IT for students; and
2. how do the three components (learning, shadowing/ training, and IT experiential project) impact students pursuing IT fields of study?

Twelve students participated in the pilot study. The results of the pilot were as follows:

- 100% displayed an increase in knowledge of IT
- 100% completed the course
- 100% remained in the Department of Computer Science
- 100% are working in the CS/IT related field

The Department of Computer Science and the Office of Information Technology at the institution benefit from having a close working relationship among their staff and faculty. Members of the IT department serve as adjunct faculty and are familiar with the students in the CS program. By incorporating the IT department into the learning process, the authors are encouraging a strong workforce development approach by providing students with real-world experience. This approach may help long-term goal of adequately preparing students for careers in IT.

For example, our institution's IT department manages a Residential Networking program (HawkNET) that employs students as technology assistants during the school year. HawkNet assistants provide support in areas such as the residence halls, the Help Desk, labs, and media. This course provided excellent preparation for students to become members of the HawkNet team and qualified them to deal with more complex issues. The institution's IT department benefited from having these skilled students as part of their support workforce for their remaining undergraduate years after taking the course.

6 RESULTS AND CONCLUSIONS

The three components in this engaged IT course: learning, shadowing/training, and IT experiential project are scalable to larger populations and can be modified for application to other courses in different majors. The IT component, while unique to CS/IT, can be replicated at institutions across the country, since most institutes of higher learning have an IT department. Student populations will benefit from this type of course because it gives them real-world experience coupled with curricular rigor. Students have the opportunity to apply curricular concepts in a practical sense throughout the course. Meaningful, hands-on work in a vibrant real-world IT environment allows them to see themselves as contributing members of an IT organization. The students in the pilot course were exposed to different tiers of a centralized IT enterprise. They observed how the customer support model works, learned about network (wired and wireless) administration, enterprise software development and the role of instructional technology. This type of course may give students the confidence to complete their CS/IT degree which ultimately will lead to higher numbers of graduates in the field and thus a larger IT-capable workforce. The authors acknowledge that CS and IT are different academic fields but have significant overlap in the ACM/IEEE curricula guidelines [14]. An enterprise IT organization is a multi-occupational organization spanning several academic disciplines and an excellent vehicle for learning and career exposure. The model is feasible and can be implemented in most colleges. We will continue this study in the next iteration of this course offering at our college. The authors hope that this type of hybrid course will:

1. attract more students to CS/IT majors,
2. increase retention rates and the number of students completing CS/IT undergraduate degrees; and
3. adequately prepare students for careers in IT.

7 ACKNOWLEDGMENTS
The authors would like to thank all the members the IT department at our institution who volunteered to be mentors for this pilot course.

REFERENCES
[1] Freeman, Richard B. 2006. Does globalization of the scientific/engineering workforce threaten US economic leadership? Innovation Policy and the Economy, Volume 6. The MIT Press, 2006. 123-158.
[2] Eric Roberts. 2000. Computing education and the information technology workforce. SIGCSE Bull. 32, 2 (June 2000), 83-90. DOI = http://dx.doi.org/10.1145/355354.355383.
[3] U.S. Department of Labor Statistics. 2016. Employment by Detailed Occupation. Accessed May 2017 from Occupational Employment Statistics: http://www.bls.gov/emp/ep_table_104.htm.
[4] United States Congress Joint Economic Committee. 2012. STEM Education: Preparing for the Jobs of the Future. Accessed May 2017 from http://www.jec.senate.gov/public/_cache/files/6aaa7e1f-9586-47be-82e7-326f47658320/stem-education---preparing-for-the-jobs-of-the-future-.pdf.
[5] Joel C. Adams and Randall J. Pruim. 2012. Computing for STEM majors: enhancing non CS majors' computing skills. In Proceedings of the 43rd ACM technical symposium on Computer Science Education (SIGCSE '12). ACM, New York, NY, USA, 457-462. DOI=http://dx.doi.org/10.1145/2157136.2157270.
[6] Barry Lawson, Doug Szajda, and Lewis Barnett. 2013. Introducing computer science in an integrated science course. In Proceeding of the 44th ACM technical symposium on Computer science education (SIGCSE '13). ACM, New York, NY, USA, 341-346. DOI: http://dx.doi.org/10.1145/2445196.2445298.

[7]   Carnevale, A. P., Smith, N., & Melton, M. 2011. STEM. Accessed May 2017 from Georgetown University Center on Education and the Workforce: https://cew.georgetown.edu/wp-content/uploads/2014/11/stem-complete.pdf.

[8]   Chen, Xianglei.2015. STEM Attrition: College Students' Paths into and out of STEM Fields. Statistical Analysis Report. NCES 2014-001.

[9]   Mary Anne L. Egan and Timoth Lederman. 2011. The impact of IMPACT: assessing students' perceptions after a day of computer exploration. In Proceedings of the 16th annual joint conference on Innovation and technology in computer science education (ITiCSE '11). ACM, New York, NY, USA, 318-322. DOI=http://dx.doi.org/10.1145/1999747.1999836.

[10]   K. Belt, Engaged Learning: Accessed on May 2017 from http://www.members.tripod.com/~ozpk/000.

[11]   Dweck, C. S. (1986). Motivational processes affecting learning. American Psychologist, 41, 1040–1048.

[12]   Bonwell, Charles C.; Eison, James A , 1991. Active Learning: Creating Excitement in the Classroom. ASHE-ERIC Higher Education Reports.(1991)
http://eric.ed.gov/?id=ED336049.

[13]   Kristy Elizabeth Boyer, E. Nathan Thomas, Audrey S. Rorrer, Deonte Cooper, and Mladen A. Vouk. 2010. Increasing technical excellence, leadership and commitment of computing students through identity-based mentoring. In Proceedings of the 41st ACM technical symposium on Computer science education (SIGCSE '10). ACM, New York, NY, USA, 167-171. DOI: http://dx.doi.org/10.1145/1734263.1734320.

[14]   Russell McMahon. 2016. A Comparison between the ACM/IEEE Computer Science Curriculum Guidelines and the Information Technology Curriculum Guidelines. In Proceedings of the 17th Annual Conference on Information Technology Education (SIGITE '16). ACM, New York, NY, USA, 13-13. DOI: http://dx.doi.org/10.1145/2978192.2978206.

Predicting Academic Success Based on Learning Material Usage

Leo Leppänen
University of Helsinki
Helsinki, Finland
leo.leppanen@helsinki.fi

Juho Leinonen
University of Helsinki
Helsinki, Finland
juho.leinonen@helsinki.fi

Petri Ihantola
Tampere University of Technology
Tampere, Finland
petri.ihantola@tut.fi

Arto Hellas
University of Helsinki
Helsinki, Finland
arto.hellas@cs.helsinki.fi

ABSTRACT

In this work, we explore students' usage of online learning material as a predictor of academic success. In the context of an introductory programming course, we recorded the amount of time that each element such as a text paragraph or an image was visible on the students' screen. Then, we applied machine learning methods to study to what extent material usage predicts course outcomes. Our results show that the time spent with each paragraph of the online learning material is a moderate predictor of student success even when corrected for student time-on-task, and that the information can be used to identify at-risk students. The predictive performance of the models is dependent on the quantity of data, and the predictions become more accurate as the course progresses. In a broader context, our results indicate that course material usage can be used to predict academic success, and that such data can be collected *in-situ* with minimal interference to the students' learning process.

KEYWORDS

element-level web logs, web log mining, academic success prediction, online learning materials, educational data mining

ACM Reference Format:
Leo Leppänen, Juho Leinonen, Petri Ihantola, and Arto Hellas. 2017. Predicting Academic Success Based on Learning Material Usage. In *Proceedings of SIGITE'17, Rochester, NY, USA, October 4–7, 2017,* 6 pages.
https://doi.org/10.1145/3125659.3125695

1 INTRODUCTION

Large amounts of research effort has been directed towards developing methodologies for detecting students who struggle. This line of research is of special importance in institutions with classes of hundreds of students, where instructors can rarely keep up with the performance of individual students. If struggling students can be identified early, appropriate resources for targeted help and guidance can be allocated, which can help the students succeed in their studies. This type of research is especially popular in the context of learning programming [21], where various types of questionnaires and tests [16, 38, 45], machine learning based methods [2, 11], and methods whose construction has required programming-specific expert knowledge [7, 9, 22, 44] have been proposed for the task.

As these methodologies can be highly context- and domain sensitive [35], we set out to investigate how a simpler and more generalizable data source – student material usage – could be used to build predictive models for identifying at-risk students. Other approaches with more generic data sources include the works by Kennedy and Cutts [24], Porter et al. [37] and Liao et al. [30], who have used data from in-class questions for predicting course outcomes. The task has also been studied on data from learning management systems [31, 39] – however the data at our disposal is more detailed.

The underlying hypothesis of this article is that fine-grained online learning material usage – that is, *information on the time each paragraph and image in an online course material is visible to a user* – can be used to predict learning outcomes.

All such predictive models are only useful if they can make sufficiently accurate predictions at a sufficiently early stage: late predictions are largely useless for the educators as they do not allow timely interventions to help the struggling students. At the same time, more data is available towards the end of the course, resulting in a situation where predictive models balance between "early" and "accurate". To this end, we are also interested in understanding how much data is needed to, or more concretely "at what point during the course" can we, predict the learning outcomes at a useful accuracy. Our research questions are as follows:

RQ 1: Can one predict student performance based on the relative amounts of time each element of the online learning material is visible on students' screens?

RQ 2: How far into the course must data be collected before these models achieve useful accuracy levels?

This article is organized as follows. In the next section, we overview the related work in predicting academic success within the context of computing and information technology. In Section 3 we detail the research design, including the context, data, and the methodology used for conducting the research. The results are discussed in Section 4, which includes also a discussion on limitations of the study and possible future venues. Finally, Section 5 presents some final conclusions.

2 RELATED WORK

This section presents an overview of previous work on predicting student learning outcomes both in general and more specifically in the context of learning to program. While factors such as motivation [1, 28, 38] and self-perceptions [5, 23, 40, 45] and metacognitive abilities [18, 19, 32] have been linked to learning outcomes and academic success, they are difficult to quantify without questionnaires. Within the context of this study, we are more interested in predictors than can be measured automatically.

First, perhaps unsurprisingly, deliberate practice has been connected to becoming an expert in a subject by Ericsson et al. [14]. Their finding is supported by, for example, a study by Minaei-Bidgoli et al. [34] where student learning outcomes are predicted based on a multitude of features extracted from logs of an intelligent tutoring system used in an introductory university level physics course. They report relatively high accuracies in both the binary classification case of classifying students to those who fail and those who pass the course as well as when classifying students to three groups: high, middle and low grade. In their model, the most important features for the 3-class classification turned out to be the total number of correct answers and the total number of tries. Total time spent was among their top five predictors. Similarly, previous research [17] has shown that the effort a student takes is well correlated with learning outcomes.

The programming process itself can also be used to predict learning outcomes in computer science and programming. Piech et al. [36] used a complex model of the students' programming process to classify students into groups that exhibited statistically significant different midterm scores. Similarly, Ahadi et al. [2] were able to correctly classify students into high-performing and low-performing students with Matthew Correlation Coefficients in the range from 0.71 to 0.81 based on features extracted from previous academic success, past programming experience and "programming assignment specific source-code snapshot attributes that potentially reflect students' persistence and success with the course assignments" [2]. When the same model – trained on data from the initial course – was used to classify students in a subsequent course, accuracies in the range of 71 % to 80% were observed [2]. These results are in line with reports that the mental models students have of programming are predictive of, or at least related to, their course outcomes [12, 45] and that novice and expert programmers employ different types of mental models [42].

Other studies have identified a multitude of other predictors. Leppänen et al. [26] found correlations between the types of pauses students take from writing program code and exam scores in a CS1 course. Leinonen et al. [25] were able to predict student learning outcomes based on the key press latencies in their typing. Porter et al. [37] predict course exam scores from in-class student clicker answers. Similar work has been done by Liao et al. [30]. Finally, multiple researchers have constructed metrics from source code snapshots that explain parts of students' course performance [7, 9, 21, 22, 25, 37, 43, 44].

Previous works have also extracted small amounts of higher level features from online learning management systems and predicted learning outcomes from said features [27, 31, 39].

3 RESEARCH DESIGN

This section overviews the design of this study in detail. The first subsection introduces the context of this study, and especially the context of the data used in the study. The second subsection details the methodologies used to answer the research questions.

3.1 Context and Data

The data used in this article comes from a seven week Introduction to Programming course held in the fall of 2016 at the University of Helsinki, a European research-first university. The course teaches the students the basics of Object Oriented programming in Java, and has no pre-requisites. It is mandatory for Computer Science majors, and can be taken by anyone who wishes to learn programming.

The online course material consists of seven content pages (HTML documents), each corresponding to one week of the course. These pages are somewhat analogous to chapters of a course book, but they also have dynamic content such as visualizations. Programming assignment handouts are also embedded to the content pages, but they are completed in a separate programming environment.

A client-side data gathering component that was built using Javascript was embedded to the material for the purposes of this study. The component records students' movements within the material page and stores time-based information on each larger HTML element (paragraph, image, etc.) that is visible on the users' screen. More specifically, the JavaScript component listened for scroll events, where the user's screen moved, and click events, where the user clicked on an element of the web page. After each event, the visibility of each HTML element – such as paragraphs and images – was analyzed, and information on what elements were visible was stored. Similar events were recorded every 2500 milliseconds if the user did not interact with the browser, provided that the browser window was visible. Collection was paused if the user was completely idle for a longer period of time to remove outliers such as long pauses where the user had left the page open but was not actually reading the material.

The course had 2 hours of weekly lectures, and the students were free to complete their weekly assignments wherever they wished to. As a part of the course, the teaching staff – mainly teaching assistants – provided over 20 hours of weekly support in specific on-campus computer labs. The grading was based on course assignments (55% of overall score) and three exams (45% of overall score). In order to pass the course, the students had to receive at least one half of the overall score as well as one half of the exam score. A total of $n = 271$ participants participated in the final exam and provided data for the study.

Due to the way the data collection and the learning sessions were organized, our data collection happened completely *in-situ*. This method therefore avoids many of the potential issues related to *ex-situ* data collection schemes, where the act of collecting data may influence the behavior of the participants.

3.2 Methodology

In this section, we outline the method we use to determine the answers to our research questions.

3.2.1 Data Preprocessing. First, the recorded events were parsed. For each student and each HTML element with visible content, the number of events where the student had the HTML element visible on their screen were counted. The event counts were then normalized for each student so that the overall sum of effort for each week – in terms of proportionate events in elements – was one. This resulted in a data set, where the data effectively described element popularities for each student.

Then, in order to make the data behave better with the support vector based models (discussed below), both the inputs and the outputs were transformed to have unit variance and zero mean. Finally, The data was split into two parts. A training set containing 70% of the students, and a test set containing the remaining 30% of the students.

3.2.2 Classification and Regression. The main difference between classification and regression is that classification is about determining a label for each data point – for example, whether the student will pass the course based on the material usage or not. Regression on the other hand is about trying to determine a scalar value for each data point – for example, determining the exam score of a student based on the material usage.

While there can be no "best" classification algorithm over the set of all possible scenarios [46], empirical research suggests that certain algorithms perform better than others when "common" scenarios are considered [10, 15]. Based on the above suggestion, we utilize Support Vector Classifiers (SVC) [13] and ϵ-insensitive Support Vector Regressors (ϵ-SVR) [6] for the purposes of predicting academic success[1]. In all cases, we evaluate three types of kernels commonly used with support vector methods: a linear kernel, an RBF kernel and a sigmoid kernel.

3.2.3 Predicting academic success. We label as "at-risk" all students who would obtain a grade of 0, 1 or 2 on a scale from 0 (fail) to 5 (best). This decision was influenced by the introductory nature of the course: failing to achieve a moderate grade in such a course would raise serious concerns about the student's ability to succeed in the subsequent courses.

To answer our first research question of "*Can one predict student performance based on the relative amounts of time each element of the online learning material is visible on students' screens?*", we build and evaluate predictive models that take the participants' material usage data as an input, and output whether the participant is "at-risk" or not. The previous is done as a classification task. We also predict three other variables from the usage data as a regression task: course exam scores, programming assignment scores and course total scores.

The second research question – "*How far into the course must data be collected before these models achieve useful accuracy levels?*" – requires us to build such models using multiple data sets, so that we can identify the point in time during the data collection when the models become practical. We simulate this by constructing multiple training sets, each containing only data from first w weeks of the 7-week-long course, for $w \in [1, 7]$ and report the results for research questions 1 and 2 using all of them.

---

[1]For a more in-depth discussion on support vector classification and regression, see e.g. [8, 41].

3.2.4 Evaluation. To prevent overfitting, the input set was split into a training and test sets. A 10-fold cross validated grid-search was conducted over the training set to determine good parameters for the predictive models that used support vector classifiers. This procedure was completed separately for each classifier – once good parameters were identified, the performance of the predictive model was evaluated with the test data.

The performance of the classifiers was evaluated and reported using F1 Score, which is the harmonic mean of precision and recall and receives values in the range from 0 (worst) to 1 (best). This measure, however, suffers from a bias. Namely, the F-measure is not invariant on the classification problem being "flipped" so that the "positive" and "negative" class labels are reversed. We thus report the F1 score for both options as the "positive" label. Regression models are evaluated and reported using R-squared, which is the percentage of variation in the data that is explained by the predictive model. R^2 takes values from positive 1 to negative infinity, with 1 indicating a model with no error and smaller values indicating increasingly larger errors.

4 RESULTS AND DISCUSSION

In this section we display the results obtained using the research methodology described in Section 3.2. The aggregated results are shown in Table 1.

4.1 Summary of Results

In the classification task where the goal was to predict whether the student will be at-risk based on the material usage, we notice that the F1-scores for cases where not-at-risk students are considered to be the positive label ($F1_0$) start at 0.83 after only the first week and quickly raise to a maximum of 0.95 when three weeks of data is used. In the case where at-risk students are considered the positive label ($F1_1$), the F1-scores raise much more slowly, but eventually reach up to $F1 = 0.76$ when all available data is used. Essentially, this means that it is harder to correctly identify the students who are at-risk ($F1_1$) and easier to identify the students who are not at-risk ($F1_0$).

We further note that significant bumps in the $F1_1$ score are observed once the third and the fourth weeks' data are added. In other words, only minor gains in classification accuracy are achieved by adding the data from the fifth and the sixth weeks. This indicates that an intervention for struggling students could be conducted at around halfway through the course (after week 3 or 4).

In the regression cases, we notice that R^2 values for students' total scores and programming assignment scores reach fairly significant heights at $R^2 = 0.56$ for programming scores and $R^2 = 0.67$ for total scores when all data is used. Exam scores, however, exhibit significantly lower R^2 scores maxing out at $R^2 = 0.29$ when all data is used. Outside the first week, the total scores produce better regression results than either of its component scores, i.e. the exam and programming assignment scores.

The exam score regression accuracy behaves similar to the classification accuracy in that after the fourth week of data is available, further weeks seem to provide only minor improvements. Such a phenomena is not, however, so clearly apparent in the programming assignment score and total score regression tasks.

Table 1: Performance in classifying students into high and low performers, predicting students' exam, programming, and total scores from the material usage data using different amounts of data from the start of the course. Only the best model for each task is reported. $F1_1$ and $F1_0$ are the F1-scores wherein "at-risk" is considered to be the positive label and the negative label, respectively.

Weeks of data	Binary classification		Exam score	Progr. score	Total score
	$F1_1$	$F1_0$	R^2	R^2	R^2
1	0.15	0.83	0.08	0.09	0.05
2	0.22	0.90	0.14	0.17	0.18
3	0.43	0.95	0.19	0.26	0.40
4	0.60	0.94	0.25	0.31	0.52
5	0.64	0.94	0.25	0.45	0.59
6	0.64	0.94	0.25	0.52	0.66
7	0.76	0.94	0.29	0.56	0.67

4.2 Material Usage Predicts Success

Based on the results, we observe that the element-level material usage statistics can be used to predict student learning outcomes in terms of both identifying at-risk students and predicting the total course scores of students. As the data is normalized so that the effort in each week sums up to one, this predictive power is independent of the total study effort. This means that we can answer the first research question *"Can one predict student performance based on the relative amounts of time each element of the online learning material is visible on students' screens?"* in the affirmative. These results, together with results in [27], indicate that researchers should pay attention to what the students are reading instead of coarse grained movement data.

To determine our answer to the second research question, *"How far into the course must data be collected before these models achieve useful accuracy levels?"* we observe the changes in the values of Table 1 as more data is made available. The R^2 and F1 values of the models vary based on the concrete task, but a small trend is nevertheless visible. Namely, we note that most models see a somewhat significant bump in their accuracy at around weeks three and four. Beyond this, the increase in predictive power is largely constant. This finding suggests that some basic predictions are possible already after three or four weeks of data are available – that is, soon after the course's halfway-point – but waiting longer allows for better predictions.

4.3 A Bump in Predictive Power

In the online course material that we used for the study, the students start to familiarize themselves with object-oriented programming during weeks three and four, while the first two weeks are focused on procedural programming. That is, during the first two weeks, the students always program to the same file throughout the assignment, and are not specifically required to maintain a broader view of the functionality of their program. While the students use input and output -related objects during the first week, and lists during the second, they do not yet need to construct their own objects.

We hypothesize that one of the reasons for the bump in the predictive power in weeks three and four is the relative bump in the effort that students need to invest in order to understand the course contents: objects have previously been noted as a challenging

topic [4, 20, 33], and it is meaningful to assume that the predictive models can – to some degree – separate those who struggle with object oriented programming constructs from those who do not.

4.4 On the Generalizability of our Approach

It appears that the methodologies presented here can provide valuable information to educators. Whilst our materials include a specific area that is challenging – namely the introduction of object-oriented programming – nothing in the actual data used in this study is inherently programming-related: the data contains information on the relative element popularity, not about the content of the said elements. Therefore, such element data should be collectible from any online learning material and from other learning management systems such as Moodle or Blackboard. As such, the system appears to be a candidate for usage in other educational contexts as well.

When one considers the fairly strong learning outcome prediction results presented in this study, a question arises: exactly how complex models are required to automatically identify struggling students? Is a very domain-specific tool such as source code analysis really required to notice that a student is failing to learn a concept, or can we simply identify that the student keeps returning to sections of material that discuss that concept when most of his or her peers no longer need to refer to that section?

It is the authors' view that a further study should be conducted to find out a set of learning outcome predictors that are as general and simple as possible. We hypothesize that such a minimal set of features would achieve a very good generalizability between subjects and thus make it easier for educators in any field where online material is used to notice struggling students and take suitable actions.

4.5 Limitations

The methods used in and the results reported by this study are not without limitations. This sections overviews the most crucial of these limitations.

4.5.1 Internal and External Validity. The model selection procedure used in this study was specifically chosen so as to prevent issues of overfitting the model to the data. As the test data set was kept completely separate from the data set used in model selection, there is no possibility of the model selection having overfitted to the test data. As such, the procedure is expected to generalize well to other data sets. Furthermore, the models in this study were learned using a rather limited set of data; it is reasonable to expect that a larger quantity of data – perhaps from multiple instances of the same course – would produce better results.

As the data comes from a single course, there exists a possible external validity issue regarding whether the results or the model will generalize to other, different, populations. For example, the participants' age distribution is rather narrow, and the participants are all university students in a country with a largely homogeneous population. Furthermore, as all the participants have specifically chosen to attend the course – they are either computer science majors of their own volition, or voluntarily taking a course outside of their major – questions of participant self-selection arise. These possible threats to the external validity of the results suggest that further study should be conducted to assess the generalizability of the methods and results presented herein.

A further threat to the internal validity of the study, regarding the reported scores of the models, is that the data used for the study does not include students who dropped out of the course prior to the final course exam. The inclusion of these students could affect the accuracies of the models. Additionally, the material used in this study was constructed so that the assignment prompts were embedded within the reading material. It is unclear how a different kind of setup – e.g. chapter-final assignment prompts or completely separate assignment prompt documents – would change the results.

4.5.2 Data Validity. As the data is collected *in-situ* on the user's computer, we surrender control of the collection process to the user. As such, the user is able – if they wish – to either block the data collection completely or even to send malicious data to the server. This is an inherent issue of any client-side data collection scheme and as such is unlikely to be solved easily.

4.6 Future Work

As noted above, future work should try to identify a minimal set of learning outcome predictors and investigate whether such a minimal set can generalize well to the educational field in general.

Online learning material movement data is a prime target for sequential pattern mining as it is essentially a sequential list of events. The fact that each event contains a range of visible elements rather than a singular value can complicate sequential pattern mining, but is not prohibitive. As a concrete example, one could determine which sequences of type "start exercise $\Rightarrow$ view element $X \Rightarrow$ finish exercise" were the most common to determine which sections of the material map to which exercises. This data could then be used, for example, to facilitate social navigation by providing users links to the material locations most commonly visited by previous students while working on the same exercise.

A similar approach to that mentioned above could be used to expand information about what knowledge each assignment requires from the student. If such a transfer or mapping was possible, it could potentially be used with student modeling algorithms to automatically detect which knowledge components – sections of the material – are related to which course assignments.

It should be investigated whether students fall into movement archetypes that correspond to certain styles or patterns of movement. If such archetypes were to exist, their relations to learning outcomes should be investigated. The feasibility of this approach is supported by research from Amershi & Conati [3] who clustered student actions in a learning environment to identify strategies that resulted in better or worse than average learning outcomes.

Finally, the models proposed herein are unable to distinguish deliberate practice – which has been connected to becoming an expert [14] – from simply browsing Facebook on the phone while having the material open. The ability to distinguish between these two could feasibly improve the predictive power of the models drastically. At the same time, identifying deliberate practice from "idling" without drastically violating the privacy of the participants is an open problem.

5 CONCLUSIONS

In this study we use element-level usage data that was collected from the online learning material of an university level introductory programming course for prediction of student learning outcomes. We answer the concrete research questions: (1) *"Can one predict student performance based on the relative amounts of time each element of the online learning material is visible on students' screens?"* and (2) *"How far into the course must data be collected before these models achieve useful accuracy levels?"*.

The results show the the answer to the first research question is affirmative: based on just three to four weeks of data containing information on what elements of the online course material were visible on each student's screen at what times, it is possible to identify at-risk students with some accuracy. Furthermore, it seems possible to predict student programming assignment scores and total course scores with a somewhat high accuracy. Simultaneously, models based on material usage statistics showed some light predictive power in predicting student exam scores. Curiously, better predictions were observed when predicting the total score, which is a simple sum of the programming and exam scores than when predicting either of the component scores.

As for the second research question, our results show indications that the models reach a certain "maturity" with regard to accuracy once data from the first three or four weeks of the seven week course are available. That is, providing more data beyond this point only results in slight improvements in predictive power.

As our models are built on effort-normalized data – data from which any indication of absolute study time has been removed – our model is not based on how long students study, but rather on what sections or elements of the material they study.

The fact that the models investigated herein were successful raises questions of whether extremely complicated student models are necessary in the first place: it might be possible to predict student learning outcomes with very high accuracies based on very few simple and non-intrusive metrics that can be collected in-situ and in a completely online learning environment and that do not require installing software on students' computers.

ACKNOWLEDGMENTS

This work was partially funded by Academy of Finland under grant number 303694 *Skills, education and the future of work*. This work is based on the MSc thesis [29] of the first author.

REFERENCES

[1] Philip C Abrami, Bette Chambers, Sylvia d'Apollonia, Mona Farrell, and Christina De Simone. 1992. Group outcome: The relationship between group learning outcome, attributional style, academic achievement, and self-concept. *Contemporary Educational Psychology* 17, 3 (1992), 201–210.

[2] Alireza Ahadi, Raymond Lister, Heikki Haapala, and Arto Vihavainen. 2015. Exploring machine learning methods to automatically identify students in need of assistance. In *Proc. of the 11th Annual International Conference on International Computing Education Research.* ACM, 121–130.

[3] Saleema Amershi and Cristina Conati. 2009. Combining unsupervised and supervised classification to build user models for exploratory. *Journal of Educational Data Mining* 1, 1 (2009), 18–71.

[4] Vladimir Bacvanski and Jürgen Börstler. 1997. Doing Your First OO Project: OO Education Issues in Industry and Academia. In *Addendum to the 1997 ACM SIGPLAN Conference on Object-oriented Programming, Systems, Languages, and Applications (Addendum) (OOPSLA '97).* ACM, 93–96.

[5] Albert Bandura. 1977. Self-efficacy: toward a unifying theory of behavioral change. *Psychological review* 84, 2 (1977), 191.

[6] Debasish Basak, Srimanta Pal, and Dipak Chandra Patranabis. 2007. Support vector regression. *Neural Information Processing-Letters and Reviews* 11, 10 (2007), 203–224.

[7] Brett A Becker. 2016. A new metric to quantify repeated compiler errors for novice programmers. In *Proc. of the 2016 ACM Conference on Innovation and Technology in Computer Science Education.* ACM, 296–301.

[8] Christopher JC Burges. 1998. A tutorial on support vector machines for pattern recognition. *Data mining and knowledge discovery* 2, 2 (1998), 121–167.

[9] Adam S Carter, Christopher D Hundhausen, and Olusola Adesope. 2015. The normalized programming state model: Predicting student performance in computing courses based on programming behavior. In *Proc. of the 11th annual International Conference on International Computing Education Research.* ACM, 141–150.

[10] Rich Caruana and Alexandru Niculescu-Mizil. 2006. An empirical comparison of supervised learning algorithms. In *Proc. of the 23rd international conference on Machine learning.* ACM, 161–168.

[11] Karo Castro-Wunsch, Alireza Ahadi, and Andrew Petersen. 2017. Evaluating Neural Networks As a Method for Identifying Students in Need of Assistance. In *Proc. of the 2017 ACM SIGCSE Technical Symposium on Computer Science Education (SIGCSE '17).* ACM, 111–116.

[12] Cynthia L Corritore and Susan Wiedenbeck. 1991. What do novices learn during program comprehension? *International Journal of Human-Computer Interaction* 3, 2 (1991), 199–222.

[13] Corinna Cortes and Vladimir Vapnik. 1995. Support-vector networks. *Machine learning* 20, 3 (1995), 273–297.

[14] K Anders Ericsson, Ralf T Krampe, and Clemens Tesch-Römer. 1993. The role of deliberate practice in the acquisition of expert performance. *Psychological review* 100, 3 (1993), 363.

[15] Manuel Fernández-Delgado, Eva Cernadas, Senén Barro, and Dinani Amorim. 2014. Do we need hundreds of classifiers to solve real world classification problems. *J. Mach. Learn. Res* 15, 1 (2014), 3133–3181.

[16] Sally Fincher, Anthony Robins, Bob Baker, Ilona Box, Quintin Cutts, Michael de Raadt, Patricia Haden, John Hamer, Margaret Hamilton, Raymond Lister, and others. 2006. Predictors of success in a first programming course. In *Proc. of the 8th Australasian Conference on Computing Education-Volume 52.* Australian Computer Society, Inc., 189–196.

[17] Sandra L Fisher and J Kevin Ford. 1998. Differential effects of learner effort and goal orientation on two learning outcomes. *Personnel Psychology* 51, 2 (1998), 397–420.

[18] John H Flavell. 1979. Metacognition and cognitive monitoring: A new area of cognitive–developmental inquiry. *American psychologist* 34, 10 (1979), 906.

[19] J Kevin Ford, Eleanor M Smith, Daniel A Weissbein, Stanley M Gully, and Eduardo Salas. 1998. Relationships of goal orientation, metacognitive activity, and practice strategies with learning outcomes and transfer. *Journal of applied psychology* 83, 2 (1998), 218.

[20] Mark Guzdial. 1995. Centralized Mindset: A Student Problem with Object-oriented Programming. In *Proc. of the 26th SIGCSE Technical Symposium on Computer Science Education (SIGCSE '95).* ACM, 182–185.

[21] Petri Ihantola, Arto Vihavainen, Alireza Ahadi, Matthew Butler, Jürgen Börstler, Stephen H Edwards, Essi Isohanni, Ari Korhonen, Andrew Petersen, Kelly Rivers, and others. 2015. Educational data mining and learning analytics in programming: Literature review and case studies. In *Proc. of the 2015 ITiCSE on Working Group Reports.* ACM, 41–63.

[22] Matthew C Jadud. 2006. Methods and tools for exploring novice compilation behaviour. In *Proc. of the 2nd international workshop on Computing education research.* ACM, 73–84.

[23] Young-Ju Joo, Mimi Bong, and Ha-Jeen Choi. 2000. Self-efficacy for self-regulated learning, academic self-efficacy, and Internet self-efficacy in Web-based instruction. *Educational Technology Research and Development* 48, 2 (2000), 5–17.

[24] Gregor Kennedy and Quintin Cutts. 2005. The association between students' use of an electronic voting system and their learning outcomes. *Journal of Computer Assisted Learning* 21, 4 (2005), 260–268.

[25] Juho Leinonen, Krista Longi, Arto Klami, and Arto Vihavainen. 2016. Automatic inference of programming performance and experience from typing patterns. In *Proc. of the 47th ACM Technical Symposium on Computing Science Education.* ACM, 132–137.

[26] Leo Leppänen, Juho Leinonen, and Arto Hellas. 2016. Pauses and spacing in learning to program. In *Proc. of the 16th Koli Calling International Conference on Computing Education Research.* ACM, 41–50.

[27] Leo Leppänen, Juho Leinonen, Petri Ihantola, and Arto Hellas. 2017. Using and Collecting Fine-grained Usage Data to Improve Online Learning Materials. In *Proceedings of the 39th International Conference on Software Engineering: Software Engineering and Education Track (ICSE-SEET '17).* IEEE Press, 4–12.

[28] Mark R Lepper and Diana I Cordova. 1992. A desire to be taught: Instructional consequences of intrinsic motivation. *Motivation and emotion* 16, 3 (1992), 187–208.

[29] Leo Leppänen. 2017. *Using element-level website usage data to improve online learning materials and predict learning outcomes.* Master's thesis. University of Helsinki, Helsinki, Finland.

[30] Soohyun Nam Liao, Daniel Zingaro, Michael A Laurenzano, William G Griswold, and Leo Porter. 2016. Lightweight, Early Identification of At-Risk CS1 Students. In *Proc. of the 2016 ACM Conference on International Computing Education Research.* ACM, 123–131.

[31] Leah P Macfadyen and Shane Dawson. 2010. Mining LMS data to develop an "early warning system" for educators: A proof of concept. *Computers & education* 54, 2 (2010), 588–599.

[32] Christoph Mengelkamp and Maria Bannert. 2010. Accuracy of confidence judgments: Stability and generality in the learning process and predictive validity for learning outcome. *Memory & cognition* 38, 4 (2010), 441–451.

[33] Craig S. Miller and Amber Settle. 2016. Some Trouble with Transparency: An Analysis of Student Errors with Object-oriented Python. In *Proc. of the 2016 ACM Conf. on International Computing Education Research (ICER '16).* ACM, 133–141.

[34] Behrouz Minaei-Bidgoli, Deborah A Kashy, Gerd Kortemeyer, and William F Punch. 2003. Predicting student performance: an application of data mining methods with an educational web-based system. In *Frontiers in education, 2003. FIE 2003 33rd annual,* Vol. 1. IEEE, T2A–13.

[35] Andrew Petersen, Jaime Spacco, and Arto Vihavainen. 2015. An exploration of error quotient in multiple contexts. In *Proc. of the 15th Koli Calling Conference on Computing Education Research.* ACM, 77–86.

[36] Chris Piech, Mehran Sahami, Daphne Koller, Steve Cooper, and Paulo Blikstein. 2012. Modeling how students learn to program. In *Proc. of the 43rd ACM technical symposium on Computer Science Education.* ACM, 153–160.

[37] Leo Porter, Daniel Zingaro, and Raymond Lister. 2014. Predicting student success using fine grain clicker data. In *Proc. of the 10th annual conference on International computing education research.* ACM, 51–58.

[38] Steven B Robbins, Kristy Lauver, Huy Le, Daniel Davis, Ronelle Langley, and Aaron Carlstrom. 2004. Do psychosocial and study skill factors predict college outcomes? A meta-analysis. (2004).

[39] Cristobal Romero, Pedro G. Espejo, Amelia Zafra, Jose Raul Romero, and Sebastian Ventura. 2013. Web usage mining for predicting final marks of students that use Moodle courses. *Computer Applications in Engineering Education* 21, 1 (2013), 135–146.

[40] Dale H Schunk. 1981. Modeling and attributional effects on children's achievement: A self-efficacy analysis. *J. of educational psychology* 73, 1 (1981), 93.

[41] Alex J Smola and Bernhard Schölkopf. 2004. A tutorial on support vector regression. *Statistics and computing* 14, 3 (2004), 199–222.

[42] Elliot Soloway and Kate Ehrlich. 1984. Empirical studies of programming knowledge. *IEEE Transactions on software engineering* 5 (1984), 595–609.

[43] Arto Vihavainen. 2013. Predicting students' performance in an introductory programming course using data from students' own programming process. In *13th Int. Conf. on Advanced Learning Technologies (ICALT).* IEEE, 498–499.

[44] Christopher Watson, Frederick WB Li, and Jamie L Godwin. 2013. Predicting performance in an introductory programming course by logging and analyzing student programming behavior. In *Advanced Learning Technologies (ICALT), 2013 IEEE 13th International Conference on.* IEEE, 319–323.

[45] Susan Wiedenbeck, Deborah Labelle, and Vennila NR Kain. 2004. Factors affecting course outcomes in introductory programming. In *16th Annual Workshop of the Psychology of Programming Interest Group.* 97–109.

[46] David H Wolpert, William G Macready, and others. 1995. *No free lunch theorems for search.* Technical Report. Technical Report SFI-TR-95-02-010, Santa Fe Institute.

Exploring the Landscape of Data Science

Deborah Boisvert	Heikki Topi	Michael D. Harris	Kim Yohannan
University of MA Boston	Bentley University	Bunker Hill CC	Dell/EMC
Boston, MA USA	Waltham, MA USA	Charlestown, MA USA	Hopkinton, MA USA
deborah.boisvert@umb.edu	htopi@bentley.edu	mdharris@bhcc.mass.edu	kim.yohannan@dell.com

ABSTRACT

The panel will discuss and answer questions the landscape of employment and education pathways in data science and analytics. The panel will also talk about the current discussions within ACM and the role(s) the information technology discipline should have in the field. Finally the panel will solicit feedback from the audience on current work and desired next steps in order to address the global education and workforce needs.

Keywords

Big Data; Analytics; Tools; Education Pathways; Workforce Development

1. INTRODUCTION

The recovery from the 2007-2009 Recession has been characterized by a growing demand for workers with technical skills. According to an analysis published by the US Dept. of Commerce in March 2015, private sector industries with the highest concentration of data occupations added 1.8 million jobs over the last decade, representing about 31% of total private job growth, which was four times faster than in private industries overall [8]. McKinsey and Company was one of the first to place a national spotlight on the term Big Data describing it as the next frontier for innovation, competition and productivity. Their May 2011 report made the case that 15 of 17 industrial sectors in the U.S. have more stored data per company than the U.S. Library of Congress and the increasing volume and detail of information captured by enterprises, the rise of multimedia, social media and the Internet of Things will fuel exponential growth in data for the foreseeable future. The growing demand is partially fueled by employers in health care, retail marketing, business operations, financial services, and other fields who are rapidly increasing their use of data and digital technologies to survive and prosper in the 21st century globally-connected economy.

According to the U.S. Department of Commerce 2015 report, employment, where data is central to the job, was about 10.3 million in 2013, or about 7.8% of all employment. [8] The power and potential of Big Data depends on the availability of both talent and technology to harness its value. Big Data is an evolving field that can benefit from a strong partnership between business and academia. This panel will explore the landscape of Big Data programs and offer insights that will aid in the development of dynamic, innovative academic programs and a pipeline of workforce talent that support the industry needs for trained professionals.

In additional, the panel will cover findings and solicit feedback and interest on an ACM Education Council data science education project funded through NSF (DUE 1545135). The project leads convened a workshop entitled "Strengthening Data Science Education through Collaboration" in Fall of 2015 and a follow-up meeting of professional and academic societies in Spring 2017.

2. PANELISTS

A brief background for each panel member follows:

Deborah Boisvert is the Principal Investigator for BATEC, an NSF-funded National Center for Computing and Information Technologies, focused on creating computing pathways from high school to community college to university in urban areas across the country. She has extensive experience in developing and implementing educational programs for secondary school, community college and university that advance the educational and professional objectives of our area students, current workers and community residents. She has developed and/or conducted numerous workshops, summer institutes, and graduate courses that advance the content and pedagogical capabilities of educators across the levels. She maintains close ties to industry to bring together stakeholders in IT, Security, Big Data, Finance, Informatics and other areas to better prepare students for the future careers.

Heikki Topi is Professor of Computer Information Systems and Director of Bentley Data Innovation Network at Bentley University in Waltham, MA. His teaching interests include advanced systems analysis and design, systems modeling, data management, and IT infrastructure. His current research focuses on systems development methodologies for enterprise-level systems, information systems education, and human factors and usability issues in the context of enterprise systems. His research has been published in journals such as *European Journal of Information Systems*, *JASIST*, *Information Processing & Management*, *International Journal of Human-Computer Studies*, *Journal of Database Management*, *Small Group Research*, and others. He is co-author of *Modern Database Management*, editor of *IS Management Handbook* and *Computing Handbook, 3rd Edition: Information Systems and Information Technology*, and co-editor of *Education Department of CAIS*. He has been actively involved in national computing curriculum development and evaluation efforts since early 2000s (including *IS 2002, CC2005 Overview Report*, and as task force co-chair of *IS 2010* and *MSIS 2016*, the latest IS curriculum revisions). Currently, he is leading an interorganizational initiative related to data science education and contributing to *CC2020* as task force member representing AIS. He served on ACM's Education Board and Council from 2006 until 2016 and represented first AIS and then ACM on CSAB's Board from 2005 until 2015. In 2015, he earned the *AIS Award for Outstanding Contribution to IS Education* and in both 2015 and 2016 the *CSAB Outstanding Contribution Award*. He serves currently as Association of Information Systems VP of Education.

Michael Harris, Assistant Professor at Bunker Hill Community College, is developing curriculum and building an associate's degree based on work done in the Creating Pathways for Big Data NSF grant with EDC. He has developed two courses – Intro to Big Data with R and R Studio, and Data Analytics and Predictive Analysis – and is currently developing Hadoop with Spark, and Data Visualization with Tableau courses. He is also in the process of creating an AS degree in Big Data which follows the data management and data analytics certificates. Along with the course development, he is currently pursuing a MS in Analytics at Georgia Tech.

Kim Yohannan is responsible the Dell EMC Academic Alliance program in the Americas (North, Central and South) and the Caribbean which is part of the Dell EMC External Research and Academic Alliances ecosystem. Previously, she managed the global Centera ISV Partner Program. Before Dell EMC, she worked at Xplana Learning, an educational software company, as their Senior Director of Operations and at Nortel Networks where she was part of the certification exam team and was responsible for the NetKnowledge Program which provided curriculum to academic institutions. Before Nortel, Kim spent seven years as a primary school teacher with a focus in English as a Second Language (ESL).

3. REFERENCES

[1] Burning Glass Technologies and BATEC (November 2015). *Middle Skill Employment: Understanding the Opportunities and Skill Requirements for an IT Workforces*. Retrieved from: http://batec.org/publications/request-middle-skill-employment-report/

[2] Burning Glass Technologies and BATEC (April 2016). *Big Data: Ground-Breaking Analysis of Employment in the Information Economy*. Retrieved from: http://batec.org/publications/request-big-data-report/

[3] Curriculum development for business intelligence, big data and analytics by the information systems community (http://aisel.aisnet.org/cais/vol36/iss1/23/)

[4] Data Science and Analytics by Business-Higher Education Forum (http://www.bhef.com/publications/investing-americas-data-science-and-analytics-talent)

[5] Dell EMC Data Science and Big Data Analytics (https://education.emc.com/guest/campaign/data_science.aspx)

[6] Envisioning the Data Science Discipline: The Undergraduate Perspective; Jon Eisenberg, PI. (https://nsf.gov/awardsearch/showAward?AWD_ID=1626983)

[7] European EDISON Project (http://edison-project.eu)

[8] Hawk, William, Regina Powers, and Robert Rubinovitz (March 12, 2015). *The Importance of Data Occupations in the U.S. Economy*, Economics and Statistics Administration Office of the Chief Economist, ESA Issue Brief #01-15.

[9] Learning Big Data Analytic Skills through Scientific Workflows (Yolanda Gil, PI) (https://www.nsf.gov/awardsearch/showAward?AWD_ID=1355475)

[10] Oracle Big Data Predictions 2017. Retrieved from http://www.oracle.com/us/dm/oracle-big-data-predictions-p1-3438670.pdf?elq_mid=75895&sh=&cmid=WWMK160603P00063C0003&elqTrackId=e7fd86ee34704bf2b3df93a1c06b8bb0&elq=bee507bce6ee438ba20fc177f21bb625&elqaid=75895&elqat=1&elqCampaignId=48190

[11] Park City Math Institute curriculum: http://www.annualreviews.org/doi/pdf/10.1146/annurev-statistics-060116-053930

[12] The Roundtable on Data Science Post-Secondary Education organized by the National Academies of Sciences, Engineering, and Medicine and sponsored by Moore Foundation, NIH, National Academies Kellogg Foundation Fund, ACM, and ASA (http://sites.nationalacademies.org/DEPS/BMSA/DEPS_180066)

Educational Approach to Cyber Foundations in an Undergraduate Core Program

Jason Hussey and Jacob Shaha
United States Military Academy
West Point, NY 10996
USA
jason.hussey@usma.edu, jacob.shaha@usma.edu

ABSTRACT

Maximizing [1] a student's learning in a general education information technology course is critical when teachers have only a little time to cover numerous topics within the discipline. It is therefore paramount that programs utilize the most effective pedagogical approach to educating students on these topics. This allows teachers to take full advantage of this limited time per topic. The principal contribution of this paper is a statistical analysis of student performance in an intermediate-level information technology course when exposed to two popular methods of teaching information technology concepts. This course is part of the larger cyber education model at the United States Military Academy. Our study implemented and analyzed the results from a control group educated with systematic, skills-based instruction versus a treatment group where a problem-centered learning approach was utilized. Our experimental results provide statistically significant reinforcement of the idea that problem-centered learning is superior to skills-based instruction for educating students in information technology topics as a part of their cyber education.

KEYWORDS

ACM proceedings; cyber; cyber education; problem-centered learning; multi-discipline cyber education; general education requirement; core program; database education; databases

1 INTRODUCTION

When information technologies become a mainstay of any discipline, undergraduate programs that prepare future professionals in those disciplines must develop curriculum educating students on the concepts and application of these technologies. Now, with the ubiquity of data across virtually every industry and the emergence of the cognitive computing era, it is important that all undergraduates emerge from their educational experience armed with an understanding of cyberspace and the tools within to achieve one's organizational goals.

Covering the main topics of a given discipline in a single semester is a major challenge for any type of general education or core course. We often refer to these courses as 'survey' courses, highlighting their emphasis on breadth, not depth. The necessarily limited time that instructors get to spend on any one topic can lead to overly brief exposure for the students and thus little knowledge acquired in the subject.

Adding to the challenges of teaching information technology to a large portion of all undergraduates, Christopher Brown et al. point out that students often enter the course with a lower level of base computer skills than expected [1]. When instructors have to spend time building these base computer skills, it further detracts from time spent with the subject matter.

It is clear that a cyber component is critical to every modern undergraduate's education. What is not always clear is the most effective way to utilize the limited time in each module to maximize student learning. Therefore, we demonstrate how different pedagogical approaches to information technology topics in a general education course can maximize the performance of students given the limited time we have in any individual module. Our research compares a problem-centered learning approach with the more common systematic, skills-based method for learning information technology concepts and applications. Specifically, we present a statistical analysis of 376 students' performance in the database module of an intermediate-level general education course in Cyber Foundations, based on whether they received problem-centered or skills-based instruction.

2 RELATED WORK

Throughout the first decade of the 2000s, Dr. Catherine Chen authored several papers concerning pedagogical approaches to teaching databases to business students. In 2004, Chen and Ray identified elements of systematic, step-by-step instruction that hold students back from being able to apply their knowledge to new situations [2]. The subjects of her study "stated that it was easy to follow the instructions in the book" but had trouble applying the same techniques later on their own [2]. She also concluded that for students to recognize the capabilities that databases provide for decision-making and problem-solving, it is vital that there be real-world context to the problems they are

SIGITE'17, October 4–7, 2017, Rochester, NY, USA
ACM ISBN 978-1-4503-5100-3/17/10 .
https://doi.org/10.1145/3125659.3125691

asked to solve in class. Our own study builds upon this work in that we seek to measure the actual improvement in student performance and confidence when exposed to problem-centered learning as opposed to skills-based instruction.

In 2010, Chen revisited the topic of teaching database skills and problem-solving with databases [3]. She studied the impact that different pedagogical approaches had on problem-solving transfer capabilities in business students. She concludes that problem-solving instruction and problem-solving discovery had no impact on a student's ability to transfer their knowledge to a new problem. Chen suggests that there are three levels in which students need proficiency in order to be able to transfer their skills to new problems. The first is learning simple procedures required to manipulate databases. The second is knowing when and why to apply these procedures. The final level is understanding problem-solving processes. When considering the time constraints in a survey-style course, it's possible students will not be able to progress through the first two tiers that Chen suggests are necessary for problem-solving transfer.

Chen points out that more research is needed as her conclusion runs counter to what Phye suggests in a similar study in 2001. In that study, Phye demonstrates and concludes that "without doubt, instruction and practice with problem-solving strategies promote problem-solving transfer" [4].

On the other hand, some studies suggest that for an introductory course teaching highly structured topics where students have little-to-no prior knowledge of the subject matter, worked examples are superior to problem-solving instruction. Halabi and Tuovinen studied the effects of these two pedagogical approaches on students participating in computer-based learning for an introductory accounting course [5]. They conclude that the reduced cognitive load required for the worked examples led to higher instructional efficiency. This approach is supported by Kalyuga et al. when learners have no prior knowledge of the subject [6].

Acknowledging that there is some precedent for implementing problem-based or problem-centered learning in information technology curricula, several papers have gone on to explore what that looks like in the classroom. Laware and Walters provide the cyber education community with a thorough review of lessons learned in their course over a three year period where they experimented with various active learning strategies [7].

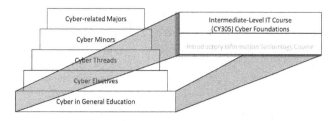

Figure 1: CY305 – Cyber Foundations is the subject of this study. It is the second of two general education cyber-related courses at USMA. This model for cyber education was initially presented by Sobiesk et al. [9]

L'Heureux et al. describe a course in which they implemented information technology problem solving to develop computational thinking in students [8]. Where many of these types of studies evaluated the suitability of this problem-centered approach via student feedback on surveys, we seek to measure it against more traditional methods of teaching information technology via statistical analysis of data from course assessments.

Christopher Brown et al. provide some helpful lessons learned from the process of constructing and delivering a cyber-security curriculum in a core sequence at the United States Naval Academy. They conclude that a technically oriented core course would benefit from more "real-world contextual reinforcement of the technical concepts discussed" [1]. Whether or not introducing real-world problems into the curriculum will tangibly improve student performance is largely what we demonstrate in this paper.

In this study, we build upon these and other works by analyzing student performance when exposed to problem-centered learning pedagogy. This study was implemented in a core requirements course with 376 student samples. Using this large sample set, we conduct statistical analysis of student academic performance in order to assess whether problem-centered learning has a significant, measureable impact as compared to more structured, skills-based instruction typical of information technology courses.

3 BACKGROUND

The ideas and focus of this paper are nested within the multi-level, multi-discipline approach to cyber education presented by Sobiesk et al. [9]. The authors set forth a model for cyber education in an undergraduate curriculum. This model is based on the implementation at the United States Military Academy (USMA), the same institution at which we teach. Sobiesk describes integrating aspects of cyber education across an undergraduate student's entire educational experience. The goal of such an approach is to ensure that graduates have the "foundational knowledge, skills, and abilities needed to succeed in the 21st Century Cyber Domain" [9].

Our work presents methods successfully used within this paradigm. We focus on the base level of the cyber education model depicted in Figure 1, the general education program. Specifically, this study centered on an intermediate-level information technology course required of approximately two-thirds of the junior class at USMA. This course is the second of a two-course sequence that comprises the general education component of cyber education at USMA.

4 METHODOLOGY: COURSE STRUCTURE AND PEDAGOGY

We hypothesized that a problem-centered learning approach to teaching databases to non-STEM majors (hereafter, "non-majors") in a constrained timeframe would result in better understanding of how and when to use databases to meet organizational goals. Further, we hypothesized that students in the treatment group would have a higher degree of self-reported confidence in recognizing situations where databases could help them solve organizational problems.

4.1 The Course

The course used for this study, CY305 - Cyber Foundations, is a core requirement for juniors at USMA. CY305 is the second of a two-course sequence required of most non-majors at USMA. Therefore, students in CY305 have already taken the introductory-level information technology course, IT105, where the emphasis is on introductory computer programming. IT105 also briefly exposes students to computer architecture, networks, and security and privacy.

CY305 is primarily populated by non-majors. Those that do not take our course are generally in technically-oriented majors and satisfy the cyber education goals of the institution with another, more focused course. Enrollment is between 350 and 400 students during the fall and spring semesters. The course educates students on leveraging information technology to achieve organizational goals and improve decision-making. Topics in this course include digitization, web development, databases, computer networks, and concepts in cyber security.

For this study, we focused on the database module of the course. This module is comprised of six 55-minute lessons and a single 55-minute project work period. Students gain exposure to the concept of relational databases followed by hands-on experience working with Microsoft Access, a desktop database management system.

4.2 The Control Group

In its current format, the unit takes a systematic, skills-based approach to teaching students how to use Microsoft Access. Each lesson, the teacher discusses a set of concepts and demonstrates corresponding features in the application at the beginning of the lesson. Following the demonstration, the students conduct a practical exercise in class. These exercises consist of step-by-step instructions on how to accomplish various tasks within the program and are designed to expose students to the concepts and features presented by the instructor.

4.3 The Treatment Group

We designed a problem-centered curriculum around three problem scenarios. One of the established goals of this curriculum revision was to maximize students' exposure to different situations where database solutions could be applied. Each of the three scenarios were explored in various portions of the unit: one scenario was used for in-class lectures and demonstrations, another was used for homework assignments, and the third was used for the database project.

The in-class scenario is modeled after cadet life at USMA to lend immediate familiarity with the problems being described. For homework assignments, students were given a commercial business scenario to familiarize them with transferring concepts and skills learned during in-class exercises to a new and slightly different situation. Finally, the culminating project introduces a third problem environment modeled after their future careers as junior officers in the U.S. Army.

At the start of each lesson in the treatment groups, instructors spent 10-15 minutes posing questions to students to illuminate the problem that the class was to solve that day. As an example, in the first lesson students received several spreadsheets containing related data and were asked to answer a series of increasingly complex questions, requiring information from multiple spreadsheets. As the instructor asked more complicated questions, the students realized that the act of retrieving information from many discrete spreadsheets can quickly become a challenge. Armed with that realization and understanding the nature of the problem, the students were then introduced to the basic concepts of relational databases. Then, the students imported the data into a database and constructed the corresponding relationships. After a quick primer on query building, the students were able to begin producing answers to the instructor's earlier, complex questions. They recognized the power of the tool and its potential for application in their own careers as students and, eventually, as military officers.

4.4 The Assessments

Student learning and understanding was assessed through performance on projects and tests covering the database module's material. In order to gauge the impact on the performance of the treatment group as compared to that of the control group, we held all of the major graded assessments constant between the two. The primary change for the treatment group was the pedagogical approach in the classroom. Additionally, it was necessary to modify the content of the in-class and homework assignments to better fit the pacing and ordering of topics under the treatment curriculum.

4.4.1 Short-term assessments. Immediately following the completion of the database module of CY305, students complete an approximately 4-6 hour project. This project requires students to answer specific questions by designing queries against a starting database. Students then expand the database given a design diagram. Finally, they are required to write more complex queries against the newly expanded database.

This project is designed to test students' ability to independently apply what they have learned in the database module to a real-world scenario modeled around their future careers as junior officers.

In addition to a hands-on project, students are evaluated on their understanding of database concepts through 20 multiple-choice style questions on a mid-term examination. These questions specifically focus on the theory behind databases and database design, leaving the practical application for the project.

4.4.2 Long-term assessments. As part of the 3.5-hour final examination, students complete another set of multiple-choice questions. One-sixth of these questions cover high-level database concepts. This representation of database questions corresponds to the percentage of CY305's overall curriculum that databases occupied.

As the next part of their final examination, students have to complete a much simpler version of the database practical application. Tasks include expanding a small database and developing two moderately difficult queries to answer specific questions.

5 EXPERIMENTAL DESIGN

5.1 Sample Selection

CY305 is taught to multiple sections of 16-18 students, by multiple instructors, using a single unified curriculum. Lesson presentation varies per instructor, but all assignments, exams, and projects are standardized between sections.

At the outset of each semester, CY305 students are grouped by Cumulative Quality Point Average (CQPA), an academy performance measure analogous to Grade Point Average (GPA). Students are then randomly assigned to sections such that like-CQPA students are tracked together; the assignment algorithm minimizes the CQPA variance within a single section. The result is sections of pseudo-randomly assigned students with highly similar academic performance records. These sections are the experimental units in this study.

Instructors are then assigned to sections based on schedule availability and previous experience with the curriculum; more experienced instructors are generally assigned to sections with lower mean CQPAs.

The cohort sections for our experimental groups were generated in this manner, at the beginning of the semester. Prior to commencing the database module of the course, we designated instructors to teach either the control curriculum or the treatment curriculum. To prevent crossover effects between the treatment and control curricula, each instructor was assigned to only one of the two versions, to be used in all that instructor's sections. Instructors were assigned to satisfy three criteria:

1. The student sample size between the treatment and control groups should be roughly equivalent. The resulting sample sizes were: $N_{ctrl} = 207$, $N_{tmnt} = 169$.

2. The treatment and control groups should have roughly equivalent numbers of high-performing sections and low-performing sections. The control group and treatment group included both high-CQPA and low-CQPA sections, with high defined as a 3.0 or above CQPA. However, the previously stated constraint (a given instructor teaches only one version of the curriculum) prevented full balance in this regard. More low-performing sections were placed in the treatment group than the control group, and as a result, *the control group had a higher mean CQPA than the treatment group,* as summarized in table 1.

3. The treatment groups were specifically assigned to instructors with a strong knowledge of both the CY305 curriculum and the general theory and application of databases. Conversely, the most experienced instructors – those with the most previous iterations of CY305 – were deliberately placed in the control group. This was done to ensure that the treatment curriculum was presented as strongly as the control curriculum.

Table 1: CQPA Descriptive Statistics

Cohort	N	Avg CQPA	Median CQPA
Control	207	3.079	3.041
Treatment	169	2.739	2.665

5.2 Outcomes

We measured two primary outcomes: raw academic scores, and self-reported confidence and comfort scores.

5.2.1 Academic Scores. Academic scores were collected on two occasions, via two separate methods. Short-term scores were assessed immediately following the conclusion of the teaching block, via a multiple-choice exam and a database project. The exam and project together assessed a student's familiarity with database principles, and with the specifics of Microsoft Access database implementation. Long-term scores were assessed using a similar multiple-choice exam and a simplified database practical application, of the same type as the initial project but of greatly reduced scope. These long-term assessments were conducted roughly six weeks after the conclusion of the instruction block, during final examinations.

In the analysis, short-term, long-term, and total raw scores were considered only in aggregate; scores from a respective interval's exam and practical application were summed into a single cumulative score for that interval. We refer to this total point value as the "raw" score. Raw academic scores are represented as a percentage, total points earned over total points possible.

5.2.2 Grade Ratio. As an additional academic outcome, we calculated each student's "grade ratio." This was calculated by translating the student's raw numeric score to the corresponding grade value on a 4.33-point scale. This "effective grade" was then divided by the student's CQPA to find the student's grade ratio. The CQPA represents the average of the student's previous performance and thus can be interpreted as a predictor of the student's CY305 performance. To ensure the validity of this approach, we calculated the Pearson's correlation coefficient between CQPA and the student's total effective grade (considering all exams and projects). The calculated value was $\rho=0.46$, $p<0.000$. The CQPA is strongly correlated to the student's final grade and therefore serves as a strong estimate of a student's performance in the course.

The grade ratio, as calculated, is the proportion of the student's anticipated performance that was actually achieved. So, a student with a 3.00 CQPA (a B average) who achieved an 85% (a B) in the raw academic scores would have a grade ratio of 1.0, having performed as predicted by the CQPA. A grade ratio of greater than 1.0 indicates the student performed better than their historical performance would have predicted. Conversely, a student with less than a 1.0-grade ratio failed to perform as well as expected.

The use of this calculated variable was a deliberate *a priori* decision to compensate for the disparity in CQPA between the cohorts. This metric better captures how much improvement was seen in each student, *relative to that student's previously measured capability.* We hypothesized that raw scores would be equivalent between cohorts – indeed that was a design specification, as it would be unethical to disadvantage either cohort in an academic setting. However, achieving raw numeric equivalence would be a greater accomplishment if one cohort was lower-performing on average. As this was the case, the grade ratio was devised as an effective measurement of the treatment's academic impact.

5.2.3 Confidence Scores. Confidence and comfort scores measured a student's self-reported familiarity, confidence, and ease with databases as an information technology tool. Scores were collected using an online survey. Hypothetical scenarios requiring complex information tracking and reporting were presented. Students then used the Likert scale to report their confidence and preparedness to succeed in those scenarios. These reported scores were used to calculate each student's "composite confidence", the normalized average of each Likert response. We designed the survey such that each question was asking for a similar measurement using different wording, with the intent of averaging the resulting scores to produce a general metric for a student's self-assessed capability with databases.

6 RESULTS AND ANALYSIS

All statistical analyses were done using Minitab 17.2.1 [10].

6.1 Raw Academic Scores

Raw academic scores (denoted "Raw" in Table 2 and described in 5.2.1) were compared between cohorts using two-sample T-tests. Raw scores are computed as the percentage of points earned on the assessments for the specified interval. Comparisons were made for raw scores in the short-term, long-term, and the total of the two scores. The results are summarized in Table 2.

Table 2: Raw Academic Score Analysis

	Short-term	Long-term	Course Total
Raw_{CTRL}	85.72%	87.3%	86.39%
Raw_{TMNT}	85.61%	85.4%	85.53%
$Raw_{CTRL} - Raw_{TMNT}$	0.11%	1.93%	0.86%
Deg freedom	369	337	349
p-value	0.895	0.125	0.276

6.2 Grade Ratio

Grade ratio (GR) scores (described in 5.2.2) were compared between cohorts using two-sample T-tests. Comparisons were made for grade ratios computed using the short-term, long-term, and course total raw academic scores. The results are summarized in Table 3.

Table 3: Grade Ratio Score Analysis

	Short-term	Long-term	Course Total
GR_{CTRL}	1.076	1.117	1.087
GR_{TMNT}	1.202	1.175	1.187
$GR_{CTRL} - GR_{TMNT}$	-0.1258	-0.0585	-0.0998
Deg freedom	337	321	337
p-value	**0.000**	0.195	**0.001**

6.3 Confidence Scores

Composite confidence (CC) scores (described in 5.2.3) were compared between cohorts using two-sample T-tests. Comparisons were made for the pre-instruction and post-instruction scores. The results are summarized in Table 4.

Table 4: Confidence Score Analysis

	Pre-block	Post-block
CC_{CTRL}	3.665	3.932
CC_{TMNT}	3.836	4.094
$CC_{CTRL} - CC_{TMNT}$	-0.171	-0.162
Deg freedom	234	255
p-value	0.099	0.098

7 DISCUSSION

No significant difference was found in raw academic scores. Average scores favored the control group, as expected due to that group's higher average CQPA. However, effect sizes were small and statistically insignificant (all p>0.1). This confirms we achieved the goal of providing similar instruction and measurement metrics to the two cohorts; *neither cohort was disadvantaged.* In other words, neither cohort received deliberate, assessment-oriented instruction; both cohorts had similar academic performance.

However, the lower CQPA of the treatment group means that this equivalent performance is, in fact, significant. This is evident in viewing the grade ratio analyses. Both cohorts achieved average grade ratios greater than 1.0, meaning students in either group, on average, performed better than their CQPAs forecasted. However, the average grade ratio was in favor of the treatment group for all assessments. The effect, however, was strongest at the short-term; in the long-term, the two groups were no longer statistically distinct. *Both scores show the treatment group performing, on average, better than projected, based on CQPA; and, the treatment group exceeded expectations by a significantly greater margin than the control group.* This is strong evidence that the treatment curriculum may be more effective in communicating database concepts and practice, although the effect seems to diminish with time. This diminishment may be explained, in part, due to: student familiarity with the topic by the time the final exam is taken; the final exam being open-note and open-book; or the relatively trivial practical application on the final due to the time constraints students face during the final.

The small effect size in grade ratio, 0.0998, might seem underwhelming. However, we must consider the observed performance difference this indicates. Considering the course total results (reflecting all measured database assessments), on average, students in the control group scored 108.7% of their anticipated score, as projected by their incoming CQPA. We contrast this to students in the treatment group, who scored, on average, 118.7% of their anticipated score. As a practical example, consider an average student with a 3.0 incoming CQPA; his anticipated overall grade and thus for each individual module is a 3.0 equivalent, a B. In the control group, this student was likely to achieve a 3.261 equivalent grade, just under a B+. In the treatment group, however, this student was likely to achieve a 3.561 grade, almost an A-. In these terms, the significance of the observed effect is clear.

Both groups showed an increase in average reported confidence. The treatment group had, on average, higher confidence scores, both before and after. The results are marginally significant (p≈0.1), and the effect size is roughly equivalent between groups. *This fails to support our hypothesis* that the treatment curriculum would provide greater confidence. We expected to see equivalent confidence prior to the block, and significantly greater confidence in the treatment group afterward. The obtained results may indicate a systemic flaw in the measurement methodology for confidence. The results may also fail to account for presentation variation between instructors; it is likely that the treatment instructors were more enthused about the block than the control instructors, and may have imparted undue initial confidence to their students.

8 CONCLUSION AND FUTURE WORK

In this paper, we presented an analysis of a large sample of performance measurements across a control and treatment group with the major graded assessments held constant between them. Our experimental results indicate that those students who were exposed to problem-centered learning versus skills-based instruction significantly outperformed their counterparts relative to their incoming CQPA.

Because our study examined primarily 3rd-year students in the 2nd semester of the academic year, we believe CQPA to be largely indicative of a student's capabilities. Indeed, our statistical analysis shows this correlation between an incoming CQPA and a final grade in the course. Because the correlation is not perfect it allows for other factors, such as the method of instruction, to contribute to the outcome. Thus, the problem-centered learning method used in our course appears to have improved students' performance above what was anticipated.

While the volume of work is robust regarding problem-centered learning's benefits over traditional skills-based instruction for information technology concepts and applications, much of it is domain-specific to information technology, computer science, or traditional business courses. Additionally, a number of the studies relied solely on student feedback or instructor-observations to evaluate the success of the particular pedagogical approach. We demonstrated with statistical significance that the problem-centered learning methodology does improve a student's ability to perform. This

reinforces the notion that problem-centered learning is preferable for information technology topics in courses supporting a student's cyber education.

As institutions implement core education requirements in the cyber or computing domain as part of their multi-level cyber education programs, curriculum caretakers must be mindful of the impact such a compressed timeline can have on the quality of learning. As demonstrated in this paper, one method for improving the efficient use of the limited time allocated to each topic is to utilize a problem-centered pedagogical approach.

Because of the constraints placed on section distribution amongst teachers in either the control or treatment groups, it is possible that stronger instructors influenced the results. To further demonstrate the benefit of problem-centered learning in cyber topics, future research will attempt to control more strongly for bias amongst instructors. We seek to implement this problem-centered learning methodology across all modules within our course based on these results while continuing to evaluate student performance.

REFERENCES

[1] Brown, C., Crabbe, F., Doerr, R., Greenlaw, R., Hoffmeister, C., Monroe, J., Needham, D., Phillips, A., Pollman, A., Schall, S., Schultz, J., Simon, S., Stahl, D. and Standard, S. Anatomy, dissection, and mechanics of an introductory cyber-security class's curriculum at the united states naval academy. *Computers in Education Journal*, 22 (2012), 63-80.

[2] Chen, C. and Ray, C. The systematic approach in teaching Database Applications: is there transfer when solving realistic business problems ? *Information Technology, Learning and Performance Journal*, 22 (2004), 9-21.

[3] Chen, C. Teaching problem solving and database skills that transfer. *Journal of Business Research*, 63 (2010), 175-181.

[4] Phye, G. D. Problem-Solving Instruction and Problem-Solving Transfer: The Correspondence Issue. *Journal of Educational Psychology*, 93 (2001), 571-578.

[5] Halabi, A. K., Tuovinen, J. E. and Farley, A. A. Empirical Evidence on the Relative Efficiency of Worked Examples versus Problem-Solving Exercises in Accounting Principles Instruction. *Issues in Accounting Education*, 20 (2005), 21-32.

[6] Kalyuga, S., Chandler, P., Tuovinen, J. and Sweller, J. When problem solving is superior to studying worked examples. *Journal of Educational Psychology*, 93 (2001), 579.

[7] Laware, G. W. and Walters, A. J. Real world problems bringing life to course content. *Proceedings of the 5th conference on Information technology education - CITC5 '04* (2004), 6.

[8] L'Heureux, J., Boisvert, D., Cohen, R. and Sanghera, K. IT problem solving. *Proceedings of the 13th annual conference on Information technology education - SIGITE '12* (2012), 183.

[9] Sobiesk, E., Blair, J., Conti, G., Lanham, M. and Taylor, H. Cyber Education: A Multi-Level, Multi-Discipline Approach. In *Proceedings of the Proceedings of the 16th Annual Conference on Information Technology Education* (Chicago, Illinois, USA, 2015).

[10] *Minitab 17 Statistical Software*. Minitab, Inc., City, 2010.

Starships and Cybersecurity

Teaching Security Concepts through Immersive Gaming Experiences

Carianna J. Cornel
Cybersecurity Resarch Laboratory
Brigham Young University
Provo, Utah, USA
cj.cornel@byu.edu

Dale C. Rowe
Cybersecurity Resarch Laboratory
Brigham Young University
Provo, Utah, USA
dale_rowe@byu.edu

Caralea M. Cornel
Cybersecurity Resarch Laboratory
Brigham Young University
Provo, Utah, USA
cara.cornel@byu.edu

ABSTRACT

As the world grows more technology involved, teaching some measure of cybersecurity has become imperative. Our research lab aims to help increase the cybersecurity interest and awareness among those of all ages. To aid us in this endeavor, we decided to introduce an interesting method that gamifies cybersecurity.

Our methodology tests whether our new method is a viable vehicle for cybersecurity education. To do this, we asked participants to take surveys and included our own observations. We conclude our paper with our analysis of survey results and future improvements for an effective educational tool.

1 INTRODUCTION

These past few years, the popularity of games that implement an educational standpoint such as Dust, Black Cloud, and World Without Oil, has increased [4]. These activities teach scientific skills, environmental issues, and more. Many of these games fall under a category called Alternate Reality games, defined as "an immersive story-game hybrid whose core mechanics are collaborative problem-solving and participatory storytelling" [1]. Studies show that in addition to being effective, these games are enjoyed by participants, resulting in a wave of new games constantly being created. In addition, these games are able to "promote 1) critical thinking and information literacy skills, and 2) collaborative problem-solving and sense-making" [ibid] [2].

We have designed an experiment to measure the validity of an immersive gaming experience derived from Escape the Room (ETR) challenges of a similar composition. We anticipate this being a viable vehicle for IT education, specifically cybersecurity. Our research has indicated that within the cybersecurity space this area of activity represents a novel approach. We believe it will provide a different approach to gamified cybersecurity education than current offerings.

Existing games in cybersecurity education include an abundance of alternate reality games, Capture the flag, and Cyber Defense Competitions [5, 6], generally involving multiple days of activity by participants. In contrast to this, ETR challenges are short high-intensity experiences that involve multiple challenges. Our approach has been to design an adaptive framework to provide an effective learning environment and compare this with traditional approaches.

We have designed our experience to be adaptive with each overall storyline accompanied by a series of challenges available in varying difficulties. As an initial proof-of-concept, we selected a target audience of young women in grades 8-12. This represents an age range of 13 – 18 years old. Challenges will be based on concepts of privacy and passwords, programming, incident response, forensics and situational awareness. The methodology and implementation of the challenge is included in this paper along with our measures and findings.

2 METHODOLOGY AND APPROACH

The National Taiwan University of Science and Technology has demonstrated the learning potential for ETR challenges. In their study, challenges were created to teach concepts and assembly skills of electromagnets. Participants were instructed to search for objects to escape the room using electromagnetic methods, such as use electromagnetism to pick up a key. Most of the 100 senior high school students who participated in this project found this game useful, thus suggesting that it could be a plausible instrument for learning [3].

Our approach involved elements of traditional ETR design fused with cybersecurity learning challenges. Approximately 80 female high school students would serve as our participants in teams of eight for an immersive experience.

Although based on ETR style challenges, we avoided the typical ETR approach of escaping a confined area. While these are a popular form of entertainment, we decided to simulate a survival scenario that while intense, did not present any real perceivable form of danger or entrapment to minimize unnecessary anxiety.

A starship simulation will form the underlying environment for the ETR challenges. This was selected for several reasons:

1. Familiarity with an existing immersive space-simulation experience using the Artermis starship engine.
2. Desire to focus primarily on cybersecurity elements and integrate these with an existing framework.
3. Advanced scripting/injection capabilities in the Artemis engine that allow for flexible development with external activities.
4. Excitement in the target audience range about space exploration.

SIGITE'17, October 4-7, 2017, Rochester, NY, USA
© 2017 Copyright is held by the owner/author(s). Publication rights licensed to ACM.
ACM 978-1-4503-5100-3/17/10...$15.00.
DOI: http://dx.doi.org/10.1145/3125659.3125696

A room has been allocated to and adapted for suitability to the experience. This includes creating a look-and-feel environment that is representative of a spaceship. The exact modifications will be discussed in Section 3.

The ETR experience was designed to run as part of our annual reach out Girls Cybersecurity Camp (GCC). The GCC is a week-long camp with a beginning and advanced track in cybersecurity. The schedule for the 2016 camp was adapted to overlay with the ETR experience to facilitate a simple comparison of performance between workshop instruction and ETR learning.

A specific learning outcome was addressed each morning in GCC via educational workshops. At the same time as this, two teams were excluded from the workshop to participate in the ETR experience. This provided us with control data by each day removing relevant classroom learning from ETR teams in a learning outcome.

While it was intended to include a scoring engine to measure the time and approach taken to solve each challenge and corresponding learning outcome(s), this was not completed in time for the initial pass and will be incorporated for our 2017 camp.

These scores will be normalized into a 1000-point per outcome maximum for easy comparison. The engine will also measure whether or not the team used instructional video material. Entry and exit surveys provided data-points to evaluate the effectiveness of the experience.

The complete ETR experience is designed to take 60-90 minutes and involve teamwork in a high-stress, parallel environment where participants must prioritize their tasks in accordance with their knowledge, skills and capabilities. We anticipated a level of artificially created stress as the challenges were completed. To alleviate frustrations that may result, we injected hints and partial solutions into each challenge that provide increased guidance with a reduced score. The objective for teams was to feel a measure of success by the completion of the experience. As a backup measure, mentors were providing additional support in the environment should puzzles be too difficult. With this, we were able to provide a safe environment that encourages enjoyment for learning rather than frustration.

3 IMPLEMENTATION

The location for the ETR experience is a small theater room adjacent to the cybersecurity laboratory. The room was originally designed for theatrical projections and has a rear projection booth, soundproofed walls and a large silver screen with graduated steps for tiered seating.

The glass to the projection booth has been covered with a one-way translucent film to remove visibility from the booth. This was used for monitoring the participants and providing interactive assistance when necessary.

Six computers based on the Intel NUC platform were used with touchscreen displays as various command consoles. The Artemis engine included varied roles such as communications, science, helm, captain, weapons and engineering, all of which will be statically assigned to each station.

Scenery and theatrical elements were added to increase the immersive experience including various physical challenges (defeating electronic pin-codes and mechanical locks, identifying potential saboteur hiding locations, restoring life-support and weapons capabilities by repairing damaged cabling etc.).

Challenges were designed to require the participation of multiple team-members. For example, in order to repair the life-support cabling, a team-member must enter a 2'x 4' constructed crawlspace, proceed 7' and reconnect a series of wires in the correct sequence. Progress was monitored by a connection to the GPIO pins of a Raspberry Pi which reported to the scoring engine using a network python script. Instructions on the correct sequence to reconnect were acquired by a system on the opposite side of the room. Further events in this challenge require the participation of each team-member to correctly solve the challenge.

An overview of the proposed storyline is included in Figure 1. Multiple paths to a victorious ending are provided to help minimize frustrations while allowing a more comprehensive solution to increase the effectiveness of the experience. Semi-autonomous execution of the scripted scenarios allows external control over encouragement of new scenarios. Mentor involvement when necessary takes place using a communications link to a nearby space station.

3.1 Camp Schedule

In order to measure the effectiveness of the intended learning outcomes, the aligned camp was an essential part of the scenario. This section provides a brief overview of the learning objectives of the camp that are aligned with the ETR scenario. A tentative schedule is shown in Figure 2.

Overall Objective: Understand the basic principles of cybersecurity and how these can be studied and used both as life skills and a field of expertise.

3.2 Day 1: Authentication and Privacy
Workshops:

Cybersecurity will be defined and introduced. Participants will learn how to protect themselves from hackers as well as learn what ethical hackers do.

Participants will learn the first step of a Penetration Test: Open Source Intelligence (OSINT) will be introduced. Participants will research and find information on their given target.

Participants will learn how social engineering is used and how to be aware of social engineering. This will be during an implemented activity.

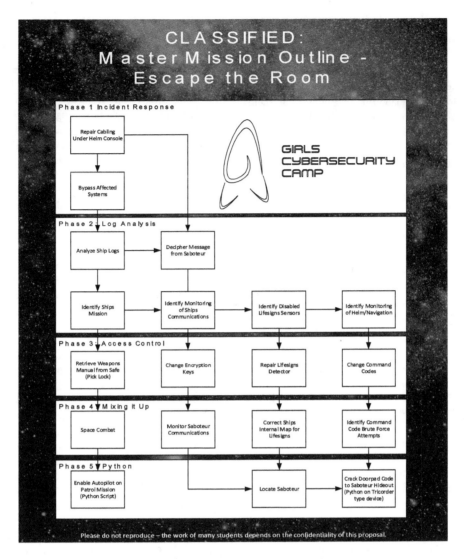

Figure 1: Escape the Room (ETR) Outline

	Tuesday - Privacy & Passwords		Wednesday - Programming		Thursday - Incident Response		Friday - Log Analysis	
8:30am	Sponsor Keynote		Sponsor Keynote		Sponsor Keynote		Sponsor Keynote	
9:00am	Daily Briefing - What to Expect							
9:30am	Introduction & Welcome		Icebreaker - Who is the best liar?		Icebreaker - Name Game		Icebreaker	
10:00am	What is Cybersecurity	Escape the Room	Alien Code	Escape the Room	Scavengers	Escape the Room	Forensics	Escape the Room
10:30am								
11:00am								
11:30am								
12:00pm	Lunch - CTB Lounge Area							
12:30pm								
1:00pm	Social Engineering		Tour		Tour		Q&A Session	
1:30pm							Professional Group Photo	
2:00pm	Staying Safe Online						Wrap Up and Closeout	
2:30pm	Command Line		OSINT		Capture The Flag			
3:00pm			Electronics		Networking			
3:30pm	Finalize and Finish up - help those struggling to finish day's goals & Escape the Room						Pick Up	
4:00pm	Daily Wrap Up & Escape the Room							
4:30pm	Fun with Pi's/Other Projects & Escape the Room							
5:00pm	Pick Up							

Figure 2: Girls Cybersecurity Camp 2016 Schedule

3.3 Day 2: Cryptography
Workshops:

Participants will learn some programming concepts in Python that will enable them to decode a message.

Participants will learn Command line that will enable them to use the keyboard for shortcuts on the computer and learn how files are stored (pre-requisite knowledge).

3.4 Day 3: Incidence Response
Workshops:

Participants will learn how to prioritize key tasks in investigating and handling cybersecurity events.

Participants will participate in a scavenger hunt prompting them to learn more aspects of cybersecurity as well as utilize their knowledge gained from the camp thus far. Clues will be provided using a variety of metadata sources.

Participants will learn how to analyze logs to recognize what traffic is going in and out of the network.

3.5 Day 4: Log Analysis
Workshops:

Participants will learn what forensics is and how it is used to solve cases in a timely manner.

Participants will learn how memory is stored in a computer and how this can be beneficial for a case and detrimental to privacy.

4 FINDINGS

A total of 48 girls participated in the ETR. The participants were asked to complete pre and post surveys to determine how effective the methods were in achieving its objectives.

For any indication questions, the assessment choices were as given: strongly agree, agree, somewhat agree, neither agree nor disagree, somewhat disagree, disagree, strongly disagree.

Sample questions from the pre and post surveys to determine effectiveness were as follows:

Question 1:

Indicate how much you agree with or disagree with the following statement: "I feel confident in my ability to learn new technologies" (Figure 3).

Comparing results from pre and post ETR there is a 5.88% increase of participants strongly agreeing with the above statement, with a minimal decrease in those somewhat agreeing, a decrease of 4.53% agreeing , and a 2% decrease of neither agreeing nor disagreeing. Because there has been a significant increase of participants strongly agreeing, compared to the rest of the changes, there is a positive jump towards the desired end of the spectrum: agreement – mainly strongly agreeing.

Question 2:

Indicate how much you agree or disagree with the following statement: "The Escape the Room experience helped me learn concepts taught in classes" (Figure 4).

Many of the girls agreed with this statement, where 10.87% strongly agree, 32.61% Agreeing, and 34.78% somewhat agreeing. The difference between Strongly Agree and Agree being a significant 21.74%. This being the case, most were not fully satisfied with the help for learning the cybersecurity concepts chosen for the camp. There is necessary improvement needed which will be discussed later on in the paper.

Furthermore, there is a small amount that neither agree nor disagree (10.87%) and disagree (2.17%) making it about 13% of the participants being unsatisfied. However, because majority of the girls picked some level of agreement, with a total of 78.26%, we can safely say that our ETR had a great beginning.

Indicate how much you agree or disagree with the following statement: "The Escape the Room experience was engaging" (Figure 5).

Over half of the participants (56.52%) strongly agreed that the experience was engaging. The rest agreed (32.61%) and somewhat agreed (10.87%). There were none who agreed with any level of disagreement or neither agreeing nor disagreeing. Thus, the TTR had some success in retaining attention.

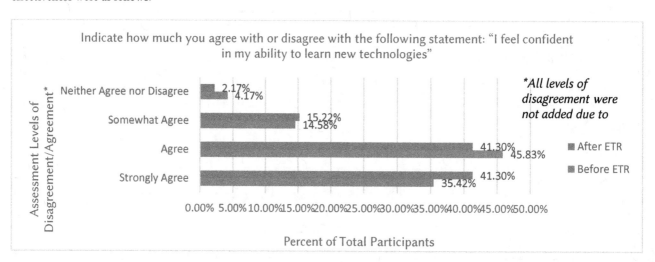

Figure 3: "I feel confident in my ability to learn new technologies" before and after the ETR.

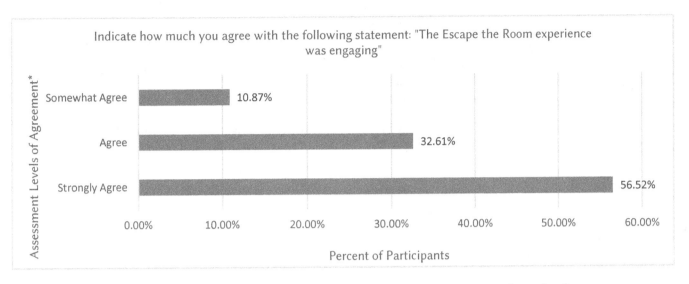

**Figure 4: "The Escape the Room experience helped me learn concepts taught in class."
These answers were given post participation of the ETR**

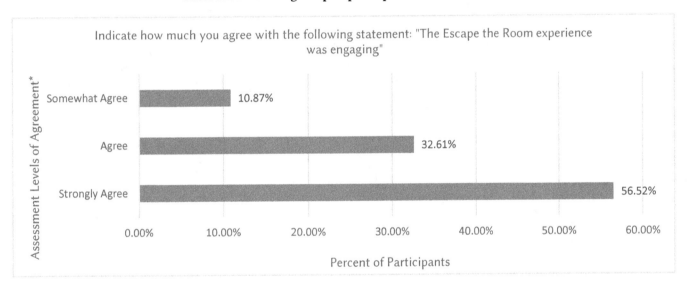

Figure 5: "The Escape the Room experience was engaging." These answers were given post participation of the ETR.

5 FUTURE IMPROVEMENTS

Our initial efforts were an extremely productive prototype and gave us valuable feedback into how this can be improved in future years. Most significantly, we believe there is sufficient data to state that ETR games such as this are an effective vehicle for cybersecurity education.

To gain further feedback, we posted the following questions to participants.

What do you feel you learned from the "escape the room experience"?

The most popular responses included: Teamwork, working under pressure, and communication.

Identified Improvement

These three concepts will be kept within the ETR experience. We will include teamwork in all challenges.

What did you enjoy most about the experience? Why?

The top three responses included: Teamwork, atmosphere, and everything.

Identified Improvement

These three concepts will be kept within the ETR experience.

What did you enjoy least about the experience? Why?

Popular responses included: Too much pressure, poor teamwork, difficult/confusing, technical difficulties.

Identified Improvements

Because teamwork was mentioned twice as something learned and enjoyed most, this will be one of the main focuses to encourage in the ETR. Because the ETR is new, technical difficulties were had and many activities had yet to be tested on female high school students. Thus, the tasks will be made more clear and framed to the desired level.

Additionally we are incorporating more challenges with 'tactile feedback' that use timers to provide hints or suggestions if attendees are struggling with challenges.

What one thing would have made your experience better? Why?

Top 3 – better training, less technical difficulties

Identified Improvement

Training that is more concise before beginning the ETR will be provided as well as refining the technology of the room.

6 CONCLUSIONS

We implemented a physical ETR to assess its plausibility in security assurance education. Participants included about 60 female high school students from the BYU Girls Cybersecurity Camp (GCC) who were split into groups of 8 for the ETR with a time limit of 90 minutes. Puzzles covered the topics of the GCC - privacy and passwords, cryptography, incident response, and situational awareness. Each participant was given a survey before and after the camp to assess how much they enjoyed and learned from the ETR. They were asked skill questions assessing how well they learned each topic: privacy and passwords, programming, incident response, and log analysis.

We have validated ETR experiences as an effective mechanism for cybersecurity education and are looking to extend our research by a more thorough evaluation over a larger participant group. Most of the recommendations have already been incorporated into the experience and we will begin gathering this data in the near future.

Most participants agreed that the ETR was engaging and aided in learning the concepts from the camp classes. It was exciting to note that most participants reported feeling more confident in their ability to learn new technology.

In contrast to this, a small number of groups struggled with team cooperation to the point that the overall experience was impacted. While this did not discourage them, it did not provide the encouragement, education or experience desired. As part of our future efforts, we will look into different methods to assist teams that have difficulty working collectively. Advancements include perfecting the technology within the ETR, clearer

training, and teaching effective teamwork. These improvements will be ready for the next year.

Thus the ETR had some desired results for becoming an agent in learning security assurance concepts and will be improved and further tested in the next BYU GCC in July 2017. This is to insure its capability of officially becoming a prosperous module for learning.

ACKNOWLEDGMENTS

We wish to thank the following sponsors for providing funding to host and run this event:

Palo Alto Network Academy, 3M, Adobe, Fireeye, Microsoft, Red Sky Solutions, Utah Open Source (UTOS), Raytheon, Heroic.

REFERENCES

[1] Bonsignore, E. et al. 2012. Alternate Reality Games: Platforms for Collaborative Learning. *Proceedings of the Tenth International Conference of the Learning Sciences* (Sydney, 2012).

[2] Goodman, B. et al. 2001. A Framework for Asynchronous Collaborative Learning and Problem Solving. *Proceedings of the 10th International Conference on Artificial Intelligence in Education* (2001).

[3] Hou, H.-T. and Chou, Y.-S. 2012. Exploring the technology acceptance and flow state of a chamber escape game - Escape the lab© for learning electromagnet concept. (2012).

[4] Jagoda, P. et al. 2015. Worlding through Play: Alternate Reality Games, Large-Scale Learning, and The Source. *American Journal of Play* 8, 1 (2015), 74–100.

[5] White, G.B. and Williams, D. 2005. Collegiate Cyber Defense Competitions. *Ninth Colloquium for Information Systems Security Education* The ISSA Journal.

[6] White, G.B. and Williams, D. 2006. The National Collegiate Cyber Defense Competition. *Tenth Colloquium for Information Systems Security Education*.

Information Technology as a Cyber Science

Joseph J. Ekstrom, Barry M. Lunt
Information Technology Program
Brigham Young University
Provo, Utah, USA
[jekstrom, luntb]@byu.edu

Rajendra K. Raj
Department of Computer Science
Rochester Institute of Technology
Rochester, New York, USA
rajendra.k.raj@rit.edu

Allen Parrish
Department of Cyber Science
United States Naval Academy
Annapolis, Maryland, USA
aparrish@usna.edu

Edward Sobiesk
Army Cyber Institute
United States Military Academy
West Point, New York, USA
edward.sobiesk@usma.edu

ABSTRACT

Emerging technologies are proliferating and the computing profession continues to evolve to embrace the many opportunities and solve the many challenges this brings. Among the challenges is identifying and describing the competencies, responsibilities, and curriculum content needed for cybersecurity. As part of addressing these issues, there are efforts taking place that both improve integration of cybersecurity into the established computing disciplines while other efforts are developing and articulating cybersecurity as a new meta-discipline. The various individual computing disciplines, such as Computer Science, Information Technology, and Information Systems, have increased and improved the amount of cybersecurity in their model curricula. In parallel, organizations such as the Cyber Education Project, an ACM/IEEE Joint Task Force, and the accrediting body ABET are producing such artifacts as a multi-disciplinary Body of Knowledge and accreditation program criteria for cybersecurity writ large.. This paper explores these various cybersecurity initiatives from the perspective of the Information Technology discipline, and it addresses the degree to which cybersecurity and Information Technology are both similar and different.

CCS CONCEPTS

• **Social and professional topics** → Accreditation • **Social and professional topics** → Computing education programs • **Social and professional topics** → Information technology education

SIGITE'17, October 4–7, 2017, Rochester, NY, USA
© 2017 Association for Computing Machinery.
ACM ISBN 978-1-4503-5100-3/17/10...$15.00
https://doi.org/10.1145/3125659.3125697

KEYWORDS

Information technology programs; cybersecurity programs; computing programs; program accreditation

1 INTRODUCTION

Information Technology (IT) has existed as a discipline since the early 2000's. Cybersecurity quickly became a critical component of any reasonable view of IT as a discipline. As demand for cybersecurity professionals has increased, however, there has been an interest in increasing the amount of cybersecurity within the IT discipline while simultaneously defining cybersecurity as a multi-disciplinary meta-discipline that has its own Body of Knowledge and its own accreditation criteria.

The emergence of cybersecurity as both part of computing disciplines and as a separate multi-disciplinary corpus raises questions about the role of cybersecurity within the IT discipline itself. How is cybersecurity part of IT, how is it a separate discipline, and do the answers to these questions provide yet unrecognized opportunities and insights?

Viewing cybersecurity as a separate concept is potentially a useful way to create a security specific educational path and increase the volume of the security workforce pipeline. However, it is impossible to reasonably separate security from the other computing disciplines. To do so would weaken the other disciplines, as it would imply that they can be conducted without security and accountability, which is not so.

To address this conundrum, we first describe the continued evolution of IT, and then we consider the growth and emergence of cybersecurity as a meta-discipline. We next analyze how the two fields intersect as well as the circumstances under which they can be considered as separate. We conclude with suggested opportunities and a summary of the current context.

2 BACKGROUND ON INFORMATION TECHNOLOGY

The academic discipline of Information Technology is the youngest of the computing disciplines cataloged in CC2005 [3]. The IT discipline was developed by a group of interested parties that started as an independent effort and eventually evolved into SIGITE. From the very beginning, there were two goals: (1) document a body of knowledge for four-year IT programs and (2) define and obtain official recognition of accreditation criteria for IT programs through ABET. The efforts got off the ground in 2001 with the first CITE (Conference on Information Technology Education) conference. The effort initially culminated with IT2005, which was the basis for IT in the CC2005 document and was officially accepted as an ACM/IEEE document in 2008 with the official publication of the IT2008 curriculum report [5].

A meeting at SIGITE 2013 discussed an update to the content of IT2008. Due to evolution of the discipline and especially the acceptance of standard terms to describe some important evolving concepts, a task force was formed under the auspices of the ACM Education Board. The task force was joined by the IEEE Computer Society. The key concepts that had emerged were:

1. Cybersecurity had emerged as the accepted name of what IT2008 called Information Assurance and Security. The terminology and conceptual foundation had evolved significantly.

2. The Internet-of-Things had emerged as a concept, as embedded systems that were connected to the Internet in large numbers.

3. Virtualization concepts and platforms had become central to IT operations and planning.

4. Cloud computing had emerged as the preferred label for describing outsourcing of computing infrastructure to organizational services (private clouds) and external providers (public clouds).

5. The need for infrastructure to support Big Data had emerged as a key requirement for organizations.

6. IT infrastructure was being used by mobile devices more than by traditional, stationary end stations.

These trends were anticipated in 2008 but the terminology and conceptual frameworks had now evolved to the point where they were key IT knowledge areas that were driving the IT practice [10]. IT2017 observes that students who have been educated under the IT2017 model will not graduate until 2020 at the earliest. Thus, IT programs need to plan for significant evolution as the IT2017 model curriculum is published in final form. New draft ABET program criteria for cybersecurity [6] are currently being piloted to accredit a small set of cybersecurity programs. Even the definition of IT as an academic discipline has evolved as a set of research questions have emerged that are the clear domain of IT, as shown by the following quotes:

Information Technology (IT) in its broadest sense encompasses all aspects of computing technology. IT, as an academic discipline, is concerned with issues related to advocating for users and meeting their needs within an organizational and societal context through the selection, creation, application, integration and administration of computing technologies [5].

Information Technology is the study of systemic approaches to select, create, apply, integrate, and administer secure computing technologies to enable users to accomplish their personal, organizational, and societal goals [10].

IT programs must evolve their curriculum as these trends emerge. One of the key areas of evolution is the term Information Assurance and Security evolving to Cybersecurity. Concepts used in both are equivalent, but there is no consensus definition for either term.

3 BACKGROUND ON CYBER SCIENCES/ CYBERSECURITY

This section presents the current status of the efforts to develop college-level curriculums in cybersecurity. To address the high demand for cyber sciences professionals, both in the civilian and non-civilian sectors, training via certification-based courses and targeted corporate courses has helped to deliver cybersecurity skills to current practitioners or ramp up the cybersecurity workforce. However, such training does not reduce the benefits of traditional undergraduate or graduate education [7].

Multiple efforts have attempted to provide guidance and resources for undergraduate cybersecurity education. On the governmental side, the NSA/DHS Center of Academic Excellence designations [8] and the NICE Cybersecurity Workforce Framework [9] have described the knowledge units needed for security. Their focus has been substantially, though perhaps not wholly, on governmental workforce requirements. For example, CAE designations require institutions, not degree programs, to map institutional curriculum to a set of technically-oriented requirements per the specific requirements of the NSA and DHS. NICE similarly provides government job classifications with associated knowledge, skills and abilities. In any event, neither of these describes what constitutes an effective cybersecurity degree program.

On the non-governmental side, the Cyber Education Project (CEP) [2] emerged much like IT had. A group of like-minded individuals worked together to define a domain and highlight curriculum for at least one degree program in this space. They used the term "cyber sciences" to refer to a broad, meta-disciplinary notion of cybersecurity. CEP helped to develop (1) curricular guidance and (2) a case for accrediting degree programs in the cyber sciences. Its immediate successor, the ACM/IEEE Joint Task Force on Cybersecurity Education (JTF) was charged with the task of developing Cybersecurity Curricula 2017 to provide "comprehensive curricular guidance in cybersecurity education" [4]. CSEC2017 defines cybersecurity as "a computing-based discipline involving technology, people, information, and processes to enable assured operations in the context of adversaries. It involves the creation, operation, analysis, and testing of secure computer systems. It is an interdisciplinary course of study, including aspects of law, policy, human factors, ethics, and risk management" [4]. Although the CSEC 2017 guidelines use the common term "cybersecurity" instead of "cyber sciences" to label this broader effort, the two terms are viewed as "conceptually consistent."

Despite the development of CSEC2017, degree programs in cybersecurity need a narrower definition of what constitutes an appropriate cybersecurity curriculum. The two uses of "cybersecurity" could be distinguished as "big cybersecurity" for the broader meta-disciplinary notion of CSEC2017 and "little cybersecurity" for the narrower notion of a program, similar to the usage of "big IT" and "little IT" in CC2005 [3]. However, as it is clearer to use different names for the two concepts, this paper uses the term "cyber sciences" to refer to the broader notion and "cybersecurity" for the narrower one.

The CSEC2017 report describes a family of cybersecurity programs, making it akin to the ACM Computing Curricula 2005 report [3] that provides an overview of curricular guidelines for five computing disciplines: computer engineering, computer science, information systems, information technology and software engineering [3]. The CSEC2017 report thus is intended to provide comprehensive cybersecurity curricular guidance to academic institutions to develop a broad range of college cybersecurity programs, not just one cybersecurity program [4].

The CSEC2017 report presents cybersecurity curricular guidelines in three parts: knowledge areas, cross-cutting concepts and a set of disciplinary lenses. Table 1 lists these components. The six knowledge areas collectively provide the full body of cybersecurity knowledge. The crosscutting concepts provide the basis for exploring interconnections between the knowledge areas and lead to "a coherent view of cybersecurity" [4]. Finally, CSEC2017 uses the disciplinary lens to customize the curricular approach, content and learning outcomes based on the needs of the computing discipline involved. CSEC2017 does not place boundaries on what cybersecurity programs need to provide, only defining the substrate in which such programs may exist.

While CSEC2017 does an excellent job in describing cyber sciences broadly, it does not provide sufficient guidance to academic institutions in defining cybersecurity programs designed to produce well-rounded, competent cybersecurity graduates. To address this need, the program criteria for cybersecurity being developed by ABET view cybersecurity more narrowly as one of the many possible implementations of the CSEC2017 [6]. The current draft of these program criteria has been influenced heavily by CSEC2017, but adds language that provides the needed guidance.

Building on the ABET general criteria used for accrediting any computing program including computer science, information systems and information technology, the program criteria for cybersecurity impose additional requirements. They require additional student learning outcomes for the program, additional curricular coverage based on the knowledge areas and cross-cutting concepts of CSEC2017, and other requirements such as appropriate mathematics. Table 2 provides a high-level summary of the current evolution of the ABET program criteria for cybersecurity -- the full version may be found in a presentation by Blair, Ekstrom and Stockman [6]. It is anticipated that these Cybersecurity Program Criteria will evolve, as several cybersecurity programs are piloted by ABET and public feedback for the current criteria draft is received.

Left out of the ABET Program Criteria for Cybersecurity is the disciplinary lens from the CSEC2017 thought model. This was intentional -- to allow each accreditable cybersecurity program to have the flexibility to drive the approach, content, and learning outcomes in each knowledge unit, the crosscutting concepts, and their interplay. That is, an institution could use one of the underlying computing disciplines to form the foundation of its cybersecurity program. One cybersecurity program thus could have IT emphasis while another program could have a computer science disciplinary lens.

Table 1: CSEC2017 Building Blocks

Knowledge Areas	Crosscutting Concepts	Disciplinary Lenses
• Data Security	• Confidentiality	• Computer Science
• Software Security	• Integrity	• Computer Engineering
• System Security	• Availability	• Information Systems
• Human Security	• Risk	• Information Technology
• Organizational Security	• Adversarial Thinking	• Software Engineering
• Societal Security		• Mixed Disciplinary

Table 2: Summary of Proposed ABET Program Criteria for Cybersecurity [6]

Criterion	High-level Description
Student Outcomes	• Ability to apply security principles and practices across the multifaceted aspects of a system.
	• Ability to ensure system operation in the presence of risks and threats.
Curriculum	Computing and cybersecurity course work covering:
	• Crosscutting concepts of confidentiality, integrity, availability, risk, and adversarial thinking.
	• Fundamental topics in each knowledge area: data security, software security, system security, human security, organizational security, and societal security.
	• Advanced cybersecurity topics built upon crosscutting concepts and fundamental topics.
	Mathematics course work including discrete mathematics and statistics.

4 INTERSECTION OF INFORMATION TECHNOLOGY AND CYBER SCIENCES

CSEC2017 specifies Information Technology as one of the disciplines that view cybersecurity through a disciplinary lens. As of this writing, no disciplinary lenses have been provided in CSEC2017, however, IT2017 contains a significant core of cybersecurity knowledge and associated competencies. A full 10% of the IT2017 curriculum is in the two cybersecurity domains.

Table 3 is a rough mapping of IT2017 cybersecurity related subdomains to the CSEC2017 knowledge areas. Two of the cross-cutting concepts also were used as containers for subdomains. Though the mapping is rough and several of the subdomains could easily apply to more than one Knowledge area, it is clear that the IT2017 subdomains significantly intersect with all of the CSEC2017 knowledge areas.

The subdomains come from three IT2017 domains, Cybersecurity Principles, Cybersecurity Emerging Challenges and Social Responsibility. These were chosen because they seemed to be the most closely related to cybersecurity curriculum for illustrative purposes. A complete mapping of all of the IT domains would provide much more in-depth coverage of the technical underpinnings of computing infrastructure.

From this analysis, it is clear that there is substantial overlap between IT programs and the emerging Cybersecurity programs. From an organizational perspective, an IT program provides a natural partner for a Cybersecurity program. There could be significant sharing of coursework and faculty.

5 IMPLICATIONS FOR ABET ACCREDITED PROGRAMS

Since Information Technology and Cybersecurity both are computing programs, both disciplines must meet the general computing criteria for ABET accreditation. In addition, each must meet the associated program-specific criteria. As we observed above, there is significant coverage of Cybersecurity topics in the Essential Domains of IT and more advanced coverage in the Supplemental subdomains. It is likely that the Disciplinary Lens that will be defined for IT in the final version of CSEC2017 will be similar to the cybersecurity domains in IT2017, after all IT2017 is a disciplinary lens for four-year IT programs applied to "Big IT."

Table 3: Mapping of IT Subdomains to Cybersecurity Knowledge Areas

CSEC 2017	IT2017 Sub-domains		
Cross-cutting Concepts	ITE-CSP-01 Perspectives and impact [L1]		ITS-CEC-05 Cloud security [L1]
Confidentiality, Integrity, Availability	These concepts do not really map as containers of subdomains but rather form the conceptual foundation of all of them.		ITS-CEC-12 Cyber-physical systems and the IoT [L1
Risk	ITE-CSP-06 Vulnerabilities, threats, and risk [L2]		ITS-CEC-11 Security implementations [L1]
	ITS-SRE-02 Goals, plans, tasks, deadlines, and risks [L2]		ITE-CSP-04 Cyber-attacks and detection [L2]
	ITS-SRE-05 Risk management [L1]	**Human Security**	ITE-CSP-08 Usable security [L1]
Adversarial Thinking	ITS-SRE-04 Global challenges and approaches [L1]		ITE-CSP-12 Personal information [L1]
			ITS-CEC-09 Personnel and human security [L1]
Data Security	ITE-CSP-09 Cryptography overview [L1]	**Organizational Security**	ITE-CSP-02 Policy goals and mechanisms [L1]
Software Security	ITE-CSP-10 Malware fundamentals [L1]		ITE-CSP-11 Mitigation and recovery [L1]
	ITS-CEC-07 Malware analysis [L1]		ITE-CSP-13 Operational issues [L2]
	ITS-CEC-08 Supply chain and software assurance [L1]		ITE-CSP-14 Reporting requirements [L1]
System Security	ITE-CSP-03 Security services, mechanisms, and countermeasures [L2]		ITS-CEC-01 Case studies and lessons learned [L1]
	ITE-CSP-04 Cyber-attacks and detection [L2]		ITS-CEC-06 Security metrics [L1]
	ITE-CSP-05 High assurance systems [L2]	**Societal Security**	ITE-CSP-07 Anonymity systems [L1]
	ITS-CEC-02 Network forensics [L2]		ITS-CEC-10 Social dimensions [L1]
	ITS-CEC-03 Stored data forensics [L2]		ITS-SRE Social Responsibility [2%]
	ITS-CEC-04 Mobile forensics [L1]		ITS-SRE-01 Social context of computing [L2]
			ITS-SRE-03 Government role and regulations [L1]

Many existing departments have CS, IT and IS programs that share infrastructure and faculty resources. Many programs also have formal emphasis tracks in cybersecurity associated with some of their programs. It is reasonable to assume that an accredited IT program with a track in cybersecurity might accredit that track as a Cybersecurity program. It may also be advantageous to create a Cybersecurity Program with a different mix of courses that do not meet the specific criteria for any other program, thereby providing a richer, and possibly more multidisciplinary, Cybersecurity experience for the students with minimal impact on Departmental resources. A potential strength of the emerging ABET Cybersecurity Program Criteria is that they account for and enable both types of Cybersecurity programs.

6 CONCLUSION

This paper provided an update on the evolving discipline of Information Technology and the emerging meta-discipline of Cybersecurity. A key component of the Cybersecurity discipline is the realization that, as the term Cyber Sciences informs, it is actually many disciplines, that span the various computing and STEM disciplines as well as the social sciences, human factors, law, ethics, and risk management.

This paper argues that there is significant intersection between IT2017 and CSEC2017, as seen through an IT disciplinary lens. The paper thus provides both insight into the continued evolutions of the disciplines as well as pointing out opportunities for the disciplines to support, benefit, and reinforce each other.

The model curricula and accreditation criteria for computing that were described will continue to rapidly evolve. It is anticipated that the curriculum reports currently in process will be published this year (2017). The ABET program criteria for cybersecurity [6] being reviewed and piloted will be finalized and implement over the next couple of years. This paper helps to highlight and contribute to these critical efforts.

REFERENCES

[1] ABET, Criteria for Accrediting Computing Programs, 2017-2018. on the Internet at http://www.abet.org/accreditation/accreditation-criteria/criteria-for-accrediting-computing-programs-2017-2018/, accessed: August 7, 2017.

[2] Cyber Education Project, on the Internet at http://www.cybereducationproject.org/ accessed: August 7, 2017.

[3] Russell Shackelford, Andrew McGettrick, Robert Sloan, Heikki Topi, Gordon Davies, Reza Kamali, James Cross, John Impagliazzo, Richard LeBlanc, and Barry Lunt. 2006. Computing Curricula 2005: The Overview Report. In *Proceedings of the 37th SIGCSE technical symposium on Computer science education* (SIGCSE '06). ACM, New York, 456-457. DOI=http://dx.doi.org/10.1145/1121341.1121482, accessed: June 17, 2017.

[4] Diana L. Burley, Matt Bishop, Scott Buck, Joseph J. Ekstrom, Lynn Futcher, David Gibson, Elizabeth Hawthorne, Siddharth Kaza, Yair Levy, Herbert Mattord, and Allen Parrish, Cybersecurity Curricula 2017, Version 0.75 Report, 12 June 2017. on the Internet at https://www.csec2017.org/, accessed: August 7, 2017.

[5] Barry M. Lunt, Joseph J. Ekstrom, Sandra Gorka, Gregory Hislop, Reza Kamali, Eydie Lawson, Richard LeBlanc, Jacob Miller and Han Reichgelt, Information Technology 2008: Curriculum Guidelines for Undergraduate Degree Programs in Information Technology, November 2008. on the Internet at http://www.acm.org/education/curricula/IT2008%20Curriculum.pdf, accessed: August 7, 2017.

[6] Jean Blair, J.J. Ekstrom, and Mark Stockman. Breakout: Developing Accreditation Criteria for Undergraduate Cybersecurity Programs. In *21*st *Colloquium for Information Systems Security Education (CISSE 2017)*, Las Vegas. June 2017.

[7] US President's Council of Advisors on Science and Technology, Engage to Excel: Producing One Million Additional College Graduates with Degrees in Science, Technology, Engineering, and Mathematics. 2012, on the Internet at http://files.eric.ed.gov/fulltext/ED541511.pdf, accessed: August 7, 2017.

[8] National Centers of Academic Excellence in Cyber Defense (CAE-CD) Designation Program Guidance on the Internet at https://www.iad.gov/NIETP/documents/Requirements/CAE_Program_Guidance.pdf, accessed: August 7, 2017

[9] National Initiative for Cybersecurity Education, on the Internet at http://csrc.nist.gov/nice/framework/, accessed: August 7, 2017

[10] Mihaela Sabin, Svetlana Peltsverger, Cara Tang, and Barry M. Lunt. 2016. ACM/IEEE-CS Information Technology Curriculum 2017: A Status Update. In *Proceedings of the 17th Annual Conference on Information Technology Education* (SIGITE 2016). ACM, New York, 102-103.

The Roles of IT Education in IoT and Data Analytics

Tae (Tom) Oh
Dept. of Information Sciences and Technologies
Rochester Institute of Technology
Rochester, NY 14623
tom.oh@rit.edu

Sam Chung
The School of Information Systems and Applied Technologies
Southern Illinois University
Carbondale, IL 62901
samchung@siu.edu

Barry Lunt
Dept. of Information Technology
Brigham Young University
Provo, UT 84602
luntb@byu.edu

Russell McMahon
Dept. of Information Technology
University of Cincinnati
Cincinnati, OH 45221
russ.mcmahon@uc.edu

Rebecca Rutherfoord
Dept. of Information Technology
Kennesaw State University
Kennesaw, GA 30144
brutherf@kennesaw.edu

ABSTRACT

The recent growth of the Internet of Things (IoT) and the expanding use of Data Analytics have both had a tremendous impact on information technology companies. A combination of IoT and Data Analytics have been used to monitor physical infrastructures, manage performance evaluation of networks and systems, integrated into personalized healthcare systems, and many more. Many information, technology-related companies have already embraced the technology. This panel discusses how IT education should embrace and approach teaching IoT and data analytics to undergraduate and graduate students. The panel will also discuss how educators should prepare students to be ready to adapt to the IoT and data analytics workforce in the industry.

CCS CONCEPTS

• Hardware~Sensor applications and deployments • Hardware~Wireless integrated network sensors • Information systems~Data analytics • Social and professional topics~Information technology education

KEYWORDS

IoT, Data Analytics, and IT Education

---

*Produces the permission block, and copyright information
†The full version of the author's guide is available as acmart.pdf document
1It is a datatype.

SIGITE'17, October 4-7, 2017, Rochester, NY, USA
© 2017 Association for Computing Machinery.
ACM ISBN 978-1-4503-5100-3/17/10...$15.00.
DOI: http://dx.doi.org/10.1145/XXXXXXX.XXXXXXX

1 INTRODUCTION

Internet of Things (IoT) has been a part of the disruptive technologies and has been impacted many areas in our life. By 2020, a number of IoT devices expected to grow to 20 to 30 billion. [1] Because of this growth, our economy could be impacted massively. [2] Also, data has been creating opportunities for Information Technology (IT) students like never before. In the last decades, emerging data technologies and tools made possible for the business to receive huge benefits from their data sets.

In this panel, we have information technology (IT) education experts with many years of experience. The panel will discuss what IT educators consider before teaching IoT and data analytics. What are the benefits and how should educators should approach including IoT and data analytics contents in IT curriculums and programs? A list of the possible discussion topics will be shared at the panel discussions, and the discussion will be tailored toward the audience interests.

2 PANELISTS' BIO (Alphabetical order)

The panelists are carefully selected and have a wealth of IT education experience. Here is a brief background of each panelist.

Dr. Sam Chung:

Dr. Chung is interested in teaching web design and development, web services, software engineering, information assurance, cyber security, penetration testing, cloud computing, and predictive analytics. His research field encompasses two areas: 1) developing software reengineering methodologies and their application to legacy information systems modernization due to emerging computing paradigms and 2) modernizing insecure legacy information systems with software reengineering-based smart and secure computing for Information Assurance and Cybersecurity. Dr. Chung directs a Smart & Secure Computing (SSC) Research Laboratory with undergraduate and graduate students. Also, he serves a student organization for minority students called Minority in Computing (MiC). He earned his Ph.D. in Computer Science from the University of South Florida (USF) in Tampa, Florida and has two MS degrees in Computer Science from George Washington University (GWU) and the Korean Advanced Institute of Science and Technology (KAIST). He graduated with a BS from the Department of Electronics/Computer Engineering track at Kyungpook National University (KNU).

Dr. Barry Lunt:

Dr. Lunt has taught electronics engineering technology and information technology at Brigham Young University since 1993 where he now serves as full professor and Director of the School of Technology. He has also taught electronics at USU and Snow College. Prior to academia he worked for seven years as a design engineer for IBM in Tucson, AZ. He has consulted for several companies and has worked summer internships for Bell Labs (now Lucent Technologies), Larson - Davis (Utah), IBM (Vermont), and Micron Technologies (Utah and Idaho). His research areas are permanent digital data storage and engineering/computing education.

Dr. Lunt is the author of "Electronic Physical Design" (Pearson Prentice Hall, 2004) and "The Marvels of Modern Electronics" (Dover, 2013) and has produced more than 70 peer-reviewed publications in the areas of electronic physical design, engineering education, and permanent data storage. He has seven U.S. patents and 20 more applied for.

Dr. Russ McMahon:

Dr. McMahon has been teaching IT related subject matter for over 35 years and is a faculty member in the School of Information Technology at the University of Cincinnati. He has been teaching full-time at University of Cincinnati since 1999 and helped create the BS Information Technology degree which started in 2004 and ABET accredited in 2006. Prior coming to UC he has taught at several area high schools and spent more than 8 years in the IT world. He teaches courses in computer programming, database administration, business intelligence, and cybersecurity. He is very active in the IT user group community having served on the boards of multiple groups (currently on the Cincinnati Chapter of Infragard) and helped create TechLife Cincinnati. In 2014, he spent 6 months working at three universities in three different countries (Rwanda, Kenya, and South Africa) in Africa performing curriculum review and development. At Nelson Mandela University in South Africa, he helped developed the first bachelors of IT degree based upon the ACM-IEEE Information Technology guidelines in all of Africa. He maintains a blog about the local IT groups and another on UC's computing history.

Dr. Tae (Tom) Oh:

Dr. Oh is an Associate Professor and Graduate Coordinator (Networking and System Administrations Program) of Information Sciences and Technology (IST) Department at Rochester Institute of Technology. He joined RIT in 2008, and his research focus has been in IoT security, sensor networks, vehicular area networks (VANET), mobile device security, and access technology. He has over 18 years of experience in networking and telecommunication as an engineer and researcher for several telecom and defense companies such as Nortel Networks, Ericsson, Ceterus Networks, Raytheon and Rockwell Collins. Also, he taught at Southern Methodist University for 7 years as an adjunct faculty. While he was working for Rockwell Collins, he was a key contributor in developing assistive technology for military soldiers on the battlefield. While at RIT, he has received funding from Office of Naval Research, Safe and Secure Mobile, Electronics and Electronics and Telecommunication Research Institute (ETRI, Korea), Rochester General Hospital, Department of Defense and American Packaging Corporation.

Dr. Rebecca Rutherfoord:

Dr. Rutherfoord is the current Interim Assistant Dean for the College of Computing and Software Engineering, and Department Chair for Information Technology at Kennesaw State University. She has been at Kennesaw State University (at the former Southern Polytechnic State University campus) for over 34 years. She began the undergraduate and graduate IT programs at the university and helped create the new Data Management and Analytics graduate certificate. Her research interests include data management, adult learners and current issues in IT.

REFERENCES

[1] Harald Bauer, Mark Patel, and Jan Veira. *"The internet of things: Sizing up the opportunity"*. http://www.mckinsey.com/insights/high tech telecomsinternet/the internet of things sizing up the opportunity, 2015.

[2] Siemens, *"Picture of the Future Magazine. Facts and forecasts: Billions of things, trillions of dollars."* http://www.siemens.com/innovation/en/home/pictures-of-the-future/digitalization-and-software/internet-of-things-facts-and-forecast.

Try-CybSI: An Extensible Cybersecurity Learning and Demonstration Platform

Rajesh Kalyanam
Research Computing
Purdue University
West Lafayette, Indiana 47907
rkalyana@purdue.edu

Baijian Yang
Department of Computer and Information Technology
Purdue Polytechnic Institute
West Lafayette, Indiana 47907
byang@purdue.edu

ABSTRACT

The increasing use of web applications for tasks such as banking, social media, and travel reservations and the frequent news of hacker attacks has brought cybersecurity to the forefront of public discussion. It is vital to ensure that the new generation of programmers is aware of the importance of cybersecurity and the various solutions in existence that address these issues. While college instructional programs incorporate optional courses on cybersecurity, the enrolled students may not receive sufficient hands-on experience or have access to resources that foster writing secure code. The goal of the Try-CybSI project is to provide a web platform that demonstrates various cybersecurity flaws and solutions, while providing users with access to containerized environments to explore and develop secure coding practices. We believe that this platform can be incorporated as a requirement in college instruction and security certification programs. In addition, researchers can contribute new applications to the platform that will enable them to publicize their work while supporting research reproducibility.

CCS CONCEPTS

• **Security and privacy** → **Software and application security**; • **Information systems** → *Web applications*; • **Software and its engineering** → *Reusability*;

KEYWORDS

Cybersecurity; instruction; containerized; cloud computing; secure coding; reproducible research

ACM Reference format:
Rajesh Kalyanam and Baijian Yang. 2017. Try-CybSI: An Extensible Cybersecurity Learning and Demonstration Platform. In *Proceedings of SIGITE'17, Rochester, NY, USA, October 4–7, 2017,* 6 pages.
https://doi.org/10.1145/3125659.3125683

1 INTRODUCTION

Cybersecurity has increasingly featured in news recently, due to several high profile hacker attacks and vulnerabilities discovered in

security libraries. For instance, the HeartBleed bug [2] discovered in the OpenSSL library required immediate patches to vulnerable systems. While researchers and graduate students at the forefront of security research are quickly aware of these vulnerabilities as they occur, there is still a large number of users who use vulnerable systems and rely on automatic security updates to secure their systems against such issues. We believe that by educating future software engineers and developers on these issues, the occurrence of such vulnerabilities can be reduced in the future.

A large gap still exists between the demand for a cybersecurity workforce and the supply of graduates with the requisite skills [14]. While several studies have been conducted into expanding and standardizing cybersecurity education [8, 10, 13], most college programs in computer science and technology still do not require a course in computer security for graduation [5]. The case has also been made for more depth in cybersecurity education, including a hands-on component [11]. Thus, a platform that provides users with constantly updated examples of security vulnerabilities and the ability to explore and apply fixes for these vulnerabilities would allow instructors to employ this platform in their instruction and also generate broader interest in the topic. A recent survey has shown that such hands-on exercises increase student interest and help them engage the material better [6]. Such a "learn-by-doing" platform can also aid reproducible research while enabling researchers to publicize their work. By hosting recent applications from security research on such a platform, interested users can replicate results published in scholarly work without having to install the necessary dependencies and code on their local machines.

Due to security concerns about the insecure applications being demonstrated, any such platform would have to sufficiently isolate these applications, preventing malicious users from exploiting these flaws. The recent *container* paradigm allows such isolation by enabling code to run in silos to which various resource and networking constraints can be applied. To support high availability of these containerized applications, they need to be deployed into an extensible resource pool. The Amazon Web Services (AWS) platform supports easy resource allocation and destruction via its load-balancing control of server instances. The Try-CybSI platform[1] uses AWS cloud computing to host easily extensible and deployable container-based demonstrations of examples of security vulnerabilities. The rest of this paper is organized as follows: we describe the design and implementation of the Try-CybSI platform, provide a brief overview of the various cybersecurity flaws and applications currently demonstrated, include analytics data from

---

[1]http://try.cybersecurity.ieee.org

global usage patterns and feedback from pilot users, and finally conclude with proposed future work.

2 DESIGN AND IMPLEMENTATION

The Try-CybSI platform is designed as a web application to provide users with simplified and centralized access to the various cybersecurity applications. In order to quickly respond to user requests for a particular application, a cluster of AWS Elastic Compute Cloud (EC2) machines is used to host (on-demand) containers for the various requested applications. While there are several container frameworks to choose from, the Docker framework is the most popular and widely supported framework of choice. Our cybersecurity applications and demonstrations are packaged as Docker *container images* and uploaded to the central DockerHub repository from where they can be downloaded and launched on any machine running the Docker daemon engine. A Docker *container* is just a runtime instance of one such image, ensuring reproducible experience in each container based on that *image*. None of the software or dependencies of the application need to be present on the machine where the container runs, the container image completely encapsulates all of the software and dependencies for the application. Thus, the same container image can be used on a Windows, Linux or Mac OS machine as long as it is running the Docker engine.

Each application's container is designed to be accessible from a web browser, lowering the barrier to entry for exploring these applications. While this requirement may seem restrictive, there are publicly available Virtual Network Computing (VNC)-based containers that provide a complete Linux desktop environment. Applications that require the full power of a desktop interface can still be deployed and accessed from the web by leveraging these containers. While we do not provide a complete description of the Docker container framework here, we briefly describe our reasons for choosing this approach, contrasting it to the well-known virtual machine paradigm. We then continue on to describe the design of the Try-CybSI website, and the typical system flow when launching Docker containers for our hosted applications.

2.1 Docker Containers versus Virtual Machines

There have been various studies comparing the performance of Docker containers against traditional Virtual Machines (VMs) [9, 12]. We believe that Docker containers work better for our requirements for several reasons:

(1) Docker containers are *lightweight*, leveraging the host machine's infrastructure for most kernel level functionality. Conversely, VMs provide a complete guest operating operating system, requiring more resources. This lightweightedness translates into our ability to host multiple application containers on a single AWS EC2 instance, increasing resource efficiency. In addition, Docker containers start up quickly which is a significant consideration when building interactive demonstration platforms.

(2) Docker containers are *extensible*, allowing users to easily start with a preexisting Docker image and add their own functionality onto it. For one, this enables incremental development using reusable building blocks. Specifically in the case of incremental demonstrative or educational

applications, the same base image can be extended incrementally with the necessary software for each subsequent demonstration or educational activity. Moreover, the ease of versioning Docker images simplifies the task of selecting the desired base or application image. While VMs are extensible as well, the task of updating a VM with new software and packaging it for use is not as trivial as the creation of new Docker images.

(3) Docker containers are easily *portable*, enabling them to be moved to a different platform or downloaded (as Docker images) and started on a user's host machine. This portability translates into more flexibility in potential system redesigns, while also enabling interested users to easily get up and running with an application on their own resources.

2.2 Try-CybSI Website

The Try-CybSI website was built using the Phalcon-PHP Model-View-Controller (MVC) framework. This allows us to separate the business logic of the website (container launching, monitoring, etc.) from the user interface. Each hosted application has three *views* or interface pages corresponding to an initial exploration page providing a brief overview of the security flaw being demonstrated and a fix (if one exists), a page listing the containers created for the user with their corresponding web access URLs and finally a help page with detailed instructions on reproducing the security flaw and fixing it to verify the solution (if one exists). The *controller* handles user interaction and page transitions. The Google ReCaptcha library is used to prevent automated bot access to these applications by requiring the user to solve a captcha query before a request for the desired application container is processed. The *model* is responsible for all the business logic, including the launching and monitoring of containers and the construction of the access URLs for the containers in response to an application request. We describe this process of launching and managing containers next.

2.3 Container Launching and Monitoring

While any EC2 instance with the Docker engine installed can support remote launching of Docker containers, AWS simplifies the task of launching sets of Docker containers and sustaining their high availability via the EC2 Container Service (ECS). ECS can manage a cluster of EC2 machines and automatically launch a predefined set of Docker containers in a load-balancing fashion on that cluster. ECS Docker container definitions can specify the Docker image to use as well as CPU, memory, and disk requirements. In addition, sets of Docker containers can be grouped into an ECS *task*, abstracting the operation of launching multiple containers as just launching the corresponding ECS task.

For each application hosted by Try-CybSI, a corresponding ECS task was defined that abstracts the set of Docker containers that need to be launched for that application. Most applications typically have a hacker and server component, thus requiring at-least two containers. ECS APIs are available for programmatic control of operations such as launching a task, monitoring a container's startup status, and determining which EC2 instance the container was launched into for various programming languages. The public access URL for a container can be constructed using information about the EC2 server hosting that container. Our model implements the business logic of launching, monitoring and constructing the access URL for the containers for each requested application using these APIs.

In general, ECS can deploy multiple containers (from different application requests) on a single EC2 instance as long as the memory and CPU requirements can be satisfied. While this approach works for most of our applications, such shared hosting has some shortcomings when additional security is required for some of the application containers. We describe this specific issue and our solution for it as well as other security considerations that arise in the context of some applications.

2.4 Additional Container Security

Docker containers typically access the outside world via a bridge network interface to the host machine that is connected to the outside world. By default, the Docker engine attaches each container on a machine to the same bridge network interface. This has the side effect of enabling the containers to communicate with each other by referencing the other's internal IP address. However, this is undesirable in certain scenarios when more than one user's container is launched into the same EC2 instance and thus attached to the default bridge network. In the special case of network security applications, this would allow a malicious user to utilize the network security exploit tools installed in their container to target containers belonging to other users.

Docker already addresses the requirement of isolating containers on a host machine by providing the ability to define additional Docker network interfaces and specify the desired network interface when launching a container. No communication is possible between distinct Docker networks. However, ECS does not yet support Docker networking, preventing its use for managing such applications requiring additional container security.

We address this issue by maintaining a separate cluster of EC2 machines that have a small number of Docker networks created by hand. Whenever a network security application is requested, the containers are launched in this separate cluster and attached to a distinct, free network on an instance in the cluster. Since we can no longer rely on ECS to automate the task of launching and monitoring the containers for such applications, a Python webservice was developed to implement these same operations. The Try-CybSI website business logic decides between ECS and the Python webservice when launching containers for a requested application based on the security requirements of the application.

It is important to note that by default, Docker containers are significantly reined in and run in an unprivileged mode. This prevents access to devices on the host machine and in particular prevents containers from running the Docker daemon to start their own containers. However, in the case of the network security demonstrations, it is sometimes necessary for containers to perform certain network-related tasks, for instance allow a hacker container to modify IP tables to set up port redirects. Rather than allow the container to run in the fully-capable privileged mode, we instead grant it certain capabilities via the fine-grained control afforded by the Docker capabilities framework. In particular, when starting a hacker container for some network security demonstrations,

we add the NET_ADMIN capability allowing it to perform certain network-related operations.

Figure 1 illustrates the overall system design and control flow diagram of the Try-CybSI platform, including the choice between the two handlers for application requests.

3 HOSTED SECURITY APPLICATIONS

There are four categories of applications currently hosted on the Try-CybSI website: network security, secure coding, security research projects and cryptography projects. We briefly describe each of these categories next.

3.1 Network Security Applications

There are three network security applications currently hosted on the Try-CybSI website and are intended to be explored in sequence:

(1) **ArpSpoof:** An ARP (Address Resolution Protocol) poisoning attack enables a hacker to mislead a victim into communicating with it by pretending to be a target server. It is a canonical example of a man-in-the-middle attack where a hacker can intercept communications between a server and the victim of the attack.

(2) **SSLStrip:** Once a hacker can intercept communication between a victim and server; (s)he can circumvent secure communication (via SSL) by using a technique called SSL stripping [1] where HTTPS links in a response from the server are replaced with HTTP, forcing the client to communicate with the server via plain text. The hacker then adds back the HTTPS headers; misleading the victim and server into thinking that they are still using secure communication.

(3) **HSTS:** A solution to the SSL stripping attack is the use of the HSTS (HTTP Strict Transport Security) protocol in all communication [3]. Specifying HSTS via the message header causes all communication to a server to necessarily use HTTPS, preventing a fallback to insecure HTTP.

In each of these applications, three containers are created; one each for the victim, server and a hacker with the necessary ArpSpoof and SSL strip programs installed.

3.2 Secure Coding Applications

Several hacker attacks often exploit vulnerabilities in systems resulting from insecure code. The secure coding applications demonstrate real-world examples of insecure coding and methods to fix such vulnerabilities. Our intent is to demonstrate how simple errors in code can have far-reaching consequences in widely used applications.

(1) **HeartBleed:** The HeartBleed bug was a vulnerability discovered in the OpenSSL library [2]. A missing validation step in the code can cause any server using the library to reveal the contents of some parts of its internal memory to a hacker exploiting the vulnerability. This flaw is demonstrated using an EC2 machine running an older (unpatched) version of the OpenSSL library and compared against a patched server.

(2) **SQL Injection:** SQL injection attacks exploit improper validation in SQL queries allowing hackers to insert their

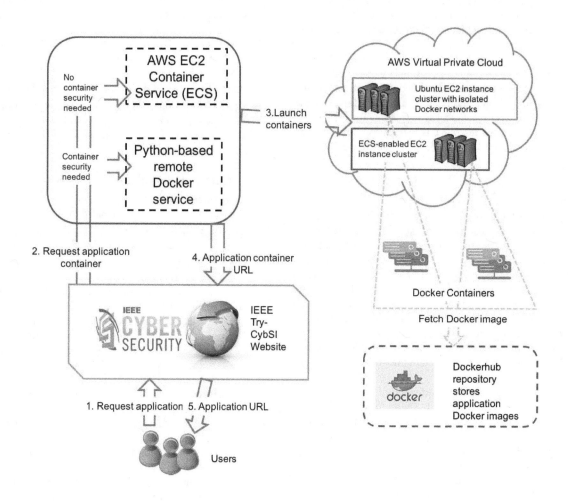

Figure 1: System Flow Diagram

own database modification statements. Applications that directly insert user typed strings into SQL queries run the risk of allowing hackers familiar with SQL syntax to run arbitrary SQL queries, inserts or deletions on a database. Sample insecure code of this nature is demonstrated along with a proposed fix that validates user input before inserting it into the SQL query.

(3) **Resource Authorization:** Resource authorization underlies one of the top ten security design flaws. Access to restricted resources must always be authorized. This is demonstrated using an insecure application where unauthorized users with knowledge of the URL to a secure resource can still access it. This vulnerability is then addressed by requiring a valid and authorized login in the session parameters, which is cleared upon a user logging out of the secure application.

3.3 Research Projects

One of the goals of the Try-CybSI platform is to foster research visibility and reproducibility by hosting applications produced as a result of cybersecurity research. Hosted research applications can be referred to in scholarly publications and conference presentations, allowing readers to better engage the research findings. Towards this goal, there are three research applications that are currently hosted on Try-CybSI.

(1) **T-DNS:** The DNS (Domain Name System) service that translates simpler website names into their IP addresses uses insecure UDP for all its communication. The T-DNS [15] project is intended to rectify this by using TCP and TLS for secure communication between a DNS client and server. We include a simple demonstration of a very small piece of this research project where network traffic can be monitored to verify that the communication is indeed using TCP.

(2) **Longtail SSH Honeypot:** The Longtail SSH honeypot [4] is used to detect and analyze unauthorized access to a secure system. The default sshd port is changed from 22 to a different number and all authorized users are informed of this change. However, connections to port 22 are still allowed, tricking an attacker into believing that they are making progress in attacking the system. The attacker's IP address, attempted user name and password can be logged for further analysis.

(3) **OFuzz:** OFuzz [7] is an example of a fuzzing platform that generates a large quantity of random data for testing file-processing applications. OFuzz focuses on flexibility, allowing a user to substitute in testing components or fuzzing algorithms. A simple configuration file is provided that generates several mutations of a sample text file. The goal of this demonstration is to make users aware of the existence of such platforms which can be used to generate useful test data for their applications to unearth security flaws resulting from unhandled input conditions.

3.4 Cryptography Projects

It is our intent and belief that Try-CybSI will find increasing use in classroom instruction, providing instructors with a platform to host programming assignments while providing all students with a uniform coding environment with the necessary libraries and skeleton code installed. As a first step towards this goal, Professor Jonathan Katz from the University of Maryland graciously provided us with two sample assignments from his cryptography course.

4 USAGE ANALYTICS AND FEEDBACK

4.1 Usage Analytics

Google Analytics was employed to collect usage statistics for the various hosted applications. Tables of both global usage patterns (number of hits, average session duration) and usage counts for each application are included below for the period from Jan 1, 2016 through May 1, 2017 [2] [3]. Table 1 provides data on the number of site visits from each country as well as the average session duration across these visits for the top 15 (in number of site visits) countries.

It is evident from Table 1 that most of our users are based in the United States. Monthly usage statistics indicate a steep decline in users from China and Japan after the first month. Future plans include integration of page translations to attract non-English speakers. Also, further outreach is required to publicize our platform and attract more visitors from around the world.

Usage data for each of our hosted applications over the same time period is provided in Table 2.

A couple of conclusions can be drawn from the application usage data in Table 2 and indicate the need for future work to attract more usage of the Try-CybSI platform.

(1) While the ArpSpoof and SSLStrip applications were used, HSTS was never explored even though the description page had several hits. We expect each of these examples to take around 5 minutes to complete. Based on the average

Table 1: Global Usage Data

Country	Number of Sessions	Avg. Session Duration (mins.)
United States	3293	04:01
South Korea	429	02:53
Turkey	328	01:54
India	212	03:48
Russia	184	04:30
Germany	126	03:39
Japan	106	02:01
Jamaica	84	01:50
Australia	76	01:17
Spain	73	04:21
France	69	13:37
China	124	02:09
Brazil	55	02:36
Canada	51	02:45
South Africa	51	05:12

Table 2: Application Usage Data

Application	Number of uses
ArpSpoof	627
SSLStrip	51
HSTS	0
HeartBleed	251
SQL Injection	296
Resource Authorization	41
T-DNS	18
SSH Honeypot	27
OFuzz	0
Padding Oracle	50
CBC-MAC	11

session duration, it is clear that not many users stayed long enough to go through the complete sequence of ArpSpoof, SSLStrip and HSTS in one sitting. It is necessary to attract return users to our platform to allow exploration of the more advanced applications.

(2) Each of the secure coding examples are fairly self-contained and possibly more familiar to lay users due to their mention in news and public discourse. Quickly deploying any new instances of well-known security flaws can attract more visitors to our platform, improving the chances of the other hosted applications being tried.

(3) Unfortunately, the research project applications did not attract much usage, probably due to user unfamiliarity with the project. We expect that if these applications were deployed prior to a conference for each accepted publication, then conference attendees would be interested in testing out the application both over the course of the conference, and beyond if the applications were constantly updated.

(4) The cryptography assignments have not yet received much usage, but it is our expectation that once Try-CybSI is

---

[2] Only countries with average session durations longer than a minute are included.
[3] Only sessions where users reached the container listing page are counted.

incorporated as a requirement in college courses, such applications would find more usage.

4.2 Feedback

The authors performed some preliminary studies on the learning outcomes of the Try-CybSI project. In Fall 2016 and Spring 2017, 24 graduate students and 45 undergraduate students enrolled in courses on Networking and Security were asked to try out the ArpSpoof and SSLStrip applications. Feedback was collected using brief anonymous surveys and the students' grades on the related final exam questions were also studied. The surveys show that 67 out of the 69 students strongly agree that the Docker-based Try-CybSI applications were easy to launch and use. In contrast, only 27 out of the 69 students strongly agree that a virtual machine-based homework assignment on password cracking was easy to launch and use. The data also shows that 41 out of the 69 students thought that the Try-CybSI applications were user friendly, whereas 38 out of the 69 students strongly agreed that the virtual machine-based homework was user friendly. The primary complaint about the Try-CybSI platform's usability was that the instructions were not on the same page as the list of containers access URLs. It should be noted, that the virtual machine-based homework assignments often had unintended issues such as the virtualized OSes auto updating, defeating the purpose of some of the attack/defense tools.

To evaluate the effectiveness of the Try-CybSI platform, results from two ARP related questions (one from Bloom category 1 and another from Bloom category 3) were compared based on whether or not students had hands-on experience with the platform. Prior to using the Try-CybSI applications, the correct rate on the Bloom category 1 question was about 91%, and about 42% on the category 3 question. After the hands-on homework exercises on the Try-CybSI applications, the correct rate on category 1 increased to 93% and rose to 68% on category 3. Based on these observations, it can be inferred that the "learn-by-doing" approach helped students better understand the concepts at higher Bloom levels and in general the Try-CybSI platform was easy to use as a learning mechanism.

5 CONCLUSIONS AND FUTURE WORK

The Try-CybSI platform is intended as both an educational resource, providing hands-on experience in various cybersecurity flaws and solutions, as well as a demonstration platform enabling researchers to publicize and deploy their applications for wider usage and testing.

While a majority of our current hosted applications do not require significant coding effort from the users, successful adoption in classroom environments will require support for users to easily save their work and continue at a later time. Future work will involve designing solutions for automatically saving user work to a mounted file system and then re-mounting the files into a new container when requested.

ACKNOWLEDGMENTS

We would like to thank Faheem Zafari, Tian Wang and Kelu Diao for developing the cybersecurity application containers. Dr. Greg Shannon, Dr. Robert Cunningham, Dr. Ulf Lindqvist and Mr. Brian Kirk from the IEEE Cybersecurity Initiative provided invaluable support during the course of this project. We would also like to thank Dr. Jonathan Katz, Dr. Anthony Joseph, Dr. Casimer DeCuastis and Mr. Eric Wedaa for graciously helping expand the content on our platform. Finally we would like to thank Dr. Carol Song and Lan Zhao from Purdue Research Computing and Dr. Eugene Spafford, Dr. Dongyan Xu and Mr. Joel Rasumus from Purdue CERIAS as well as Purdue CIT faculty and students for their initial feedback on this platform.

REFERENCES

[1] 2012. SSLStrip. (2012). https://moxie.org/software/sslstrip Accessed 05/14/17.
[2] 2014. HeartBleed bug. (2014). http://heartbleed.com Accessed 05/14/17.
[3] 2014. HSTS. (2014). https://https.cio.gov/hsts Accessed 05/14/17.
[4] 2015. SSH Honeypot. (2015). http://longtail.it.marist.edu Accessed 05/14/17.
[5] 2016. CloudPassage Study Finds U.S. Universities Failing in Cybersecurity Education. (2016). https://www.cloudpassage.com/company/press-releases/cloudpassage-study-finds-u-s-universities-failing-cybersecurity-education/ Accessed 05/14/17.
[6] S. Bell, E. Sayre, and E. Vasserman. 2014. A longitudinal study of students in an introductory cybersecurity course. In *Proceedings of the 121st Annual ASEE Conference and Exposition*.
[7] S. K. Cha, M. Woo, and D. Brumley. 2015. Program-adaptive mutational fuzzing. In *Proceedings of the IEEE Symposium on Security and Privacy*. 725–741.
[8] S. Cooper, C. Nickell, V. Piotrowski, and et al. 2010. An Exploration of the Current State of Information Assurance Education. *SIGCSE Bull.* 41, 4 (2010), 109–125.
[9] W. Felter, A Ferreira, R. Rajamony, and J. Rubio. 2015. An updated performance comparison of virtual machines and linux containers. In *Proceedings of the IEEE International Symposium on Performance Analysis of Systems and Software (IS-PASS)*.
[10] L. Hoffman, D. Burley, and C. Toregas. 2012. Holistically building the cybersecurity workforce. *IEEE Security & Privacy* 10, 2 (2012), 33–39.
[11] D. Manson and R. Pike. 2014. The case for depth in cybersecurity education. *ACM Inroads* 5, 1 (2014), 47–52.
[12] R. Morabito, J. Kjallman, and M. Komu. 2015. Hypervisors vs lightweight virtualization: a performance comparison. In *Proceedings of the IEEE International Conference on Cloud Engineering (IC2E)*.
[13] NIST. 2012. National Initiative for Cybersecurity Education Strategic Plan. In *National Institute of Standards and Technology (NIST)*.
[14] J. Vijayan. 2013. Demand for IT security experts outstrips supply. (2013). ComputerWorld.
[15] L. Zhu, Z. Hu, J. Heidemann, D. Wessels, A. Mankin, and N. Somaiya. 2015. Connection-oriented DNS to improve privacy and security. In *Proceedings of the IEEE Symposium on Security and Privacy*. 171–186.

Using Capture-the-Flag to Enhance the Effectiveness of Cybersecurity Education

Kees Leune
Salvatore J. Petrilli, Jr.
leune@adelphi.edu
petrilli@adelphi.edu
Adelphi University
Garden City, New York, United States of America

ABSTRACT

Incorporating gamified simulations of cybersecurity breach scenarios in the form of Capture-The-Flag (CTF) sessions increases student engagement and leads to more well-developed skills. Furthermore, it enhances the confidence of students in their own abilities. Our argument is supported by a study in which undergraduate students taking a cybersecurity class were surveyed before and after participating in a CTF.

GENERAL TERMS

cybersecurity; education; capture-the-flag

1 INTRODUCTION

There is ample opportunity to improve the current state of cybersecurity defenses. We argue that many breaches are, at least partially, caused by human error, which, in turn, is regularly the result of insufficient and/or ineffective education [5].

In this paper, we argue that incorporating gamified simulations of cybersecurity breach scenarios in the form of Capture-The-Flag (CTF) sessions strongly support traditional lecture-style instruction, and that it significantly enhances confidence of students in their own abilities.

Three types of CTF games are generally distinguished: quiz-based, in which participants score points by answering questions; scavenger-hunt, or flag-based, in which participants locate and exploit vulnerabilities in systems security in order to gain access to files which contain "flags" in the form of random strings, and king-of-the-hill, or castle-based, in which participants score points by defending a server against attackers. The study presented in this paper combines quiz-based questions and flag-based questions, and does not include a king-of-the-hill component.

We present our statistical findings from a single observation. Although based on a single experiment, we hope that this study begins an on-going discussion and may lead to recommendations for further research regarding the benefits of gamification for students pursuing a career in cybersecurity.

SIGITE'17, October 4–7, 2017, Rochester, NY, USA.
© 2017 ACM. 978-1-4503-5100-3/17/10...$15.00
DOI: https://doi.org/10.1145/3125659.3125686

The remainder of this paper is structured as follows: section 2 explains the rationale for our study and provides background. Section 3 described the methods and objectives of our study and section 4 presents our findings. Section 5 summarizes the main conclusions that can be drawn from our work, and section 6 shows possibilities for future research.

2 BACKGROUND

Popular media have been reporting extensively how, despite the availability of many highly advanced technical products and solutions, human decision-making is a key component of data breaches. The point is made very clearly in a survey of approximately 80,000 recent systems breaches that have been summarized in Verizon's annual Data Breach Investigation Reports [15, 16], in which human error, deliberate actions, or insufficient training and awareness are all identified as factors that lead to security breaches.

While these highly visible breaches have led to fragmented legislation [12] and increased awareness of the general public concerning the importance of achieving and maintaining cybersecurity, the methods for teaching cybersecurity at institutes for higher education have not kept up with the high pace of developments. In fact, human error, which may have been minimized through better education and training, has played some role in each of the breaches that were referenced.

Hence, since systems breaches are commonplace, and the root cause of many breaches involves human decision making, engaging in an attempt to improve human decision making skills with regards to cybersecurity problems is a worthy effort. One way by which human decision making skills can be influenced is through education. As such, the goal of this research project is to find new and innovative ways to engage student learning, especially in the arena of cybersecurity.

The problem of lacking education in cybersecurity is a global problem. In "The UK cyber security strategy: Landscape review" [9], the authors observed that it could take up to 20 years to address the skills gap at all levels of education.

Among the many top issues that are facing higher education, a skills gap between the outputs of colleges and universities and the needs of employers [1] is frequently mentioned. Higher Education is not always equipped to respond rapidly to changing demands in labor force skills, and the cybersecurity domain is no exception to that. By embracing traditional teaching methods, which may not align with the needs of potential employers, or with the emerging interests of students, colleges and university do not always produce the best outcomes.

Research shows that student motivation is a key predictor of successful educational outcomes. If students are intrinsically motivated to learn something, they may spend more time and effort learning, feel better about what they learn, and use it more in the future [8].

The most notable causes of student disengagement with learning include boredom, alienation, and disconnection between learning activities and real life application of knowledge [11]. Gamification has the ability to address many of these causes: it focuses students on relevant content, provides timely feedback, which improves retention, and supports students' multiple styles of learning [4].

Usually, there are two approaches to using games in education. The first approach seeks the engagement that commercial and widely available games have to foster learning outside the school environment. Games such as *Sid Meier's Civilization* or *World of Warcraft* can provide a challenging and motivating world that requires analyzing, planning, communication skills and others, contributing to improving the problem solving abilities of players. On the other hand, games can be specifically designed to convey traditional content in a different, untraditional form [7].

Intrinsic learning requires the embedding of learning outcomes of a teaching program within the mechanics of a game. It appears crucial that the task learned in the game maps directly onto the challenge faced in the real world [6].

Projecting these findings onto cybersecurity education, we posit that a carefully designed gamified cyberbreach simulation can be incorporated into the traditional university classroom, and used to capture interest and engagement by a variety of audiences. Furthermore, we believe that participation in these simulations can address the root causes identified by [11]. Specifically, we anticipate that students will be more engaged and have an increased understanding how their classroom skills related to realistic real-world scenarios. Consequently, we anticipate that learning outcomes using this approach enhance traditional teaching methods based on lectures followed by written exams.

3 METHODOLOGY

3.1 Research question and Hypotheses

In our study, we set out to answer the following research question:

RESEARCH QUESTION. Does the inclusion of realistic simulations of offensive attack scenarios — in the form of capture-the-flag exercises — demonstrably increase the effectiveness of cybersecurity education?

In order to find an answer to this question, we defined a number of hypotheses:

HYPOTHESIS 1. *Self-confidence of students will improve by participating in a capture-the-flag (CTF).*

We are interested in finding out if participating in the CTF helps students gain self-confidence in their skills. Our hypothesis is that participants will generally feel more accomplished and more secure in their abilities after having spent some time in a realistic, but controlled environment.

HYPOTHESIS 2. *Students enjoy participating in a CTF.*

By introducing gamification components, such as the ability to choose 'hacker handles', a shared scoring system to encourage some friendly competition, and the ability to buy hints using points that were scored by solving previous challenges, we anticipate that students will enjoy participation in the CTF. Our expectation is that, by active participation, students will spend more time learning and develop stronger outcomes.

HYPOTHESIS 3. *Students develop stronger practical skills by participating in the CTF.*

Reinforcing theoretical knowledge of cybersecurity methods and techniques by experimenting with them in a controlled environment is expected to reinforce and/or develop strong practical skills in students.

HYPOTHESIS 4. *Participating in the CTF reinforces theoretical concepts.*

Similar to reinforcing practical skills, we expect that participation in the CTF will solidify student's understanding of general concepts and improve learning outcomes.

3.2 Participants

This study was conducted in an elective undergraduate course entitled 'Cybersecurity', which had $N = 24$ students enrolled. Students were asked to fill out a consent form indicating their willingness to participate in this study. A sample of ($n = 10$) undergraduate students agreed to complete a baseline questionnaire after a theoretical block had been completed, but before the block was reinforced using a two-week long capture-the-flag scenario. The questionnaire consisted of seven Likert-scaled questions (scale: 1–5) and 11 free-response questions. In the free-response questions, participants were asked to properly phrase definitions of security-related terms and techniques. After completion of the questionnaires, these questions were subsequently graded out of five points to facilitate analysis.

A large part of our students consisted of male (90%) junior-level (47.6%) and senior-level (33.3%) undergraduate computer science (76.2%) majors. However, since this was a class without prerequisites, other majors (Physics, Mathematics, Business Administration and Information Systems) also participated.

3.3 Materials and Procedures

In the questionnaires[1] we assessed knowledge of the students concerning different attack vectors, and we asked them to identify how confident they were in their skills to recognize, execute and prevent attacks.

Students were provided access to a virtual network, on which a variety of (virtual) servers had been installed. In all, students were tasked to gain access to all servers that they could find, identify flags, elevate privileges to achieve administrative access, and provide a writeup of their activities in which they summarized their case notes and provided recommendations for hardening the environment so that the techniques that they successfully used could not be reproduced.

---

[1]Questionnaires available via http://cs.adelphi.edu/~leune

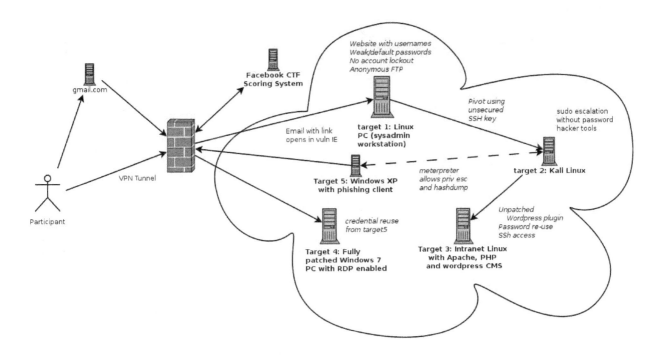

Figure 1: Capture-the-Flag overview

As shown in Figure 1, the virtual network was only accessible via a Virtual Private Network (VPN) tunnel and contained six target virtual machines, running a combination of Ubuntu Linux, Microsoft Windows 7 and Microsoft Windows XP.

With minimal additional instruction, students were asked to play out a variety of scenarios, ranging from simple default passwords (target 1), which allowed access to a server from which students can then pivot their attack by using an unprotected secure shell (SSH) key to pivot their attack to a Kali Linux server running a variety of offensive tools (target 2), to an unpatched Wordpress plugin vulnerabilities hosted on target 4, which re-used the same password for the database access and access to an account capable of elevating privileges using the Linux sudo command.

Furthermore, in an attempt to mimic realistic contemporary attack scenarios, we created a small program that would download email via the POP protocol so that passwords could be intercepted using a packet sniffer (target 5). The server on which the program ran according to a predetermined schedule actively filtered inbound traffic and was offering no externally available services.

As an added twist, the email download program ran on a vulnerable Microsoft Windows XP virtual machine that would open any URLs using Internet Explorer that were contained in the incoming email. Students were able to craft messages and send them from their regular email accounts. Upon receipt, the URL that was opened resulted into a downloaded exploit, which would give students access to the target. On that target, elevating privileges and obtaining a copy of the encrypted password store (SAM) was a logical next step.

Flag category	Amount	Percentage
weak configuration	5	26%
reconnaissance	4	21%
vulnerability	4	21%
password	3	16%
privilege escalation	2	11%
phishing	1	5%
	19	100%

Table 1: Flags per category

The encrypted passwords can be cracked off-line, yielding additional credentials that can were re-used on a fully patched Windows 7 virtual machine, which permitted Remote Desktop Connections.

As shown in Table 1, students were able to collect 19 flags, ranging from easy ones, to ones that required lateral attacks and privilege escalation. The flags were placed on to seven virtual machines, running three different operating systems, and students were able to gain access to and escalate privileges on five of them. Samples of each flag category are described in Table 2.

Vulnerabilities introduced in this simulation mostly focused on insufficiently patched software, password re-use, weak and default passwords, phishing, and weak operational security practices.

In addition to recognizing and exploiting vulnerabilities, students were asked to answer a range of quiz questions. In the CTF design, the flags questions were intended to reinforce skills, while the quiz questions were designed to reinforce knowledge. The quiz questions area broken down by category in Table 3.

Flag category	Sample challenge
weak configuration	Target 2 (Kali Linux) allowed remote login using an unprotected SSH key.
reconnaissance	Target 1 published a staff directory, including usernames, email addresses and job titles to an unprotected website.
vulnerability	Target 3 was running Wordpress with an vulnerable plugin that allowed unauthenticated remote code execution.
password	User on target 1 had easy to guess password.
privilege escalation	User was allowed sudo without password challenge.
phishing	Emailing a special account with trigger opening an arbitrary web page using a vulnerable web browser.

Table 2: Sample questions per flag category. Network architecture depicted in Figure 1

Quiz category	Amount	Percentage
news & general	6	35%
networking	6	35%
definitions	2	12%
attacks	1	6%
cryptography	1	6%
law & ethics	1	6%
	17	100%

Table 3: Quizzes per category

Table 4 includes samples of the quiz questions that students were asked. In scoring, quizzes were generally awarded one point, while flags commonly yielded five points.

Gamification components were introduced by encouraging students to work in competitive teams. A shared score board was kept using Facebook's CTF platform, a publicly available scoring system [2].

4 FINDINGS

Based upon the responses to the pre and post questionnaires, we were able to examine outcomes from participating in the capture-the-flag. Here we share some of our observations. We should note that majority of our results come from an analysis of the post-assessment questionnaire.

We found a direct correlation between the level of enjoyment that participants reported after participation in the CTF activity and an increased confidence in their ability to execute attack methods that were simulated during the exercise. Furthermore, we found that an increased confidence almost directly translates to increased outcomes.

4.1 Strong Confidence in Abilities

[10] found that gamification in the educational setting has the added benefit of increasing student self-esteem with respect to the content area. Our numbers support that statement; we posit that a gamified environment contributes to increased participation, which, in turn, leads to a significant increase in the participant's confidence and abilities to execute cyberattacks.

Our surveys showed that, prior to participating in the activity, students expected to enjoy the exercise. The post-activity assessment demonstrated that students were not disappointed; the data

indicates that participants clearly enjoyed taking part in the exercise. This is evident most strongly in the responses to question 7 *Did you enjoy participating in a hands-on capture-the-flag exercise?*, in which students reported a strong affirmative median score of 5 out of 5 in the post-CTF assessment questionnaire.

In addition, our repeated-measures study discovered a significant correlation between a participant's enjoyment in participating and their self-confidence in their ability to perform cybersecurity defense tactics.

The participant's new-found confidence is most strongly illustrated by the answers to question 1 from the pre- and post-questionnaire (*How confident are you in your abilities to execute a typical attack that follows the phases discussed in class?*). A Wilcoxon test found a significant increase in the mean ranks in the repeated-measures study ($Z = 2.719, p < .05$).

All confidence-related questions were significantly correlated, suggesting that confidence is built broadly, and includes confidence in participants' ability to execute, recognize and defend against cyberattacks.

In particular, question 1 was significantly correlated with question 2 *How confident are you in your abilities to recognize a typical attack that follows the phases discussed in class? You may assume that you have sufficient visibility into the infrastructure?*, question 3 *How likely are you to execute certain attack types after reading about them? You may assume that you have permission to do so, and a platform to conduct the attacks on?*, question 4 *Do you feel prepared to defend against real attacks on an actual enterprise network?*, and question 6 *Did participating in a hands-on capture-the-flag exercise enhance your understanding of how attacks are conducted?* ($r = +.716$ and $p < .05, r = +.779$ and $p < .05, r = +.824$ and $p < .05, r = +.857$ and $p < .05$, respectively).

Additionally, we found that students gained an increased appreciation for learning about new cyber-defense techniques. In particular, the answers to question 5 *How prepared are you to keep up with learning about new vulnerability types and attack trends?*, and question 6 *Did participating in a hands-on capture-the-flag exercise enhance your understanding of how attacks are conducted?* were significantly correlated with question 7 *Did you enjoy participating in a hands-on capture-the-flag exercise?* ($r = +.672$ and $p < .05$, and $r = +.701$ and $p < .05$, respectively).

These strong results were matched by students' self-assessments. In particular, question 2 from our survey *How confident are you in your abilities to recognize a typical attack that follows the phases discussed in class? You may assume that you have sufficient visibility*

Quiz category	Sample question	Answer
news & general	What global organization of volunteers aims to advance the state-of-the-art of application security by publishing tools?	OWASP
networking	What protocol is expected to be found in a network flow that involves TCP port 25?	smtp
definitions	In which access control model is the creator of the resource the owner?	discretionary
attacks	What kind of attack will try all possible combinations of a key/passphrase?	bruteforce
cryptography	What hashing algorithm was recently proven to be insecure?	SHA1
law & ethics	Which if the following is a federal law enforcement agency: CIA, NSA, DHS, or US Secret Service?	US Secret Service

Table 4: Sample questions per quiz category

into the infrastructure. was scored with a median score of 4 in the post-CTF assessment, and it was significantly correlated with question 4 *Do you feel prepared to defend against real attacks on an actual enterprise network?* (median: 2.5), and question 6 *Did participating in a hands-on capture-the-flag exercise enhance your understanding of how attacks are conducted?* (median: 4.5) The correlations were $r = +.703$ and $p < .05$ and $r = +.773$ and $p < .05$, respectively.

4.2 Strong Observed Outcomes

Participants spent more time on the CTF than they anticipated: in the pre-assessment, an anticipated median time commitment of ten hours was reported, but in the post-assessment, students reported having taking a median 20 hours to participate.

Their efforts paid off. After completing the post-CTF assessment questionnaire, participants generally scored high. Overwhelmingly, participants were able to define and explain the consequences of password re-use (median: 5), phishing (median: 4) and weak configurations (median: 4). Significant increases in outcomes were observed in participants' ability to describe the risks of using weak passwords (median: 4).

Interestingly, when examined jointly, the quiz and flag components were not contributing to the post-assessment score. However, when examined separately, they were contributors to the post-assessment score. This indicates that quizzes and flags measures two different educational aspects: quizzes measure terminology and flags measure application.

A multiple linear regression model was constructed to predict participants' post assessment score on their quiz score and categorization of the quiz topics. A significant regression equation was found ($F(2, 36) = 7.374$, $p < .05$), with an R^2 of .291. Participants' predicted post score is equal to 31.188 + .968(QUIZSCORE) + .418(CATEGORY). Participants' post score increased by a factor of .968 for every point they scored on a quiz in the CTF. Both QUIZSCORE and CATEGORY significant contributors to the regression model.

Additionally, a multiple linear regression model was constructed to predict participants' post assessment score on their flag score and categorization of the flag topics. A significant regression equation was found ($F(2, 36) = 6.412$, $p < .05$), with an R^2 of .263. Participants' predicted post score is equal to 31.831 + .145(FLAGSCORE) + .332(CATEGORY). Participants' post score increased by a factor of .145 for every point they scored on a flag in the CTF. Both FLAGSCORE and CATEGORY are significant contributors to the regression model.

These findings are consistent with those that were found by [3], who found that gamification in the classroom makes computer science education more interesting and effective for students.

4.3 Reality vs. Perception

One post-assessment question asked students to describe the risk of weak passwords, and to provide suggestions how to mitigate the risk. One students answered that "weak passwords are a vulnerability caused by the use of a generic, default, or otherwise easily guessed password for an account. These can include common passwords (e.g., password, qwerty) or easily accessed personal information (e.g., last name, birth year, pets name). This is dangerous as there are methods where you can guess millions of passwords for a single account and a weak password can be easily guessed/cracked. You can prevent this by educating users on what a secure password should be and also implementing password controls like length on users when they are creating passwords."

This answer is interesting, given that the issue of weak passwords (password=*password*), as well as password re-use were central to successfully completing the simulation exercise. This answer clearly indicates that the student understood this aspect of securing a system.

In another question, students were asked to describe *port scanning*, explain when the technique would be used, and what preventative measures can be taken. One student responded that port scanning happens "when someone scans a computer on a network to determine what ports are open on that computer. This will help determine what protocols are running behind those ports, and in turn what software is running behind that protocol. Nmap is a popular tool. To prevent this, you can monitor incoming traffic and blacklist IPs that try scanning too many nodes. You can also prevent direct access to your network from the outside through a firewall/IPS."

Since the students were provided access to the test network without knowing any additional information, the first step they were expected to perform was to conduct a portscan. This student clearly understood not only how to run a tool (nmap), but also understood its significance.

Other questions were not answered as well as these two examples were. For example, when asked to discuss lateral attacks, which were not prominently present in the CTF, answers ranged from ones that exhibit little or no understanding ("Always keep your eyes on the server. Investigate suspicious IP.") to ones that indicate a more sophisticated view ("Using a vulnerable computer to branch over to another computer on the same network. getting into a 3rd party company to attack the target company through the unprotected connection. Can be defended by implementing controls all along the network.").

Most students were able to successfully execute the attacks that were prominently features in the CTF, which appears to support the hypothesis that participation in CTF-like exercises positively impacts the ability to execute and recognize offensive cyber techniques.

The responses showed clear correlation between the perceived level of understanding (questions 9–18) and enjoyment (question 7) that students obtained from participating in the CTF and the actual understanding of vulnerability types *weak configuration, weak passwords* and *unpatched software vulnerabilities*, as evidenced by their ability to define and describe these vulnerability types.

The significant correlation between increased confidence in the ability to recognize and the ability to respond to cyberattacks is relevant, since these vulnerability categories were prominently present in the CTF exercise. Students were asked to recognize and exploit vulnerabilities in Symposium, a Wordpress Plugin [14], as well as in Microsoft Windows XP [13].

5 CONCLUSION

Our first hypothesis was that self-confidence of students will improve by participating in a capture-the-flag (CTF). The study confirmed that this is indeed the case. Having the ability to practice — potentially dangerously — techniques in a controlled environment solidified students' confidence in their own ability to execute, recognize and defend against attacks.

Our second hypothesis was that students enjoy participating in a CTF. First and foremost, one of the main conclusions from this experiment was that students overwhelmingly enjoyed participating in the exercise. Most students were very engaged and spent a significant amount of time in trying to solve the exercises. Research has shown that engaged students generally have improved learning outcomes; this study confirmed that CTF-like events positively contribute to student's enjoyment in the course work and their engagement with it.

While perception and enjoyment are important factors in teaching, the end-result is what really matters. Our third hypothesis was that students develop stronger practical skills by participating in the CTF. This was confirmed as well. Student's understanding, as measured by the post-CTF assessment, of attack scenarios that were played out during the CTF was higher than the scenarios that were not.

Lastly, our fourth hypothesis was that participating in the CTF reinforces theoretical concepts. This hypothesis was less clearly proved. While post-CTF assessment outcomes were generally high, they were not necessarily significantly higher than during the pre-CTF assessment. It appears that a CTF in which flags (skills assessments) and quizzes (knowledge assessment) are combined do not have a strong positive outcome on learning theoretical concepts. However, based on the data presented in section 4.2, we suspect that

separating exercise in a knowledge-based CTF and in a skill-based CTF will lead to improved outcomes.

Having tested out hypotheses, we can now answer our research question: "Does the inclusion of realistic simulations of offensive attack scenarios — in the form of capture-the-flag exercises — demonstrably increase the effectiveness of cybersecurity education?" Taking into consideration what we learned, we must answer this positively. CTF exercises increase the effectiveness of cybersecurity education, provided that they are designed appropriately. If the desired learning outcomes include strong practical skills, a CTF that is flag-based is good use of time. Combining flag-based questions and quiz-based questions in a single CTF may be less effective.

6 FUTURE WORK

Future research can and will hopefully entail collecting longitudinal data on the effects of gamification in a cybersecurity major/track. It is still to be determined which of the suggested course content and activities are most effective. One way to approach a broader study might include tracking incoming freshmen and the influence of gamification until the end of their senior year. By means of such a study, researchers might be able to determine if gamification has statistically significant influence in better preparing students to enter the field of cybersecurity. In addition, a larger quantitative and qualitative study across areas in computer science could prove illuminating.

Furthermore, investigating under which circumstances different CTF forms (quiz, scavenger hunt, king-of-the-hill) are most appropriate is a worthwhile endeavor.

REFERENCES
[1] Ebersole, J. (2014). Top issues facing higher education in 2014. *Forbes*.
[2] Facebook (2017). Facebook CTF Platform. Available at https://github.com/facebook/fbctf.
[3] Firdausi, N., Prabawa, H., and Sutarno, H. (2017). Improve student understanding ability through gamification in instructional media based explicit instruction. *IOP Conference Series:* Journal of Physics.
[4] Geelan, B., de Salas, K., Lewis, I., King, C., Edwards, D., and O'Mara, A. (2015). Improving learning experiences through gamification: A case study. *Australian Educational Computing*, 30(1).
[5] Liginlal, D., Sim, I., and Khansa, L. (2009). How significant is human error as a cause of privacy breaches? an empirical study and a framework for error management. *Computers & Security*, 28:215–228.
[6] Linehan, C., Kirman, B., Lawson, S., and Chan, G. (2011). Practical, appropriate, empirically-validated guidelines for designing educational games. In *Proceedings of the SIGCHI Conference on Human Factors in Computing Systems*, pages 1979–1888.
[7] Lopes, R. (2014). Gamification as a learning tool. *International Journal of Development and Educational Psychology*, 2:565–574.
[8] Malone, T. (1981). Toward a theory of intrinsically motivating instruction. *Cognitive Science*, 4.
[9] National Audit Office (2013). The UK cyber security strategy: Landscape review.
[10] Richter, R., Raban, D., and Rafaeli, S. (2015). Studying gamification: The effect of rewards and incentives on motivation. *Gamification in Education and Business*.
[11] Shernoff, D., Csikszentmihalyi, M., Schneider, B., and Shernoff, E. (2003). Student engagement in high school classrooms from the perspective of flow theory. *School Psychology Quarterly*, 18(2).
[12] Stevens, G. (2012). Data Security Breach Notification Laws. Technical report, Congressional Research Service.
[13] The MITRE Corporation (2008). CVE-2008-4250. Available from MITRE, CVE-ID CVE-2008-4250.
[14] The MITRE Corporation (2014). CVE-2014-10021. Available from MITRE, CVE-ID CVE-2014-10021.
[15] Verizon Business (2015). 2015 data breach investigations report.
[16] Verizon Business (2016). 2016 data breach investigations report.

EZSetup: A Novel Tool for Cybersecurity Practices Utilizing Cloud Resources

Yanyan Li
Department of Computer Science
University of Arkansas at Little Rock
Little Rock, AR, USA
yxli5@ualr.edu

Dung Nguyen
Department of Computer Science
University of Arkansas at Little Rock
Little Rock, Arkansas, USA
dvnguyen@ualr.edu

Mengjun Xie
Department of Computer Science
University of Arkansas at Little Rock
Little Rock, Arkansas, USA
mxxie@ualr.edu

ABSTRACT

Recent years have witnessed fast growth of interests and efforts in developing systems and tools for cybersecurity practices, especially with the rapid advancement of cloud computing. However, those systems either suffer from issues in scalability, customization and setup complexity or are constrained by a specific cloud technology and limited customization support. In this paper, we present a novel Web based tool called EZSetup that can create and manage user-defined virtual environments for various types of cybersecurity practices on demand and at scale. Distinct from previous cloud-based systems, EZSetup does not rely on a particular type of cloud platform or technology. It is able to interact with multiple clouds and instantiate virtual environments in multiple clouds simultaneously. EZSetup allows for easy customization and significantly reduces the overhead in creating and using practice environments through carefully designed Web interfaces. The experimental results are quite positive in general and indicate that EZSetup can also be applicable to other computer science and engineering subjects.

KEYWORDS

Cybersecurity Practice; Security Lab; Cloud Computing; Tool Development

1 INTRODUCTION

The gap between demand and supply for cybersecurity professionals is huge [10]. According to Forbes [8], the number of cybersecurity job openings is expected to rise to 6 million by 2019 and one quarter of them, roughly 1.5 million jobs, are projected to be unfilled. Meanwhile, cyber attack and data breach events occur constantly (e.g., [4, 6]). Therefore, training and enhancing current and next-generation cybersecurity professionals via effective, affordable, and scalable mechanisms is vital to fill in the gap.

Hands-on cybersecurity practices are indispensable to cybersecurity education and training. They can be applied in various forms such as regular course labs and extracurricular cyber defense competitions. The system settings of those practices can range from a

SIGITE'17, October 4-7, 2017, Rochester, NY, USA
© 2017 Association for Computing Machinery.
ACM ISBN 978-1-4503-5100-3/17/10...$15.00
https://doi.org/10.1145/3125659.3125699

simple virtual machine to a complex network with multiple subnets and server systems. Although a cybersecurity practice environment built with physical hardware is usually effective, the high cost and low scalability make it less popular and only adopted by well-funded activities (e.g., collegiate cyber defense competition or CCDC [12]). With the advancement of virtualization technologies, virtual machine (VM) based approaches to building cybersecurity practice environments become popular and there exist a number of VM-based solutions such as SEED Labs [3], Open Cyber Challenge Platform (OCCP) [13], ISERink [5], V-NetLab [11], and Platoon [7]. Those tools and systems have greatly facilitated the widespread of cybersecurity practices due to their much reduced cost in environment setup and scenario creation. However, they suffer from the following issues: 1) They are not designed for large-scale deployment of practices; 2) The deployment of those systems still requires nontrivial effort and beyond entry-level system and networking knowledge and skills, which becomes a barrier to their wide adoption; 3) They lack strong and user-friendly support for customization.

The rapid development of cloud computing also brings cybersecurity practices into clouds. Recent years have witnessed the flourish of cloud-based security practice platforms and systems such as the training system at the Center for Systems Security and Information Assurance (CSSIA) [2], NICE Challenge Project [9], and V-Lab [14]. Those systems are able to support large-scale deployment of security practice scenarios. However, they usually are built using a specific cloud technology and do not expose an interface to their users for customization.

In this paper, we propose a novel Web application called EZSetup, which is capable of creating a variety of user-defined cybersecurity practice environments (e.g., labs and competition scenarios) in one or multiple computing clouds (e.g., OpenStack and Amazon AWS). Distinct from previous cloud-based solutions, EZSetup does not rely on a particular type of cloud platform or technology. It is able to interact with multiple clouds and instantiate virtual environments for security practices in multiple clouds simultaneously, which makes EZSetup flexible and scalable. EZSetup provides a Web user interface for practice designers to visually create a practice scenario (drag and drop icons and link them) and separates the Web interface for practice designers, namely admin panel, from the one for practice executors (i.e., end users), namely user panel. By doing so, EZSetup allows for customization and at the same time significantly reduces the overhead in creating and using practice environments. Completely hidden from the complexity in creating practice environments, end users can enjoy a quick start and fully concentrate on security practices. We recruited nine volunteers to evaluate the current prototype of EZSetup in both lab creation as a lab manager and lab exercise as a lab user. The experimental results are in general quite positive and indicate that EZSetup can also be applicable to other computer science and engineering subjects.

The rest of this paper is organized as follows: We briefly describe the related work in Section II. We then present the design of EZSetup in Section III and its implementation in Section IV. We detail the evaluation of EZSetup in Section V and conclude this paper in Section VI.

2 RELATED WORK

Recent years have witnessed the growing interest in applying virtualization technologies to cybersecurity learning and practices. Many tools have been proposed and used in security education and training. Based on the architectural model of those tools, they can be roughly classified into the following categories: hosted hypervisor based (e.g., [3, 13]), bare metal hypervisor based (e.g., [5, 7, 11]), and cloud based (e.g., [1, 14]).

A hosted hypervisor refers to a hypervisor program running on top of an existing OS (e.g. Linux or Windows), e.g., Virtual Box, VMware Workstation, and Parallels Desktop. Tools relying on this type of hypervisor include SEED Labs and OCCP [3, 13]. SEED Labs are a collection of security labs designed primarily for security courses and individual practices. OCCP (Open Cyber Challenge Platform) is designed for various challenge scenarios such as network defense and penetration testing.

A bare metal hypervisor refers to a hypervisor that directly controls physical hardware, e.g., VMware ESXi, Citrix XenServer, and Microsoft Hyper-V. Tools relying on this type of hypervisor include V-NetLab, ISERink, and Platoon [5, 7, 11], all of which run on top of VMware ESXi. V-NetLab is a virtual network lab platform designed for networking courses and network related labs. ISERink is a virtual system that is initially designed to support cyber defense competitions. Platoon is a team-oriented cybersecurity exercise platform for both security labs and competitions.

Cloud-based platforms are the new trend where complex networks and labs can be created at scale using public or private cloud resources. Example systems of this type include V-Lab and DETER Lab [1, 14]. V-Lab is a cloud-based virtual lab education platform for hands-on course experiments. The DETER Lab (Cyber-Defense Technology Experimental Research Laboratory) is a research testbed mainly for cyber defense research on large-scale network attacks such as DDoS and botnet.

One uniqueness of our work is that EZSetup supports not only private clouds but also public clouds, which is not available in other security practice tools and systems. In addition, the capability of working with multiple clouds and on-demand lab creation and server auto-configuration features make EZSetup highly flexible and scalable.

3 SYSTEM DESIGN

The overview of EZSetup is shown in Figure 1, where EZSetup consists of a frontend (Web-based user interface (UI)) and a backend (the internal database not shown in the figure). EZSetup is a Web application. It can be deployed on a physical or virtual Web server. In order to use EZSetup to create a virtual cybersecurity practice

environment in a computing cloud (e.g., an OpenStack cloud), a user is required to have access to the target cloud and have necessary cloud resources (such as computing, networking, and storage resources) for the environment.

EZSetup aims to make it easy to create and deploy a cybersecurity practice scenario (e.g., a lab or a competition) in a cloud by providing a user-friendly frontend and hiding all the technical complexity in the backend. A lab instructor/manager or a competition creator only needs to fill in the cloud access credentials and a few parameters (e.g., a specific practice scenario and the number of users) to instantiate a scenario. EZSetup automates the deployment process by utilizing the specified cloud resources. Once the deployment is finished, people seeking practice can log into EZSetup and select a scenario (called lab in the prototype) to join. By doing so, complexity in configuring a cybersecurity practice environment (e.g., setting virtual networks, routers and servers) is hidden to EZSetup users whose interest is in security practices instead of environment setup. In addition, the burden for instructors or managers is also significantly reduced. EZSetup is designed to provide the following features.

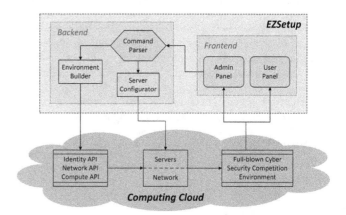

Figure 1: System Overview of EZSetup

- **Scalable and on-demand service.** EZSetup is able to deploy security practice scenarios at scale (e.g., creating labs for a few students as well as hundreds of students) by leveraging elasticity of computing clouds. Moreover, EZSetup deployment is on demand, making it flexible and cost effective.

- **Customizable scenarios.** EZSetup uses YAML based scenario templates, in which the network topology and system configurations can be clearly defined. With the Web-based visualization UI, a scenario can be easily created by dragging and dropping network and server icons onto a canvas and making specific settings on them.

- **Multi-cloud support.** EZSetup is not designed for a particular cloud. Instead, it can work with multiple cloud providers, e.g., OpenStack, Amazon AWS, Google Cloud Platform. Lab managers and competition organizers can choose the most appropriate cloud for their needs.

- **Open source.** EZSetup is an open source tool, aiming to benefit the cybersecurity education community and facilitate anyone interested in cybersecurity.

- **Portability.** EZSetup is a Web application and supports all major Web browsers.
- **Flexible user management.** EZSetup adopts a multi-layer user management scheme, which is illustrated in Figure 2. All users can be divided into three categories, i.e., EZSetup manager, lab manager, and lab user (lab here refers to a general practice scenario). Lab managers and lab users are based on group and managed by a EZSetup manager. Groups are created based on course offerings or competition needs. For example a computer security course can have its own group with all registered students as lab users for that group and the course instructor or teaching assistant who create and manage security labs serving as the lab manager. A lab manager is able to create, modify, and delete one or more labs. A lab user can only join one or multiple existing labs but cannot create a lab. A EZSetup manager is able to create, modify, and delete lab managers and lab users. For a cyber defense competition scenario, competition organizers can act as the lab manager, and each participating team joins as a lab user, with all team members sharing the same lab user account. In addition, a lab user can join in multiple groups if he or she registers multiple courses. Similarly, a person can serves as multiple lab managers (e.g., a TA for multiple courses).

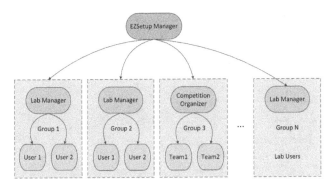

Figure 2: Multi-layer user management structure

3.1 Frontend Functions and Design

The frontend UI contains two different webpages: admin panel and user panel. The admin panel is for EZSetup manager and lab managers where they can manage groups and labs. Several components are used in the admin panel including scenario designer, deployment management, and lab management. The Scenario designer component helps a lab manager design lab scenarios through a visualization UI (i.e., via drag and drop on a canvas). The deployment management UI helps deploy labs onto a cloud by providing a webpage for deployment parameters and interacting with the specified cloud. The lab management UI receives network and server status information from the target cloud and displays the status of each created slice in EZSetup. A slice is a collection of the resources dedicated to a user account. The number of slices in a lab depends on the number of user accounts in need to access that lab.

EZSetup provides a user panel for each lab user helping him or her interact with all available and joined labs within the group. The user panel aims to provide necessary information for users and make them concentrate on practices instead of lab management. Two main components–lab listing and lab viewer–are included in the user panel. Lab listing is able to retrieve the lab user's group information from the internal database and to display all the labs created within the group. Joining in one lab essentially make a user get one slice from the lab's reserved resources. After joining a lab, the lab user can see the lab's network topology as well as detailed network and server information through the lab viewer.

3.2 Lab Scenario

In EZSetup, we use scenarios to describe and manage different types of security exercises such as labs and competitions. A scenario consists of a scenario template file describing necessary networking and computing resources and a number of server configuration files specifying the software packages to be installed and the system settings to be applied. Scenario creation and customization is supported through EZSetup Web GUI to cater to the needs of different users and to encourage creation of new scenarios. EZSetup is aimed to support a wide spectrum of security labs and competitions to save its users' time in building practice environments. For instance, the scenarios under development include network security labs (e.g., SYN Flooding attack and DNS attack scenarios), Web security labs (e.g., Cross-Site Scripting attack and SQL Injection attack scenarios), and a CCDC-style cyber defense competition scenario. The list of scenarios is expected to grow quickly once EZSetup is officially released.

3.3 Backend Functions and Design

The main function of the backend is to parse the input specified on the admin panel by a lab manager and to interact with the target cloud through specific cloud API to instantiate the scenario(s) in the cloud. The backend consists of three types of modules: a command parser, environment builders, and a server configurator. The command parser is able to not only select an appropriate environment builder based on the specified cloud provider, e.g., OpenStack or Amazon AWS, but also reconstruct the scenario template based on the specified number of users or teams (slices) so that the reconstructed scenario template defines all the resources required by users or teams. Essentially, a scenario template created on EZSetup Web GUI only includes the resources needed for one slice. The total resources that are actually needed are calculated by the command parser based on the slice information filled in by a lab manager.

An environment builder generates the required networks and VM instances for the specified scenario. Several environment builders are provided in EZSetup, each responsible for interacting with one particular cloud. For example, there is one builder for OpenStack and one for Amazon AWS. The environment builders essentially enable EZSetup to support multiple clouds. A separate session is created and maintained for each lab deployment request, which makes multiple simultaneous deployments possible. To fulfill a deployment request, one environment builder needs to employ at least three types of APIs provided by a cloud: identity API, network API, and compute API. The identity API is needed because the initiator's identity has to be verified before resources are granted. The network and compute APIs are for requesting for the networking and computing resources from the cloud.

The server configurator is mainly used to set up servers based on the specified configuration, e.g., installing a particular software

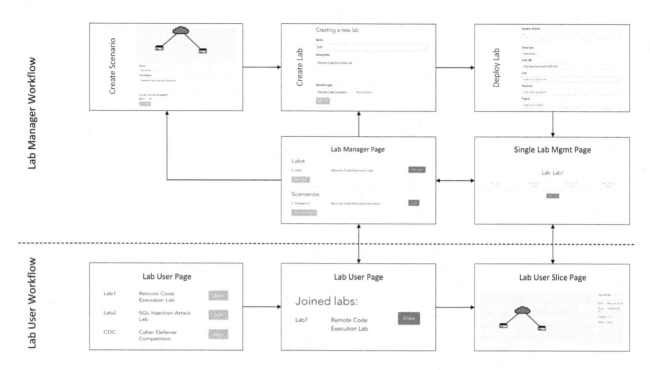

Figure 3: Workflows for a lab manager (upper) and for a lab user (lower)

package or adjusting an application or system setting. The server configuration is conducted using Ansible playbooks, which define all the actions to be performed on the server so that the configuration is automated without human intervention.

Last but not least, an SQL database is internally employed in the backend to bookkeep user and system information including user and manager account information, group information, and lab settings.

3.4 Usage

Similar to other Web applications, EZSetup is accessed through a web browser and a user has to pass the login page for access. Once logged in, the admin panel will be displayed for a lab manager or admin and the user panel will be displayed for a normal end user. A lab manager on the admin panel can either choose an existing scenario from a a drop-down list or create a custom one on the scenario design canvas. After that, a lab manager can create a lab based on the selected scenario and then deploy it to a cloud (e.g., OpenStack or Amazon AWS) by supplying their cloud credentials. The last step is to define the number of slices for the lab. A separate slice will be created for each user afterwards.

After logging in, regular lab users can find the groups they belong to and the labs they have joined. They can find the network topology information of their registered lab such as IP addresses and SSH command. Console access and snapshot creation are realized via the compute APIs provided by the different cloud services. The workflows for both lab managers and lab users are illustrated in Figure 3.

```
- network: LAN
    cidr: 192.168.0.0/24
- network: DMZ
    cidr: 192.168.1.0/24
- network: WAN
    cidr: 172.32.1.0/24
- server: Email
    interfaces:
      - network: LAN
        ip: 192.168.0.11
    playbook: email_server.yml
- server: Web server
    intefaces:
      - network: DMZ
        ip: 192.168.1.11
    playbook: web_server.yml
- router: Shorewall
    interfaces:
      - network: LAN
        ip: 192.168.0.1
      - network: DMZ
        ip: 192.168.1.1
      - network: WAN
        ip: 172.32.0.1
```

Figure 4: A Sample scenario template

4 IMPLEMENTATION

The core of EZSetup was implemented in Python 3. The Web UI is based on Vue, a modern Javascript framework. The internal database uses PostgreSQL. Certain frameworks and libraries have to be installed before running EZSetup, e.g., Flask, Flask-Login, psycopg2, argon2-cffi, boto3, cloud sdk, and openstacksdk. Flask is a python microframework for developing Web applications. Flask-Login helps manage user sessions for Flask. psycopg2 is a PostgreSQL adapter for Python that allows using Python code to manage PostgreSQL databases. argon2-cffi provides an efficient password hashing function. The three Python-based SDKs boto3, cloud sdk, and openstacksdk are provided by Amazon AWS, Google Cloud Platform and OpenStack respectively, and they allow for EZSetup to communicate with their respective cloud platform.

```
- name: Install nginx
  apt: name={{item}} state=installed
  with_items:
    - nginx
- name: Copy index.html file
  template: src=index.html.j2 dest=/usr/share/nginx/html/index.html
- name: Create the nginx configuration file (non-SSL)
  template: src=site.conf.j2 dest=/etc/nginx/sites-available/{{prj_n
ame}}
  when: not use_ssl
- name: Ensure that the default site is removed
  file: path=/etc/nginx//sites-enabled/default state=absent
- name: Ensure that the application site is enabled
  file: src=/etc/nginx/sites-available/{{prj_name}} dest=/etc/nginx/
sites-enabled/{{prj_name}} state=link
  notify: reload nginx
- name: Ensure nginx service is started, enable service on restart
  service: name=nginx state=restarted enabled=yes
- name: Stop nginx for local dev, disable service
  service: name=nginx state=stopped enabled=no
  notify: stop nginx
  when: not enabled
- name: Allow incomming http request
  ufw: rule=allow port=http
```

Figure 5: Ansible playbook file (web_server.yml)

Our scenario file uses a YAML-based domain specific language, an example of which is shown in Figure 4. This example defines a blue team network for a cyber defense competition scenario. There are three subnets defined in a blue team network, i.e., LAN, DMZ, and WAN. Inside each subnet, there are servers with basic networking information. The configuration of these servers is defined in separate Ansible playbooks.

One example of an Ansible playbook for an nginx Web server is given in Figure 5. The installation and configuration process involves multiple tasks, each of which has a name and a specific action or a state check, e.g., using apt to install nginx, copying a pre-defined web page to a specific location and enabling it, and removing the default webpage. With its own Ansible playbook, each server can be quickly and automatically configured to the desired state.

5 EVALUATION

In this section, we first conduct a comparison between EZSetup and other virtual solutions to cybersecurity practices and then present users' feedback on using EZSetup both as a lab manager and as a lab user.

5.1 Feature Comparison

We compare EZSetup with other similar solutions that offer virtual machine (VM) based security practices including SEED Labs, V-Lab, OCCP, ISERink, Platoon, V-NetLab and DETER Lab. Those solutions are evaluated against the features important for hosting cybersecurity practices. The detailed comparison results are shown in Figure 6.

From Figure 6, we can see that not all the systems support security competitions. This is due to the fact that competition environments are usually more complex and demand more resources and efforts to build. All the platforms that support competitions also support teamwork. Self-hosting is desirable in that it allows users to deploy environments themselves and have full control. Based on the complexity of installing and configuring the system itself, only Platoon and EZSetup have "easy deployment" marked in that both provide installation scripts for automating system deployment, which is critical for self-hosting. On-demand creation is an

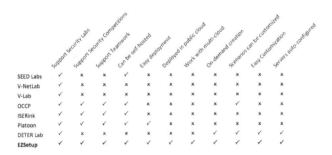

Figure 6: Comparison of systems for security practices

appealing feature of EZSetup as it gives users a fine-grained control over scenario creation and allows them to flexibly create and delete scenarios. The level of scenario customization is important for instructors and scenario creators. EZSetup gains the easy scenario customization feature by using scenario template and visualization UI. Another attractive feature of EZSetup is that the configuration of the systems specified in a scenario can be automated through Ansible playbooks.

EZSetup has two unique features: the ability to be deployed in public clouds and multi-cloud support. The ability to deploy in public clouds empowers users in short of hardware resources to host security practice labs or competitions at scale. Working with multiple clouds gives users a great flexibility to select appropriate target cloud(s) for deployment from different clouds so as to maximize their benefits.

5.2 User Feedback

We also collected user feedback via a survey given to the voluntary testers immediately after they completed two tasks: creation of a security lab as a lab manager and the following lab exercise as a lab user. In the test, EZSetup was deployed on a virtual Web server and was able to interact with a small private OpenStack testbed that was built using 4 old Dell R410 servers.

The evaluation was conducted in June 2017. We recruited 9 science and engineering students for it. The task of lab creation is to create a remote code execution lab through EZSetup Web UI. Two virtual machines (VMs) are used in the lab, with one Kali VM serving as the attacking machine and one Ubuntu VM serving as the victim. Both VMs are in the same LAN, as illustrated in Fig. 3. The task of lab exercise is to conduct an attack against the Ubuntu VM where an old and vulnerable version of Java installed. In the evaluation, the volunteers played both roles of lab manager and lab user. Thus they experienced the entire life cycle of a lab in EZSetup. A detailed lab manual was provided for both tasks. As a lab manager, a participant is first instructed to create a lab using the pre-built scenario, and then asked to deploy the lab onto the OpenStack cloud with the given cloud credentials. Once the lab is deployed, the same participant is required to log in EZSetup as a lab user, join the newly-created lab, and launch a remote attack following the lab manual. Specifically, a user has to first log into the Kali VM through SSH or web-based console and then use the social engineering toolkit (SET) to launch a browser exploit attack. By doing so, whoever accesses the vulnerable webpage hosted on the

Kali VM will be compromised, and a reverse shell will be established from the Ubuntu victim VM to the attacking Kali VM.

A survey was given out to each participant after the test. In total, 15 questions were included in the survey with 9 questions for lab manager and 6 questions for lab user. Likert scale (strongly disagree to strongly agree) is used for all questions. The survey results are presented in Figures 7 and 8.

Q1. The interface of this webapp is user-friendly for creating labs
Q2. The process of creating a lab is straightforward and smooth
Q3. Creating the remote code execution lab with one slice only needs several minutes
Q4. It is more cost-effective for deploying labs using clouds than using physical servers
Q5. The concept of scenario makes it easy to re-deploy labs
Q6. I would like to use this webapp for creating security and/or networking labs in the future
Q7. I would like to use this webapp for creating cs or engineering labs in the future
Q8. I would like to contribute scenarios for more diverse security labs when possible

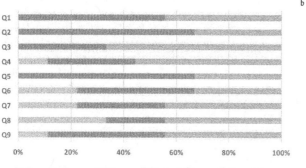

Figure 7: Results of survey questions for lab manager

From Figure 7, we can see that participants have very positive feedback about the interface, operation, efficiency of EZSetup in creating labs. In addition, the scenario concept and time-saving feature of EZSetup are widely recognized. Some participants gave neutral feedback about using EZSetup for creating security or engineering labs. A major reason is that in the test they used an existing scenario instead of creating one themselves. So they did not fully understand the capability and potential of EZSetup in other settings.

From Figure 8, we can see that the participants can complete the lab exercise smoothly and the security knowledge conveyed by the lab can be gained quickly. This is a highly positive sign given that most of the participants were security novice, having no prior experience of security practice. This survey also reveals that the participants are willing to use EZSetup in other computer science and engineering labs, which indicates that EZSetup can also be applied to other online practices other than cybersecurity ones.

6 CONCLUSION

In this paper, we have presented a new Web application called EZSetup that can create and manage virtual environments for various types of cybersecurity practices using one or more cloud computing platforms. EZSetup provides an easy and user-friendly mechanism to create virtual environments for cybersecurity practices on demand and at scale. EZSetup can be applied to both academic curriculum (e.g., security labs) and extracurricular activities (e.g., cyber defense competitions). Given its unique features and positive user feedback from experimental results, EZSetup is expected to further lower the barriers in promoting hands-on cybersecurity practices and help address the shortage of cybersecurity professionals.

Q1. Performing the tasks in this lab exercise using this webapp is more convenient than performing them using my own computer
Q2. I have completed this lab exercise smoothly with the provided lab instruction
Q3. I have completed this lab exercise in less than 20 minutes
Q4. I am satisfied with the security knowledge (especially hacking knowledge) gained in such a short time
Q5. I would like to use this webapp in other security and/or networking labs in the future
Q6. I would like to use this webapp in cs or engineering lab exercises in the future

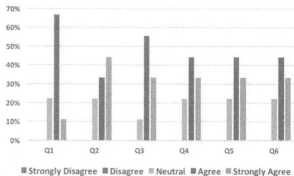

Figure 8: Results of survey questions for lab user

ACKNOWLEDGMENTS

This work was supported in part by the National Science Foundation (Grant Numbers: 1338102 and 1623628), National Security Agency (Grant Number: H98230-17-1-0273), and Amazon with an AWS in Education Research grant. Development of EZSetup also used the Chameleon testbed supported by the National Science Foundation.

REFERENCES

[1] Terry Benzel. 2011. The Science of Cyber Security Experimentation: The DETER Project. In *Proc. 27th ACSAC*. 137–148.
[2] CSSIA. n.d.. National Center for Systems Security and Information Assurance. http://www.cssia.org. (n.d.).
[3] Wenliang Du and Ronghua Wang. 2008. SEED: A Suite of Instructional Laboratories for Computer Security Education. *J. Educ. Resour. Comput.* 8, 1 (March 2008), 3:1–3:24.
[4] Jim Finkle and Dustin Volz. 2015. Database of 191 million U.S. voters exposed on Internet: researcher. http://www.reuters.com/article/us-usa-voters-breach-idUSKBN0UB1E020151229. (December 2015).
[5] ISU. 2015. ISERink. http://www.iserink.org. (2015).
[6] Kif Leswing. 2016. Yahoo confirms major breach - and it could be the largest hack of all time. http://www.businessinsider.com/yahoo-hack-by-state-sponsored-actor-biggest-of-all-time-2016-9. (September 2016).
[7] Yanyan Li and Mengjun Xie. 2016. Platoon: A Virtual Platform for Team-oriented Cybersecurity Training and Exercises. In *Proceedings of the 17th Annual Conference on Information Technology Education*. ACM, 20–25.
[8] Steve Morgan. 2016. One Million Cybersecurity Job Openings In 2016. https://www.forbes.com/sites/stevemorgan/2016/01/02/one-million-cybersecurity-job-openings-in-2016. (January 2016).
[9] National Initiative For Cybersecuriy Education. n.d.. NICE Challenge Project. https://nice-challenge.com. (n.d.).
[10] Jon Oltsik. 2016. High-demand cybersecurity skills in 2017. http://www.networkworld.com/article/3152023/security/high-demand-cybersecurity-skills-in-2017.html. (December 2016).
[11] W. Sun, V. Katta, K. Krishna, and R. Sekar. 2008. V-NetLab: An Approach for Realizing Logically Isolated Networks for Security Experiments. In *Proc. USENIX CSET*. 5:1–5:6.
[12] UTSA. n.d.. CCDC. http://www.nationalccdc.org/. (n.d.).
[13] Richard H. Wagner. 2013. *Designing a Network Defense Scenario Using the Open Cyber Challenge Platform*. MS thesis. University of Rhode Island.
[14] Le Xu, Dijiang Huang, and Wei-Tek Tsai. 2013. Cloud-Based Virtual Laboratory for Network Security Education. *IEEE Trans. Educ.* 57, 3 (Oct. 2013), 145–150.

Reimagining and Refining Campus Cultures: Promoting Vibrant Learning Environments at RIT

Margaret Bailey
Kate Gleason College of Engineering
Rochester Institute of Technology
mbbeme@rit.edu

Linda Manning
Centre on Governance
University of Ottawa

Elizabeth Dell
College of Applied Science
and Technology
Rochester Institute of Technology

Carol Marchetti
College of Science
Rochester Institute of Technology

Maureen Valentine (Moderator)
College of Applied Science
and Technology
Rochester Institute of Technology

ABSTRACT

This interactive session explores the journey of a university to intentionally and strategically transform its campus culture. Many organizations exclusively approach cultural change by creating and enforcing rules and regulations to promote gender equity and inclusion. Within this session, we will explore the possibility of augmenting this well-established campus paradigm with intentional organizational development initiatives. Through understanding best practices and developmental models utilized at other ADVANCE funded universities, we reimagine the campus culture and develop possible strategies to achieve the desired state. The AdvanceRIT team shares the story and impacts of their five-year effort to refine and influence campus culture to support a more inclusive campus environment. Campus efforts have included the creation and administration of interactive and high-energy unconscious bias education workshops, theatrical productions that explore navigating key faculty career milestones, bystander awareness sessions using Playback Theater, theatrical readings with discussion forums, and a new campus organization to actively engage faculty men in the cultural transformation process. Data related to these sessions will be shared, including participation numbers and workshop evaluations. The team feature the work of key partners from aligned organizations both within and external to RIT who have worked closely with the project team throughout this journey.

Keywords
Diversity; women; faculty; STEM; ADVANCE; gender

1. INTRODUCTION
The National Science Foundation looks to strengthen the advancement and representation of women faculty in STEM through the ADVANCE Institutional Transformation program [1]. Specifically, the goals of the program are to:

(1) develop systemic approaches to increase the representation and advancement of women in academic STEM careers; (2) develop innovative and sustainable ways to promote gender equity in the STEM academic workforce;

and (3) contribute to the development of a more diverse science and engineering workforce. ADVANCE also has as its goal to contribute to and inform the general knowledge base on gender equity in the academic STEM disciplines [2].

The AdvanceRIT Institutional Transformation project (NSF ADVANCE 1209115), awarded in 2012, aims to increase the representation and advancement of women STEM faculty by removing barriers to resources that support career success and by creating new interventions and resources. Three of the five AdvanceRIT principal investigators will serve as the leads for this panel, and one will serve as moderator.

AdvanceRIT has adopted a multi-frame organizational analysis approach from Bolman and Deal [3] to improve understanding of organizational matters at RIT. This approach integrates several aspects of organizational theory, including structural, human resources, political, and symbolic perspectives, and suggests the use of each as a "frame" or "lens" for viewing the organization and for devising strategic interventions to change the organization [4]. The multi-year, multidimensional approach to this institutional transformation project incorporates over 20 interventions which impact processes related to faculty recruitment and advancement, cultural change, and resource allocation.

The AdvanceRIT team shares the story and impacts of their lengthy effort to refine and influence campus culture to support a more inclusive campus environment. Data related to these sessions will be shared, including participation numbers and workshop evaluations.

2. PANELISTS

2.1 Dr. Margaret Bailey
Dr. **Margaret Bailey**, P.E. is a professor of Mechanical Engineering and conducts research in Thermodynamics, engineering and public policy, engineering education, and gender in STEM. Dr. Bailey serves as PI for the AdvanceRIT grant, co-PI for the NSF Advocates and Allies award (NSF ADVANCE 1500604) and Senior Faculty Associate to the Provost for ADVANCE. In her panel presentation, Dr. Bailey will focus on the overarching AdvanceRIT program goals and the unconscious bias education effort underway.

2.1.1 Unconscious Bias Education

RIT institutionalized unconscious bias (UB) education for faculty search committees over the past seven years, although its delivery style varied by college. In 2012, AdvanceRIT began collaboratively working with key campus partners to raise the collective level of understanding regarding best practices within RIT in regards to UB education. AdvanceRIT also began hosting UB education workshops for various audiences on campus. There have been over ten different educational experiences offered since 2012, with varying program lengths, styles, and intended learning outcomes. This discussion will explore the UB education activities, future work and recommendations.

2.2 Dr. Linda Manning

Dr. **Linda Manning** is a Senior Fellow at the University of Ottawa and has more than 20 years of experience in teaching and training worldwide. Her current work focuses on creating strategic and inclusive talent management practices for optimal organizational capacity. Dr. Manning serves on the AdvanceRIT external advisory board and has facilitated several unconscious bias education workshops at RIT.

2.2.1 Model for Change

The developmental model of intercultural sensitivity (DMIS), created by Dr. Milton Bennett, explains reactions that people have to cultural differences. The DMIS stages form a continuum that ranges from ethno-centric to highly ethno-relative, based on the theory that increased cultural awareness is accompanied by improved cognitive sophistication (i.e., growth). Dr. Manning will discuss how this model facilitates discussions on inclusivity.

2.3 Professor Elizabeth Dell

Professor **Elizabeth Dell** is a professor in the Department of Manufacturing and Mechanical Engineering Technology. Her interests include characterization of biodegradable plastics and environmental considerations in materials selection for product design. Professor Dell serves as co-PI, leading the *Connectivity* Series and PI for the NSF Advocates and Allies award. In her panel presentation, Professor Dell will focus on the *Connectivity* Series and the Advocates and Allies Program.

2.3.1 Connectivity Series

The *Connectivity* Series consists of workshops, speakers and panel sessions sponsored by the AdvanceRIT project. The series offers resources and strategies to support faculty recruitment and career success. Objectives include developing strategies and competencies related to career satisfaction and navigation, work-life balance, leadership development, recognition of work, and scholarship. Discussion will focus on the series evolution.

2.3.2 Advocates & Allies

In 2015, the AdvanceRIT team embarked on the Advocates & Allies program as part of North Dakota State University NSF ADVANCE Plan D (1500604) [5]. This signature program from NDSU looks to improve gender equity through the proactive engagement of male faculty with two components: Senior male faculty who research and learn about issues of gender inequality, train others and serve as Advocates; and the Allies, male faculty trained by the Advocates who become proponents for gender equity, this project focuses on men as change agents. By ensuring fair and equitable treatment of women, men actively and vocally promote gender diversity. Discussion will focus on goals and benefits of engaging male faculty in transformation efforts.

2.4 Dr. Carol Marchetti

Dr. **Carol Marchetti** is a professor in the School of Mathematical Sciences and an associate of the Research Center for Teaching and Learning. Dr. Marchetti's conducts research in statistics education, deaf education, and online learning. She is directly involved in numerous externally funded projects focused on improving access and learning for deaf and hard-of-hearing students. In her panel presentation, Dr. Marchetti will discuss the role of faculty data, such as faculty indicator data and results from faculty salary studies, in supporting the change initiative.

2.4.1 Indicator Data

The National Science Foundation's ADVANCE program requires institutions to collect and report on a set of indicators, that is, measures of the representation of women faculty in terms of recruitment, retention, advancement, and leadership. This provides NSF with information on the success of the project. But more importantly, dissemination of this data ideally elicits productive discussions on campus and, ultimately, use of data in decision-making processes.

2.4.2 Salary Study

The AdvanceRIT team assembled a Resource Allocation Committee (RAC) in 2013 to revise and improve the process for evaluating resource equity by gender, beginning with RIT's salary equity study. Previous salary equity studies lacked transparency and campus-wide representation to inform decision- making. The RAC engages faculty and administration from across campus to understand resource allocation concerns and perceptions of the process. Collaborators include members from the AdvanceRIT leadership team, the VPt for Strategic Planning, the Assistant VP for Institutional Research and Human Resources, the Senior Associate Provost, a Department Head, and an Associate Dean. Comments and discussion will focus on how inclusivity in the process fostered campus discussions.

ACKNOWLEDGMENTS

Support for this research is provided by the NSF ADVANCE Institutional Transformation Catalyst program under Award No. 0811076 and the Institutional Transformation program under Award No. 1209115. Any opinions, findings, and conclusions or recommendations expressed in this material are those of the authors and do not necessarily reflect the views of the NSF.

3. REFERENCES

[1] N. S. Foundation. (July 2). *NSF ADVANCE: Increasing the Participation and Advancement of Women in Academic Science and Engineering Careers.* Available: https://www.nsf.gov/funding/pgm_summ.jsp?pims_id=5383

[2] M. Bailey, C. Marchetti, S. Mason, and M. Valentine, "NSF ADVANCE Institutional Transformation," ed. Rochester, NY: National Science Foundation, 2012.

[3] L. Bolman and T. Deal, *Reframing organizations: Artistry, choice, and leadership.* San Francisco, CA: Jossey-Bass, 1991.

[4] A. Austin, S. Laursen, A. Hunter, and M. Soto, "Organizational Change Strategies to Support the Success of Women Scholars in Science, Technology, Engineering, and Mathematics (STEM) Fields: Categories, Variations, and Issues.," presented at the *Proc. Annual Conference of the American Educational Research Association*, New Orleans, LA., 2011.

[5] (Nov. 3). *ADVANCE North Dakota State University.* Available: http://www.ndsu.edu/forward/advance_forward_initiatives/forward_advocates_and_allies/

Shaping a Wearable and Ubiquitous Computing Curriculum

Bryan French
Rochester Institute of Technology
1 Lomb Memorial Drive
Rochester, NY 14623
bdfvks@rit.edu

Daniel Bogaard
Rochester Institute of Technology
1 Lomb Memorial Drive
Rochester, NY 14623
dan.bogaard@rit.edu

Stephen Zilora
Rochester Institute of Technology
1 Lomb Memorial Drive
Rochester, NY 14623
stephen.zilora@rit.edu

ABSTRACT

Creation of a Wearable and Ubiquitous computing curriculum is an apt response to the rapid growth of the Internet of Things and its subsequent devices around the world. The authors have created an advanced concentration in Wearable and Ubiquitous Computing at the Bachelor of Science level.

KEYWORDS

Internet of Things; curriculum development; wearable computing; ubiquitous computing, IT concentrations

ACM Reference format:

B. French, D. Bogaard, S. Zilora. 2017. SIG Proceedings Paper in word Format. In *Proceedings of ACM SIGITE conference, Rochester, New York, October 2017 (SIGITE/17)*, 1 page.
DOI: 10.1145/3125659.3125668

1 INTRODUCTION

The faculty at the authors' institution strive to keep up with the current and future trends in the industry, to help the students prepare for not only the current job market, and also to prepare the students for a career of life-long learning. A concentration in Wearable and Ubiquitous Computing is an extension of the core concepts learned in the Information Technology field, utilizing all five pillars of IT.

The projections of the growth of the number of Internet connected devices vary, but most project 20+ billion Internet connected things by the year 2020 [2]. This projected continued growth leads to an increase in the number of jobs that the industry is going to need to help create, design, connect, develop, and implement solutions. The industry is just coming out of its infancy and is preparing for future skyrocketing growth [1].

2 CONCLUSIONS

We found that for students (and instructors) to be successful in a Wearable and Ubiquitous Computing curriculum they need to have to following foundational background:

- Expectations/Attitude
- Programming Concepts
- Web
- Database
- User Experience

We also found that the technology/materials required for courses such as these fall into two main categories: Consumable and Reusable. Consumable (one's that students purchase and keep) are based upon current trends in the industry. Reusable (the more expensive devices) were provided for student use during the course and plan on updating them on a fairly frequent basis.

A 2-course concentration has been offered for one year. Students have been very enthusiastic about the concentration commenting that they now had a better view of where things were going and what is possible in the industry—and felt better prepared for their future employment given a wider perspective of what is possible. This same emphasis on cutting-edge technology translates into a substantial work burden on the instructors and the department resources. The constantly evolving nature of the associated hardware and software necessitates constant rewrites of material and constant upgrading of supplies.

While the topics and curriculum discussed in this talk are a small part of the computing discipline, the Internet of Things, and more specifically Wearable and Ubiquitous Computing, is a concentration that captures not only the cutting edge of what is possible, but also students' interest. At the authors' university, we have seen a large percentage of students gravitate towards these areas. Being a part of the Information Technology discipline has always meant not being too rigid in adoption of the next new area or development—capturing not only the students' interest, but also invigorating the faculty.

REFERENCES

[1] Internet of Things (IoT) Outlook for 2017, Krell (January 3,2017). Retrieved June 18, 2017, from https://www.forbes.com/sites/moorinsights/2017/01/03/ internet-of-things-iot-outlook-for-2017/#1f338d7f444a
[2] Popular Internet of Things Forecast of 50 Billion Devices by 2020 is Outdated, Nordrum. August 18, 2016 Retrieved June 18, 2017 from http://spectrum.ieee.org/tech-talk/telecom/internet/popular-internet-of-things-forecast-of-50-billion-devices-by-2020-is-outdated.

Undergraduate Academic Dishonesty:
What Students Really Think is "Bad" Behavior

Hollis J. Greenberg
Department of Management
Wentworth Institute of Technology
greenbergh1@wit.edu

ABSTRACT

In school, we are taught that in order to properly analyze the best solution to a problem, one must first determine both the nature and the cause of the problem. As faculty, we know that academic dishonesty is a problem throughout not only our campuses, but rather all institutions of higher education. Perhaps the actual problem is not that students are dishonest in the generation of their coursework, but what if the problem lies deeper than that? What if the students' belief and value systems don't perceive their actions as wrong? What if the perception of using or not using technology makes these actions seem "less wrong?" Can we fight the new norms of society?

CCS Concepts

• Social and professional topics →Computing education

Keywords

Academic integrity; academic honesty; academic dishonesty; cheating; international; higher education.

1. INTRODUCTION

At Wentworth Institute of Technology, the faculty find that they are at a turning point facing increasing instances of student academic dishonesty. The school is beginning to implement tried and true methods of dealing with such incidents, from disciplinary boards to required incoming course modules, all with the hope of deterring future integrity occurrences. Independently, one faculty member is trying to understand student views on distinct types of academic dishonesty through primary research, querying both incoming freshman and outgoing graduating seniors. Current research also gathers demographic information, declared major and international student status.

2. DISCOVERY

Surveys have been administered to both freshman and senior student groups to understand the views and subsequent actions of

each group of students. This first round of surveys is to be replicated over the course of several years, as the surveys follow the freshmen through graduation and track changes in the students' value structure and their specific actions during college. The research aims to answer the following questions:

- Has the institute "corrupted" their value structure over the four years spent on campus?
- Has the institute itself lived up to the students' incoming high standards?
- How has the student conducted him/herself while earning a degree over four years?
- Are specific majors more prone to participate in questionable behavior and/or their values different than students from other majors?
- Will any of our new initiatives, created to deter academic dishonesty incidents, make a difference in the students' value structures and, subsequently, the students' actions?

3. ANALYSIS

At our institution, most majors are "technical" in nature. As such, interesting nuances in the manner of academic dishonesty are being unearthed. One such instance is that 41% of senior-level respondents answered that paraphrasing or copying a few sentences from a non-electronic or web-based source without footnoting the sources was either not cheating at all or trivial cheating. Using the same group of students, 27% said that using an electronic source was not cheating or trivial cheating. Interestingly, using the electronic source was perceived as a worse infraction than using a paper-based source. As a result, more students admitted to cheating with paper-based sources versus electronic sources.

Historically, higher education only has a one-size-fits-all approach [1] to deterrence of academic dishonesty. What if the current standard is not the correct approach? By analyzing the data and looking for statistically significant trends, research may prove that different or multi-prong approaches work best for various majors and/or other student subsets.

4. REFERENCES

[1] McCabe, D., Trevino, L. and Butterfield, K. 2001. Cheating in Academic Institutions: A Decade of Research. *Ethics & Behavior, 11(3)*, Taylor & Francis, 219-232. http://www.middlebury.edu/media/view/257513/original/Decade_of_Research.pdf

Object-Oriented Programming with DevOps

Sam Chung
Southern Illinois University
1365 Douglas Dr. Mailcode 6614
Carbondale, IL 62901
1-618-453-7279
samchung@siu.edu

DevOps is an emerging culture that emphasizes continuous collaboration between software developers and IT operators through continuous standard process with automated tools for continuous delivery. DevOps participants take diverse roles to support its values - continuous collaboration, continuous process, and continuous delivery. A development team needs to be familiar with user cases, Object-Oriented Analysis (OOA), Object-Oriented Design (OOD), Object-Oriented Programming (OOP), and software testing. A quality assurance team must know use cases, abuse cases, software testing, and penetration testing. An operation team requires understanding deployment of Application Programming Interface (API) documents and executable components, and monitoring them and sharing their monitoring outcomes with both development and quality assurance teams.

In this paper, we challenge how we can infuse DevOps into a beginning-level programming course. Instead of teaching OOP, can we teach OOP with DevOps? If so, what concepts and practices need to be included in the programming course without losing what the course originally covers? What new subjects and practices do we need in order to design an introductory OOP with DevOps?

For this purpose, we first visit the concept of DevOps and their values in terms of 'Continuous *' in which * denotes Collaboration, Process, and Delivery. In addition, we discuss Evidence-Based Practice (EBP) to identify DevOps for OOP. EBP is an approach seeking best practices that have underpinning research evidences

Second, we explore the emergence of DevOps and their related research. However, we cannot find pilot or case studies with programming that demonstrate how computing major students studying beginning-level programming can experience DevOps through reengineering a non-DevOps-aware software application to a DevOps-aware application.

Third, we seek best practices in DevOps that can fulfill the values of DevOps – Continuous *. One of the major concerns of software industry is the lack of collaboration and communication ability for teamwork between existing and newly hired software developers immediately out of college. To enhance collaboration, DevOp participants need to understand their concerns and define the concerns through architecture. We also need a standard process to manage the application project during software development life cycle – software process. Then, for continuous deployment, we can see many research outcomes in software testing, software documentation, software security, and software deployment.

Fourth, we demonstrate how we can reengineer a given legacy application to a DevOps-aware target application. We choose a simple legacy application from an introductory programming course. We apply the identified evidence-based practices to the application, 'Payroll.java' to demonstrate the OOP with DevOps.

Fifth, we collect and analyze what concepts and best practices of DevOps that we employed during the reengineering process. Then, we argue that we need to infuse those identified concepts and practices into an introductory programming course towards programming with DevOps.

The results of this research clearly show that we can teach DevOps in the introductory programming course without losing what the course covers. The curriculum of the course covers important Java practices useful for continuous collaboration such as method definition and invocation, class definition and instantiation, control statement and continuous deployment for JavaDoc comment, exception, try statement, and catch statement. We also need to expand the current curriculum for continuous collaboration by including the IPO model and the MVC architecture. The students can learn separation of concerns and software architecture through functional and object-oriented decomposition. We need to emphasize the effective use of Java package in the programming practice.

We need to introduce an agile software process for the students to learn iterative and incremental approach. If the students will use this process continuously for their programming assignments, they will learn one of the values of DevOPs – continuous process.

We need to cover more for continuous deployment by practicing software documentation, software security, and software testing. Although the introductory course covers JavaDoc comment, we need to show how we can use the JavaDoc to generate API documentation for public classes and methods. To learn how we can make an application secure, we need to show how we can define a user-defined Exception class for a Model class and can call it in a pair of Try and Catch statements within a View class. We also include new subject areas for software testing with JUnit, input data validation with pattern matching using regular expression, and software deployment with a JAR file, not class files.

MySecurityLab: A Generic Tool for Self-paced Learning of Security Controls

Amos O Olagunju
St Cloud State University
St Cloud, MN USA 56301

(320) 308-5696

aoolagunju@stcloudstate.edu

Benjamin Franske
Inver Hills Community College
Inver Grove Heights, MN 55076

(651) 450-3575

b.franske@inverhills.edu

Joseph Silman
St Cloud Tech & Community College
St Cloud, MN 56303

(320) 308-5342

JSilman@sctcc.edu

ABSTRACT

Information technology students and employees in organizations require a tool for self-paced learning of the administration of technical security controls in stand-alone and network systems. This enlightening talk presents the design and implementation of an interactive tool with a graphical user interface. The tool will enable current and future IT professionals to achieve proficiency in the applications of technical security mechanisms. The presentation provides a brief demonstration of the initial version of the tool and engages the audience to provide feedback.

Keywords

Applied Cryptography; DevOps; Security Control; IT curriculum

1. INTRODUCTION

Providing confidentiality, integrity, availability and nonrepudiation of data in information systems is crucial to the survival of any business or organization. Consequently, students who pursue associate degrees in Networking and Cybersecurity, or bachelor degrees in Cybersecurity and Information Technology, or graduate degrees in the areas of Information Assurance should be skilled in technical security designs, implementation and administration. Information technology students and security staff members in industry all require adequate knowledge of operational software safeguards, network defense and applied cryptography. Unfortunately, the in-depth understanding of security techniques and mechanisms require more mathematical ideas beyond discrete math and calculus. Moreover, most students come across learning difficulties in courses such as applied cryptography and open systems interconnection layers security. Thus, this lighting talk presents a tool called MySecurityLab for self-paced understanding of the various components of technical security mechanisms.

2. TOOL CONTENTS

The tool, MySecurityLab, is not designed to replace any course or curriculum in the areas of Cybersecurity, Information Assurance and Information Technology. The

faculty members and academic departments are still responsible for the design of course curriculum and learning objectives. The tool should be used to make learning more effective in teaching course contents.

The question certainly arises on the contents of a tool for understanding various security mechanisms. The contents of the tool were selected based on the materials in computer security analysis in [1], cryptography and network security in [2], and the areas students expressed concerns about learning in course evaluations over the years. The first version of MySecurityLab tool consists of instructional and practice modules for self-paced learning of:

1. Elements of modulus arithmetic and number theory;
2. Symmetric and asymmetric algorithms for providing data confidentiality, non-repudiation, key exchange, and digital signatures;
3. Hashing algorithms for providing data integrity;
4. Scripts for setting up alternative DevOps tools for monitoring and analyzing the security of networks; and
5. Scripts for setting up access control lists.

3. IMPLEMENTATION AND EVALUATION

Two versions of MySecurityLab tool have been designed and implemented. The standalone interactive MySecurityLab was implemented in C#; it has a graphical user interface for navigating and displaying the instruction and practice exercises of each security control module. The web-based MySecurityLab was implemented with cascade style sheets, JavaScript and HTML5.

The effectiveness of the use of MySecurityLab to teach Basic Networking and Security, OSI Layers Security, Applied Cryptography and Operational Software Safeguards is being evaluated, in terms of both student achievements and learning. Students from two and four-year institutions at Minnesota State College and University (MnSCU), and professional colleagues in academia and industry are continuing to evaluate the effectiveness of MySecurityLab on learning.

4. REFERENCES

[1] Pfleeger, C. P., and S. L. Pfleeger. Analyzing Computer Security: Threat/Vulnerability/Countermeasure Approach, Pearson Education Inc., Upper Saddle River, NJ, 2012.

[2] Stallings, W. Cryptography and Network Security: Principles and Practice, Seventh Edition, Pearson Education, Inc., Hoboken, NJ, 2017.

Reflections on Curriculating a South African Information Technology Degree

Reinhardt A. Botha
School of ICT, Nelson Mandela University
Port Elizabeth, South Africa
ReinhardtA.Botha@mandela.ac.za

Russ McMahon
School of IT, University of Cincinnati
Cincinnati, OH, 45221
russ.mcmahon@uc.edu

ABSTRACT

The South African Higher Education environment is highly regulated and has undergone significant restructurings during the last 15 years. New legislation provided the incentive to reconsider the offerings. This talk reflects on the process followed and design decisions made to create a Bachelor of Information Technology (BIT) degree for Nelson Mandela University.

CCS CONCEPTS

• **Social and professional topics** → **Information technology education**;

KEYWORDS

Curriculum design

ACM Reference format:
Reinhardt A. Botha and Russ McMahon. 2017. Reflections on Curriculating a South African Information Technology Degree. In *Proceedings of SIGITE'17, Rochester, NY, USA, October 4–7, 2017*, 1 pages.
https://doi.org/10.1145/3125659.3125667

1 INTRODUCTION

The South African Higher Education landscape is complex. Recent legislative changes have led to the formulation of a new Higher Education Qualifications Sub-Framework (HEQSF) [2]. This required universities to reconsider the programme mix.

The drive towards a Bachelor of Information Technology Degree was fuelled by two important factors: The new HEQSF requires the phasing out of BTech degrees (following a 3-year diploma) and a gap in the offerings of the School of ICT at Nelson Mandela University. Nelson Mandela University offers Computer Science (CS) and Information Systems (IS) as majors for Bachelor of Science and Bachelor of Commerce degrees driven by the Department of Computing in the Faculty of Science. The School of ICT in the Faculty of Engineering, the Built Environment and Information Technology offers diplomas in Information Technology. Expectations for IT graduates are distinct from those for IT diplomats in terms of the theoretical grounding. Seen from a 'why-how-what' perspective, the IT diplomats focus on the 'how-what' aspects, whereas the IT graduates focus on the 'why-how' aspects. The need for an IT graduate who is more versed in the theoretical aspects has also been confirmed by the School of ICT Industry Advisory Board.

The decision was made that the curriculum should be informed by the ACM/IEEE IT2008 Curriculum Guidelines [1]. We also set out to learn from the experiences of others.

2 CURRICULUM DESIGN

We aim to produce graduates who are technical all-rounders and can communicate competently, analyze complex problems, provide integrative solutions, be life-long learners and act professionally while living the Ubuntu-philosophy.

Two cross-curricular themes were chosen: Human-centeredness due to the user advocacy nature of an Information Technology Professional, and Information and Computer Security due to our in-house expertise and the overall importance of the theme.

We deem the following design decisions the most important.

Application areas are introduced. Information Technology work does not happen in isolation but in a specific context. Taking our cue from the Software Engineering degree at RIT [3] we give learners a choice of application area to allow them to apply their IT skills within a specific user context.

Design and development subjects are integrated. History taught us that during development courses some learners seem to 'forget' that they were taught proper design in another course. An overall design experience is still facilitated through the capstone project.

A *portfolio-based approach* is adopted. The portfolio is assessed as part of the capstone project. This stresses the importance of applying previous knowledge and skills, while it allows us to assess aspects of professional practice difficult to assess otherwise.

3 CONCLUSION

If we discount the time waiting for bureaucracy, the curriculation of the proposed BIT degree represents 2.5 years of research, design, and discussion between a variety of stakeholders. In the spirit of Ubuntu we hope that sharing our thoughts and ideas will help others figuring out their contexts and contribute to the greater good of the IT education community.

REFERENCES

[1] ACM/IEEE. Information Technology 2008: Curriculum Guidelines for Undergraduate Degree Programs in Information Technology. (????). http://www.acm.org/education/curricula/IT2008%20Curriculum.pdf
[2] Council for Higher Education. 2013. The Higher Education Qualifications Sub-Framework. (2013). http://www.che.ac.za/media_and_publications/frameworks-criteria/che-higher-education-qualifications-sub-framework
[3] J. Fernando Naveda, Thomas J. Reichlmayr, Michael J. Lutz, James R. Vallino, and Stephanie A. Ludi. 2009. The road we've traveled: 12 years of Undergraduate Software Engineering at the Rochester Institute of Technology. In *ITNG 2009 - 6th International Conference on Information Technology: New Generations*. LAs Vegas, NV, 690–695. https://doi.org/10.1109/ITNG.2009.290

A Comparison amongst Face-to-Face, Blended, and Mostly Online Course Options

Russell McMahon

University of Cincinnati

College of Education, Criminal Justice, and Human Services

Cincinnati, OH 45221

513-556-4873

russ.mcmahon@uc.edu

Abstract

This talk is based upon the author's observations in 4-secitons of a freshman database 1 course over a two-year period in which students were given the option of attending nearly every class, taking a blended version of the course, or taking it partially online. Attendance was kept for all classes and a comparison of the final grades were tabulated. Later, statistics were gathered on what format of class (online or face-to-face) students took for their second database course. This study only looks at Information Technology majors. This talk is designed to elicit discussion from the audience.

Keywords

face-2-face teaching; blended teaching; online teaching

1. INTRODUCTION

The Database Management I course in our IT program is a second semester freshman level course that is open to both majors and non-majors. More than 60% of our IT majors transferred into the program and the actual number of IT freshmen students in these classes was about 49%. In the Spring 2015 and 2016 semesters, a total of 4 sections were taught by the author. After the second week of class, students were given the option of continuing the course mostly online, blending the course, or attending the majority of the classes in person. All students were required to take their tests in the classroom so that was controlled. Attendance was taken for each class day.

The University of Cincinnati has 4 different mode of instruction designations for classes: In Person, Partially DL 26-74%, Mostly DL 75-99%, or DL 100% (DL = Distance Learning). The IT program currently offers the database courses only as In Person or fully Distance Learning format. For the sake of getting a better distribution of data the following attendance percentages were used: F2F – at least 90% attendance rate, Blended – between 50% - 89% attendance rate, and for Mostly Online – between 0% - 49% attendance rate. The breakdown of the numbers of students in each group was: F2F = 19, Blended = 28, and Mostly Online = 14 for a total of 61 students out of 120. Only IT majors

SIGITE'17, October 4- 7, 2017, Rochester, NY, USA
ACM 978-1-4503-5100-3/17/10.
http://dx.doi.org/10.1145/3125659.3125663

who had successfully completed the second database course were considered in this study.

2. RESEARCH

There are studies which indicate that overall students prefer F2F courses when they can attend them, but online courses give students greater flexibility. Several studies have indicated that students who opted for the F2F or blended courses had a higher average than those who did the course mostly online, but not by much.

3. FINDINGS

The distribution of those utilizing one of the three course format options was not evenly distributed between freshman and upper-level students as a larger number of freshman opted for the F2F format for both courses. The Upper level students did not outperform the freshman in the any of the 3 formats. Overall, students in the F2F classes outperformed the other two groups.

The lowest grades in this study came from the blended group. Also, the biggest and most grad drops between the first and second courses are found in this group. This may suggest those who took the blended course format for the database 1 course were not as motivated as those in the other two groups and thus struggled in their database2 class.

4. REFERENCES

[1] Shi, N et al, "Online Versus Face to Face College Courses", The Alan Shawn Feinstein Graduate School at ScholarsArchive@JWU, May 1, 2011

[2] Young, S, Duncan, H, "Online and Face-to-Face Teaching: How Do Student Ratings Differ?", MERLOT Journal of Online Learning and Teaching Vol. 10, No. 1, March 2014

[3] Study says many online students prefer face-to-face classes April 25, 2013 http://articles.latimes.com/2013/apr/25/local/la-me-ln-study-online-20130425

[4] Virtual classrooms and MOOCs (massive open online courses) are growing rapidly, but students still prefer face-to-face interaction. https://www.usatoday.com/story/news/nation/2013/06/11/real-classrooms-better-than-virtual/2412401/

[5] The Benefits of Face-to-Face Interaction in the Online Freshman Composition Course, Samuel B Howard http://jolt.merlot.org/vol5no4/howard_1209.htm

A LinkedIn Analysis of IT Students and Alumni

Ye Diana Wang

Information Sciences and Technology Department

George Mason University

Fairfax, VA 22030, USA

ywangm@gmu.edu

ABSTRACT

This talk discusses a creative and effective way for collecting and analyzing student and alumni data by leveraging LinkedIn and provides evidence to address quality-related questions regarding the employment and career advancement of graduates from the Bachelor of Science in Information Technology (BSIT) program at an American university.

Keywords

LinkedIn Analysis; Degree Quality; IT Alumni; Employment

1. INTRODUCTION

With the rising costs of higher education, university administrators are facing increasing pressure to demonstrate the quality of their degree programs. Alumni employment rates and career advancement are useful indicators of the quality of the education provided [1]. Traditionally, programs only have limited information on their alumni's employment. Most departments rely on paper-based or electronic alumni surveys, which are conducted within several years after graduation. However, the lack of current contact information of the alumni and the ineffectiveness of the process are well-known problems.

The purposes of the current talk are to present a creative and effective way for collecting and analyzing student and alumni data by leveraging LinkedIn and to provide evidence to address quality-related questions regarding the employment and career advancement of graduates from the Bachelor of Science in Information Technology (BSIT) program at an American university.

2. METHOD

LinkedIn is currently the world's largest professional network and a valuable information repository. Although the Alumni Tools on the University Page uncover career insights of alumni from a university, it is impossible to break down the statistics at the department or program level. More and more students have joined LinkedIn Groups of their colleges, departments or programs, which have been a viable way for the educational units to maintain relationships with students and harvest alumni data for the past few years. However, LinkedIn has recently eliminated the Group API for general use and removed the functionality of exporting a list of group members and their email addresses for privacy reasons.

In order to collect data from the current and past students in the BSIT program effectively and efficiently, the author resorted to the connection list of her own LinkedIn profile, which has grown tremendously as the result of her teaching a 1-credit mandatory junior transition course between January of 2013 and May of 2017. During the course, the students are required to create a complete LinkedIn profile that consists of a list of required sections, such as education and working experience, and they must have at least three connections including the instructor. With just a click of a button, the LinkedIn Export Contacts functionality generated an Excel file that contained 1079 connections of the author's profile, which eventually reduced to 690 connections after all the personal connections and irrelevant data were deleted.

3. RESULTS

The data file yield five pieces of key information: the student's name, e-mail address, company, position, and connected date, which is useful in determining the graduation status of a student. Out of the 690 connections under investigation, there are 489 graduates and 201 current students from the BSIT program. The results of the analyses are able to answer the following questions:

How many people are working in the IT field?

431 or 88.14% of graduates and 39 or 19.40 % of current students are working in the IT field. The findings suggest that the graduates with a BS in IT degree have been much more successful than current IT students to find quality employment in the IT field, such as network administrators, web developers, and information assurance engineers, etc.

How many people are holding managerial positions in the IT field?

43 or 8.80% of graduates and 2 or 1 % of current students are holding managerial positions in the IT field. The findings suggest that the graduates have a much better chance of achieving high-level management positions, such as project managers, chief operating offers, and senior consultants, etc. than current students.

These findings provide evidence to support the quality of the current BSIT program and may be valuable to numerous university constituencies, such as academic administrators, career advisors, students and their parents, and IT recruiters and employers. Another potential use of the LinkedIn analysis is for the assessment and the accreditation of university degree programs.

4. REFERENCES

[1]   Case, T.L., Han, H. J., & Rimes, E. 2016. Career Paths of Computing Program Graduates: A LinkedIn Analysis. In *Proceeding of the Southern Association for Information Systems Conference*, St. Augustine, FL.

Using a Game to Teach About Phishing

Patrickson Weanquoi
Department of Computer Science
Winston-Salem State University
Winston-Salem, NC
pweanquoi115@rams.wssu.edu

Jaris Johnson
Department of Computer Science
Winston-Salem State University
Winston-Salem, NC
jjohnson514@rams.wssu.edu

Jinghua Zhang
Department of Computer Science
Winston-Salem State University
Winston-Salem, NC
zhangji@wssu.edu

ABSTRACT

Cyber security education has become increasingly critical as we spend more of our everyday lives online. Research shows that college students are mostly unaware of many online dangers. To teach students about cyber security using their preferred medium, gaming, we developed an educational 2D game called *Bird's Life* that aims to teach college students about phishing. Players will come to understand phishing attacks and how to avoid them in real world scenarios through a fun gaming context. The game can be deployed to multiple platforms such as PC, web and mobile devices. To measure the effect of this game on learning the concepts of cyber security, a pre-test, post-test and online survey were developed and used in the evaluation process. In Spring 2017, the game was used in the CSC1310 Computer programming I class and CSC3332 Fundamentals of Internet Systems class at Winston-Salem State University. Initial classroom evaluations show that students love this type of learning and they did perform better in the post-test after playing the game.

CCS Concepts

Security and privacy → Phishing; Security and privacy → Malware and its mitigation

Keywords and Phrases

Cyber security; Phishing; Game-Based Learning; mobile devices; Unity

1 INTRODUCTION

To help students understand the concepts of phishing, we developed a 2D game called *Bird's Life*. The objective of the game is to provide students with a fun environment to learn about phishing. Two undergraduate students developed the prototype using Unity3d game engine in about six months. The game was not designed for gamers. Students without prior gaming experience can complete the game within 20 minutes. There are three main levels in the game: introduction, tips, and quiz. To evaluate the potential impact of the game on student learning, we used a pre-test and post-test. We developed and used an online survey to collect the feedback from students. The game was used in two classes in spring 2017 and the initial evaluation shows promising results.

2 GAME DESIGN & DEVELOPMENT

2.1 LEVEL ONE

This section of the game aims to get the player's attention of the game. The conversation between the two birds foreshadows the general ideas the player will learn throughout the game. In order to accomplish the dialogue between the birds, we hard coded the conversation in a C# script.

2.2 LEVEL TWO

This level is designed to have the player collect useful tips on how to avoid phishing attacks. The player will be prompted to collect five good worms to obtain a tip. Once all five tips have been collected, the player will enter the next level.

2.3 LEVEL THREE

The level three is designed to test the player's knowledge of the concepts covered in the previous level. Questions are randomly selected from the question pool. The player needs to get eighty percent correct to win the game.

3 EVALUATIONS

We started the impact study with the pre-test and post-test comparison. 20 out of 30 students showed improvements in their scores. In addition to the tests, students did a survey online after playing the game to provide comments and feedback on the game. The game will be refined based on the feedback.

4 ACKNOWLEDGEMENTS

This project was supported by the Collaborative Research Experiences for Undergraduates (CREU) via iAAMCS AYUR program.

SIGITE'17, October 4-7, 2017, Rochester, NY, USA
© 2017 Copyright is held by the owner/author(s).
ACM ISBN 978-1-4503-5100-3/17/10.
DOI: http://dx.doi.org/10.1145/3125659.3125669

Creating Economy Active Learning Classrooms for IT Students

Quentrese Cole
Department of Educational
Leadership
Central Michigan University
Mount Pleasant, Michigan 48859
cole1qt@cmich.edu

Matthew Johnson
Department of Educational
Leadership
Central Michigan University
Mount Pleasant, Michigan 48859
johns9m@cmich.edu

Jesse Eickholt
Department of Computer Science
Central Michigan University
Mount Pleasant, Michigan 48859
eickholt.j@cmich.edu

ABSTRACT

Active learning and active learning classrooms can enhance students' classroom performance and experience and the technology and collaborative nature of active learning classrooms are similar to what IT students can expect to encounter during their careers. One difficulty in providing more students with access to active learning classrooms is the cost associated with creating new spaces or retrofitting existing spaces. State-of-the-art active learning classroom designs, such as those showcased elsewhere in the literature, can easily cost hundreds of thousands of dollars to construct. In this work we describe the modification of an existing IT lab to create an economical active learning classroom. Our experience is that even with limited resources it is possible to create a productive space that students find helpful and that mimics state-of-the-art active learning classrooms. Also provided is an overview of the theoretical foundations of active learning classrooms and active learning and some preliminary results from the use of such a classroom for an introductory programming course.

CCS CONCEPTS

• **Applied computing** → **Collaborative learning**; *Interactive learning environments*; • **Human-centered computing** → *Collaborative and social computing systems and tools*;

KEYWORDS

active learning classrooms, active learning, collaboration, learning environment

1 INTRODUCTION

The art of teaching has evolved greatly in recent years. Much of this progression can be credited to new innovative ways of teaching. There are many factors that can contribute to students learning in the classroom. One contributing factor, technology, has shaped best practices in education today significantly. New groundbreaking methods must be utilized to teach a new population of learners. Many institutions have been diligent in discovering new techniques, utilizing technology to improve teaching methods to accommodate

the new generation of students [16]. The traditional style of teaching has shifted to support a diverse student population. Traditional classroom environments are no longer meeting the multifaceted needs of students.

Walker, Brooks, and Baepler [18] researched technology enriched learning spaces at the University of Minnesota. This study was a follow up to a previous study on the University of Minnesota's new learning environments, active learning classrooms (ALCs) [18]. The study discovered teaching in an active learning classroom added considerably to student learning outcomes. Both students and teachers are impacted by the design of the space where learning occurs. The learning environments included large round tables constructed to accommodate nine students, each with a personal laptop. Additionally, large LCD screens were used to share work with the classroom and microphones were affixed to each of the tables, so students could share with peers across the room. The room was equipped with white boards for collaboration amongst the learners. Students could press a button that prompted a small light if they wanted to share in discussion [18].

Walker, Brooks, and Baepler had two main objectives to achieve through their research [18]. They wanted to reproduce the original study with additional samples of students and teachers. They also wanted to be more intentional about the pedagogy used in the space. The researchers sought to find factors that impacted the relationship with types of learning spaces and well as the relationship with pedagogical approaches. The study found that when the instructors adjusted their pedagogical approach to the environment by using intentional student concentrated active learning techniques, student learning improved [18]. Active learning classrooms have many benefits that help foster advantageous learning environments [13]. In active learning classrooms environmental factors are taken into account. The design of the classroom is shifted from the traditional front facing desk and chair. In active learning classrooms, technology is utilized to invoke student participation and interaction [13]. As technology has evolved in recent years, more devices have been made available for use in the spaces.

Active learning can be described in general terms as activities which attempt to make students active agents in the learning process as opposed to being passive observers or recipients [14]. While the idea of active learning is not new, it has received more attention in recent years as meta-analyses with regard to active learning show improvements for STEM students in terms of satisfaction and performance [9]. Active learning classrooms and technology are designed to directly support active learning pedagogy. Constructing new active learning classrooms or retrofitting existing classrooms can be very costly, with expenses reaching into the hundreds of thousands of dollars [13, 19]. This expense may be prohibitive to

SIGITE'17, October 4–7, 2017, Rochester, NY,USA
© 2017 Association for Computing Machinery.
ACM ISBN 978-1-4503-5100-3/17/10...$15.00
https://doi.org/10.1145/3125659.3125682

many institutions and reduces the reach of a proven approach to increase student performance in STEM fields.

This work presents an overview of the theoretical foundation of active learning and active learning classrooms as well as our experience in transforming an existing classroom into a modified active learning classroom. Provided some flexibility and ingenuity, it is is possible to retrofit an existing space to function similar to state-of-the-art active learning classrooms and do so in an economical fashion. This is particularly true in Information Technology as our lab spaces are often already equipped with movable furnishings and sufficient power. Furthermore, faculty, staff and students often possess the skills needed to adopt commodity hardware to support active learning. Initial feedback from students that made use of our economical active learning space has been largely positive.

2 ACTIVE LEARNING CLASSROOMS

Bonwell and Eison suggested approaches that produced active learning classrooms [4]. They referred to active learning as a learning approach that causes students to be active while thinking about the material they learning. In an active learning classroom, teachers facilitate student learning and support the process of gaining knowledge. In these spaces teachers are better able to educate students compared to traditional classrooms. They promote the ideal of students being actively engaged in interactive class sessions. As a result, students are capable of taking ownership of their learning. When students are actively engaged, they not only add to their learning of concepts, but they enhance learning for their peers. The role of teachers and learners in classroom settings have been more clearly defined through this research. As a result, instructors are better prepared to serve and educate newer generations of students.

Social constructivist theory sets the theoretical framework for active learning classrooms. This theory promotes the idea that students learn best by being active. Through actions in a group setting, knowledge is produced collaboratively [17]. Through these collaborative interactions each individual is a stakeholder in the development of learning. Each student takes a part in shared ownership of the process rather than one person maintaining it. Social constructivist theory delivers a firm pedagogical foundation for active learning classrooms [7]. Grabinger and Dunlap introduced the concept, Rich Environments For Active Learning (REALs) [11]. REALs are grounded in constructivist philosophies. REALs offer instructional strategies that involve students in the learning process. In this learning process students are able to take part in learning through collaborative activities that include intentional experiences and interactions. REALs are a method to foster learning practices that stimulate the growth of inert knowledge. Active learning frequently aligns with constructivist philosophies, that were originally fostered by John Dewey [6].

In Experience and Education, Dewey addresses how students learn information most effectively [6]. Dewey argued that there is a necessary relationship between experience and education. Dewey believed that students must actually do hands-on work to benefit educationally. Dewey highlighted the importance of interaction between both the student and the teacher. In this view, teachers shift from controlling learning in the classroom to fostering an environment where students can learn. The teacher can shape the entire learning of a student by obtaining certain skills and maintaining the important concepts. According to Dewey, knowledge and skills are transferred to students through the facilitation of the instructor [6]. The space where students gain knowledge can be as imperative as the content they are learning. The idea of experiences in the classroom ties in directly with the role of active learning classrooms. Active learning classrooms have created the space for a new type of educational experience. Through an intentional approach, active learning classrooms have developed places of learning to be more inclusive to students.

While the spaces can create positive learning experiences, researchers discovered that instructors must also use new innovative ways to reach students [18]. The research found that traditional teaching pedagogies in active learning spaces were not as effective as active learning techniques. Instructors in active learning classrooms must integrate active learning to their teaching techniques [18]. Student learning evolves when teachers are able to acclimate their teaching style to the design of the classroom, utilizing active learning techniques which are focused on the student [18].

Barr and Tagg wrote on the need to transform the way students learn at universities [1]. They emphasized behaviors to convert traditional instructional teaching to quality knowledge construction for students. The authors compare past practices in the "instruction paradigm" to what Barr and Tagg called the "learning paradigm" [1]. In the learning paradigm students are able to take ownership of the learning experience. In the learning paradigm, the goal of education is not to just impart knowledge, it empowers students to construct knowledge for themselves. Students are able to be a part of the process and collaborate with others in the space to shape the knowledge created. When educators utilize interactive learning practices, students receive a more beneficial education. These paradigm shifts in learning should be a requirement for the education of today. As universities work to support the whole student, these practices transform the learning environment to a more intentional and robust learning space [1].

One of the first models of active learning classrooms started with North Carolina State University's Student-Centered Activities for Large Enrollment Undergraduate Programs (SCALE-UP) [2]. The SCALE-UP space was created to increase interaction in the learning process for students and faculty [2]. In SCALE-UP, the classroom design consisted of large round tables, laptop connections, projectors and tabled microphones for students to use. In these spaces, students were able to collaborate on work with others in the class [2]. The researchers found that the design of the course had positive impact on student learning. They found that the spaces amplified student understanding of content as well as heightened critical thinking proficiencies [2].

Evans and Cook explored the impact of environment on classroom instruction [8]. Their research sought to find the dynamics of design on pedagogical practices. Evans and Cook studied how educational spaces are shaped by technology. With society shifting to a technology driven world, integrating technology into education is imperative [8]. The design of innovative educational spaces has the potential to influence the future of student learning. These innovations brought about the creative learning spaces at Queensland University of Technology.

In these learning environments, an assortment of furniture and technologies were utilized to create a classroom [8]. The technology utilized in the space included a camera to share documents, lectern, projector, as well as recorders [8]. The space also featured touch-screen computers on wheels for each student. Along with the space modification, a learning program called Learning and Teaching in Collaborative Environments (LATICE) was implemented. The goal of LATIACE was to create a set of measurable innovative and assessable learning and teaching prototypes that supported university goals [8]. After a semester of teaching in these environments, teachers were surveyed about their teaching experiences. The results of this study found a positive influence on engagement and interaction. These learning environments have created an advantageous space for collaboration. Evans and Cook highlight a need for more research to find interventions that may have large impacts on learning experiences.

Constructing active learning classrooms can require a substantial commitment of resources from an institution [5]. For example, a classroom with 100 seats was renovated to an active learning classroom for 30 students with the overall cost totaling $100,000 [13]. While renovations for active learning classrooms can be costly, Rands and Gansemer-Topf (2017) found that low-cost features including transportable whiteboards and moving chairs provide numerous opportunities for active learning and student engagement [15].

3 MODIFYING CLASSROOMS FOR PALS

In this work we modified an existing classroom to support active learning. It is certainly true that active learning can be achieved in a number of settings, even without specific supporting technology or spaces. Still, from the perspective of enhancing collaboration and the ability to easily share the types of digital artifacts that information technology students produce, this supporting technology and specific active learning spaces have value. Two principle components to creating an active learning classroom are the physical space (e.g., classroom layout, desks) and technology (e.g., screensharing, whiteboards, audiovisual systems). Here we focus primarily on modifications that can be made to the physical space to support active learning and accommodate the associated technology.

3.1 Classroom Layout

The classroom selected for modification was an average sized computer lab that could accommodate up to 30 students. Prior to modifications, each student had his or her own desk equipped with a monitor, keyboard, wired network connection and power tap. The instructor station was a large desk towards the front, right corner of the classroom and an overhead projector and screen occupied the front, left half of the classroom wall. Figures 1 and 2 display the arrangement of the classroom prior to modifications.

The principle physical modifications to the classroom were designed with improved collaboration in mind. The desk were arranged into pods and moved the periphery of the room. This made moving around the room easier, particularly from the view point of the instructor. It also indicated to the students that group collaboration would be key and foundational to the class. A number of whiteboards were also installed on the walls. Finally, the footprint

Figure 1: Student work stations before PALS transformation.

Figure 2: Instructor station before PALS transformation.

of the instructor station was greatly reduced and placed along the front wall. Figures 3 and 4 show the new arrangement of the room, instructor station and the PALS system when deployed.

3.2 Practical Active Learning Stations

Augmenting the physical modifications to the classroom was technology to support collaboration and active learning. A system termed PALS (i.e., Practical Active Learning Stations) was developed and deployed in the classroom. This system mimics the technology found in state-of-the-art active learning classrooms. Two student PALS were placed on each pod and allowed students to connect their device via HDMI and share content with a local display. The instructor can monitor student progress via an instructor station and select content to broadcast throughout the classroom on the larger LCDs. The PALS system was designed using open source, community licensed software and commodity hardware to minimize cost. An existing, wired local area network was used to connect the PALS and the LCDs.

Figure 3: Arrangement of student desks after transformation. A smaller instructor station can be seen against the back wall.

Figure 4: A laptop connected to a student station. Content is mirrored locally and to the larger wheeled LCD in the background.

4 DISCUSSION

4.1 Design Considerations

The initial plan for modifying the classroom relied heavily on leveraging the existing infrastructure as much as possible. This is necessary to minimize cost. As a result, the existing audiovisual system was used and a few additional large LCDs were to be mounted to the walls. The existing student desks were reused and the instructor station was to be replaced with a smaller podium located in the center of the classroom. Student collaboration would be supported through wall mounted whiteboards and the PALS system. Initial consultations with facilities management indicated that these modifications could be achieved within our budgeted amount of approximately $10,000 and the end result would be an environment to support active learning and collaboration.

As the project moved forward, it became clear that several of the structural modifications (e.g., moving the instructor station) would not be possible. This was due to the fact that in addition to the planned modifications, a number of additional changes may have been needed to bring the space into compliance with changes in code which had transpired over the years. This is an important consideration that needs to be taken into account for any planned renovation and likely to be faced by many institutions. Modifications that seem simple (e.g., mounting LCDs on walls) may trigger more extensive renovations for older buildings when building permits are sought. These ancillary renovations can quickly dominate the budget and scuttle plans for modest, economical modifications. In this work, we were able to accommodate these limitations by placing the LCDs on large wheeled carts and left the instructor station in its previous location but reduced its size. Figures 3 and 4 show the transformed PALS classroom with group seating, smaller instructor station and one of the large LCDs.

Initially, it may seem that a number of factors worked in our favor (e.g., the existing student furniture was movable and could form larger tables, an existing wired network was present to support the PALS). In reality, when cost is the driving factor some flexibility and ingenuity is needed to manage cost. In this work, that meant using existing furniture and network connectivity. In other settings

with larger fixed tables or immovable desks, wireless networking and wheeled student stations could be employed. Another option would be limited runs of CAT5 cable in conjunction with HDMI over CAT5 receivers/transmitters. There is an increasing amount of commodity hardware available which can replicate the supporting technology often found in active learning classrooms. While such approaches are not turnkey, they can offer tremendous savings, provided some flexibility at the institutional level.

4.2 Comparison to a Traditional Active Learning Classroom

The physical modifications made to the classroom presented in this work along with the PALS system are meant to mimic the environment found in a typical, state-of-the-art active learning classroom exemplified by designs such as SCALE-UP [3] and TEAL [7]. The physical layout places the focus of the student on their neighbor and not the instructor. The instructor has easy access to each group and can move unimpeded throughout the classroom and interact locally with each group. Digital (e.g., code, diagrams) and analog (e.g., whiteboard notes) artifacts can quickly and easily be shared locally and with the entire class. This supports collaboration and peer learning.

4.3 Limitations

In terms of the physical space, there are two limitations of this work. First, in order to make a space group centric, the student furniture will need to be movable and the space will need to allow repositioning of the instructor station and student furniture. Some spaces are more receptive to repositioning then others. The need to purchase new student furniture, particularly of the variety that are need for IT labs (e.g., capable of supporting workstations, monitors, etc.), will quickly inflate any budget. Second, space will be needed to mount (or store if wheeled options are selected) whiteboards and large LCDs.

Flexibility in terms of institutional policies is also needed. The amount of flexibility is dependent on the extent of the modifications but most institutional offices of information technology (OIT) prefer software and hardware which are, at minimum, supported by the manufacture. Direct support and turnkey solutions for supporting technology come at a substantial cost which will stand in contrast to economy options. Specific active learning or classroom technology may also lack flexibility in deployment which may necessitate more expensive renovations to install properly. Thus, flexibility in what can be purchased and how it will be deployed is needed. Faculty and students may need to help with the maintenance of the support technology as well.

There are of course limitations in what the active learning space will provide in and of itself. Simply placing students in an active learning space will not necessitate that students partake in active learning or that faculty will use it properly. Some technological and pedagogical training and willingness on the part of faculty is needed.

4.4 Initial Student Perceptions

To gauge students' initial perceptions of the modified classroom and PALS learning stations, we asked several Likert scale and open-ended questions on an end-of-the-semester post-survey, which was administered by a professor in another department in order to avoid bias. This was conducted in an introductory programming course. Post-surveys were administered in week 14 of the 16-week semester. Two of the open-ended questions are relevant to this manuscript: (1) What role did the active learning aspects of this course (e.g., group/pair programming activities, think-pair-share) have in your learning?, and (2) What role did the in-class technology and classroom used in this course have on your learning?

Of the 25 students in the PALS classroom in Spring 2017, 23 participated in the post-survey, netting a response rate of 92%. In analyzing their open-ended responses to the survey, several themes emerged. The first and most prominent theme was that the PALS system allowed students to see different solutions to problems, which was more than a traditional classroom would allow. Having the opportunity to see how several different peers approached or solved a problem benefited student learning. The PALS system allowed for students to share their work easily to the rest of the class, which provided examples to other students and helped them when they were stuck. This ease of sharing afforded students prompt feedback on their work. This is markedly different from a traditional model where students complete assignments individually and await instructor feedback several days later and similar to the interactions found in state-of-the-art active learning classrooms. Many students appreciated learning the material from peers rather than the instructor as evidenced by one student who said, "Also [the PALS system] helped me learn the material better sometimes because my peer explained it to me in an easier way." Learning from more advanced peers was especially important in this course because students had varying levels of efficacy in problem-solving and coding prior to the course. Additionally, instead of becoming bored or isolated, more advanced peers could help others learn different ways to solve problems. The PALS system helped ameliorate some of the issues that often arise with differentiating instruction to varying levels of knowledge in a course. The positive benefits associated with learning from peers was the strongest theme from the respondents.

Seeing multiple solutions to a problem also had an ancillary effect of normalizing confusion and a lack of confidence in problem-solving. When students were able to see that others were having difficulty solving problems, they felt less anxious and out of place. One student remarked, "[The active learning aspects of the course] helped me see that I am not the only one that may be having problems with the course." The format that the PALS system allowed also created an environment for students to "ask questions in a non-fearful way," as one student stated.

Not all students appreciated the active learning setup because it forced them into a learning pedagogy that was not their preferred way of learning. One student offered that the PALS system was "very unhelpful and made learning more difficult. I am a person that prefers a lecture and note-taking." This view was held by only two students, while the rest found the PALS system had a positive effect on their learning.

4.5 Next Steps for Active Learning with PALS

While the PALS classroom can provide a cost-effective option for ALCs, it does not take away from the needed preparation to operate in the space. One next step in the process of bring more active learning technology to more students would be through faculty training. With the economic savings of a PALS classroom compared to ALCs, department funds can be leveraged in other meaningful ways such as professional development or specialized training for teaching methods in the PALS classroom. In ALCs, learning does not happen on its own and the use of ALCs requires innovative instruction [10]. Educators must experience pedagogical training to be able to properly facilitate in ALC spaces. Faculty training and construction costs are arguably the largest barriers to wider scale adoption of active learning classrooms and technology. This work begins to address the issue of construction costs but more will be needed to help the larger community with training options.

Another next step with the PALS classroom is to explore the potential of the room in terms of its flexibility. IT educators can utilize PALS classrooms to create a space of knowledge construction and sharing of ideas. These spaces present an advantageous space for high student engagement and learning. One of the greatest benefits of the PALS classroom is the ability for instructors to utilize mobility in the space. In most classrooms, a whiteboard is mounted to the front of the classroom and is utilized by the instructor in one location [12]. In the PALS classroom, there are numerous white boards around the room as well as LCD projectors. While many ALCs may have a movable whiteboard in the space, PALS instructors can utilize the entire space of the classroom with displays on multiple, varying surfaces.

5   CONCLUSION

We have described our experience in modifying an existing classroom to support active learning and provided an overview of the theoretical foundations of active learning classrooms and active learning. Typical modifications required to create an active learning classroom include rearranging the student seating, changing the focal point of the classroom (i.e., shifting it away from the instructor) and adding technology that can be used to support collaboration. New construction or renovations that make use of turnkey systems to support active learning can be expensive, often to the point of being cost prohibitive. Nevertheless, provided some flexibility and leveraging the expertise of IT students and faculty, it is possible to create economy active learning spaces which function similar to state-of-the-art ALCs. Our initial results indicate that students enjoy working in our modified classroom and they report it had an overwhelmingly positive effect on their learning.

ACKNOWLEDGMENTS

This material is based on work supported by the National Science Foundation under Grant No. 1608043.

REFERENCES

[1] Robert B Barr and John Tagg. 1995. From teaching to learning - A new paradigm for undergraduate education. *Change: The magazine of higher learning* 27, 6 (1995), 12–26.

[2] Robert J Beichner, Jeffery M Saul, David S Abbott, Jeanne J Morse, Duane Deardorff, Rhett J Allain, Scott W Bonham, Melissa H Dancy, and John S Risley. 2007. The student-centered activities for large enrollment undergraduate programs (SCALE-UP) project. *Research-based reform of university physics* 1, 1 (2007), 2–39.

[3] Robert J Beichner, Jeffery M Saul, Rhett J Allain, Duane L Deardorff, and David S Abbott. 2000. Introduction to SCALE-UP: Student-Centered Activities for Large Enrollment University Physics. (2000).

[4] Charles C Bonwell and James A Eison. 1991. *Active Learning: Creating Excitement in the Classroom. 1991 ASHE-ERIC Higher Education Reports.* ERIC.

[5] Sehoya Cotner, Jessica Loper, JD Walker, and D Christopher Brooks. 2013. It's Not You, It's the Room - Are the High-Tech, Active Learning Classrooms Worth It? *Journal of College Science Teaching* 42, 6 (2013), 82–88.

[6] J Dewey. 1938. *Experience and Education.* MacMillian, New York, NY.

[7] Yehudit Judy Dori and John Belcher. 2005. How does technology-enabled active learning affect undergraduate students' understanding of electromagnetism concepts? *The Journal of the Learning Sciences* 14, 2 (2005), 243–279.

[8] Richard Evans and Roger Cook. 2014. In the right space: exploring the dynamics between design, environment and pedagogy. In *Proceedings of 31st ascilite Conference" Rhetoric or Reality: Critical perspectives on educational technology".* ascilite, 713–716.

[9] Scott Freeman, Sarah L Eddy, Miles McDonough, Michelle K Smith, Nnadozie Okoroafor, Hannah Jordt, and Mary Pat Wenderoth. 2014. Active learning increases student performance in science, engineering, and mathematics. *Proceedings of the National Academy of Sciences* 111, 23 (2014), 8410–8415.

[10] Xun Ge, Yu Jin Yang, Lihui Liao, and Erin G. Wolfe. 2015. *Perceived Affordances of a Technology-Enhanced Active Learning Classroom in Promoting Collaborative Problem Solving.* Springer International Publishing, Cham, 305–322. https://doi.org/10.1007/978-3-319-05825-2_21

[11] R Scott Grabinger and Joanna C Dunlap. 1995. Rich environments for active learning: A definition. *ALT-J* 3, 2 (1995), 5–34.

[12] Matthew Koehler and Punya Mishra. 2009. What is Technological Pedagogical Content Knowledge (TPACK)? *Contemporary Issues in Technology and Teacher Education* 9, 1 (March 2009), 60–70. https://www.learntechlib.org/p/29544

[13] Elisa L Park and Bo Keum Choi. 2014. Transformation of classroom spaces: traditional versus active learning classroom in colleges. *Higher Education* 68, 5 (2014), 749–771.

[14] Michael Prince. 2004. Does active learning work? A review of the research. *Journal of engineering education* 93, 3 (2004), 223–231.

[15] Melissa L Rands and Ann M Gansemer-Topf. 2017. The Room Itself Is Active: How Classroom Design Impacts Student Engagement. *Journal of Learning Spaces* 6, 1 (2017), 26.

[16] A Twigg. 2003. Improving Quality and Reducing Cost: Designs for Effective Learning. *Change: The Magazine of Higher Learning* 35, 4 (2003), 22–29.

[17] Ernst von Glasersfeld. 1987. The construction of knowledge: Contributions to conceptual semantics. Seaside. (1987).

[18] JD Walker, D Christopher Brooks, and Paul Baepler. 2011. Pedagogy and space: Empirical research on new learning environments. *Educause Quarterly* 34, 4 (2011), n4.

[19] Aimee L Whiteside, Linda Jorn, Ann Hill Duin, and Steve Fitzgerald. 2009. Using the PAIR-up model to evaluate active learning spaces. *Educause Quarterly* 32, 1 (2009), n1.

Enhancing Human-Computer Interaction and User Experience Education through a Hybrid Approach to Experiential Learning

Andrew B. Talone
University of Central Florida
4000 Central Florida Blvd
Orlando, FL 32817
atalone@knights.ucf.edu

Prateek Basavaraj
University of Central Florida
4000 Central Florida Blvd
Orlando, FL 32817
prateek.basavaraj@ucf.edu

Pamela J. Wisniewski
University of Central Florida
4000 Central Florida Blvd
Orlando, FL 32817
pamwis@ucf.edu

ABSTRACT

This paper introduces the concept and implementation of a hybrid experiential learning approach to building a User Experience (UX) Lab at a large public university (the University of Central Florida). The UX Lab @ UCF (UX Lab) is intended to bridge the gap between traditional project-based courses and full-time industry internships to provide Information Technology (IT) undergraduates (and students from other disciplines and levels) with the opportunity to apply their Human-Computer Interaction (HCI) knowledge and hone their UX skills by working in partnership with local companies. Specifically, students work as part-time, paid UX consultants for local companies while receiving guidance, mentoring, and feedback from a faculty mentor and graduate student with expertise in HCI and UX. Thus, the UX Lab contributes to IT pedagogy by providing students with a unique opportunity to apply what they've learned in their HCI coursework to real products in development by actual companies. Our approach complements other pedagogical approaches, such as industry-sponsored project-based courses and capstone courses. In this paper, we describe the conceptual model upon which the UX Lab was built, and the success of the first proof-of-concept project that was recently completed in May 2017.

1 INTRODUCTION

The Information Technology (IT) discipline faces new challenges and opportunities everyday due to fast-paced changes and the rapidly growing importance of technology in our society [9]. These changes not only require IT professionals to adapt but also necessitate that undergraduate IT curriculums adapt to reflect these changes. One way in which undergraduate IT programs have been working to improve their curriculum is to use industry-sponsored project-based learning in the classroom [8]. Such

SIGITE'17, October 4–7, 2017, Rochester, NY, USA
© 2017 Association for Computing Machinery.
ACM ISBN 978-1-4503-5100-3/17/10...$15.00
https://doi.org/10.1145/3125659.3125685

applied approaches work well for training IT students' skills necessary to enter the workforce [3]. Thus, many accredited IT programs in the United States are trying to incorporate industry partnerships to supplement their curriculum and help students get hands-on experience working on real-world projects [2].

Meanwhile, Human-Computer Interaction (HCI) has been recognized as a core discipline to be included in IT undergraduate education [7]. One domain in which HCI is critically important is User Experience (UX) [4]. As noted by Kuniavsky [4], HCI principles and methods are relevant to UX because they are used to create products that accommodate end user's abilities and goals. HCI and UX are, therefore, important aspects of IT undergraduates' education, and continued effort should be taken to improve students' HCI and UX knowledge, skills, and employment opportunities. To improve the recently ABET (Accreditation Board for Engineering and Technology) accredited undergraduate IT program at our university (University of Central Florida; UCF) and to help students get real-world experience applying HCI principles and methods to the design of software-based products, we created a User Experience laboratory.

The UX Lab @ UCF (http://www.cs.ucf.edu/ux/) offers local businesses an opportunity to partner with our university to receive high-quality, low-cost UX services. In turn, client engagements provide students with unique experiential learning opportunities working as UX consultants or interns for the industry partners. Students are trained to apply the concepts and methods learned in their HCI coursework to the enhancement of software-based products that the companies intend to bring to market. The UX Lab provides students with practical experience that is not available through course offerings or internships alone. The novelty and effectiveness of our approach comes from the guidance and mentoring the IT undergraduate students receive from graduate students and faculty members affiliated with the UX Lab. Since small to mid-size companies often do not have the in-house capabilities or expertise in HCI or UX concepts; this mentoring bridge provides valuable benefits to both the industry partners and IT students.

In this paper, we discuss related work and provide an overview of the concept behind the UX Lab. Then, we describe our first proof-of-concept project with the UX Lab's inaugural client and discuss how the project was perceived by both the undergraduate students and the client. We conclude by summarizing the success of the project/lab thus far, and the next steps we are taking to continue to improve the UX Lab.

2 RELATED WORK

Prior literature has shown 1) the importance of engaging students through interactive exercises and projects when teaching HCI and UX as part of an IT curriculum [1,8] and, 2) the benefits that real-world project experience has on IT students' motivation and learning outcomes [3,5,6]. We briefly discuss each of these perspectives below.

2.1 Engaging Students in the Classroom

Prior work has identified ways in which HCI and UX instruction can be more effective. One approach to enhancing HCI courses is to engage students in interactive exercises and projects. For instance, Bačíková [1] provided recommendations to help design HCI and UX coursework that is more engaging and meaningful to IT undergraduates. Two of Bačíková's recommendations were to 1) involve industry UX experts when possible, and 2) make the course more engaging to students by making the lectures and class exercises more interactive. In addition, Preston [8] demonstrated that real-world projects that are based upon industry practices are crucial for IT students to strengthen their understanding of HCI and other critical IT subjects. Through the use of real-world lab style software courses, students were motivated, and the efforts were deemed successful. The average pass rate improved to 91% with these changes.

2.2 Project-Based Learning

Based on interviews with IT employees, there is a need for students to obtain practical, project-oriented skills and experience in the form of internships and coursework involving experiential learning [6]. The benefits of engaging IT undergraduates in project-based learning have been demonstrated within academia. Laware et al. [5] implemented project-based learning or project-centered learning for courses in the computer technology program at Purdue University. The benefits of project-centered learning were that it helped students 1) obtain practical experience, 2) understand why planning is a critical step during a project, and 3) understand the importance of communication skills, and other soft skills, when working within a team.

Project-based learning is particularly effective in capstone courses [3]. Team-based projects in capstone courses are important for learning teamwork, etiquette, and improving project management skills. Gorka et al. [3] highlighted the benefits of industry-sponsored capstone projects for students, industry partners, and educational institutions. Students benefit from these projects by being more motivated to work on real-world problems and having materials to place in their professional portfolio. The industry partners benefit by receiving solutions at no (or little) cost to them, as well as multiple solutions to consider. Finally, educational institutions benefit by obtaining feedback from industry to improve their programs to ensure graduates meet industry expectations.

3 THE CONCEPT BEHIND AN EXPERIENTIAL LEARNING UX LAB

3.1 Overview

The UX Lab connects both undergraduate and graduate students with local companies through part-time, paid UX consulting engagements. Each project is individually negotiated and led by the faculty mentor who is primarily responsible for the success of the client engagement. Thus, local companies pay students through a university account that is owned by the faculty member within the UX Lab, as opposed to adding students directly to their own payroll as interns. Therefore, faculty expertise plays a large role in companies' desire to work with the students, as they are not only provided with low-cost resources, but also Ph.D. level expertise and oversight provided by the faculty mentor. The faculty mentor is then responsible for putting together a team of students with the capabilities needed to deliver the services requested by the client. Students then provide UX services at a reduced rate (compared to the average $150/hour for UX consulting companies), while under the supervision and direction of a graduate student and their faculty mentor. This structure affords students the opportunity to apply what they have learned in their HCI coursework to existing (or in-development) products while receiving guidance and mentoring from experts in HCI and UX. Thus, IT student involvement in UX Lab projects provides students with unique practical experience that is not obtainable through their HCI coursework, nor through UX internships that do not provide in-house UX mentoring.

3.2 Guided Experiential Learning

3.2.1 UX Lab Structure. The uniqueness of the UX Lab comes from the way Dr. Wisniewski (co-author on this paper) structures and manages projects to facilitate student learning. Students who apply to work in the lab are matched to projects based on their prior experience and specific interests. Through the UX Lab, they are paid hourly for their work and complete projects while under the supervision and mentorship of Dr. Wisniewski, or in the future, additional faculty mentors experienced in HCI and UX. Undergraduates are directly supervised by a graduate (M.S. or Ph.D. level) student, so they receive additional support and mentoring throughout a given project. This tiered structure reduces the need for micro-management on behalf of the faculty mentor but leaves enough flexibility for bi-directional communication channels between all stakeholders of the project (Fig. 1).

This structure for the UX Lab was chosen to provide undergraduates with a strong experiential learning environment in which they can 1) work within a team with fellow students, 2) receive feedback and mentoring from experts in HCI, 3) work on real-world projects for actual companies, and 4) maintain full-time student status (i.e., maintain a full course load). Thus, UX Lab projects provide an intermediate or hybrid approach between two typical approaches by which students gain HCI or UX experience: project-based coursework and full-time industry internships.

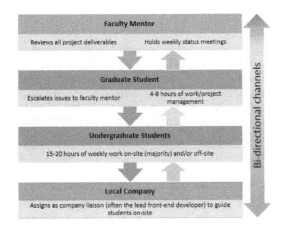

Figure 1: UX Lab structure on a weekly basis.

3.2.2 Benefits over Project-Based Coursework. Project-based coursework is beneficial to students because it provides them an opportunity to apply course principles to more realistic situations while in a controlled learning environment. This approach also allows the faculty to have more control over the structure and outcomes of the projects. This approach, however, is limited in its ability to simulate the challenges faced when working on an actual product for a real company (e.g., shifting priorities, convincing stakeholders). While our approach takes some of the control out of the hands of the faculty, it also provides students with valuable real-world experience and more one-on-one mentoring from the faculty.

3.2.3 Benefits over Full-Time Internships. In contrast, full-time internships immerse students within an organization and provide them with the most realistic introduction to working within an industry setting as an HCI or UX professional. However, full-time industry internships have their own limitations. One important constraint for students is that internships are highly variable in terms of the mentorship provided by more senior HCI or UX professionals. Another limitation is that students are often required to take a semester off from their coursework or to temporarily move for a position. This poses challenges for students who cannot afford to delay graduation or the cost of temporary living accommodations.

In summary, UX Lab projects bridge the gap between project-based coursework and full-time internships by utilizing a hybrid approach that incorporates the strengths of these approaches while mitigating their limitations.

4 CONTRIBUTIONS TO IT PEDAGOGY

The UX Lab is part of a larger initiative, led by Dr. Wisniewski, to enhance HCI education at our university. Our ABET accredited undergraduate IT program currently only requires students to complete one course dedicated to HCI topics and principles. This course is a 4000-level course and, thus is typically not taken by students until the latter half of their undergraduate education. While this provides students with an introductory understanding of HCI topics, principles, and methods, it does not prepare students for entry-level UX careers. As such, our university

recently hired Dr. Wisniewski (a new tenure-track Assistant Professor who specializes in HCI). She has been working to adjust the IT curriculum to enhance HCI education, so that students interested in pursuing UX careers are well prepared upon graduation. First, she proposed that the current 4000-level course be changed to a 3000-level course so that students can be exposed to it earlier in their academic careers. She has also proposed a new 4000-level project-based course in user-centered design. Her end goal is to create a curriculum track of HCI courses designed for students interested in UX-related career paths. The lab thus complements students' HCI coursework and brings what they have learned out of the classroom and into the real world. The UX Lab contributes and enhances IT pedagogy relevant to HCI education as summarized in Fig. 2.

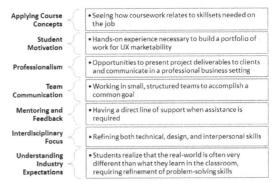

Figure 2: Contributions to IT pedagogy.

5 BENEFITS TO STAKEHOLDERS

We apply HCI principles of user-centered design to present a stakeholders analysis that shows the unique benefits to each party involved in or affected by the UX Lab: 1) Students, 2) Industry Partners, 3) Faculty, and 4) the University as a whole.

5.1 Benefits to Students

There are multiple benefits to IT undergraduate students who participate in the UX Lab. HCI and UX encompass a wide variety of skills, ranging from interpersonal communication skills, leadership and time management skills, technical skills, and design skills. Students have the opportunity to refine these skills so that they are more marketable upon graduation. Furthermore, students are matched to projects in which they can apply their strengths (e.g., design, front-end development, business analyses), while simultaneously improving upon their weaknesses (e.g., lack of research experience). This process is facilitated by creating cross-functional teams with students of different backgrounds and expertise (e.g., IT students with a more technical background may be working with Psychology students who are familiar with user research). Consequently, the UX Lab also benefits students from other disciplines and graduate students.

Another benefit for students is that the structure of the projects allows students to participate while still maintaining a full-time class schedule. The number of hours expected of students can vary from project to project (depending on the client's needs), but students are restricted to working no more than 20 hours per week to ensure a proper balance between coursework and UX Lab projects. Students also can complete a portion of their hours remotely and at their convenience (e.g., outside of typical business hours) which further helps them to balance their UX Lab obligations with their coursework. Additional benefits to students include expanding their professional portfolio, networking, and the potential for job placement after graduation.

5.2 Benefits to Industry Partners

One of the primary benefits to clients of the UX Lab is that they obtain UX consulting services at a discounted rate. They pay the university, which offloads human resource management tasks, such as hiring and payroll to the faculty mentor and university. In addition, the faculty mentor reviews and approves all deliverables to ensure quality is maintained. This is particularly helpful for companies that do not have in-house UX expertise and resources as it helps ensure they are obtaining quality service and actionable results from the students. The second major benefit to clients is that UX Lab projects can help them to identify talented students for potential hire upon graduation.

5.3 Benefits to Faculty Mentors

Admittedly, the UX Lab structure can be a time-intensive and heavy burden for the faculty mentor because they essentially are responsible for the quality of the consulting services on top of their faculty duties. However, a value proposition for the faculty is that the university has agreed to give credit for dollars brought in through the UX Lab toward tenure and promotion. Another key benefit to faculty is that it increases their future marketability should they want to transition to industry-based UX roles or another HCI academic research position in the future.

5.4 Benefits to the University

Our university highly values partnerships with local industry. These connections may begin as a partnership between the UX Lab and a specific company, but successful projects can open up opportunities for increased company interest in engaging with the university for other needs. Another major benefit is that the IT department and university can use the lab as an opportunity to stay apprised of current and emerging industry needs and trends. This information can help faculty to continually update their HCI coursework to stay at pace with industry. Finally, the UX Lab recruits undergraduates and graduate students from varying disciplines (e.g., Information Technology, Computer Science, Design, Psychology) due to the interdisciplinary nature of UX work, and thus, the lab helps to foster connections and partnerships across different university departments.

6 AN EXAMPLE OF A UX LAB PROJECT

6.1 Project Description

6.1.1 Overview. The UX Lab recently completed its first proof-of-concept project in May 2017 (the project began in August 2016). Bogen Communications, Inc. (a local company specializing in audio and sound systems; http://www.bogenedu.com/) was seeking UX services to enhance the usability of an in-development, non-disclosure agreement (NDA)-protected product. The UX team consisted of a faculty mentor (last author), one graduate student (first author, who managed the undergraduate students), and two undergraduate students. During the project, the team evaluated the usability of a product for three different user archetypes. The process students followed for each user archetype was as follows: 1) create a realistic persona, 2) develop a prioritized list of representative tasks, 3) obtain approval from the client to move forward with user testing based on the agreed upon set of tasks, 4) for each task, conduct a detailed task analysis, 5) perform heuristic evaluations and cognitive walkthroughs, 6) prepare a report detailing the team's findings and recommendations (required creation of wireframes and mockups), and 7) document findings and recommendations into the client's issue tracking software. This process was completed over the course of two semesters. The students also conducted think aloud user testing with company employees who were otherwise unfamiliar with the feature set of the new product.

6.1.2 UX Team Organization and Responsibilities. The undergraduates worked 15 hours per week with the majority of their time (approx. 10-12 hours) spent on-site at the company. The remainder of their hours could be completely remotely. This arrangement ensured students were actively engaged in the project and interfacing with the client while simultaneously granting them flexibility with their class schedules. It also reinforced the need for good team communication especially when work was being completed remotely. The undergraduates were primarily responsible for 1) performing the aforementioned UX services and process, 2) serving as the primary point-of-contact (POC) with the client, and 3) keeping the graduate student and faculty mentor apprised of any issues or concerns.

Mr. Talone (the graduate student) worked 4-8 hours per week (either on-site or remotely) and was responsible for 1) directly managing the undergraduates (e.g., assigning tasks, tracking progress), 2) providing the undergraduates with daily guidance, and 3) obtaining and sharing client feedback with the team. Dr. Wisniewski (the faculty mentor) worked 2-4 hours per week and was responsible for 1) facilitating weekly meetings, 2) providing higher-level guidance, mentoring, and feedback, and 3) managing project logistics (e.g., contract negotiations, budget). Mr. Talone handled the majority of the day-to-day project management activities, so Dr. Wisniewski could focus on providing higher-level guidance and deliverable reviews.

6.1.3 Interaction with Client. Students on the project primarily interacted with a small development team. The team consisted of four individuals with one serving as the primary POC regarding development progress, upcoming development deadlines, and other development updates. Students were expected to maintain a professional demeanor (e.g., dressing appropriately, and being respectful of other employees' time and work), maintain consistent and clear communication with the client (e.g., provide weekly updates on their progress), and work diligently to provide value to the client (e.g., produce deliverables and actionable results in a timely manner). These expectations were established at the beginning of the project and continually emphasized to the students throughout the project.

6.1.4 Faculty Mentorship and Guidance. To facilitate student learning during the project, Dr. Wisniewski held a weekly meeting with the students to 1) ensure that the project was on track, 2) provide feedback to the students, 3) assist with deliverable and presentation preparation, and/or 4) provide HCI and UX resources/expertise. In addition, Dr. Wisniewski was available throughout the week to assist with questions and concerns.

6.2 Evaluating Project Success

Project success was evaluated based on feedback obtained from the students and the client, as described below.

6.2.1 Undergraduate Student Feedback. At the end of the project, the two undergraduates were asked to share their feedback regarding the project. One of the students was a senior and graduated during the same semester that the project ended. This student received a job offer as a web developer during the final semester of the project. The other student began the project as a junior and had already completed two full-time internships prior to participating in the UX Lab project.

Table 1 compiles quotes from the undergraduate students regarding how they benefitted from the project. As evidenced by their feedback, the students felt the project benefitted their job marketability, ability to work within a professional setting, skill acquisition (e.g., soft skills), and HCI education. The students also shared feedback regarding how they felt the project could be improved. Areas for improvement included: 1) having a dedicated UX Lab space on-campus for meetings and completing work for the client, and 2) soliciting feedback from clients via alternative methods (besides weekly surveys).

6.2.2 Industry Partner Feedback. Feedback from the client regarding the students was solicited on a weekly basis using a web-based survey (Table 2). The feedback survey included eight items in total (four Likert items and four free response items). The Likert items could be answered using one of four response options: 1=*Unacceptable*, 2=*Below Expectations*, 3=*Met Expectations*, 4=*Exceeds Expectations* (an additional option, "*N/A: No deliverables were assigned this week*," was provided for the 4th survey item).

Table 2: Client Weekly Feedback Survey

Questions
1. **Attendance**: The students attended all scheduled meetings and were on time. (*Likert*)
2. **Professionalism**: The students presented themselves professionally and appropriately. (*Likert*)
3. **Communication**: The students clearly and promptly communicated with the team. (*Likert*)
4. **Work Products**: The students made progress and delivered high quality work products. (*Likert*)
5. Please provide additional details for ANY time when the students did NOT meet or exceed expectations. If there is a problem with a particular student, please indicate which student here. (*Free response*)
6. Do you have any concerns or suggestions you would like us to address with the students? (*Free response*)
7. Do you have any positive feedback about the students? (*Free response*)
8. Your Name (*Free response*)

This survey helped the faculty to assess how the students were performing, and identify areas where improvements could be made. In total, we received 24 responses. Fig. 3 provides a summary of the survey responses to each of the Likert items. Overall, the students met or exceeded the client's expectations during the project.

Upon completion of the project, the client provided the students and UX Lab with a letter of recommendation. The letter highlighted several areas in which the students exceeded the

Table 1: Undergraduate Student Feedback

Benefits	Quotes
Job Marketability	Senior: "The project increased my chances of being hired as a web developer as it was a big talking point during my interview." Junior: "This was a great opportunity to show future employers I didn't just take a class in user experience, but employed the material I learned in that class to improve a product of an actual company. I got to network and learn alongside industry individuals, which is a great opportunity so early on in my career."
Professionalism in a Real-World Environment	Senior: "From a UX perspective, I was able to see how some of our findings could be downplayed as opinions rather than data driven decisions. This was beneficial in that I learned that different people respond to information differently depending on how it's displayed or presented to them. Understanding this early on in my next project could give me a leg up." Senior: "The project helped to improve my confidence speaking and interacting in a professional environment." Senior: "One valuable experience I took from working with the client was how to handle a situation where someone may not agree with your work and to not be discouraged by it."
Skill Acquisition	Senior: "This project in combination with my studies and other commitments required an improvement to my task prioritization and time management skills." Junior: "I learned many soft skills that we didn't have enough time to cover thoroughly in class, like how to give constructive criticism in a way that wasn't going to offend the development team, how to come across professionally to clients, and making sure we had clear communication with them at all times."
Application of Coursework to Real-World Projects	Senior: "I was finally able to apply topics I learned in my coursework at the university to actual projects outside of the classroom." Junior: "Working on the project helped me understand how to apply UX principles I learned in the classroom in industry. For example, the development process of software engineers was very different to the process we employed, and finding a middle ground between the two to be the most effective to the company was something that the class couldn't really teach and one that was best experienced on the job."

clients' expectations, which included: 1) the students' subject matter expertise (HCI and UX expertise), 2) professionalism, and 3) ability to produce actionable results.

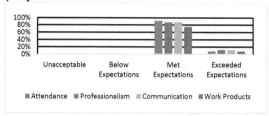

Figure 3: Client responses to weekly feedback survey.

6.3 Lessons Learned

While the inaugural project of the UX Lab was largely successful, there were some valuable lessons learned. First, it took almost a year to negotiate the initial contract due to the project being framed as academic research. By framing new projects as experiential learning experiences, this sped up and simplified the contract negotiation process. Second, a third undergraduate student was initially assigned to the project and had to be replaced after the first semester. We learned that it is crucial that students understand the expectations of each project and that they will be quickly replaced if there is a lack of fit with the project team or client. Third, students, at times, felt uncomfortable providing constructive criticism regarding the client's product, as they were unsure how the client would react to their recommendations. We found that it is important to encourage students to speak their mind and be open to defending their recommendations, as this is a normal part of working within a team.

7 CONCLUSION

Engaging IT undergraduates in real-world projects to assist companies in enhancing the UX of their products is a valuable mechanism by which experiential learning can be facilitated. In this paper, we described the development of a UX Lab intended to enhance undergraduate IT students' HCI education. Overall, the first proof-of-concept project for the UX Lab was a success. The students were satisfied with the experience they gained (with one obtaining a full-time job upon graduating the following semester). In addition, the students consistently met or exceeded the client's expectations and were noted as significantly improving the UX of their product. Finally, the project helped form a stronger connection between the university and the client's organization, with the client expressing interest in engaging in future collaborations with the UX Lab.

The results of the UX Lab's inaugural project demonstrate that our hybrid approach to experiential learning provides a unique bridge between traditional project-based coursework and full-time industry internships. In terms of next steps for the UX Lab, we recently acquired dedicated lab space for future projects. We are

also developing formal student assessment instruments (e.g., surveys) that can be used to better gauge the impact the UX Lab has on students' education and professional development. In addition, we are working with the university to see if students who participate in the UX Lab can also receive course credit for their time/effort. Dr. Wisniewski is now working with a local start-up company, who is bringing a new product to market at the end of this year. Thus, the UX Lab and the student team assigned to the project will be an integral part of the product launch and the ultimate success or failure of the start-up company.

ACKNOWLEDGMENTS
We thank Bogen Communications, Inc. and the undergraduate students (Tyler Martin and Meenakshi Karthikeyasundaram) who were pivotal to this successful proof-of-concept. This work was funded by Bogen Communications, Inc. (ID 1060294), the Florida High Tech Corridor Council's Industry Matching Funds (ID 1061662), and UCF's Quality Enhancement Program. The opinions expressed in this paper are our own and do not necessarily reflect those of our sponsors.

REFERENCES

[1] M. Bačíková. 2015. User experience design: Contrasting academic with practice. In *Proceedings of the 13th International Conference on Emerging eLearning Technologies and Applications (ICETA)*. IEEE, 1-6. DOI: http://dx.doi.org/10.1109/ICETA.2015.7558493

[2] Brian H. Cameron. 2008. Enterprise systems education: New directions & challenges for the future. In *Proceedings of the 2008 ACM SIGMIS CPR Conference on Computer Personnel Doctoral Consortium and Research*. ACM, New York, NY, 119-126. DOI: http://dx.doi.org/10.1145/1355238.1355269

[3] Sandra Gorka, Jacob R. Miller, and Brandon J. Howe. 2007. Developing realistic capstone projects in conjunction with industry. In *Proceedings of the 8th ACM SIGITE Conference on Information Technology Education*. ACM, New York, NY, 27-32. DOI: http://dx.doi.org/10.1145/1324302.1324309

[4] Mike Kuniavsky. 2007. User experience and HCI. In *The Human-Computer Interaction Handbook: Fundamentals, Evolving Technologies, and Emerging Applications* (2nd. ed.), Andrew Sears and Julie A. Jacko (Eds.). Lawrence Erlbaum Associates Inc, New York, NY.

[5] Gilbert W. Laware and Andrew J. Walters. 2004. Real world problems bringing life to course content. In *Proceedings of the 5th Conference on Information Technology Education*. ACM, New York, NY, 6-12. DOI: http://dx.doi.org/10.1145/1029533.1029536

[6] Craig S. Miller and Lucia Dettori. 2008. Employers' perspectives on IT learning outcomes. In *Proceedings of the 9th ACM SIGITE Conference on Information Technology Education*. ACM, New York, NY, 213-218. DOI: http://dx.doi.org/10.1145/1414558.1414612

[7] Barry M. Lunt, Joseph J. Ekstrom, Sandra Gorka, Gregory Hislop, Reza Kamali, Eydie Lawson, Richard LeBlanc, Jacob Miller, and Han Reichgelt. 2008. *Information Technology 2008: Curriculum Guidelines for Undergraduate Degree Programs in Information Technology*. Retrieved June 19, 2017 from http://www.acm.org//education/curricula/IT2008%20Curriculum.pdf

[8] Jon A. Preston. 2005. Utilizing authentic, real-world projects in information technology education. *ACM SIGITE Newsletter 2*, 1 (2005), Article 4. DOI: http://dx.doi.org/10.1145/1869667.1869671

[9] Charles R. Woratschek and Terri L. Lenox. 2009. Defining CS, IS, and IT: Are we there yet? *Information Systems Education Journal 7*, 59 (2009), 1-30.

Evolutionary Curriculum Reconstruction

Process Model and Information System Development

Vangel V. Ajanovski

Ss. Cyril and Methodius University

Faculty of Computer Science and Engineering

Rugjer Boshkovikj 16, P.O. Box 393

Skopje 1000, Macedonia

vangel.ajanovski@finki.ukim.mk

ABSTRACT

The paper proposes a new evolutionary curriculum development process based on a structured approach. The process uses ideas from the Rational Unified Process (RUP) – a well-known software development methodology in the field of software engineering. The process that is proposed in this paper is customized from the point of view of an institutional-wide curriculum reconstruction project. This process should have a spiral approach in several iterations, whereas each iteration will go into more depth with the curriculum specifications and finally produce study plans and syllabi that will be ready for accreditation and put into production. The rationale behind the introduction of such a process is the deepening of the institutional knowledge on the curricula structure and contents. A system architecture is described that enables the introduction of such a process within an institution and the information system that was implemented on top of this base architecture is presented.

CCS CONCEPTS

• **Social and professional topics** → **Model curricula**; **Computing education programs**; *Information systems education*; • **Information systems** → *Information systems applications*; *Open source software*;

KEYWORDS

Curricula guidelines; curriculum development; curriculum analysis; course enrollment; curriculum development process

ACM Reference format:
Vangel V. Ajanovski. 2017. Evolutionary Curriculum Reconstruction. In *Proceedings of SIGITE'17, Rochester, NY, USA, October 4–7, 2017*, 6 pages.
DOI: http://dx.doi.org/10.1145/3125659.3125698

1 INTRODUCTION

As science is advancing rapidly, reforms in education quickly follow, especially in higher education. A century ago digital computing was a concept, now almost all universities have at least one department

specializing in this field. As an implication, changes in curricula are omnipresent and gaining in frequency everywhere.

Being in a department that was constantly under reconstruction and one that warranted even faster and easier changes in curricula, the author witnessed 5 major reconstructions in 15 years – changes introducing completely new study programs, dozens of new courses, new course syllabi and even changes in the overall structure of existing programs. Some reconstructions were forced by new laws, some were mandated by organizational structure changes and some were driven by the desire for improved teaching, better content and following some well-known international practices and trends.

To some readers this might not seem as a big issue, until it is put into the right perspective. In our model, the students have a flexible workload, allowing enrollment of varying number of credits each term and re-enrollment of unsuccessful courses, so that many scenarios are possible in which a student can study for more than 4 years. Each student has the right to keep studying by the same rules that were in place during first admission for a minimum of 8 years, as a guarantee that she won't feel negative impact due to frequent changes in the study programs. Of course, the student can switch to the most modern revision voluntarily. Therefore, although a revision in the curricula has occurred recently, many students will continue to study old-style.

As an example, a student admitted in 2006 will start the studied according to the study plans and rules from 2005, and will be allowed to continue studying according to those rules even until 2014, although 3 revisions took place in the meanwhile (in 2009, 2011 and 2013). This is not just an administrative problem, but teachers feel the consequences too, since it can happen that a course (that has several revisions) could take place for students that study according to each of those several revisions of the study plans, all at the same time. While it might seem specific for the situation in the country of the author, this example can easily become the case of any institution working according to the principles behind the European Credit Transfer System (ECTS) and the Bologna process[6], that offers flexible education and at the same time tries to make faster changes to curricula in order to keep pace with progress.

One important implication of the problems occurring due to the multitude of changes can be the "self-censorship" within the institution and drop in quality. Teachers can not cope anymore with understanding the breadth of choice that all the students have, and the content that is behind all those choices. Hence, they no longer know what exactly do the students learn overall, and how prepared they are. Teachers that are put into position to teach the same course to different groups of students in different plans, will often try to lessen the burden and merge all the groups (although the course was revised and meant to be taught another way). Decisions might creep up that put everything into strict form although illogical (e.g, all curricula should be taught in the same format, all curricula should have the same number of credits, all should have the same number of lecture hours, all should have the same type of grading, testing, exams, etc). The administration will start to push such changes in order to make their jobs easier (e.g. easier calculation of the sum of received credits, easier creation of lecture schedules, etc). Finally, although needed, new revisions might get postponed, in order not to increase the administrative workload.

Generally universities and regulatory bodies treat curricula reconstructions as a one-off process, that is necessity-mandated, rarely-happening, deal-as-it-occurs, unusual situation, that mostly generate administrative problems and warrant bureaucratic procedures that prohibit change. The state of change is never considered as ever-lasting. This paper has the goal to break this barrier by dealing with the problems and issues of working under a constant curricula change. One possible solution is presented for the two main aspects of the problem – the complexity of ever-lasting change and the ability to learn from change itself. The proposed solution is based on concepts from the software life-cycle management field in software engineering. Understanding that we should base our solution on the knowledge acquired from gathered data about processes, that we should embrace and manage change instead of avoiding it, it was clear that a model-based solution is better suited to the problems. Thus, having as a base a simpler but flexible database model will be better than an overly fitted specialized model.

1.1 Related work

Curriculum design and revision is not a new topic, and it has been covered at many levels, however it was never treated in literature from the point of view of perpetual state of change. The idea to use a software-oriented development process for a curriculum reconstruction project, supported by a process management software that enables evolutionary development and implementation of curricula has never been encountered by the author before, so this needed further investigation in the field in order to gather information on all the necessary elements a successful solution would need. The efforts to develop curriculum guidelines that are led by the Association for Computing Machinery (ACM) are one of the most distinguished, so a decision was made to start the investigation in the field of computing with the rationale that the constructive long-term process of development of curricula guidelines have spurred related works discussing experiences, processes, designs and experiments related to the process of implementation of such guidelines. Search within the digital libraries of the ACM and the IEEE (Institute of Electrical and Electronics Engineers) produced several dozens of papers that could influence this process, of which we note only those that were helpful towards the proposed methodology.

One of the earliest publications relevant to curriculum development that discusses a process methodology is [7]. The authors propose gathering the data-processing environment needs in a company, and use them to define requirements for training. While this is definitely a methodological process, it does not cover all the typical phases of a curriculum life-cycle, it is not applicable to all subject

domains, and it is too specific to certain types of curricula. Also, higher education institutions usually do not have requirements that can be expressed in such a manner.

A systematic approach to gathering stakeholder requirements for new curricula is explained in much detail by [9], with specifics on topic, themes and surveys that were discussed with different stakeholder types (teachers, students, companies and others) and the outcomes of this process of elaborating. Some papers deal with the phase of the life-cycle of a curriculum when there is need for assessment. More direct methods of assessment of the state of a single curriculum or even the state of whole study programs are discussed in [19], and [5]. One of the most prominent techniques for planning and assessment of a single curriculum, but can also be applied to analyze the effects of curricula running in parallel, is the curriculum mapping, described extensively in literature and has been applied quite often in educational institutions (see [8][10]). Curriculum mapping is employed in the proposed process and is implemented in the system prototype. There are also some authors that discuss indirect assessment of curricula, by analysis of learner behavior and results, or process results overall [25][15].

There are more than few publications that present case studies on specific curriculum development projects within their institution (see for example [16][12]). For this project, the most interesting ones focus on participatory design during curricula development, especially on inclusion of students in the process (see [18][17]). These are relevant, as practices intended for inclusion in the iterations of the proposed process, when additional stakeholder input or opinions are required.

Finally, there are works that present tools relevant to curriculum development as a process: tools for curricula analysis, tools for visualization of the structure of curricula and study programs, databases of curricula and others (see [24][4][20][21][22]). None of them discussed the scenarios of curriculum revision projects that happen so frequently that there is life-cycle overlaps. All of them could be helpful, if integrated in a general framework.

Up to the knowledge of the author, there are no tools that support the whole life-cycle of curriculum revisions and are specifically designed to cope with multiple life-cycle overlaps within a single institution. This paper discusses a process that includes gathering requirements, discussing opinions, disseminating results and covering the whole life-cycle of a curriculum, but being at the same time effective and simple enough to be used in an evolutionary style through many iterations – driving multiple curricula reconstruction efforts in parallel. When setup in proper way, the process can be beneficial in increasing the self-awareness at institutional level, so that the final goal is not just to have newly developed curricula in the end (since there is no end), but the journey itself.

2 PROPOSED PROCESS

The proposed evolutionary curriculum development process borrows from some already established practices in software development process methodologies. Then it redefines those practices into a curriculum development process that enables better management of curriculum reconstruction projects. The whole life-cycle of a curriculum development process will be managed with the use of methods from the overall software development life-cycle that these methodologies propose. The Rational Unified Process (RUP)[13] was chosen as a model process, because it is known to address the biggest issues and risks first, while actively managing changes in requirements, ensuring overall process and artifact trace-ability from problem towards solution space and vice-versa.

The main driver of the development process should be the collaborative effort where all the teachers and students representatives (as high-priority stakeholders) are actively involved and freely exchange ideas, proposals, discussions, critique and in the end – work towards the finalization of the accreditation materials. After curricula are accredited and enrollment starts, they collaborate in the implementation and deployment of the curricula proposals in specific courses. Three main principles lead this effort: *Free exchange of ideas* – everyone has the right to have a voice, at a systematically defined point in time; *Joint* collaborative and open effort – not a competitive one *Iterative process* that welcomes discussion and change, ensuring trace-ability between results and requirements.

A *Steering Committee (SC)* consisting of *Process Engineers* and *Quality Assurance Managers* controls the process and ensures the other members follow the proposed workflows. The process itself resembles the typical phases and objectives from the RUP as used in software projects, setup for an evolutionary development.

Phase 1: Inception – Seed Proposals.

(1) *Joint Vision*: Discuss the most important issues in the existing study programs and agree on biggest problems.

(2) *Environment preparation*: Setup of templates, access-rights to the system, define roles in the system, establish of content repository of related materials.

(3) *Program Inception*: Short proposals are submitted on new study programs and/or reconstruction of existing ones.

(4) *Curriculum Inception*: Gathering of short proposals on new curricula or reconstruction of existing curricula.

(5) *Curriculum Mapping*: Preliminary curriculum mapping is established based on the short proposals as to the coverage of content in the proposals with respect to standards, international curricula guidelines and recommendations.

(6) *Phase 1 Assessment*: The discussions are analyzed and the mapping reports are investigated, producing a project status report. Each of the study program and curriculum proposals are tagged based on general opinion as "Acceptable", "Minor issues" or "Major issues".

(7) *Phase 1 Review*: Items tagged with status "Major issues" are evaluated through a further discussion in which the proposers address the noted issues with specific arguments and offer possible fixes. At the end there is online voting if the fixes are accepted to be incorporated in the proposal. Items that are not accepted are dropped.

Phase 2: Elaboration – Elaborate Proposals.

(1) *Elaboration teams*: For each of the proposals that were deemed acceptable for elaboration, teams are formed from participants that have interest to continue development.

(2) *Environment preparation* Templates, structures, access and administrative rights to the system, roles of users within the system, establishment of a content repository, revisions of Phase 1 proposals are activated.

(3) *Program Elaboration*: Detailed overview is written for each study program by volunteers from the respective team.

(4) *Curriculum Elaboration*: *Step 1*: Detailed contents for each of the curricula are prepared by volunteers from the team (written from scratch, or based on former contents that are under reconstruction or renown curricula guidelines) *Step 2*: Review discussion is open to all for all the contents. *Step 3*: Revision of the content is performed based on the discussion. Curriculum mapping is refined based on the new contents. Inter-dependencies and prerequisites are defined for each curriculum.

(5) *Debate*: The elaborated contents and curriculum maps are frozen for discussion by participants from all the groups (including student boards and organizations). Since the proposals have already received a pass in Phase 1, this discussion and critique is focused towards checks on the knowledge coverage and completeness.

(6) *Phase 2 Assessment*: Similar process as in Phase 1 Assessment except that the process allows several iterations, hence the additional status "Not finished".

(7) *Phase 2 Review*: Similar to Phase 1 Review. The Items tagged with status "Major issues" are evaluated thoroughly based on the documents and reviews. The proposers address the noted issues with arguments and offer fixes. Online voting at the end is used to decide which fixes will be incorporated in the proposal. Items that are not accepted are dropped. The results from the assessment reports, are used by the SC to decide if another iteration is needed.

Phase 3: Construction – Implementation-level Prototypes.

(1) *Construction Teams*: Formed among participants that have interest to further develop the acceptable proposals from elaboration. Participation is voluntary.

(2) *Environment preparation*: Templates, structures, access and administrative rights to the system, roles of users within the system, establishment of a content repository, revisions of Phase 3 proposals are activated.

(3) *Program Construction Step 1*: Detailed description is written for each study program by volunteers from the teams, focusing on semester programming, layout of the curricula and inter-dependencies in order to create optimal programming that increase choice the students will have in each semester. Profiles and specialization tracks are clearly defined, with rules of achievement.

(4) *Curriculum Construction Step 1*: Detailed contents for each of the curricula are written: week-by-week topics are defined, reading materials are listed, decisions on plan of activities, learning methods, exam types and all requested details. The objectives and learning goals are mapped with respect to curriculum guidelines, preferably with a week-by-week curriculum mapping.

(5) *Program Construction Step 2*: Prerequisites receive special second focus, graphs of inter-dependencies are constructed and analyzed as a mandatory part of the process in order to investigate possible deadlocks, non-pass or delay-provoking constraints in the study program overall.

(6) *Curriculum Construction Step 2*: Revision of the contents is performed based on the program-level decisions. Curriculum mapping is refined based on the new contents.

(7) *Debate*: Final implementation level contents, graphs and maps are frozen and discussion is started by participants from all groups (also representatives from student boards and organizations). The curriculum proposals have already received a pass in Phase 2, so this discussion focuses on checks over newly added details, especially prerequisites and inter-dependencies. Week-by-week program-level investigation is performed to detect possible overload – too many exams or too many assignments at the same time.

(8) *Phase 3 Assessment*: Similar process as in Phase 2 Assessment. Since the curriculum proposals have already received a pass in Phase 2, this report only checks completeness.

(9) *Phase 3 Review*: Similar process as in Phase 2 Review, except that no items are dropped in this phase. Those which are not approved will simply be subject of following iteration. Based on the results from the assessment reports, a decision is made by the SC if another iteration will be needed for Phase 3 or the project will continue.

Phase 4: Transition – Courses.

(1) The SC exports the final version of the curricula from the system, prepares final accreditation materials and initiates the respective process at the board.

(2) In case of issues reported by the accreditation board, an additional iteration from Phase 3 is needed. The cycle repeats until all issues are solved and materials are approved.

(3) Once in production and students have enrolled in courses from the new proposals, versioning is frozen but access to discussions is given to all students for critique and review of the curricula based on real experiences from classes.

(4) At the end of each semester the SC creates overview-level evaluation reports focusing on the strengths and weaknesses of the study programs and gathered ratings from discussions. To increase objectiveness, the committee asks for two complementary reports for each curriculum – report by the teachers that were involved, and reports by volunteers from the initial team members that did not have teaching assignments.

(5) The reports are considered as an input in the following life-cycle of the process, starting from Phase 1.

3 SYSTEMS SUPPORT FOR THE PROCESS

A functional prototype of a system that supports the proposed curriculum development process was developed by the author. The prototype enables to implement and track the whole of the process as discussed in the previous section. The system itself was initially founded on top of an existing open-sourced term enrollment solution, developed by the author.[1] The original system was used for term enrollments at the authors home institution for several years. Its central database model was extended with support for flexibility in curricula definitions and links among them, support for discussions and versioning of curricula enabling trace-ability. In this paper the focus is only on the extensions that enable the evolutionary process of curricula revisions.

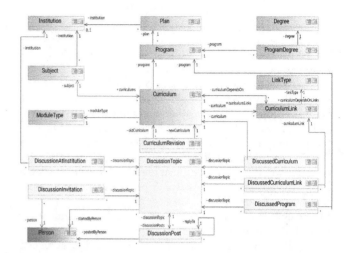

Figure 1: The core of the architecture that defines the curriculum management system

Figure 2: Editing curriculum definition as a proposal.

3.1 Curriculum management modules

The core of the developed information system, that defines the structure of higher-education institutions, their study programs and curricula and enables support for the proposed iterative process is given in Fig.1. The core consists of the following parts – study programs and curricula structure (top left part of the figure), curriculum definitions (right), discussion moderation process (bottom), and versioning curricula, links and inter-dependencies (middle).

The design of the system core gives a flexible architecture that opens many possibilities, envisioned to be used in varying scenarios. Some features that are possible: Institutions are modeled as a hierarchical tree, each one can have as many study plan reconstructions as needed (for separate accreditation and other reconstruction processes). Each study plan reconstruction can modify as many study programs as needed, with varying sets of curricula. Links between curricula can be established both within a single study program and across different programs. Groups of curricula can be established and group-based prerequisites can be defined (Fig.2).

Versioning of curricula is supported by design and the scheme can be customized. The process of discussion is supported on several levels – over specific reconstruction plans, over study programs, over curricula and their specifics of implementation.

The heart of the concept lies in the ability to trace-forward and backward the change-requests and implications they provoke. Stakeholders start to discuss the issues at the level of a single curriculum, continue at the level of study program, and do this for each study program, for each plan revision. Tags denote certain discussions as phase or iteration coordination, change requests or solution proposals. Special curriculum link types allow to indicate the thread of changes from one to another curricula revision, and implement rules of behavior regarding the changes (such as to consider two implementations of similar contents as equivalent and preventing the students to enroll to both at the same time). The system allows tagging various statuses to the study plans, programs and curricula, in order to serve as steps between transitions or denote state of phase or iteration in the process.

3.2 Curriculum links visualization and editing

As mentioned previously, there are many types of prerequisites and other types of associations among curricula. These associations that form links among curricula form a structure of significance in a study program, or even across several study programs. There are several link types that should be mentioned as important for this discussion. *Hard Prerequisite Link* $a \rightarrow b$ is when the student can enroll b, only if she has a passing grade on a. *Soft Prerequisite Link* $a \dashrightarrow b$, when it is not mandatory to have a passing grade on a to enroll b, and it will suffice to just have attended a. *Parallel Link* $a \upuparrows b$, when a and b should be enrolled at the same time. *Equivalence Link* $a \equiv b$, when a and b cover the same knowledge and competencies and can be considered as the same or equivalent. *Group Link* $a := b$, when a is a virtual container that includes b (and possibly others).

While the prerequisites are traditionally defined in the curriculum definition form as a list, this is not a good solution. There are thousands of links, so the stakeholder should be able to inspect the underlying structure in a visual form. A special module was implemented to ease the visualization and understanding of the formed graph structure, to filter it and easily define new links within it. The editor was based on the of [26], but being web-based it is integrated in several applications – in the curriculum management subsystem (to ease the process of curriculum development) and the enrollment subsystem's virtual academic adviser (to check if students have met the prerequisites and display a map of possible future enrollments for each student, taking into account the eligibility even after eventual transfers from one to another study program).

The visualization implementation uses a method that is a combination of initial topological sorting and later force-directed graph layout. As the first step topological sorting is performed (similar to [14], the difference being that transitive dependencies are kept in the graphs since we want to see all links, as part of the QA process), and the results are used to calculate initial vertical position of the nodes in the graph. The vertical "levels" represent the semester in which a curriculum can be placed the earliest. The graph uses live data and automatically rearranges itself during interaction, keeping restrictions based on the topological sorting.

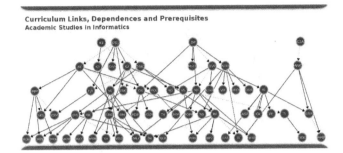

Figure 3: Real-time visualization of the graph of curriculum links of two prerequisite type within a study program.

The generated graphs are not trees, and in fact need not be planar, so that there is no automatic solution that will generate a satisfactory visualization in all cases. Because of this, an initial graph based on randomized positioning and force-directed rearrangement is presented to the user, still keeping the topological ordering layout restrictions. After the graph rearranges itself and stabilizes, it can be tweaked by the user to fine tune the layout. At all times, the curricula will be properly sorted and divided into "levels" corresponding to semesters. Fig. 3 presents the graph of hard and soft prerequisites for one of the study programs at the author's department.

3.3 Quality assurance by curriculum mapping

Curriculum mapping takes central part in the assessment and quality assurance steps of the proposed reconstruction process. The idea is to track, topic-by-topic, week-by-week, how a curriculum covers the Body of Knowledge (BoK) in the field.

Some authors use mapping as a tool to investigate the timeliness of introduction of a certain concept in an investigated course as compared to the overall gained knowledge prior to that moment in that course and other prior or parallel courses [23]. In this curriculum reconstruction process only a week-by-week or topic-by-topic mapping should suffice. See also [11]. First, the BoK of a certain field (e.g. computing) is imported into the system. Then, in each iteration, for each of the proposed curricula, the syllabus is analyzed and its weekly topics are mapped to certain knowledge areas, units or topics from the BoK. The curriculum mapping is enabled by a previously developed module of the system, as a result of the ISISng[3] project in 2015/16.[2]

The reports resulting from the curriculum mapping process enable introspection into the coverage of the BoK and use it as a measure to compare new curricula proposals against their earlier revisions, or comparison to the expected coverage defined in well-known curricula guidelines published by international organizations, such as ACM, IEEE and others. The system was refactored to enable versioning in an iterative process, so that the institution can track the evolution of curricula definitions from one to another curriculum reconstruction project, from one to another phase within the project or from one to another revision in each iteration of each phase. Figure 4 is a screenshot of the report that shows how complete is the coverage of the BoK at a certain moment in the curriculum development process. Similar reports list the exact weekly topics in each curriculum proposal covering a specific BoK element.

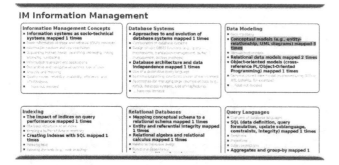

Figure 4: Coverage of a knowledge area in a study program proposal, with a heat map indicating the extent of coverage.

These reports, together with the ones gathered from voting and expressed opinions during the discussions, are used when making decisions how to proceed with the curricula revisions.

4 CONCLUSIONS AND FUTURE WORK

The proposed process and system should not be considered a solution for every problem and issue, but instead as a framework towards solutions that will be more satisfactory than typical administratively organized university management systems. The system is open-sourced and is made available from the ISISng project website[3], after each successful phase is completed.

Future development will continue in several directions. Most relevant to this paper is is the goal to develop a new quality assurance assessment model that measures the effects that the structure of a study program and curricula have over learner success (ideas similar to [15], but expanded in a more global context). The idea is to track the success of both active students and alumni and evaluate the real-world impact of the changes in the curricula. Another direction for investigation are model proposals for accreditation boards that can enable the evolutionary process in a formal way.

ACKNOWLEDGMENTS

This work is a result of the project ISISng[3], partially financed by the Faculty of Computer Science and Engineering.

REFERENCES

[1] Vangel V. Ajanovski. 2010. Information System of the Institute of Informatics - IS for Students by the Students. In *Proceedings of the 7th International Conference for Informatics and Information Technology (CIIT 2010)*. Institute of Informatics, Molika, Bitola, Macedonia, 129–132.

[2] Vangel V. Ajanovski. 2017. Information System for Mapping the Coverage of Reference Curriculum Guidelines in the Teaching Curricula of a Higher-Education Institution. In *Proceedings of the 14th International Conference for Informatics and Information Technology (CIIT 2017)*. Faculty of Computer Science and Engineering, Mavrovo, Macedonia, (in press). http://ciit.finki.ukim.mk

[3] Vangel V. Ajanovski. 2017. ISISng: Integrated Student Information System of the Next Generation – Official Project Website. (June 2017). https://develop.finki.ukim.mk/projects/isis

[4] Tapio Auvinen, Juha Paavola, and Juha Hartikainen. 2014. STOPS: A Graph-based Study Planning and Curriculum Development Tool. In *Proceedings of the 14th Koli Calling International Conference on Computing Education Research (Koli Calling '14)*. ACM, New York, NY, USA, 25–34. DOI:https://doi.org/10.1145/2674683.2674689

[5] Lucía Camilloni, Diego Vallespir, and Mark Ardis. 2015. Using GSwE2009 for the Evaluation of a Master Degree in Software Engineering in the Universidad De La RepÚBlica. In *Proceedings of the 37th International Conference on Software Engineering - Volume 2 (ICSE '15)*. IEEE Press, Piscataway, NJ, USA, 323–332. http://dl.acm.org/citation.cfm?id=2819009.2819062

[6] EU. 2017. How does the Bologna Process work? - European Higher Education Area and Bologna Process. (Aug. 2017). http://www.ehea.info/pid34247/how-does-the-bologna-process-work.html

[7] Michael M. Gorman, John F. Rogers, and Edward A. Embick. 1970. A data processing curriculum development methodology. ACM Press, 27–47. DOI:https://doi.org/10.1145/800162.805171

[8] Heidi Hayes Jacobs. 1997. *Mapping the Big Picture: Integrating Curriculum and Assessment K-12 (Professional Development)*. ASCD. https://www.amazon.com/Mapping-Big-Picture-Integrating-Professional/dp/0871202867

[9] Nicole Herbert, Julian Dermoudy, Leonie Ellis, Mike Cameron-Jones, Winyu Chinthammit, Ian Lewis, Kristy de Salas, and Matthew Springer. 2013. Stakeholder-led Curriculum Redesign. In *Proceedings of the Fifteenth Australasian Computing Education Conference - Volume 136 (ACE '13)*. Australian Computer Society, Inc., Darlinghurst, Australia, Australia, 51–58. http://dl.acm.org/citation.cfm?id=2667199.2667205

[10] Heidi Hayes Jacobs and Association for Supervision and Curriculum Development. 2006. *Getting results with curriculum mapping*. Association for Supervision and Curriculum Development, Alexandria, VA. OCLC: 73516036.

[11] Heidi Hayes Jacobs and Association for Supervision and Curriculum Development (Eds.). 2010. *Curriculum 21: essential education for a changing world*. Association for Supervision and Curriculum Development, Alexandria, Va. OCLC: ocn435711210.

[12] M. R. K. Krishna Rao, S. Junaidu, T. Maghrabi, M. Shafique, M. Ahmed, and K. Faisal. 2005. Principles of Curriculum Design and Revision: A Case Study in Implementing Computing Curricula CC2001. In *Proceedings of the 10th Annual SIGCSE Conference on Innovation and Technology in Computer Science Education (ITiCSE '05)*. ACM, New York, NY, USA, 256–260. DOI:https://doi.org/10.1145/1067445.1067515

[13] Philippe Kruchten. 2004. *The Rational Unified Process: An Introduction* (3rd ed.). Addison-Wesley, Boston. OCLC: ocm53038793.

[14] John G. Meinke and Charles R. Bauer. 1976. Topological Sorting As a Tool in Curriculum Planning. *ACM SIGCSE Bulletin* 8, 3 (July 1976), 61–66. DOI:https://doi.org/10.1145/952991.804757

[15] Gonzalo Mendez, Xavier Ochoa, and Katherine Chiluiza. 2014. Techniques for Data-driven Curriculum Analysis. In *Proceedings of the Fourth International Conference on Learning Analytics And Knowledge (LAK '14)*. ACM, New York, NY, USA, 148–157. DOI:https://doi.org/10.1145/2567574.2567591

[16] Steven Nordstrom, Arisoa Randrianasolo, Eddy Borera, and Fortune Mhlanga. 2013. Winds of change: toward systemic improvement of a computer science program. ACM Press, 201. DOI:https://doi.org/10.1145/2512276.2512298

[17] Lisa Romkey and Laura Bradbury. 2007. Student Curriculum Mapping: A More Authentic Way Of Examining And Evaluating Curriculum. In *2007 Annual Conference & Exposition*. ASEE Conferences, Honolulu, Hawaii.

[18] Esperanza Román-Mendoza. 2016. Engaging students in curriculum development: the case of an undergraduate course in digital humanities. ACM Press, 965–969. DOI:https://doi.org/10.1145/3012430.3012633

[19] Dale C. Rowe, Barry M. Lunt, and Richard G. Helps. 2011. An Assessment Framework for Identifying Information Technology Programs. In *Proceedings of the 2011 Conference on Information Technology Education (SIGITE '11)*. ACM, New York, NY, USA, 123–128. DOI:https://doi.org/10.1145/2047594.2047630

[20] Julio Santisteban and Danet Delgado-Castillo. 2016. Comparing Topics in CS Syllabus with Topics in CS Research. ACM Press, 360–360. DOI:https://doi.org/10.1145/2899415.2925483

[21] Takayuki Sekiya, Yoshitatsu Matsuda, and Kazunori Yamaguchi. 2010. Analysis of Computer Science Related Curriculum on LDA and Isomap. In *Proceedings of the Fifteenth Annual Conference on Innovation and Technology in Computer Science Education (ITiCSE '10)*. ACM, New York, NY, USA, 48–52. DOI:https://doi.org/10.1145/1822090.1822106

[22] Takayuki Sekiya, Yoshitatsu Matsuda, and Kazunori Yamaguchi. 2015. Curriculum Analysis of CS Departments Based on CS2013 by Simplified, Supervised LDA. In *Proceedings of the Fifth International Conference on Learning Analytics And Knowledge (LAK '15)*. ACM, New York, NY, USA, 330–339. DOI:https://doi.org/10.1145/2723576.2723594

[23] Claudia Szabo and Katrina Falkner. 2014. Neo-piagetian theory as a guide to curriculum analysis. In *Proceedings of the 45th ACM technical symposium on Computer science education*. ACM Press, Atlanta, GA, USA, 115–120. DOI:https://doi.org/10.1145/2538862.2538910

[24] Manas Tungare, Xiaoyan Yu, William Cameron, GuoFang Teng, Manuel A. Pérez-Quiñones, Lillian Cassel, Weiguo Fan, and Edward A. Fox. 2007. Towards a syllabus repository for computer science courses. ACM Press, 55. DOI:https://doi.org/10.1145/1227310.1227331

[25] Duo Helen Wei and Arron Nappen Burrows. 2016. Tracking students' performance to assess correlations among computer science programming series courses. *Journal of Computing Sciences in Colleges* 32, 1 (2016), 9–16. http://dl.acm.org/citation.cfm?id=3007229

[26] Ron Zucker. 2009. ViCurriAS: A Curriculum Visualization Tool for Faculty, Advisors, and Students. *Journal of Computing Sciences in Colleges* 25, 2 (Dec. 2009), 138–145. http://dl.acm.org/citation.cfm?id=1629036.1629059

IT2017 Report: Putting It to Work

Mihaela Sabin
Applied Engineering and Sciences
University of New Hampshire
Manchester, New Hampshire, USA
+1 603.641.4144
mihaela.sabin@unh.edu

Svetlana Peltsverger
Information Technology
Kennesaw State University
Kennesaw, Georgia, USA
+1 470.578.3813
speltsve@kennesaw.edu

Bill Paterson
Mathematics and Computing
Mount Royal University
Calgary, AB, Canada T3E 6K6
+1 403-440-7086
bpaterson@mtroyal.ca

Ming Zhang
School of Electronics Engineering & Computer Science
Peking University
100871, Beijing, China
+86.10.62765825
mzhang@net.pku.edu.cn

Hala Alrumaih
Al Imam Mohammad Ibn
Saud Islamic University
Riyadh, Kingdom of Saudi Arabia
+966 50.549.6409
haalrumaih@imamu.edu.sa

SUMMARY

IT2017 report is the second edition of the ACM/IEEE-CS Curriculum Guidelines for Undergraduate Programs in Information Technology. The report is scheduled to replace its predecessor, the IT2008 report, by the end of this year. A twelve-member diverse task group has worked diligently to make revisions and produce an appropriately forward looking document that is globally relevant and balances perspectives from educators, practitioners, and IT professionals. The novelty of the report is its focus on industry-informed competencies that IT graduates should have to meet the growing demands of a changing technological world in the next decade. Key to the effectiveness of the report's guidelines are implementation decisions that take into account program goals and resources, institutional missions, and local contexts. The panel will elicit productive conversations around how to effectively implement the IT2017 curriculum framework in educational institutions around the world.

General Terms
Documentation; Design; Standardization

Keywords
Information Technology Education; Computing Curricula; IT2017; IT2008

1. INTRODUCTION

The computing education community expects modern curriculum guidelines for information technology (IT) undergraduate degree programs by the end of 2017. Developing such guidelines for high quality, rigorous IT educational programs benefits from a comprehensive approach that engages international perspectives and reflects needs and expectations from industry and IT professional societies [9, 10, 11]. Many new technologies have emerged and flourished since 2008 when the first ACM/IEEE-CS IT curriculum guidelines report was released [5]. The IT2017 report proposes a learner-centered framework

for programs that prepare successful IT graduates for professional careers or further academic study.

The IT2017 task group is the committee developing the IT2017 report. Its membership represents academia (nine) and industry (three), and has international composition across three continents (Asia, Europe, and North America) and five countries (Canada, China, Netherlands, Saudi Arabia, and United States). The task group has envisioned the IT2017 report as a "sought-after and durable set of guidelines for use by educational institutions around the world to help them develop IT curricula for the next ten years". The IT2017 task group holds the view that IT programs should prepare students with knowledge and skills in learning contexts that emphasize development of competencies: what students do and how they demonstrate performance with what they know.

The report includes feedback that the task group received from public comment and review solicited for report versions 0.51 (January-February 2015), 0.61 (August - September 2016), and 0.85 (May-June 2017). Some task group members participated in two international working groups who led extensive data gathering and analysis efforts with support from ACM to gauge input from academia and industry through surveys conducted in 2015 (almost 700 responses, 597 computing faculty and 91 industry respondents) and 2016 (over 350 responses from Latin America, 182 faculty and 177 employers). Report development dissemination included a variety of venues to engage educational and professional communities, such as birds of a feathers discussion group at SIGCSE'15 in Kansas City [7]; curriculum design workshop and panel at IEEE EDUCON in Tallinn, Estonia in 2015 [3] and Abu Dhabi, Saudi Arabia in 2016; panels on the report status updates at SIGITE conferences in Chicago in 2015 and Boston in 2016 [8], at the Western Canadian Conference on Computing Education (WCCE'16) in British Columbia, Canada [1], and ITiCSE'16 in Arequipa, Peru [4].

The report is undergoing its final distribution for pubic review and comment. The most recent version of the document is available on an ACM web site at http://it2017.acm.org.

2. PANEL GOALS AND ACTIVITIES

The primary goal of this panel is to provide an update on the current state of the IT2017 report, highlight main improvements, and engage the audience in discussing ways to implement the new curriculum framework.

Inspired by the IT competency model for associate degree curriculum [2] and receptive to industry demands for competent and competitive IT workforce, the IT2017 report has adopted a full competency-based approach to learning IT. The report articulates competencies grounded in content of essential and supplemental IT domains and enables faculty members to implement IT programs that articulate convincingly what student should be able to achieve by the time of graduation. Another innovative change is the elimination of hours as a measure of domain coverage. A competent graduate from an undergraduate IT degree program should experience the equivalent of at least 1.5 years of information technology studies.

IT impacts all economic sectors. The report provides advice on how to teach IT so that graduates can perform competitively in a wide variety of settings other than typical IT departments. The panel will address how to fit IT curriculum in other contexts and degrees programs including business, computer science, and cybersecurity. The panelists will also discuss the need for local adaptation of the curriculum to address institutional expectations, preparation and background of entering students, faculty expertise, and local industry demands. Curriculum adaptation in United States, Saudi Arabia, China, and Latin America will also be discussed.

Involving the SIGITE'17 audience in this panel session is particularly relevant to the IT education community. The major topics to guide the panel discussion will include the competency-based curricular framework [6], improvement and development of new IT programs that implement proposed curriculum framework, and inclusion of IT curriculum in other disciplines.

3. PANEL PRESENTERS

3.1 Mihaela Sabin

Mihaela Sabin is the Chair of the IT2017 Task Group. She serves as Vice-Chair for Education on SIGITE Executive Committee. Sabin is an associate professor of computer science at the University of New Hampshire.

3.2 Svetlana Peltsverger

Svetlana Peltsverger is a Professor and Interim Associate Dean of the College of Computing and Software Engineering at the Kennesaw State University. She is a co-author of a framework and lab-ware for teaching privacy in information assurance curriculum.

3.3 Bill Paterson

Bill Paterson is an Associate Professor and past department chair at Mount Royal University. He has been a long time active member in SIGITE. Paterson first developed an interest in the IT curriculum when helping to develop Mount Royal's Bachelor of Computer Information Systems degree program.

3.4 Ming Zhang

Ming Zhang is a Professor of computer science at Peking University. She is a member of the ACM Education Council and Chair of the ACM SIGCSE China Chapter. She is currently the vice director of CCF Educational Committee. Zhang is a member of the IT2017 Executive Committee.

3.5 Hala Alrumaih

Hala Alrumaih is a Lecturer in information systems at Al Imam Mohammad Ibn Saud Islamic University and a PhD candidate in information systems at King Saud University. Her research interests include requirements engineering and the semantic web. Alrumaih is a member of the IT2017 Executive Committee.

4. ACKNOWLEDGMENTS

The IT2017 Task Group extends its thanks to the ACM Education Board for its support for this important project.

5. REFERENCES

[1] Byers, B., Paterson, B., Hepler, C. 2016. IT2017 Report: Panel Discussion. In *Proceedings of the 21st Western Canadian Conference on Computing Education* (WCCE'16).

[2] Hawthorne, E.K., Campbell, R.D., Tang, C., Tucker, C.S., Hichols, J. 2014. *Information Technology: Competency Model of Core Learning Outcomes and Assessment for Associate-Degree Curriculum.* Technical Report.

[3] Impagliazzo, J. 2015. Curriculum Design for Computer Engineering and Information Technology. In *Proceedings of the Global Engineering Education Conference* (EDUCON).

[4] Impagliazzo, J., Cuadros-Vargas, E., Escobedo, G.B., Miranda del Solar, J.J., Sabin, M., and Viola, B. Latin American Perspectives and the IT2017 Curricular Guidelines. In *Proceedings of the 2016 ACM Conference on Innovation and Technology in Computer Science Education* (ITiCSE'16).

[5] Lunt, B. M., Ekstrom, J. J., Hislop, E., Lawson, R. LeBlanc, Miller, J., Reichgelt, H. 2008. *Information Technology 2008: Curriculum guidelines for undergraduate degree programs in Information Technology.*

[6] Wiggins, G. and McTighe, J. 2011. The Understanding By Design Guide to Creating High-Quality Units. *Alexandria, VA: Association for Supervision and Curriculum Development.*

[7] Sabin, M., Peltsverger, S., Tang, C. 2015. Updating the ACM/IEEE 2008 Curriculum in Information Technology (Abstract Only). In *Proceedings of the 46th ACM Technical Symposium of Computer Science Education* (SIGCSE'15).

[8] Sabin, M., Peltsverger, S., Tang, C., and Lunt, B. 2016. ACM/IEEE-CS Information Technology Curriculum 2017: A Status Update. In *Proceedings of the 17th Annual Conference on Information Technology Education* (SIGITE'16).

[9] Sabin, M., Snow, P., and Viola, B. 2016. Industry and faculty surveys call for increased collaboration to prepare information technology graduates. *Journal for computing Sciences in colleges,* 31, 6 (June 2016), 70-78.

[10] Sabin, M., Impagliazzo, J., Alrumaih, H., Byers, B., Gudoniene, D., Hamilton, M., Kotlyarov, V., Lunt, B., McGuffee, J.W., Peltsverger, S., Tang, C., Viola, B., Zhang, M. 2015. Multinational Perspectives on Information Technology from Academia and Industry. In *Proceedings of the 2015 ITiCSE on Working Group Reports* (ITiCSE-WGR'15).

[11] Sabin, M., Viola, B., Impagliazzo, J., Angles, R., Curiel, M., Leger, P., Murillo, J., Nina, H., Pow-Sang, J.A., and Trejos, I. 2016. Latin American Perspectives to Internationalize Undergraduate Information Technology. In *Proceedings of the 2016 ITiCSE Working Group Reports* (ITiCSE'16).

Teaching Network Administration in the Era of Virtualization: A Layered Approach

Yang Wang
La Salle University
Philadelphia, PA
wang@lasalle.edu

Thomas Blum
La Salle University
Philadelphia, PA
blum@lasalle.edu

Margaret McCoey
La Salle University
Philadelphia, PA
mccoey@lasalle.edu

ABSTRACT

Teaching network administration for undergraduate students possesses a number of challenges. On one hand, network administration requires a wide spectrum of ad-hoc technologies from service management to physical connection. It is hard to select a critical set of technologies to fit into one course as well as maintain a clear organization and flow among these technologies. On the other hand, the rapid pace of technology advancement in the field of IT requires up-to-date technologies (e.g., Cloud Computing) to be included in a timely manner. In this study, we present our design of an undergraduate network administration course. Different from the literature, the novelties of this design are multi-fold. First, we identify a group of administration tasks, which, for the first time, is presented to the students in a top-down approach according to the Internet protocol stack. Second, given our prior lesson with virtualization, we adopt a hybrid approach that combines both physical and virtual technologies in the lab design (rather than solely resorting to virtualization). Finally, being aware of the implication of desktop virtualization and network virtualization to network administration, we design labs that cover desktop virtualization, and Cloud Computing based on Amazon AWS cloud.

KEYWORDS

Network administration; course design

1 INTRODUCTION

Network administration is an important course that is offered in CS/IT majors in many universities. One major challenge in teaching network administration is the wide spectrum of ad-hoc topics (e.g., Network OSs, protocols, vendor-specific devices) that can potentially be included in this course. It is critical to identify a well-organized subset of

SIGITE'17, October 4-7, 2017, Rochester, NY, USA
© 2017 Association for Computing Machinery.
ACM ISBN 978-1-4503-5100-3/17/10. . . $15.00
https://doi.org/http://dx.doi.org/10.1145/3125659.3125678

topics that can introduce the big picture of the field to students. Likewise, the recent decade has witnessed the emergence of virtualization for the IT industry (e.g., desktop virtualization based on hypervisors, and network virtualization as Cloud Computing), which also significantly changes the traditional concept of network administration. For instance, web hosting provided by Amazon AWS [4] allows the network administrators of a company website to outsource the physical network and servers to the cloud provider while only focusing on the service deployment in the cloud. It is hence important to discuss the implication of virtualization to network administration. In this paper, we select a subset of critical administrative tasks that is organized in a top-down order of the Internet protocol stack. In addition, desktop virtualization and network virtualization (i.e. Cloud Computing) are also incorporated.

Not only is virtualization a topic that should be studied on its own right, but also it is an essential tool to facilitate the teaching of other subjects. In the literature, many studies have proposed to import virtualization software in the teaching of network courses [1, 2, 6, 7, 20, 23]. Particularly, virtualization brings a few advantages into the network administration class. First, students can obtain almost equivalent hands-on experience in rudimentary operations such as OS installation and configuration. Second, it is easy for the teachers to maintain the physical lab as students' administrative operations are done on the virtual instances. Third, it is cost-effective, space-friendly and portable as students can store multiple virtual machines on a portable drive. Our experience in an entry level network class, however, does include discomfort from students who are new to desktop virtualization. This is in line with the study in [16] where it is revealed that students do not want to take all the labs in a solely virtual manner. Moreover, virtualization can bring negative impacts to administrative operations such as performance benchmarking. For instance, the authors of [12] found that virtualization-based testbeds can negatively affect the system and network performance metrics. We hence argue that virtualization technologies should not be overused when teaching an undergraduate level course. In this paper, we present a hybrid approach that combines both physical and virtual technologies/devices.

This work overall presents our design and lesson for an undergraduate network administration class. Different from the literature, the novelties of our design lies on a few facets. First, we adopt a layered approach to teach network administration for the first time, where we design lectures and labs according to the protocol stack of the Internet in a top-down order. Second, despite the rich literature on advocating virtualization-based networking labs, we propose to adopt a hybrid approach that combines both physical and virtual instances in the lab design. Third, among the wide spectrum of potential topics, we identify a minimum subset of topics to present students a big picture of network administration, which includes coverage of desktop virtualization, as well as Cloud Computing based on Amazon AWS cloud. The rest of this paper is organized as follows. Section 2 presents the background and the major learning objectives of the network administration class. In Section 3, we discuss the major challenges in the course design, and present the detailed design in Section 4. We summarize the major principles of the course design in Section 5, and discuss the feedback of students and lessons learned in Section 6. Finally, Section 7 concludes this paper.

2 BACKGROUND AND OBJECTIVES OF THE CLASS

Our university is an urban institution, where the Math and Computer Science Department offers both Computer Science (CS) and Information Technology (IT) majors. There is a list of courses that are related to the network administration course, which are listed below.

(1) 220 Data Communications
(2) 320 LANs and Network Administration
(3) 321 Client Support
(4) 327 Administrative Scripting
(5) 422 Information Security

First, the teaching of computer networks, as a common requirement for both CS and IT majors, are broken into three courses: 220 Data Communications, 320 LANs and Network Administration, and 422 Information Security. Specifically, 220 Data Communication is an entry level networking class for freshmen, which adopts a top-down approach that covers a subset of representative protocols of the Internet protocol stack. 320 LANs and Network Administration and 422 Information Security address the adminstration and security aspects of networking, respectively. This breakdown aims to reinforce the learning of networking with gradually increased depth and difficulty. In addition, 321 Client Support contains modules that address system adminstration, and 327 Administrative Scripting are dedicated to administrative scripting skills such as *bash*, and *PowerShell*. Recently, the department is planning to design a Cloud Computing class as an elective course.

Our design presented in this paper is dedicated to the 320 Network Administration class. The major objectives of this course are: (i) Present students with a big picture of network administration; (ii) Present students with skills in protocol and service configuration. (iii)Present students with skills in LAN deployment and administration, client connectivity and troubleshooting.

3 CHALLENGES

In this section, we discuss the major challenges that we face when developing the network administration class.

First, as an urban university, we have limited space and support for the lab setup and maintenance. Also, we have limited budget for purchasing hardware and software.

Second, in prior teaching, we have observed frustrations from students when adopting virtualization technologies as tools. For instance, students are not confident or comfortable with router emulation software before first gaining familiarity with physical devices. Given the same concern, we have avoided adopting virtualization in the 220 class for freshmen and introduced virtualization for the first time in this 320 course. In addition, given the industrial need for experience in administration of desktop virtualization and network virtualization, virtualization should also be taught on its own right in this course.

Third, given the fact that network administration contains a wide variety of ad-hoc topics (e.g., Network OSs, protocols, vendor-specific devices), it is critical to identify a subset of important topics to introduce the big picture of the field. And more importantly, the selected diverse topics should be well-organized. Also, the design of this class should be tailored to the upstream and downstream related courses to maintain the flow of knowledge and avoid unnecessary overlap.

4 COURSE DESIGN

In this section, we present the detailed design of the network administration course following the top-down order of the Internet protocol stack. Given the space limitation, instead of covering all the details, we overview the major components and stress the novel features of and connections among components.

4.1 Choice of Hardware, Software and Virtualization Technologies

Table 1: Hardware, Software Selections

OS	Window Server 2012, Ubuntu Server.
Web Service	IIS, LAMP.
Hypervisors	VMVare Workstation.
Cloud	Amazon AWS.
Routers	CISCO 2600, GNS3, NETGEAR WIFI router.
Switches	CISCO 2950.
Others	USB-to-NIC converters, portable drivers.

Table 1 lists the major software (the first three rows) and hardware (and the last three rows) that are adopted in our course design. Specifically, our university has signed up to Microsoft Imagine and VMWare, and students have access to windows server images, and VMWare software. We obtained a grant from Amazon AWS to cover the cost on cloud related labs. We purchased a small number of CISCO 2600 routers, and CISCO 2950 switches to provide students physical experiences with the devices while resorting to GNS3, an emulation software that can create a virtual network (by loading images of CISCO IOS) for large scale labs. The detailed usage of the hardware and software are further elaborated in the sections below.

It is also worth noting that virtualization technologies that are covered in this class are also viewed from a layer perspective. As shown in Table 2, desktop virtualization, residing in the end system, may be considered as virtualization at the application layer. VPN, and VLAN are forms of virtualization at network layer and link layer, respectively. Finally, Cloud Computing can be viewed as an integrated application of virtualization technologies of all layers.

Table 2: Virtualization Technologies on Each Layer

Application	Desktop Virtualization.
Transport	N/A.
Network	VPN.
Link	VLAN.

4.2 Desktop Virtualization

First, we introduce desktop virtualization (using VMWare Workstation) to students as which is not only the basis for latter labs but also an essential knowledge for administrators. As this is the first course that adopts virtualization, we overview virtualization technologies and develop two labs for students to practice as listed in Table 4. In the first lab, students are directed to create Window virtual machines (VMs), where they are briefly introduced to *PowerShell*. In the second lab, we design tasks for students to create Ubuntu virtual machines. In both labs, we also ask the student to experience the difference between *Bridged* and *NAT* configurations in virtual machines (VM) settings to have a first experience on the concept of NAT.

4.3 Application Layer

As we adopt a top-down approach, this course is followed by covering administration skills at the application layer. We design four labs as listed in Table 4. In these three labs, students are asked to install and setup HTTP, DNS, DHCP and Active Directory services, respectively. As IIS has a built-in FTP functionality, students are also asked to setup the FTP services in the first lab. In addition, the students are asked to configure SSH remote access to the Ubuntu server, which aims to prepare them for the cloud labs.

4.4 Transport Layer

As shown in Table 4, at the transport layer, we design one lab to practice TCP parameters tuning and observe the performance variations under load testing. As the first author worked as a Cloud administrator and performed such tasks on a regular basis, we believe that it is a beneficial administrative task for students. An example setup is shown in Fig.

1 where a group of load generating VMs are used to generate a large volume of traffic to the target server (e.g., with tools such as Pktgen [19], Apache Bench [5], and JMeter [14]), and the target web server is tuned in TCP parameters that are associated with server performance (e.g., bound for TCP buffer size). The corresponding performance of the web server are collected and analyzed.

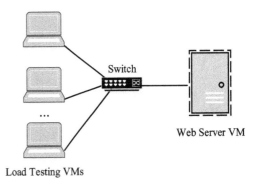

Figure 1: Load Testing Setup

4.5 Network Layer

For the network layer, we design three labs as shown in Table 4: two labs based on physical devices, and personal laptop computers (PCs) (brought by students), and one based on emulation software GNS3. As shown in Fig. 2, GNS3 allows to create a logical or virtual networks consisting of a large number of virtual devices, where each virtual device is created based on the image of the CISCO IOS. GNS3 also allows the configuration of each virtual device as physical device (via the console window shown in Fig. 2). In the first lab, students are introduced to the CISCO IOS by practicing physical connection and setup two laptops connected by a router (via crossover cables). The second lab aims to provide experience for NAT setup on CISCO routers. Note that in both physical labs, we need no more than two routers per group, which respects our budget and space constraints. In the last lab, students are directed to perform large scale routing labs (e.g., *RIP* and *BGP*). In addition, the students are exposed to ICMP protocol and network utilities such as *ping*, and *traceroute* in above labs. We also cover the concept of VPN in the lecture but leave the practice to the security class.

4.6 Link Layer

For the link layer, we design three physical labs as listed in Table 4. In the first lab, students are introduced to switch-based subnet, ARP protocol, and are asked to manually setup the IP addresses/subnet mask. The second lab introduces the VLAN configuration on CISCO switches. The last lab is designed to meet the demand from the students to learn skills on home ethernet and WIFI network setup.

Table 3: Desktop Virtualization Labs

Lab	Software/Hardware Configuration	Skills Covered
Windows Server VM	VMVare Workstation	Creation of Window VMs on a portable driver.
Ubuntu Server VM	VMVare Workstation	Creation of Ubuntu VMs on a portable driver.

Table 4: Layer-based Labs

Layer	Lab	Software/Hardware	Skills Covered
Application	HTTP(FTP) Server	VMs from prior labs	IIS configuration in Window Server, and LAMP and SSH setup in Ubuntu Server.
Application	DNS	VMs from prior labs	DNS configuration.
Application	DHCP	VMs from prior labs	DHCP configuration.
Application	Active Directory	VMs from prior labs	Active Directory, File sharing, and *Powershell*.
Transport	TCP Parameter Tuning and Web Server Load Testing	Ubuntu Server VM Apache Bench, Pktgen, JMeter	TCP parameters tuning, and web server load testing.
Network	IOS introduction	CISCO router, student PCs	Basic IOS commands, and router physical connection.
Network	NAT	CISCO routers, and switches	Configuration of NAT on CISCO routers.
Network	Routing Labs	GNS3	Configuration of routing on the emulation platform.
Link	Subnetting	CISCO Switch, student PCs	Manual configuration of IP addresses/subnet mask, and connectivity troubleshooting.
Link	VLAN	CISCO Switch	Configuration of VLAN over CISCO switch.
Link	Home Network Configuration	NETGEAR Wireless Router	Configuration of home network.

Figure 2: GNS3 for Virtual Labs

4.7 Cloud Computing

The coverage of desktop virtualization, and administration on the four layers of the Internet protocol stack prepare the students with enough background (e.g., SSH, LAMP, subnetting, public/private IP addresses etc.) before introducing network virtualization. We finally present Cloud Computing

as a form of network virtualization and discuss its implication on network administration. Currently, we have designed three labs based on the public cloud Amazon AWS as shown in Table 5. In the first lab, students are directed to create virtual machines in AWS. In the second lab, students are asked to practice LAMP and DNS configuration in AWS to achieve web hosting in cloud. The last lab is for remote access and configuration where students are asked to perform administrative tasks (such as backup, firewall configuration, load balancing and network troubleshooting) with a SSH connection to the remote instance.

5 DESIGN PRINCIPLES

In this section, we summarize the major design principles that we follow to address the challenges mentioned above.

First, given the wide spectrum of topics in network administration, we selectively cover a subset of topics that introduces the big picture to students. We exclude extensive coverage of administrative scripting and security in teaching network administration as these are covered in other downstream classes.

Second, being aware of the ad-hoc nature of administrative tasks, we adopt a top-down approach to teach network administration. This aims to present network adminstration with a clear flow as well as to maintain a consistency with the teaching of upstream networking class. Also, Cloud Computing is introduced as the last topic once students have exposure to all required background knowledge.

Third, we strive a balance between theory and practice in teaching network administration. Although it is prone to design this course as practice-oriented, we design lectures before each lab to prepare students with sufficient background, which are followed by labs that gradually train their management, administration, and troubleshooting skills.

Fourth, being aware of the side effects of adopting virtualization, we advocate a hybrid approach that combines both physical and virtual counterparts in the lab design to respect the budget and space limitations.

Fifth, we believe that both desktop virtualization and network virtualization (i.e., Cloud Computing) are essential skills each as a tool and on its own right to network administrators. Thus we design lectures and labs to ensure the coverage of these two topics.

Finally, although these design principle are introduced to address unique challenges at our institution, it can be applied (partially or all-together) to the teaching of network administration in a generic setting. The challenges of ad-hoc nature of administrative tasks, the large variety of administration topics, and the sides effects with virtualization are not unique cross different universities [15, 18, 21, 24].

6 FEEDBACK AND LESSONS

Over four semesters of following this approach, the evaluations for this course rated are 90.8% (=4.54/5) on average in terms of the overall value that it has contributed to learning. Over 62% of the surveyed students considered this course as "very valuable" (i.e., the highest rating). We list some representative (anonymous) feedback from the students below.

(1) *"Organized well which made me learn all the details about the subject."*
(2) *"This is my second experience with networking. I actually feel that the layers make a little bit of sense now."*
(3) *"Build capacity, knowledge, and skill, provide breadth and depth of study, develop practical application for comprehensive implementation."*
(4) *"There is many strength to the course the best strength of this course is the hand-on labs."*
(5) *"This course was crucial and should be necessary for all IT majors."*

Moreover, we have learned a few lessons from our practices, which are discussed below.

First, many recent laptop models do not have built-in Ethernet network interface card (NIC). For labs that requires students' own PCs, we have resolved this issue by providing USB-to-NIC converters to students when necessary.

Second, it is worth noting the lab design should be applicable to different operating systems as students may use either a MAC book or Windows computer.

Third, given the budget and space limitation, labs related to physical devices are typically organized as group labs. One

major problem is that the participation of each member cannot be guaranteed. We gradually revise the lab report to include questions that is unique for each student. For instance, when setting up the IP addresses, part of the addresses is associated with each student's birth date or student ID to ensure the uniqueness of the answers.

Finally, to ease the management of student accounts in Amazon AWS, we have resorted to AWS Identity and Access Management (IAM) service, which allows the management of student users and groups, and their access to AWS resources under one instructor account.

7 RELATED WORK

There is an extensive literature on the lab design of a networking class (e.g., [1–3, 7–11, 13, 20, 22, 28]). The proposed lab design is either general for supporting multiple networking classes (e.g., [2, 7, 8, 10]) or dedicated to a particular class (e.g., [11, 13] for wireless networking, and [17] for security auditing).

Meanwhile, only limited work has been dedicated to the teaching of network administration. The authors of [18] presented the course design models of network administration for beginning students, and experienced students, respectively. The selected lab design and setup, however, are mostly already out-of-date. Given the importance of hands-on experience for IT students, the work of [24] advocates a mix of theory and hands-on components in teaching networking administration. In [21], a survey on potential topics of network administration reveals the increased importance of server, remote system and cloud management. The authors of [15] suggested to use a combination of virtual and physical environment while no actual lab design or setup are provided.

Among the wave of virtualization, there are many literature studies on introducing desktop virtualization technologies to the classroom [1, 2, 6, 20, 23, 26, 27]. A few recent works also present lab design to include Cloud Computing. The authors of [25] discussed how to implement a private cloud based on Xen cloud platform for student labs, and the authors [3] discussed the implementation of a private cloud based on Microsoft Hyper-V hypervisor.

This study fills a few gaps in the literature. First, we present network administration with a top-down layered approach that sorts out a wide spectrum of ad-hoc administrative technologies. Second, we adopt a hybrid approach that integrates both physical and virtual labs which are also cost-efficient and space-friendly. Finally, we incorporate both the coverage of desktop virtualization and Cloud Computing into the teaching of network administration.

8 CONCLUSION AND FUTURE WORK

In this study, we present our design of an undergraduate network administration class. The major novelty of this class design includes a top-down approach that covers major administration skills on each layer of the Internet protocol stack, a hybrid approach that combines both physical and

Table 5: Cloud Computing Labs

Lab	Software/Hardware Configuration	Skills Covered
Introduction to AWS	Amazon AWS	Creation of an AWS Ubuntu virtual instance.
Web Hosting	AWS Ubuntu VM	LAMP configuration, and DNS configuration in AWS.
Remote Access and Configuration	AWS Ubuntu VM	SSH configuration, troubleshooting, firewall configuration and load balancing.

virtual technolgies/devices in the lab design, and the coverage of both desktop virtualization and Cloud Computing. Given the fast pace of technology advancement in IT, we are continually updating this class design, with a list of potential technologies that are considered to be further incorporated: OpenFlow routing and switching in Software Defined Networks, OpenStack platform, and private cloud configuration and maintenance.

9 ACKNOWLEDGEMENT

The first author thanks the generous support from Amazon Education Grant (2015-2016).

REFERENCES

[1] S. Abbott-McCune, A. Newtson, B. S. Goda, and J. Girard. Developing a reconfigurable network lab. In *Proceedings of SIGITE'08*, pages 255–258.
[2] J. C. Adams and W. D. Laverell. Configuring a multi-course lab for system-level projects. In *Proceedings of SIGCSE'05*, pages 525–529.
[3] J. Alexander, A. Dick, J. Hacker, D. Hicks, and M. Stockman. Building a cloud based systems lab. In *Proceedings of SIGITE'12*, pages 151–154.
[4] Amazon AWS, https://aws.amazon.com.
[5] Apache Benchmarking, httpd.apache.org/docs/2.4/programs/ab.html.
[6] W. Bullers, S. Burd, and A. Seazzu. Virtual machines: an idea whose time has returned. In *Proceedings of SIGCSE'06*, pages 102–106.
[7] X. Cao, Y. Wang, A. Caciula, and Y. Wang. Developing a multifunctional network laboratory for teaching and research. In *Proceedings of SIGITE'09*, pages 155–160.
[8] M. Casado and N. McKeown. The virtual network system. In *Proceedings of SIGCSE'05*, pages 76–80.
[9] S. Cosgrove. Bringing together a low-cost networking learning environment. In *Proceedings of SIGITE'11*, pages 101–106.
[10] J. Gerdes and S. Tilley. A conceptual overview of the virtual networking laboratory. In *Proceedings of SIGITE'07*, pages 75–82.
[11] B. Hartpence. Teaching wireless security for results. In *Proceedings of SIGITE'05*, pages 89–93.
[12] B. Hartpence. Curricular and performance measurement challenges in cloud environments. In *Proceedings of the 15th Annual Conference on Information Technology Education*, SIGITE '14, pages 51–54, New York, NY, USA, 2014. ACM.
[13] B. Hartpence and L. Hill. Wireless cart- an inexpensive education and research platform. In *Proceedings of SIGITE'05*, pages 79–82.
[14] JMeter, http://jmeter.apache.org/.
[15] R. Kumar and G. Singh. Learning computer networking using virtualization tools. In *Proceedings of Annual Conference of the National Advisory Committee on Computing Qualifications*, pages 52–55, 2012.
[16] E. A. Lawson and W. Stackpole. Does a virtual networking laboratory result in similar student achievement and satisfaction? In *Proceedings of the 7th Conference on Information Technology Education*, SIGITE '06, pages 105–114, New York, NY, USA, 2006. ACM.
[17] Y. Pan. Security auditing course development. In *Proceedings of SIGITE'07*, pages 259–266.
[18] S. Perez-Hardy. A unique experiential model for teaching network administration. In *Proceedings of the 4th Conference on Information Technology Curriculum*, CITC4 '03, pages 119–121, New York, NY, USA, 2003. ACM.
[19] Pktgen, https://pktgen.readthedocs.io.
[20] S. Rigby and M. Dark. Designing a flexible, multipurpose remote lab for the it curriculum. In *Proceedings of SIGITE'06*, pages 161–164.
[21] F. Shen, B. Qi, H. Li, and A. Friberg. Rethinking network administration curriculum design. In *Proceedings of the 2013 Mid-Atlantic Section Conference of ASEE*, pages 176–188, 2013.
[22] B. Stackpole. The evolution of a virtualized laboratory environment. In *Proceedings of SIGITE'08*, pages 243–248.
[23] B. Stackpole, J. Koppe, T. Haskell, L. Guay, and Y. Pan. Decentralized virtualization in systems administration education. In *Proceedings of SIGITE'08*, pages 249–254.
[24] M. Stockman and J. Nyland. A teaching pedagogy for networking/system administration courses: Freshman through senior years. In *Proceedings of the 2010 ACM Conference on Information Technology Education*, SIGITE '10, pages 15–20, New York, NY, USA, 2010. ACM.
[25] X. Wang, G. C. Hembroff, A. B. Cerier, and B. W. Perrault. Introducing cloud computing with a senior design project in undergraduate education of computer system and network administration. In *Proceedings of the 2011 Conference on Information Technology Education*, SIGITE '11, pages 177–182, New York, NY, USA, 2011. ACM.
[26] X. Wang, G. C. Hembroff, and R. Yedica. Using vmware vcenter lab manager in undergraduate education for system administration and network security. In *Proceedings of the 2010 ACM Conference on Information Technology Education*, SIGITE '10, pages 43–52, New York, NY, USA, 2010. ACM.
[27] L. Yang. Teaching system and network administration using virtual pc. *J. Comput. Sci. Coll.*, 23(2):137–142, Dec. 2007.
[28] D. Yuan, C. Lewandowski, and J. Zhong. Developing ip telephony laboratory and curriculum with private cloud computing. In *Proceedings of SIGITE'11*, pages 107–112.

Cybersecurity Should be Taught Top-Down and Case-Driven

Yu Cai and Todd Arney
Michigan Technological University
1400 Townsend Drive
Houghton, MI 49931
cai@mtu.edu,toarney@mtu.edu

ABSTRACT

This paper aims to re-engineer cybersecurity education with an innovative top-down & case-driven (TDCD) teaching model by dissecting recent high-profile cybersecurity breaches. The traditional way of teaching cybersecurity is usually bottom-up where a list of security topics are taught separately in an isolated context, with little or no effort to link these topics together. The proposed TDCD model starts with real-world cyber breaches including the Target Corporation breach, the Anthem Inc. breach, and selected Distributed Denial of Service (DDoS) attacks. Students look into the details of these attacks and learn how these attacks took place from the beginning to the end. During the process of case analysis, a list of security topics reflecting different aspects of these breaches is introduced. Through guided in-class discussion, selected readings and hands-on lab assignments, student learning in lecture will be reinforced. Overall, the entire cybersecurity course is taught top-down and driven by real-world breach cases. The proposed TDCD model is ideal for teaching cybersecurity. First, the new model can easily draw students' attention and interest with real-world cases. Second, the new model can help instructors select important and timely cybersecurity topics from a wide range of options. Third, the new model can improve student learning outcomes, particularly help students gain a holistic view of security and learn socio-technical factors.

KEYWORDS

Computer network security; security education; cyber security

1 INTRODUCTION

Cyber hacks and security breaches have dramatically increased in the past few years. People with cybersecurity skills are in great demand as the threat environment increasingly becomes more complex and challenging. Despite the continuous efforts from the cybersecurity education community, there are still mismatches between industry needs and cybersecurity education provided by universities and colleges. For example, A CloudPassage study in 2016 shows that "there is an incredible IT security skills gap... a major root cause is a lack of education and training at accredited

schools" [1]. Another ISACA reports in 2017 finds that less than 25% of cybersecurity job candidates are qualified [2].

The core idea of this paper is to re-engineer cybersecurity education with an innovative top-down & case-driven (TDCD) teaching model by dissecting recent high-profile cybersecurity breaches, including the Target breach in 2013 [3], the Anthem breach in 2015 [4], a couple of DDoS attacks [5, 6] and others.

We go far beyond the traditional case-study approach. The entire cybersecurity course, from course topic selection to course schedule arrangement, from lecture content to lab format, are all driven by these real-world cybersecurity breaches.

This new TDCD education model starts with real-world cyber breaches. Students will look into the details of these attacks, learn how these attacks took place from the beginning to the end, and study how these attacks could be prevented. During the process of case analysis, a list of related cybersecurity topics is introduced. Through guided in-class discussion, selected readings, and hands-on lab assignments, students will explore various cybersecurity offensive techniques, defensive mechanisms, and best practices.

The authors conceived the idea of TDCD in regular teaching on cybersecurity. There are so many existing high-profile cyber breaches! And there are so many lessons we could learn from those breaches! It is almost a crime itself to waste such abundant resources. To a large extent, the cybersecurity industry is driven by cyber breaches and cyber threats, so should cybersecurity education.

The TDCD model was tested in a cybersecurity course at Michigan Technology University during the fall semester of 2015 and 2016. The small-scale pilot study shows that the new course is extremely welcomed by students. Most students (80%) expressed great interest and enthusiasm on cybersecurity during and after taking the course by using this top-down and case-driven approach.

2 PROJECT RATIONALE

A top-down teaching approach focuses on providing students a big picture or a macro view of a system, then breaking down the system into many compositional sub-systems. A bottom-up teaching approach begins with the component parts of a system and gradually builds up to the whole by piecing together many sub-systems. Both top-down and bottom-up can be effective teaching methods, but operating in the opposite direction [7].

Teaching with case studies is another common pedagogy widely used in many disciplines. Study cases are usually realistic, complex, and context-rich stories used to show the application of a theory or concept in real situations. Teaching with cases can help students actively engage in classroom participation and achieve positive learning outcomes [8].

SIGITE'17, October 4–7, 2017, Rochester, NY, USA
© 2017 Association for Computing Machinery.
ACM ISBN 978-1-4503-5100-3/17/10...$15.00
https://doi.org/10.1145/3125659.3125687

The proposed model integrates two different teaching methods (top-down+case-driven) and is ideal for teaching cybersecurity. The major advantages of the new model are addressed below.

First, the TDCD model can increase students interest in cybersecurity and motivate them to study security topics. - *"Interest is the best teacher!"*.

Apparently increasing student interest is crucial to any education improvements. Students usually have a great curiosity to know what happened in real-world cyber breaches. Analyzing these high-profile breaches are an eye-opening experience for most students. The instructor can easily motivate students to explore details of these cyber breaches and study underlying security topics.

Second, the TDCD model can help instructors select cybersecurity topics to better meet industry needs. - *"The difficulty in life is the choice."*

Cybersecurity covers a wide range of topics and evolves at a very fast pace. It is always a challenging task for instructors to decide which topics to cover(scope), and to what depth(scale). Quite often the selection process becomes ad-hoc and is heavily influenced by instructor's personal preferences and background. As a result, there are growing mismatches between what professors teach in the classroom and what students need in the cybersecurity field.

By utilizing the new model, the process of topic selection is mainly determined by the importance and timeliness of these topics as illustrated in the real-world breaches, with a careful balance between fundamental theory and hands-on knowledge. We will discuss course topics in details in Section 4.

Third, the TDCD model can improve student learning outcomes, particularly help students gain a holistic view of cybersecurity and learn socio-technical factors in cybersecurity. - *"You can't see the forest for the trees."*

Traditional cybersecurity courses are usually bottom-up where security topics are taught one by one in an isolated context, with little or no final integration. The main drawback is that students will have a hard time to link these topics together and gain a whole picture of cybersecurity in enterprise networks.

In the new model, we start by dissecting the real-life cyber breaches and real-world enterprise networks. During case analysis, students are guided to follow the footprint of hackers. Students will not only get hands-on and practical experience, but also start to see how different security mechanisms are integrated into enterprise networks, and how weakest links in the system (both technical and social) are exploited by hackers, thus obtaining a comprehensive and holistic view of cybersecurity.

During case analysis, it is a natural step to draw student's attention to human, social, ethical, organizational, and economic factors, and the complex interaction among these factors. In traditional cybersecurity courses, it is less easy to find a good place to fit human and social factors. This is a key element in providing students experience with the human factor that often missing from more purely technical courses.

In summary, we believe that the proposed model is ideal for teaching cybersecurity and can better prepare students for industry needs. Figure 1 compares the proposed TDCD model with the traditional bottom-up model in cybersecurity education.

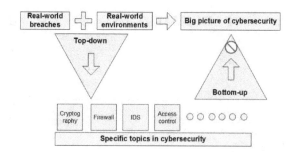

Figure 1: Top-down & case-driven vs. traditional bottom-up

3 RELATED WORK

There is a growing pool of efforts on cybersecurity education including teaching pedagogies, curriculum materials, lab platforms, and faculty training. Several effective teaching pedagogies are developed to improve student learning outcomes on cybersecurity. For example, hacker curriculum and offensive security curriculum are presented in [9, 10]. Cybersecurity games and hacking competitions / hackathons are introduced in iCTF [11] and CCDC [12]. For curriculum materials, NSF sponsored projects such as SEED [13] present a set of well-documented security labs. Also, cloud-based virtual lab platforms such as EDURange [14] and DETERlab [15] have been developed for security education.

The U.S. government has recognized the importance of cybersecurity with two efforts. The first effort is the National Initiative for Cybersecurity Education (NICE) effort led by National Institute of Standards and Technology (NIST), and the other one is the National Centers of Academic Excellence (CAE) led by National Security Agency (NSA) and Department of Homeland Security (DHS).

4 DETAILED COURSE DESCRIPTION

4.1 Selection of course topics

Table 1 compares course topics in a traditional cybersecurity course and in the new cybersecurity course with the TDCD model. The topics in a traditional cybersecurity course are extracted from the classic textbook "Corporate Computer Security (4th Edition)" by Randall J. Boyle and Raymond R. Panko [16]. This classic textbook gives great coverage on a variety of security topics. This textbook is used here for illustration purpose.

Course topics and subtopics identified by the TDCD model represent some of the most important, timely and urgent needs from the industry. These topics will be continuously updated based on real-world cyber breaches and security incidents.

4.2 Sample case study: the Target data breach

In this section, we will use the Target data breach to illustrate how real-world cases are analyzed and how course topics/subtopics are identified.

The Target data breach started around late 2013 and became publicly known around Dec. 2013. Hackers gained access to more than 40 million credit and debit card information through malware on Target's Point-Of-Sale (POS) systems [3].

Target didn't publicly release breach details, and probably will never do so. But enough information exists online and within the

Table 1: Comparison of Cybersecurity Course Topics. Strike through means topics are eliminated; underline means new topic; italic are case studies

Topics in traditional course	Topics in the new course
1. ~~Introduction~~	1. Introduction & *Case study on Target breach*
2. ~~Planning & Policy~~	2. Email phishing & social engineering
3. Cryptography	3. Web security (including SQL injection and XSS attack)
4. Network security	4. Network security (including DDoS attack)
5. Access control	5. *Case study on DDoS attacks*
6. Firewall	6. Access control (including privilege account management)
7. ~~Host hardening~~	7. Firewall (including next-generation firewall)
8. ~~Application security~~	8. Intrusion Detection Systems (including user behavior analytics)
9. ~~Data protection~~	9. *Case study on Anthem breach*
10. Incident response	10. Cryptography
	11. Malware (including ransomware)
	12. Incident response & risk analysis

The Target Breach in 2013

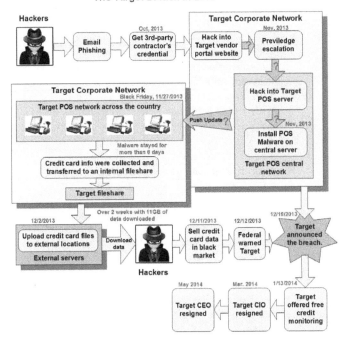

Figure 2: The Target data breach from Nov. 2013 to Jan. 2014

cybersecurity community to piece together what likely happened during the breach. By studing and analyzing this information it can help people prevent similar attacks in the future. Figure 2 is a diagram illustrating the Target data breach with a timeline. Information was collected through a number of sources [3, 17, 18].

There are several reasons to use the Target data breach as one of the representative cases. First, the Target breach represents a typical type of cyber threats named Advanced Persistent Threat (APT). Second, the Target breach happened a few years ago, short enough so that lessons learned are not out-of-dated, also long enough so that there are sufficient details available to piece things together. Third, the Target breach is a high-profile case, which can easily draw students' attention and interest. These three elements combined make for an ideal case study selection for a cyber security class analysis.

There are two ways of using the Target case. First, we can have an in-class discussion on the Target case during the semester. Students will answer questions and have discussions on the Target breach. Table 2 is a list of sample discussion questions on the Target case. Second, we can use the Target breach as an example to teach individual security topics and link them together. Table 3 shows security topics related to different stages in the Target case.

During case discussion, special attention will be given to help students understand how different security mechanisms and systems are integrated into corporate networks, what are the common weakest links, and how those weakest links would be exploited by hackers. By walking through a couple of case studies like the Target breach and the Anthem breach, students will obtain a holistic view of cybersecurity, and start to link different security topics together.

4.3 A list of case studies on cybersecurity

The authors collected a set of recent cybersecurity breaches and plan to collect more in the future. This is the scope of case studies available to be used in class analysis. Cases in List A are representative cases and should be covered with great details and in-depth analysis. This is the scale of case analysis. Cases in List B are short cases with less details (usually 10-15 minutes). Our plan is to collect as many recent high-profile cyber breaches as possible and turn them into usable cases for cybersecurity course. By having both lists available, instructors can customize courses and find an appropriate balance of covering many topics (scope) and spending time to do a deep-dive analysis (scale) on fewer topics.

List A - Cyber breaches covered with great details
- 1. The Target data breach in 2013 [3]
- 2. The Anthem data breach in 2015 [4]
- 3. A 300Gbps DDoS attack in 2013 [5]

A study package with the following materials was developed for each case in the List A:

a) A video tutorial introducing the case (typically 30-40 minutes): students need to watch the video and get a basic idea of what happened in the breach before attending the classroom discussion

b) A list of discussion questions (typically ten): students need to finish the discussion questions after watching the video and before attending the classroom discussion. See Table 2 for an example.

c) A Powerpoint presentation explaining technical details and lessons learned from the case (typically 30-50 pages): used by the instructor

Table 2: Sample questions & answers for in-class discussion on the Target breach

Discussion questions	Key points in answers
1) Use your own word to explain what happened in the Target data breach.	1) Open answer
2) The HVAC contractor's credentials were compromised by email phishing. Please propose at least two security mechanisms to guard against email phishing.	2) Email spam filter; phishing education
3) If you are the hacker, please propose a scheme for phishing email attack. Be as real as possible.	3) Open answer
4) The stolen credentials alone are not enough to access the company's POS devices. The hackers then acquired elevated rights that allowed them to navigate company's network and to deploy malware. This process is called Privilege Escalation. Name as many ways as you know to do privilege escalation.	4) SQL injection attack; buffer overflow attack; XSS attack; 0-day attack; weak or default password
5) To do privilege escalation, the hackers need to do vulnerability scanning on the Target network. Please propose as many ways as you know to do vulnerability scanning?	5) Nmap; Nessus; penetration test
6) Many POS machines on the market nowadays are vulnerable to viruses and malware. Please propose a few measures to enhance POS security.	6) Internal firewall on POS network; malware detection
7) Target admitted that they ignored many alerts from their network security devices because of alert overload. If you are the Target CTO, what would you do to alleviate the problem of alert overload?	7) Upgrade security software; better training
8) The security experts criticize Target for failing to isolate sensitive sections of their networks from those more easily accessible to outsiders. If you are the Target CTO, please propose a feasible solution to segment and categorize your networks and resources.	8) Internal firewall and IDS; privileged account monitoring; network segmentation
9) IT Weaknesses Paved the Way for Target Hackers. Please identify as many weaknesses as possible in the Target IT security.	9) Open answer
10) If you are the Target CIO, what would you do to improve IT security?	10) Open answer

Table 3: Analysis of the Target data breach

Anatomy of the Target breach	Corresponding cybersecurity topics
Step 1. Hackers launched phishing attacks on Target 3rd-party contractor	• Email phishing • Social engineering • Phishing education
Step 2. Hackers gained access to Target portal website with compromised credentials	• Two-factor authentication • Access control • Firewall
Step 3. Privilege escalation within Target network	• Vulnerability scanning • Common vulnerabilities: buffer overflow, SQL injection, XSS • Software patch management • Network segmentation
Step 4. Hackers gained control of Target POS server and installed Malware on POS machines	• Privilege account management • User behavior analytics • Host hardening • Alert overloading
Step 5. Hackers collected credit card information with malware and stored data on an internal file share	• Malware, virus, and worm
Step 6. Hackers downloaded stolen data from Target network	• Firewall • Intrusion detection system
Step 7. Hackers sold credit card data in black market	• Security regulations • Risk analysis
Step 8. Target publicly announced the breach	• Incident response • Penetration test

to guide the classroom discussion.

Each case study will take one or two lectures, mixed with student discussion and instructor comment/lecture.

d) Selected readings from publicly available sources to provide students with expanded awareness of topics. These selected readings can be either required assignment (graded), or optional (ungraded).

List B - Cyber breaches covered with fewer details

- 4. Case study: Mark Zuckerberg's social media accounts were hacked in 2016 [19]. *Corresponding topic: password management, human factors*
- 5. Case study: Panama paper breach in 2016 [20]. *Corresponding topic: web server security, software patch management*

- 6. Case study: OpenSSL heartbleed attack in 2014 [21]. *Corresponding topic: zero-day attack, https security, buffer overflow*
- 7. Case study: An Internet-of-Things DDoS attack on Dyn DNS in 2016 [6]. *Corresponding topic: DDoS attack, security on Internet-of-Things*
- 8. Case study: Ransomware on San Francisco public transportation in 2016 [22]. *Corresponding topic: Malware, Ransomware*
- 9. Case study: The JPMorgan data breach in 2014 [23]. *Corresponding topic: email phishing, end-host hardening*

- 10. Case study: The SWIFT and Bangladesh bank hack in 2016 [24]. *Corresponding topic: backdoor attack, malware*

4.4 Lab assignments

Hands-on lab assignments is an important part in the TDCD approach. The new cyber security course has 10 hands-on labs, designed to help students practice classroom learning in a simulated virtual environment. Each lab session is about 2-hour long. We recommend using cloud-based lab platform to provide virtual machines with multiple operating systems and other technical resources for students and instructors to have both a consistent and shared platform. Additionally, these virtual machines can be "quarantined" as to not allow any security research tools to affect other systems..

The labs are designed based on the TDCD principle with an emphasis on offensive security training. Students will try to follow the footprint of hackers in high-profile cyber breaches. Students will explore common offensive and defensive cybersecurity techniques. Here is a list of lab topics.

- Lab 1: Set up virtual machines for lab use
  Objectives: get familiar with cloud-based virtual lab platform; be exposed to Windows and popular Linux distributions including Redhat(Fedora, CentOS), Kali, Ubuntu and Debian.
- Lab 2: Email phishing and social engineering
  Objectives: explore different ways of sending phishing emails, such as PHP sendmail; play with email filters and try to bypass them; setup a phishing scheme.
- Lab 3: Common web vulnerabilities
  Objectives: explorer common web weaknesses; SQL injection attack; Javascript-based XSS attack; Javascript-based malicious code attack
- Lab 4: Network scanning and sniffing
  Objectives: learn the initial step of hacking - reconnaissance; introduce methods of network scanning and sniffing such as NMAP, Xprobe2, p0f, Wireshark.
- Lab 5: Vulnerability Scanning,
  Objectives: learn methods of penetration test and vulnerability scanning in simulated network; learn tools like Nessus, Nikto, and OpenVAS
- Lab 6: Password cracking
  Objectives: learn password cracking with John the Ripper; learn Cain & Abel on Windows.
- Lab 7: Spoofing and Man-in-the-Middle Attacks
  Objectives: introduce ARP spoofing and man-in-the-middle attacks with Ettercap; introduce IP spoofing and MAC address spoofing;
- Lab 8: Common backdoor attacks
  Objectives: introduce "Swiss Army Knife" Crypcat; backdoor with Crypcat; ICMP-Backdoor; Metasploit to explore common backdoors.
- Lab 9: Intrusion detection system (IDS)
  Objectives: introduce a common open source IDS - Snort; setup and configure Snort.
- Lab 10: Ethical hacking with Kali Linux
  Objectives: learn the hacker's arsenal - Kali Linux which has hundreds of cybersecurity tools; use Kali Linux for penetration test.

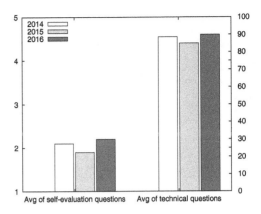

Figure 3: Pre-course survey: Avg of self-evaluation questions (on a scale of 1-5) and Avg of technical questions on prerequisite knowledge (on a scale of 0-100)

5 COURSE EVALUATION

The TDCD model was developed and tested in a cybersecurity course (SAT3812 Cybersecurity I) during the fall semester of 2015 and 2016, with a class of 20 students and 26 students respectively. The authors also taught the same course in Fall 2014 with 16 students by using the traditional method. The group of 2014 was used as a comparison group for course evaluation.

Students were asked to finish a pre-course survey at the beginning of the class to evaluate their technical background for the class of 2014, 2015 and 2016. The pre-course survey consisted of a set of student self-evaluation questions and a set of technical questions to test student's real understanding of prerequisite knowledge. The pre-course survey results were shown in Figure 3. The independent t-tests were performed on pre-course assessment data and shows no significant differences in student background when they entered the course for the class of 2014, 2015 and 2016.

For post-course assessment, the final exam and lab reports were used to evaluate student's accomplishment on content knowledge. There are eight subject areas to assess: 1. cryptography; 2. phishing & web security; 3. access control; 4. IDS & DDoS; 5. firewall; 6. various offensive security methods; 7. various defensive security methods; 8. risk analysis & incident response. The subject of phishing & web security and risk analysis & incident response were not assessed in 2014. The assessment metric is the percentage of students who score 75% or higher. The result is shown in Table 4.

The independent t-tests were performed on assessment data of content knowledge for 2014, 2015 and 2016, and show no significant differences. However, the grand average of assessment data on topic 1-8 shows slight improvement, as illustrated in Figure 4. It is too early to attribute the minor improvement to the new teaching model. However, considering that the new model covers more topics and study cases than the traditional model, the assessment results show that the new model didn't sacrifice student performance for additional content.

Table 4: Assessment of student content knowledge. The metric is the percentage of students who score 75% or higher.

Topic	2016	2015	2014
1. Cryptography	88	81	82
2. Phishing & web security	96	87	N/A
3. Access control	77	87	71
4. IDS & DDoS	77	81	76
5. Firewall	70	61	65
6. Various offensive security methods	96	87	81
7. Various defensive security methods	96	81	77
8. Risk analysis & incident response	65	68	N/A

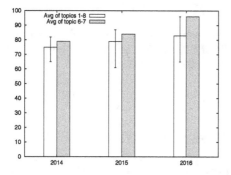

Figure 4: Avg of topic 1-8 (with maximum and minimum value) and avg of topic 6-7 of student content knowledge.

In the final exam, there were a few comprehensive case study questions designed to test student's analytic skills and problem-solving skills. The study cases include covered cases like the Target data breach as well as new cases like Office of Personnel Management data breach in 2015. The exam questions are similiar to what listed in Table 2. The student skills to assess include skills to identify the weakest links in an enterprise network; skills to analyze how the weakest links are exploited by hackers; skills to analyze socio-technical factors in cyber breaches; skills to apply multiple offensive techniques in complex contexts; and skills to apply multiple defensive techniques in complex contexts. The evaluation results of these skills were reflected in Topic 6 and 7 in Table 4 and in Figure 4. Students showed some improvements on assessed analytic skills.

Although further assessment is needed to attribute the improvement of student content knowledge and analytic skills to the new model, feedbacks at the end of the course were very positive as students reported being motivated and actively engaged during classroom and lab activities. Student self-efficacy were also improved as they were more confident in their abilities to tackle complicated cybersecurity breaches. Taken together, these findings demonstrate that the new TDCD model provided a favorable method for delivering cybersecurity content without compromising student performance.

6 CONCLUSION

This paper presents a TDCD teaching model by dissecting recent high-profile cybersecurity breaches to teach cybersecurity courses.

The successful outcome of the proposed project has a potential to re-engineer and transform cybersecurity education. It will change cybersecurity education from traditional bottom-up approach to the new TDCD approach. The new model will help bridge the existing gap between university education and industry need on cybersecurity. With the encouraging initial results, there are still many questions left open as stated in this paper. Therefore, future collaboration is needed to achieve successful innovation in cybersecurity education through the proposed TDCD model.

REFERENCES

[1] CloudPassage. Cloudpassage study finds u.s. universities failing in cybersecurity education, 2016. Available at https://www.cloudpassage.com/company/press-releases/cloudpassage-study-finds-u-s-universities-failing-cybersecurity-education/.
[2] Darkreading. Fewer than one-fourth of cybersecurity job candidates are qualified, 2017. Available at http://www.darkreading.com/vulnerabilities-threats/fewer-than-one-fourth-of-cybersecurity-job-candidates-are-qualified/d/d-id/1328244.
[3] US Senate Report. A kill chain analysis of the 2013 target data breach, 2014.
[4] Wiki. Anthem medical data breach, 2015. Available at https://en.wikipedia.org/wiki/Anthem_medical_data_breach.
[5] Blackhat USA. Lessons from surviving a 300gbps denial of service attack, 2013. Available at https://www.youtube.com/watch?v=w04ZAXftQ_Y.
[6] DDoS Attacks. Mirai IOT bonet, 2016. Available at https://www.incapsula.com/blog/malware-analysis-mirai-ddos-botnet.html.
[7] Ron Sun and Xi Zhang. Top-down versus bottom-up learning in cognitive skill acquisition. *Cogn. Syst. Res.*, 5(1):63–89, 2004.
[8] C. R. Christensen. *Teaching By the Case Method.* Harvard Business School, Boston, Massachusetts, 1981.
[9] Surgey Bratus. What hackers learn that the rest of us don't: Notes on hacker curriculum. *IEEE Security & Privacy*, 5:72–75, 2007.
[10] Zouheir Trabelsi and Walid Ibrahim. Teaching ethical hacking in information security curriculum: A case study. In *Proceedings of the 2013 IEEE Global Engineering Education Conference (EDUCON)*, 2013.
[11] Adam Doupé, Manuel Egele, Benjamin Caillat, Gianluca Stringhini, Gorkem Yakin, Ali Zand, Ludovico Cavedon, and Giovanni Vigna. Hit 'em where it hurts: A live security exercise on cyber situational awareness. In *Proceedings of the 27th Annual Computer Security Applications Conference*, pages 51–61, 2011.
[12] NCCDC. Collegiate Cyber Defense Competition, 2016. Available at http://nationalccdc.org.
[13] Wenliang Du. SEED: Hands-on lab exercises for computer security education. *IEEE Security & Privacy*, 9:70–73, 2011.
[14] Richard S. Weiss, Stefan Boesen, James F. Sullivan, Michael E. Locasto, Jens Mache, and Erik Nilsen. Teaching cybersecurity analysis skills in the cloud. In *Proceedings of the 46th ACM Technical Symposium on Computer Science Education*, pages 332–337, 2015.
[15] Peter A. H. Peterson and Peter L. Reiher. Security exercises for the online classroom with deter. In *Proceedings of the 3rd International Conference on Cyber Security Experimentation and Test*, pages 1–8, 2010.
[16] Randall J. Boyle and Raymond R. Panko. *Corporate Computer Security (4rd Edition)*. Pearson, ISBN-13: 978-0133545197, 2014.
[17] Michael Kassner. Anatomy of the target data breach, 2015. Available at http://www.zdnet.com/article/anatomy-of-the-target-data-breach-missed-opportunities-and-lessons-learned/.
[18] KrebsonSecurity. Verizon security report on target, 2015. Available at https://krebsonsecurity.com/2015/09/inside-target-corp-days-after-2013-breach/.
[19] Mark Zuckerberg Was Hacked Because Passwords Are Hard, 2016. Available at https://theringer.com/mark-zuckerberg-was-hacked-because-hes-bad-at-passwords-3c38514398b6.
[20] Jason Bloomberg. Cybersecurity lessons learned from 'panama papers' breach, 2016. Available at http://www.forbes.com/sites/jasonbloomberg/2016/04/21/cybersecurity-lessons-learned-from-panama-papers-breach/.
[21] Wiki. Openssl heartbleed, 2014. Available at https://en.wikipedia.org/wiki/Heartbleed.
[22] Ransomware locks up San Francisco public transportation ticket machines, 2016. Available at http://arstechnica.com/security/2016/11/san-francisco-muni-hit-by-black-friday-ransomware-attack/.
[23] Wiki. 2014 JPMorgan Chase data breach, 2014. Available at https://en.wikipedia.org/wiki/2014_JPMorgan_Chase_data_breach.
[24] Wiki. SWIFT banking hack, 2016. Available at https://en.wikipedia.org/wiki/2015%E2%80%9316_SWIFT_banking_hack.

The Impact of Virtualized Technology on Undergraduate Computer Networking Education

John Chamberlin, Jason Hussey, Benjamin Klimkowski, William Moody, Christopher Morrell
United States Military Academy
West Point, NY
United States
firstname.lastname@usma.edu

ABSTRACT

Virtualization technology is becoming ubiquitous in the classroom, particularly in the computing fields, and could potentially make technical education more accessible by reducing cost to the student. Does this potential gain come at the costs of quality of education? To understand the drawbacks, if any, of virtualization in the classroom, a network engineering class at an undergraduate institution is taught to two separate groups of students; one group using physical labs for evaluations and lab work, and the other group using virtual networking software. The effectiveness of both classroom teaching methods are compared and evaluated based on the performance of the students and their perceived confidence in the material. Our results indicate that there is no significant difference in student performance or perceived confidence in the course material, supporting the argument that the benefits of virtualization technology in the classroom far outweigh the drawbacks.

KEYWORDS

Computer Science, Computing, Information Technology, Education, Virtualization, Networks, Network Engineering, Pedagogy

1 INTRODUCTION

The rising costs of education in today's society continue to challenge institutions seeking to provide a relevant, applicable learning experience while keeping tuitions manageable. Computer networking education is particularly costly, as it involves investing considerable sums of money into purchasing quality networking hardware and software, as well as man-hours to configure and troubleshoot this infrastructure. With the continued increasing popularity of computer science as a discipline, as well as the dramatic coming-of-age of global cyber warfare, networking education has never been in a higher demand. Consequently, the dramatic coming-of-age of global cyber warfare, networking

SIGITE'17, October 4–7, 2017, Rochester, NY, USA.
ACM ISBN 978-1-4503-5100-3/17/10.
https://doi.org/10.1145/3125659.3125693

education has never been in a higher demand. Consequently, the number of jobs requiring a firm understanding of how computers and information systems communicate will continue to increase, which makes maintaining the accessibility of the requisite educational background paramount. It is, therefore, imperative to explore methods to cost-effectively teach this critical topic while preserving the quality of the educational experience.

The rapid emergence of virtualization in all aspects of education has provided an enticing avenue for cost reduction. Virtual laboratories, while requiring initial overhead to set-up, require less maintenance than physical labs, as well as less equipment in general. In computer science networking education, virtualized networking software has been somewhat ubiquitous for many years. It has been an integral part of the Cisco network training curricula, and many institutions of higher learning have used virtualized technologies such as GNS3 for years. Clearly, there are cost savings to the educator and potentially the student. The focus of our research is to determine if there are measurable drawbacks to the widespread adoption of virtual networking software in the classroom. Specifically, how does the use of virtualized technology impact student outcomes? In addition, our research hopes to shed light on if the students themselves prefer physical lab environment with real equipment or a virtualized environment.

2 BACKGROUND AND RELATED WORK

We conducted our study at the United States Military Academy at West Point, an undergraduate institution with a heavy emphasis on engineering disciplines. At West point, students who are not science, technology, engineering, mathematics (STEM) majors are required to complete an engineering sequence consisting of three classes in an engineering discipline. Recently, our college began offering a cyber sequence as a possible option to fulfill this requirement, which includes a course called Network Engineering and Management, or IT350. Due to the engineering sequence requirement, many students in IT350 come from a variety of non-STEM majors. As this course is also a requirement for the Computer Science and Information Technology majors at our institution, the course presented an opportunity to evaluate the effectiveness of network virtualization software as an instructional tool to a student population with a highly diverse knowledge base.

We seek to compare the quality of virtual networking instruction to that of a traditional, hands-on paradigm that uses real physical equipment, through various quantitative means that we will elucidate. We also examine the student experience in terms of perceived confidence in the course material.

Previous research conducted on virtualization in the classroom shows somewhat contradictory findings on the benefits and drawbacks of virtualization. Xu et al. discuss the advantages and disadvantages of virtual instruction with respect to network security education. While they purport that hands-on learning is indispensable in both acquiring, understanding, and building upon essential concepts, maintaining up-to-date physical infrastructure is both expensive and time consuming. A cloud-based, virtual laboratory platform called V-Lab was used to educate students in network security, and the experimenters conducted surveys to gather information about the students' level of participation, ability to complete assignments, and number of hours spent on assignments. Their results indicated that students using V-Lab were able to participate in more hands-on experiments, spent fewer hours working on assignments, and had a higher overall completion rate [1].

Gaspar et al. discuss the benefits of employing virtualization to make the classroom experience more authentic for computer science and information technology students, as they are often required to administrate their own virtual machine or network to complete the course material. This role is typically absent from most curricula utilizing physical infrastructure due to the cost and scalability issues. In particular, the VNet Lab project that this study focused on seemed to reinforce the benefits of virtualization with respect to network security classes. Costs and consequences due to student mishaps are greatly minimized, while allowing instructors additional levels of control via virtual management environments [2].

D. Brooks conducted a study somewhat similar to ours in terms of structure and methodology, where information technology researchers collected data regarding the effects of the physical classroom environment on student outcomes. An identical course was taught by the same instructor in both a typical classroom environment and an "Active Learning Classroom" (ALC). The ALC is equipped with round tables to facilitate discussion, switchable laptop technology allowing students to project content onto a display at their table, an instructor station linked to two large display screens, and wall-mounted glass marker boards surrounding the perimeter of the room. Student surveys, assignment logs, course grades, and interviews were used to evaluate the effectiveness and enjoyment levels of the new classroom environment. The students in the ALC classroom outperformed their peers by a significant margin, supporting the assertion that the physical environment of the classroom can have a profound effect on learning outcomes, independent of other variables [3].

Nedic et al. introduced NetLab, a virtual environment that allows a student to interact with real laboratory equipment remotely. It also allows real experimental data to be transferred back to the student on the remote end for further analysis. NetLab was evaluated with a test group of students, who were asked via surveys to compare and contrast their experienced to that of using a physical laboratory. The responses indicated that students generally enjoyed the virtual lab more than the physical lab because it allowed them the convenience of working at home or elsewhere, eliminated the need to familiarize themselves with the physical operation of the lab equipment, and allowed them to repeat experiments that they had conducted by booking timeslots. Students however also indicated that the NetLab experience was not similar to conducting the experiments in a real lab. Also, the interface itself took some time to master [4].

Weyang Zhu, a professor at a smaller university, evaluated the practicality of using Virtual Machines running on cloud based Amazon EC2 services as a "hands-on" approach to a Computer Networking class in contrast to the students running multiple virtual machines (VMs) on a single host locally. The students were anonymously surveyed during the course and asked if they preferred using the cloud based virtual machines. The majority of students indicated that the virtual cloud-based network environment was preferable to that of the local machines in the campus network for several reasons: the VMs allowed them to work remotely and at any time, they were able to truly simulate a disparate network infrastructure with latency separation, and they were not limited by the administrative policies of the campus network [5].

Aliane et al. discuss the drawbacks of remote virtual laboratories on learning and student outcomes, specifically highlighting the lack of collaborative learning that hands-on work in an actual lab tends to facilitate. They also discuss the effects on student motivation and the lack of familiarization with lab equipment, which is significant in that students who are taught computer networking in a purely virtual environment will not have the same experience with manipulating a physical router or switch [6].

Lastly, Jianping Pan argued that the traditional, hands-on lab experience when teaching computer networks is indispensable for effective student outcomes, while virtualization adds an unnecessary abstraction layer to the learning process and incurs additional instructor overhead for little benefit to the student. He addresses the cost and time investment issues common with physical network infrastructure by designing a practical network for experimentation using cheap, off-the-shelf products and open-source software. The students were surveyed and indicated a significant increase in satisfaction with the course while the instructors noted a significant increase in average grades. Additionally, the overhead cost of the course was calculated at roughly $100 per student [7].

Given the many perspectives on virtualization in the classroom and its effectiveness, we were excited to have the opportunity to evaluate two diverse groups of students in the same computer networking class side-by-side, one with virtual labs and the other with physical. We procced with the premise that virtualized instruction is less expensive than a hands-on experience, such as in a laboratory or, in our case, using actual networking equipment in the lab setting. This premise has been well demonstrated in previous studies, which explored the cost effectiveness of virtual instructional techniques.

3 COURSE STRUCTURE AND TEACHING METHODOLOGY

The academic course "Network Engineering and Design" is a 40-lesson undergraduate course taught at our institution to approximately 150 students per academic year. This course is required for the Information Technology majors, is one of two required networking electives for Computer Science majors, and the second of three courses in the Cyber Security Engineering sequence. Each semester approximately half of the students come from non-engineering majors, and are enrolled under the auspices of the sequence.

This course addresses the analysis, design, building, and testing of modern computer networks. Network implementation techniques and considerations are discussed and practiced extensively. Key concepts include analysis and design using standardized network models, protocols and practices such as the Open Systems Interconnect (OSI) network model, sub-netting, static/dynamic routing, switching, and access control. Practical skills implementing network designs are also reinforced through a number of hands-on laboratory exercises using commodity network hardware.

Course objectives are the following:

1. Demonstrate technical proficiency in network engineering.
2. Design, model and install a network infrastructure.
3. Secure a network infrastructure by implementing access controls.
4. Develop alternatives to solve a network engineering problem.

Students demonstrate understanding and mastery of course and lesson objectives by the completion of three in-class examinations, two out of class laboratory assignments, and a final group project. This group of graded events comprises 75% of the total points students can earn for the semester. The remaining points consist of small individual homework assignments and discretionary points award by the instructor for participation, preparation, and effort.

The three in-class examinations are given following the end of the major sections of the course. Those sections are network routing, network switching, and network security. Each section includes lectures, textbook readings, homework assignments, and ungraded in-class exercises.

Additionally, an individual lab project is completed by the students for the routing and switching sections, the security section has an extended multi-day group in-class exercise. Lab assignments require students to design a network according to a given specification, implement the network according to their design, and finally test the functionality of the network running a prescribed list of validation checks. Students generally have two weeks to complete this assignment, including a few classroom hours designated as work periods. Students submit a formal lab report as an artifact of the work completed.

The group final project is the comprehensive, culminating event for the semester. This project is significantly more difficult than the previous lab assignments, includes the network security facets not yet evaluated in a lab project, and includes multiple update briefings to the instructor and classmates throughout the process. The project covers the final three weeks of the semester and all remaining classroom time is dedicated to this project. Groups are made up of two or three students each and are determined by the course director based on previous course performance.

4 EXPERIMENTAL DESIGN

4.1 Sample Selection.

In order to understand the impact that different laboratory environments can have on computer network education, we designed and executed a semester long experiment in the spring of 2017 classes of Network Engineering and Design taught at our institution. The experiment involved pre-determined pools of students completing all laboratory assignments and the final group project in either a virtualized network environment or in the physical classroom lab environment.

A total of 45 students were enrolled in three sections of the course with two different instructors. Each section was divided into equally-sized pools designated as virtual or physical. Students then completed both labs and the final project in that respective learning environment. Each assignment was identical with regards to the learning objectives, the performance tasks, and the network to build, but had slight variations as needed to account for the platform.

Students assigned to the virtual group built their networks in Cisco Packet Tracer 7 [8]. This software is available from Cisco Networking Academy as part of their free Packet Tracer 101 course. Enrollment and completion of this introductory course was an early homework assignment for all students.

The physical implementation pool students completed the labs and group project using multiple physical Cisco 2900 series routers and Cisco 3560 switches available in the classroom. Each desk in the networking classrooms is assigned two routers and two switches, has an Apple Mac Mini Computer, and a patch panel connection to the devices. With this equipment, students are able to connect Ethernet patch cables to build their network and configure it with the Mac Mini. Each station has multiple uplinks to the internal academic network that belongs to our academic department.

Though students only complete their labs and final project in the network platform specified, all students get exposed to both environments throughout the semester. Thirteen homework assignments are completed using Cisco Packet Tracer by all students. Additionally, six lessons are dedicated to physical in-class-exercises where all students follow step-by-step instructions to build introductory networks using the classroom physical switches, routers, and workstations.

In order to build comparable experiment groups in each section, the student's academic major and incoming Cumulative Grade Point Average (CQPA), which is our institution's close equivalent to the Grade Point Average (GPA), were used to equally sized, experienced, and academic performance as possible. The breakdown of students per classroom section, per network implementation pool and the mean academic GPA can be seen in Table 1.

Table 1: Incoming CQPA of Students per Lab Type

Number of Students	Lab Type	Mean CQPA
20	Physical	3.20
23	Virtual	3.13

Data on student performance was collected in the form of raw scores and survey. Raw scores were recorded after each laboratory assignment, final project, and in class examination. Surveys were distributed to all students throughout the semester to collect data on their performance. An initial survey focused on their background with networking, experience with hands-on hobbies or activities, and their anticipated performance in the class. After each lab assignment and the final project surveys focused on the most recent assignment and the previous in class examination. Questions focused on availability to the equipment, comfort level with the material, time spent completing the assignment, and likelihood of voluntarily taking additional network classes.

4.2 Measurements.

For this study there are two types of metrics we gathered: academic results and survey responses. Academic results came from hands-on lab assignments and mid-term examinations. Self-reported survey data was gathered via an online survey research platform.

We examined academic results from each major graded event individually as well as the students' overall, aggregate performance. The first lab assignment concentrates on practical application of computer network routing protocols. The second lab assignment exposes students to computer network switching. The first two mid-terms evaluated students on the concepts associated with each of these first two labs respectively. The third mid-term is focused on the topic of cyber security. There is no lab assignment dedicated solely to this topic, however the cyber security concepts in computer networking are incorporated into the final, culminating project.

In order to establish a baseline performance potential for each student, we used the students' incoming CQPA. A Pearson correlation test reveals that a student's incoming CQPA is highly correlated to their overall academic performance in the Network Engineering and Design course. For the students in the sample set, the Pearson correlation coefficient is $\rho=0.648$ with $p=0.000$, indicating strong, though not perfect, correlation. Thus, we accept this metric as a valid predictor of a student's performance in the course but recognize other factors, such as whether they are using the physical or virtual lab infrastructure, contribute to their ultimate academic performance.

Accepting the incoming CQPA as a prediction of a student's performance in our course, we sought to establish a metric that would allow us to compare each student's relative performance based on their incoming CQPA. First, we translate the percentages of earned points in our course to a 4.33-GPA scale, giving us a course QPA. Next, we calculate the ratio between a student's performance in our course and their incoming CQPA to gauge this relative performance. We call this metric the *grade ratio*. A grade ratio of greater than 1.0 would indicate that the student performed better than his or her past performance would predict. If the grade ratio was less than 1.0, the student would have failed to perform as well in our course as their incoming CQPA would predict.

In other words, if a student enters the course with a 3.0 CQPA and earns a 3.5 in the course, they have a grade ratio of 1.17. This represents a historically B student earning a B+ in the Network Engineering and Design course. We then examine the grade ratio for each of our lab groups to assess whether the infrastructure type, physical or virtual, has any correlation to how students perform on major graded assessments.

After each major lab assignment, to include the final project, we administered an online survey to all of the students. Responses were voluntary. The survey solicited responses from the students concerning the number of hours they spent on the assignment and the overall ease of use of their respective lab environments, either physical or virtual. Students answered multiple questions about their lab environment's ease of use that had slight variations from one another. Their responses were then averaged on the Likert scale to form a composite ease of use score for each lab assignment.

The initial survey at the start of class differed slightly from this format in that it gathered background information from students relating to their preference of learning styles and baseline knowledge in computing and computer networking. Likewise, the final survey asked students to report additional information as compared to the post-lab surveys, primarily the student's overall confidence in designing, implementing, and operating computer networks in the future.

5 RESULTS AND DISCUSSION

All analysis was completed using Minitab® 17.2.1 [9].

5.1 Lab Assignment Performance

5.1.1 Results and Analysis. Mean percentages for major graded assignments were compared between the two groups using a two-sample t-test. We evaluated the differences between percentages achieved on the practical application assignments, written mid-term examinations, and the aggregate of the two. The results are summarized in Table 2.

Table 2: Major Graded Assignment Percentage-Earned Analysis

	Labs	Exams	Total
GRADE_PHYS	0.898	0.819	0.864
-			
GRADE_VIRT	0.873	0.808	0.845
= GRADE_DIFF			
	0.025	0.011	0.019
P-value	0.398	0.682	0.464

5.1.2 Discussion. No significant difference exists for percentage of points earned on major graded assignments. Students in the physical lab group tended to earn higher raw scores on the labs and exams than their counterparts in the virtual lab group did, though the advantage is small and statistically insignificant. The physical group did have a higher average incoming CQPA, but only slightly. These results indicate that neither group was disadvantaged by being assigned to the virtual or physical lab infrastructure.

5.2 Grade Ratios

5.2.1 Results and Analysis. To account for the small difference in the average incoming CQPAs for each group, grade ratios were compared using a two-sample t test. We evaluated the differences between scores achieved on the practical application assignments, written mid-term examinations, and the total of the two. The results are summarized in Table 3.

Table 3: CQPA Deltas Analysis

	Labs	Exams	Total
ΔCQPA_PHYS	1.141	0.874	1.027
-			
ΔCQPA_VIRT	1.092	0.869	0.997
=			
RATIO_DIFF	0.049	0.005	0.030
p-value	0.588	0.943	0.668

5.2.2 Discussion. There is no statistically significant difference in the students' grade ratios for the labs or the exams, and thus none for the total of the two. The average grade ratio for the physical group was 1.027 while the virtual group achieved a grade ratio of 0.997 with p=0.668. This indicates that both groups achieved almost exactly what was expected of them, based on their incoming CQPA, with no statistically significant difference between the two lab environments.

5.3 Hours Spent Per Lab and Post-Course Confidence

5.3.1 Results and Analysis. Students reported an estimated number of hours per assignment. We average these across the course and compare them with a two-sample t test. The results are presented in Table 4. Additionally, we present a visual depiction in Figure 1 of the 95% confidence interval for the mean hours reported per assignment grouped by lab infrastructure type.

For the final survey after completion of the course, students reported their confidence in their ability to correctly set up and configure computer networks in the future. The average of these responses is compared with a two-sample t test. The results are summarized in Table 5.

Table 4: Average Hours per Hands-On Assignment Grouped By Lab Infrastructure Type

N	Lab Type	Average Hours Reported Per Lab
7	Physical	9.10
9	Virtual	6.33

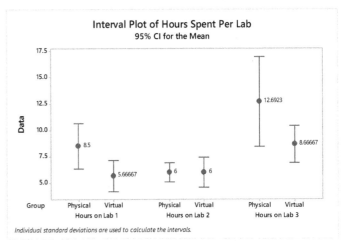

Figure 1: Interval Plot of Student-Reported Hours Spent Per Lab Assignment Grouped by Lab Environment

Table 5: Post Course Confidence

	End-of-Course
CONFIDENCE_PHYS	3.000
-	
CONFIDENCE_VIRT	3.333
=	
CONFIDENCE_DIFF	-0.333
P-value	0.134

5.3.2 Discussion. Students, on average, reported spending 2.76 hours more per lab assignment in the physical lab environment that their peers in the virtual lab environments. The number of respondents that answered these questions across all three surveys was 7 and 9 for the physical and virtual groups respectively. Due to this low sample size, we did not conclude that the physical environment will always require more time of students, but the large effect size is noteworthy. The increase in reported time might be partially explained by the physical group's students' perceptions; having to be present physically in the lab was seen as laborious to many of the students whose peers in the virtual sections could conduct their work from anywhere they desired.

There was no statistical significance between lab groups in their average confidence in setting up and configuring computer networks. The average confidence for the physical group was a 3.0, which translates to "somewhat confident" while the virtual group's 3.33 is between "somewhat confident" and "extremely confident." We conclude that no lab environment provided students with more confidence than the other; both groups report a similar level of confidence after having completed the course.

6   CONCLUSION AND FUTURE WORKS

6.1 Conclusion. Our goal was to evaluate the differences, if any, in student performance, end-of-course confidence, and time spent working on the Network Design and Engineering course between two groups: one using physical lab equipment and the other using virtual lab software. Based on our results, we conclude that there is no significant difference in either student performance or post-course confidence in the material, based on measured CQPA ratios from graded events and end-of-course surveys, between the two groups. Additionally, while students reported spending more time on the physical labs than the virtual labs, the difference was not statistically significant.

Given the expenses involved in constructing, maintaining, and utilizing computer networking labs with relevant, state-of-the-art hardware, it is crucial to ensure that these expenses are justified in terms of quantifiable student outcomes. Prior research in virtualization technology for the purposes of education, as indicated previously, shows contradictory results—while some studies suggest that the hands-on physical laboratory experience is indispensable, others indicate that students prefer the convenience and advantage afforded by a virtual lab, and in some cases even outperformed those using physical equipment.

If, as our conclusions suggest, the difference in student performance, workload, and confidence is insignificant when virtual labs are utilized in place of physical ones, then a compelling argument can be made for the continued adoption of virtual lab technology in computer networking classes. While some research shows measurable benefits from the collaborative and "real" experience offered by physical labs, the costs of these labs are, as with all educational costs, eventually absorbed by the student. Given the increasing costs of education at large, combined with the continued ubiquity of computing and network technology in all aspects of society, it is imperative that we, as educators, endeavor to make technical education as accessible as possible. This is doubly true for public institutions, such as high schools, that may not have access to the wealth of resources of major colleges and universities. Furthermore, by eliminating large sunken costs, institutions are better positioned to adapt to new releases of network products, enabling students to learn on the most up-to-date technologies.

6.2 Future Works. Our study was limited to students enrolled in our Network Engineering course, which had a total enrollment of 43 students. We are encouraged by our findings and would like to see our study extended to a similar course with a larger enrollment size to either validate our findings, or allow us to perform a contrasting analysis on methodology if the outcomes should differ. It would also be of value to repeat this experiment on classes consisting of entirely of Computer Science/Information Technology majors, in order to assess if technically-oriented

students respond more favorably to virtualization technology. Additionally, while we based our study on the outcomes of major graded events from two groups of students using virtual and physical labs, some of the minor classroom events for the virtual group involved hands-on work with networking equipment. This was part of the standard course curriculum and, while we do not feel that this unduly influenced our results, we would be interested in conducting a similar study where the virtual lab group received no exposure to physical lab equipment whatsoever.

Lastly, further studies comparing and contrasting the effectiveness of virtualization in other STEM disciplines, such as physics, chemistry or other lab-intensive fields could further elucidate the advantages or disadvantages of either approach.

ACKNOWLEDGEMENTS

The authors would like to give thanks to our department's Computer Support Group for their consistent and timely support. In addition, a special thanks to Dr. Nicholas Olijnyk at the West Point Dean's office for his assistance in helping us get our research up and running.

REFERENCES

[1] Le Xu, Dijiang Huang, and Wei-Tek Tsai. 2014. Cloud-Based Virtual Laboratory for Network Security Education. *IEEE Transactions on Education.* Vol. 57, No. 3 (Aug. 2014), 145-150. DOI:http://dx.doi.org/10.1109/ TE.2013.2282285

[2] A. Gaspar, S. Langevin, W. Armitage, R. Sekar, T. Daniels. 2008. The Role of Virtualization in Computing Education. *In Proceedings of the 39th ACM SIGCSE Technical Symposium on Computer Science Education (SIGCSE '08).* ACM Press, New York, NY, 131-132. DOI:http://dx.doi.org/10.1145/ 1352135.1352181

[3] D. Christopher Brooks. 2010. Space Matters: The Impact of Formal Learning Environments on Student Learning. *British Journal of Educational Technology.* Vol. 42, No. 5 (Sep. 2011), 719-726. DOI:http://dx.doi.org/ 10.1145/ 1352135.1352181

[4] Zorica Nedic, Jan Machotka, and Andrew Nafalski. 2003, Remote Laboratories Versus Virtual and Real Laboratories. In proceedings of the 33rd ASEE/IEEE Annual Frontiers in Education Conference (FIE '03). Boulder, CO. T3E-1-T3E-6. DOI:http://dx.doi.org/ 10.1109/FIE.2003.1263343

[5] Weyang Zhu. 2015. Hands-On Network Programming Projects in the Cloud. In Proceedings of the 46th ACM SIGCSE Technical Symposium on Computer Science Education (SIGCSE '15). ACM Press, New York, NY, 326-331. DOI:http://dx.doi.org/ 10.1145/2676723.2677257

[6] Nourdine Aliane, Rafael Pastor, and Gonzalo Mariscal. 2010. Limitations of Remote Laboratories in Control Engineering Education. *Journal of Extension* (iJOE) Vol. 6, Issue 1, (Feb. 2010), 31-33. DOI:http://dx.doi.org/ 10.3991/ijoe.v6il.1131

[7] Jianping Pan. 2010. Teaching Computer Networks in a Real Network: The Technical Perspectives. *In Proceedings of the 41th ACM SIGCSE Technical Symposium on Computer Science Education (SIGCSE '10).* ACM Press, New York, NY, 133-137. DOI:http://dx.doi.org/10.1145/1734263.1734311

[8] Cisco Systems, Inc. (2010). Cisco Packet Tracer (Version 7) [Software]. Available from https://www.netacad.com/about-networking-academy/packet-tracer/

[9] Minitab, Inc. (2009). Minitab 17 Statistical Software (Version 17.2.1) [Software]. Available from http://www.minitab.com/

Teaching Responsive Web Design to Novice Learners

Karen H. Jin
Department of Applied Engineering and Sciences
University of New Hampshire
Manchester, NH 03101
karen.jin@unh.edu

ABSTRACT

Although responsive web design has become a standard industrial requirement in recent years, it is rarely emphasized in introductory courses on web front-end development. This paper presents an integration of responsive web design topics with the traditional HTML/CSS content in an introductory course designed for non-CS major students. By working with technologies appropriate for novice learners, students with no programming experience are able to create modern-looking, user-friendly responsive websites as well as to improve their abstract thinking skills. Students' experience in software development principles and tools within the context of web development also has a positive impact on their overall confidence in computing related fields.

KEYWORDS

computing education; web development; responsive web design; novice learners

1 INTRODUCTION

Web systems are among the most important disciplines of information technology. A recent study by the Bureau of Labor Statistics estimates that the employment growth for web developers is the highest among all computing occupations projected for 2014-2024 [4]. Meanwhile, as an inherently interdisciplinary subject, web front-end development offers a unique introductory path to computing for those who might not be interested in traditional programming courses.

Introduction to web development courses typically teach students how to build static websites with HTML and CSS. Since no prior programming knowledge is required, these courses often attract a diverse body of students, including high school students and college non-CS majors. Recent studies indicate that in some states, web development courses are among the most attended computing classes in public high schools [5]. HTML/CSS is the second most commonly taught language in our state high schools, and 40% of students

SIGITE'17, October 4-7, 2017, Rochester, NY, USA
© 2017 Association for Computing Machinery.
ACM ISBN ISBN 978-1-4503-5100-3/17/10. . . $15.00
https://doi.org/http://dx.doi.org/10.1145/3125659-3125684

enrolled in all web development classes are female. At the college-level, web development courses are also popular among non-CS majors, as they are used to fulfill computing related general education requirements.

Furthermore, an important aspect of teaching web development is to provide students with an experience in software development practices, as well as to foster their basic computational thinking. Research shows that learning to build a static website with HTML and CSS can be used as an opportunity to gain basic computing skills [1, 7]. Although HTML and CSS are markup languages with limited computational expressive power compared to other languages like JavaScript, students are still presented with typical computational activities such as coding and debugging [3].

The growing popularity of mobile technologies presents web development courses with new challenges and opportunities. For the first time in October 2016, mobile devices were used more than desktop computers for web browsing as smartphone and tablet usage overtook desktop usage [6]. Modern websites must be mobile-friendly, so that a single web page can provide users with an optimal experience on both desktops and mobile devices. As a consequence, Responsive Web Design (RWD) has been defined as the application of standard-based technologies to create websites that are transformable to fit users' browsing needs, and has become the de facto standard for web front-end design. RWD has gained support from many industry leaders and has been used to enhance mobile web design everywhere including in higher education [2]. In spite of this prevalence of responsive websites, RWD is not yet commonly taught in introductory web development courses, and widely used web development tools and responsive frameworks are rarely covered. Accordingly, websites created by the students often look outdated and clunky, and the webpages designed for desktops often do not render well on mobile devices, to the point of sometime becoming unusable.

Teaching RWD enables students to build modern-looking, mobile-friendly websites. Despite their limited programming experience, most students are motivated to build websites that resemble those they regularly use on their own mobile devices. Being able to achieve this goal creates a sense of accomplishment and boosts their confidence in the field of computing. More importantly, integrated RWD content provides students with a more in-depth experience in problem solving and understanding of software development principles compared to the traditional coverage of HTML/CSS.

This paper presents the design of an introductory web development course that encompasses modern responsive web front-end technologies. The course is built as a single semester general education course for non-CS majors. Two RWD strategies, both appropriate for novice learners, are integrated with basic HTML and CSS content. The first strategy involves hard-coding responsiveness using the CSS3 flexbox and media query features. The second strategy leverages the W3.CSS framework towards a simple yet powerful responsive design. Various development tools and third-party CSS style libraries are also used throughout the course. A primary objective of the course is to enable students with limited programming experience to improve their understanding of basic computing concepts and software development practices through the coverage of RWD content.

2 RESPONSIVE WEB SOLUTIONS IN AN INTRO COURSE

One of the most appealing aspects of RWD is that it creates websites with user-friendly content and layout that can "respond" to various screen sizes, achieving optimal user experience across many devices. Teaching industry-standard RWD technologies and tools can better engage this generation of digital-native students through building more user-friendly and professional-looking responsive websites.

However, designing a RWD-integrated curriculum can be challenging especially when targeting students with limited computing background. Even in a course that covers only HTML and CSS, many students have difficulties understanding basic web development workflow, find it hard to become proficient with the development environment and can struggle with HTML/CSS language syntax. Working with RWD generally requires more in-depth understanding of computing concepts and development skills. Therefore, it is important to select suitable technologies, tools and frameworks among a plethora of choices, and in particular to take into account the limited background knowledge and programming ability of the students.

The chosen RWD topics should enable students to build a responsive website, yet remain simple enough that they do not incur a steep learning curve and an excessive workload. Being for many students their first computing course, it should also provide them with a positive and empowering opportunity to hone their abstract thinking skills and to discover important aspects of software development. Accordingly, the selected RWD content for an introductory course in web front-end development should:

- require only basic knowledge of HTML and CSS in order to accommodate students with no programming background;
- rely on simple yet powerful responsive technologies to allow students to build websites on par with what they use everyday on their own mobile devices;
- improve students' abstract thinking skills and understanding of software development practices.

In the following sections, key HTML/CSS concepts important for preparing students for RWD content are first discussed. Next, two responsive design strategies are introduced. The first one uses the CSS media query and flexbox features with external style sheets. The flexbox model layout, which enables a more convenient control of page layout compared with more traditional models, is combined with media queries so one can apply different page layouts on a same web page using queries on device sizes.

The second strategy leverages a CSS responsive framework, W3.CSS framework, to build automatically responsive webpages. HTML elements are applied with pre-defined CSS framework classes, which involves less CSS coding effort but requires a good understanding of the framework design. Students are also introduced to web development tools and other third-party CSS libraries that facilitate the development process. Students learn to apply basic software development practices such as structural design, debugging, incremental development, and code reuse. Moreover, abstract thinking skills are emphasized in problem solving of responsive design related challenges throughout the course.

2.1 Key concepts of HTML and CSS

The selected RWD content requires only basic knowledge of HTML and CSS. Nonetheless, the following topics need to be discussed prior to the introduction of the two RWD strategies. These topics, along with their underlying abstract computing concepts and software development practices, are necessary to prepare students for subsequent material.

- HTML element hierarchy: a structure abstraction.

The discussion of HTML language in introductory courses typically focuses on tags and language syntax. It is, however, essential to emphasize the HTML element hierarchy structure, also known as the Document Object Model (DOM) early on. The understanding of how HTML elements relate to each other, in the form of parent, child and sibling, are important in applying more advanced CSS features such as flexbox.

Students tend to focus on how a web page looks rather than its underlying structure as a hierarchy tree. Constructing such a tree structure is harder than learning various HTML tags since it involves abstract thinking and modeling. Activities such as hand-drawing the tree and inspecting the HTML DOM using a web browser's development tool are helpful to reinforce this understanding. Students should also practice using <div> tags to manipulate the HTML page structure without necessarily changing its appearance.

- CSS class selector: a style abstraction.

The CSS class selector is the most versatile CSS selectors. Class selectors are widely used in CSS frameworks and third-party libraries. Students should know that a CSS class selector provides an abstraction for a set of styling rules. Also, a many-to-many relationship applies between CSS class selectors and HTML elements. That is, an HTML element can be associated with multiple CSS classes, and a CSS class selector can be applied to multiple HTML elements.

- CSS external style sheet: software modularity.

While it is often convenient to introduce CSS using internal style or inline style embedded within the same HTML file, students should be able to define an external style sheet and import it into an HTML page using the **<link>** element. External style sheets not only are essential in the implementation of the responsive strategies discussed later, but also serve as an excellent example to introduce basic software development concepts such as code modularity, separation of concerns, code reuse and maintenance. Working with external CSS style sheets, students learn to view a website as a basic software system with relationships among multiple modules.

2.2 RWD with CSS Media Query + Flexbox

A first RWD strategy suitable for novice learners uses CSS media queries and flexbox features. CSS Flexible Box, or flexbox, is used to specify individual layouts for different screen sizes. Media queries are then applied to implement the page responsiveness so that layouts are conditioned on the size of the viewing screen.

Flexbox layout model

Flexbox is a CSS3 layout model that enables a convenient layout design. An HTML element, typically a **<div>** element, can become a flex container by setting its display property as **display:flex**. The position and size of elements within the flex container' will be auto-adjusted to fill the available space in the best possible way on various screen sizes. Flexbox is particularly useful to change display orientation, resize, re-order elements, or stretch and shrink element display, making it well suited for the needs of small to medium scale websites. For example, the following HTML code:

```
<div class="content">
  <div>
      <img src="one.jpg" alt="#">
      <p>One</p>
  </div>
  <div class="section">
      <img src="two.jpg" alt="#">
      <p>Two</p>
  </div>
  <div>
      <img src="three.jpg" alt="#">
      <p>Three</p>
  </div>
</div>
```

can be rendered differently by applying flexbox styles in various ways as shown in Figure 1.

Figure 1-(a) is the original layout without flexbox. Figure 1-(b) shows the layout after the **.content** class is set to a flexbox container with the default horizontal alignment. By simply adding one line of code, the three images are flipped to be displayed in a row. Figure 1-(c) shows a more complex layout designed that sets both **.content** and **.section** containers as flexbox containers and uses the **flex-direction** property to reverse the order of their children elements.

The flexbox model can be introduced after students have learned basic HTML tags, HTML element tree structure (DOM) and CSS selectors. Compared to older CSS layout models such as **float** or **inline-block**, the flexbox model

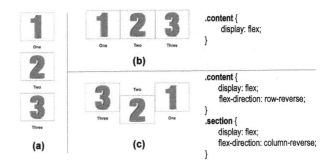

Figure 1: Using CSS flexbox to control HTML element layout.

makes it much easier to control both the horizontal and vertical alignment of HTML elements.

Working with flexbox is a good practice to improve students' abstract thinking and debugging skills. A solid understanding of HTML structural hierarchy and the parent/child/sibling relationships are essential to correctly set up the proper parent element as a flex container and its children elements as flex elements. Students often need to deal with logic errors associated with the HTML element tree structure, e.g., a misplaced ending **<div>** tag.

CSS Media Query

Media query is a RWD technique introduced in CSS3. Media queries are used to implement responsive layout design various screen sizes by limiting the scope of CSS styles by applying different media features such as screen width and height. Media queries can be applied with only a few extra lines of code. For example, the code below

```
<link rel="stylesheet"
   media="screen and (max-width:480px)" href="small.css">
<link rel="stylesheet"
   media="screen and (min-width:481px)" href="large.css">
```

uses media queries to set the screen size breakpoint to 480px. Of the two external style sheets, **small.css** and **large.css**, only one will be applied depending on whether the screen width is less than 480px or larger than 480px. Thus, the same page will be rendered differently, using layouts defined in the two style sheets.

Figure 2 shows an example of how the two different style sheets render an HTML page using user-friendly layouts on two devices. CSS flexbox is used in implementing the two different layouts. For example, the three content blocks are arranged in a row on a larger screen and the flexbox's flex-direction property is set as row display. On a smaller screen, the same content is displayed in a column and the page navigation bar is repositioned under the title image for a more convenient viewing experience.

The responsive strategy based on media queries requires only basic knowledge of HTML and CSS. Using external style sheets, media queries provide a solution of responsive page

Figure 2: Simple responsive design implemented with CSS media query and flexbox.

design appropriate for beginners. Even though the common usage of embedding media queries in an internal CSS style sheet involves less code duplication, it tends to cause CSS errors that are hard to resolve. Instead, defining the context of the media query breakpoints in separate style files reduces CSS rule conflicts. Under such a setting, students can implement simple responsive pages that consist of a number of queries and breakpoints, and apply appropriate style sheets for user-friendly layouts on different devices.

Learning media queries reinforces students' abstract thinking skills and understanding of software development practices. By working with media queries, students are required not only to reinforce their understanding of HTML element tree structure, but also to understand the basic concept of boolean logic and program control. For example, a media query with more than one breakpoint can be written as a screen width condition using the logic operator *and*:

```
<link rel="stylesheet"
  media=
  "screen␣and␣(min−width:481px)␣and␣(max−width:819px)"
  href="medium.css">
```

Such code is analogous to a "switch" statement, providing alternative behaviors in terms of CSS styles given the screen width. Debugging media queries often involves solving program control flow issues such as condition boundaries or faulty fall-through cases.

Media queries with external style sheets also reinforce the concepts of software modularity and separation of concerns. The process of implementing responsive webpages with media queries requires students' abilities to work with multiple software modules as layout designs for different sizes of devices are specified in separate style files.

2.3 RWD with W3.CSS Framework

A CSS framework consists of prepared CSS style sheets, tools and libraries that allow the easy development of modern and standard-compliant web design. The W3.CSS framework was developed by W3Schools (www.w3schools.com) using

Google's Material Design guidelines. It includes a responsive layout system that makes responsive design easier to implement compared to using media queries. W3.CSS stands out among hundreds of other CSS frameworks (e.g., Bootstrap) as a good choice for introductory courses because of its small size and smooth learning curve. It consists of a single CSS style sheet written with standard CSS without Javascript or jQuery, and thus is less intimidating to students.

The W3.CSS framework can be downloaded locally, or used from online directly by adding a single line of code in the HTML file:

```
<link rel="stylesheet"
  href="https://www.w3schools.com/w3css/4/w3.css">
```

Creating responsive layouts with W3.CSS involves using only a few framework classes to set the proper HTML elements as responsive containers (e.g., with **w3-row** class) or responsive elements (e.g., with **w3-half** or **w3-third** classes). For example, the following code creates a responsive layout with two content blocks that will be automatically scaled and displayed either side by side on a larger screen, or in a column on a smaller screen.

```
<div class="w3−row">
  <div class="w3−half">
    <h2>half of the page content</h2>
  </div>
  <div class="w3−half">
    <h2>another half of the page content</h2>
  </div>
</div>
```

W3.CSS provides novice learners with a simple yet powerful responsive solution. Learning W3.CSS after their previous experience with CSS media queries and flexbox features benefits students in several ways. First, they have a better understanding of W3.CSS framework and other web development frameworks in general. They are able to compare two different responsive implementation strategies: flexible and creative design possibilities with hand-coding of media queries vs. convenient and standard built-in responsiveness with W3.CSS.

Moreover, working with W3.CSS helps develop their software development skills as a website becomes more complex with multiple modules. Instead of creating their own CSS styles, students learn to reuse third-party code to jumpstart their development productivity. Besides its responsive layouts, W3.CSS offers a wide range of style design, typography, color classes, and other style classes such as animations and image effects, with which students are able to create impressive modern webpages with minimal effort.

Finally, W3.CSS is an excellent opportunity for students to work independently through active learning activities. Working with W3.CSS involves self-directed activities such as searching online documentation, learning from examples and tailoring templates to fit their own design needs. Students build their ability to develop understanding and master the material independently, which is particularly important in the field of ever-evolving computing technologies.

2.4 Web Development Tools

The use of web development tools is included as an essential component of the course content. Properly selected tools can ease the learning curve and facilitate the web development process for students with limited programming background. Among many choices, several tools that are appropriate to support RWD in introductory courses are listed below:

- **Text editor**: Sublime Text. It is a free cross-platform text editor. Syntax errors are highlighted with color-coding. Its auto-completion feature makes it easy to remember CSS style attributes and value names. Its "View in Browser" feature helps avoid the common beginner's mistake of viewing and editing different versions.

- **Developer tools**: Chrome DevTools. Its Element View feature helps visualize the hierarchical structure of HTML. Its CSS Box visualization is an excellent tool for learning and debugging CSS box model properties. Multiple mobile device simulators are available to evaluate responsiveness.

- **Responsiveness testing tools**: Many online services offer testing environments of a large range of mobile devices.
(e.g., `responsivewebdesigntester.com`)

- **Code validator**: HTML/CSS validators reveal hidden syntax errors and are particularly helpful in debugging.

- **Code formatter**: HTML/CSS beautifiers auto format code following standard coding style and they are also helpful in spotting syntax errors.

- **Other third party CSS libraries** : The Font Awesome icon library and the Google API fonts provide students with a wide range of modern, easy to use icons and font styles.

3 EVALUATION

An initial evaluation was designed to gauge the learning experience of students with limited programming background in working with RWD related content. The main evaluation questions are 1) What were their attitude and experience working with RWD and development tools? 2) How did the RWD content relate to students' confidence in their abilities to learn more about web development and computing in general?

A questionnaire survey was conducted in an introductory web development course designed for non-CS majors all over campus. 75% of the students enrolled in the course reported that they had none or very minimal programming experience prior taking the course. In Spring 2017, 32 students completed the course. Among them, 16 (50%) were females and 25 (78%) were non-CS majors. Students responded to the voluntary online questionnaire administered out of class at the end of the semester. Some questions were also asked during the semester to obtain a repeated observation. The detailed evaluation results are discussed below.

1. Students consider learning RWD, W3.CSS and development tools important.

Two five-level Likert scale items are used to measure stu-

dents' perception of the importance of RWD technologies and development tools. As shown in Figure 3, the 24 responses are heavily skewed toward "strongly agree", indicating that most students considered learning RWD and the usage of tools important in building their own websites.

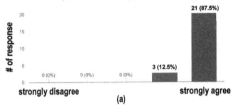

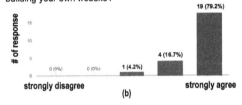

Figure 3: Response to two questions measuring the perceived importance of the RWD content and tools.

2. Most students feel confident in learning more about computing after the course.

Two five-level Likert scale items were used to evaluate students' self-reported confidence in their abilities in learning more computing related topics. As shown in Figure 4, the responses from students were highly positive. More than 75% of students were very confident that they could learn more about web development, while 63% of students felt the same way about computing and programming in general.

In particular, students felt confident in their abilities to learn new technologies despite the difficulties they have encountered. This strongly suggests that learning RWD and solving difficult responsive design challenges was effective in establishing students' confidence and self-efficacy in computing.

3. Students have gained increased confidence in learning W3.CSS independently.

Independent learning is an important skill in all computing fields. Beside classroom instruction, students had to learn much W3.CSS framework related material on their own using online documentation and other resources. The five-level Likert scale item *"How confident you feel in learning about different W3.CSS classes on your own by looking up online references"* was used to measure students' self-reported confidence level. A repeated observation was obtained based on students' response to the question in the first class when W3.CSS was introduced, and then three weeks later at the end of semester.

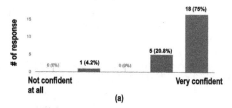

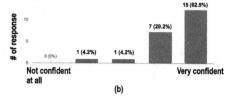

Figure 4: Response to two questions measuring confidence in learning more computing topics.

An unpaired T-test was conducted to compare the difference between the two observations. Table 1 shows that students reported a higher level of confidence in searching online references after three weeks of working with W3.CSS. The percentage breakdown of the responses from the two groups are also shown in Figure 5. The number of students who reported to be "very confident" increased significantly over the three weeks period.

	N	mean	sd	p-value
At the first W3.CSS class	29	4.31	0.60	0.03
Three weeks later	24	4.67	0.56	

Table 1: Result of T-test for measuring improvement of confidence in independent-learning.

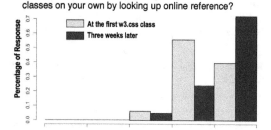

Figure 5: Reported confidence in independent-learning.

4 CONCLUSION

Students are interested in learning how to build professional-looking responsive websites, given the increasing popularity of mobile web browsing. This paper investigates how modern responsive web design technologies can be taught in an introductory web development course to novice leaners.

Two simple yet powerful responsive web design strategies, one using CSS flexbox and media queries and one using the W3.CSS framework, were integrated with basic HTML and CSS course content. Students were able to practice their abstract thinking and problem solving skills by working with responsive design technologies. Moreover, students were exposed to software development practices such as the use of tools and third-party frameworks. The W3.CSS framework was particularly well-received, thanks to its easy-to-use responsiveness and modern style design features.

A preliminary evaluation shows that students consider responsive web design an important topic when learning how to build their own websites. Students feel more confident in learning about web front-end development and computing in general by the end of the course. Moreover, students have opportunities to improve their skills in independent learning when working with the W3.CSS framework.

Building static websites with HTML and CSS has been considered less of a real programming task, whereas such courses often attract diverse groups of students who are excited about learning to "code" a website. Introducing modern front-end technologies such as responsive design makes it possible to teach computational concepts and practice within the content of web development. Meanwhile, students can gain a greater appreciation and sense of accomplishment by creating their own modern responsive websites. Further studies are needed to understand how the course can prepare students for more advanced computing topics, especially compared with traditional programming-oriented introductory courses.

REFERENCES

[1] A. F. Blackwell. 2002. First steps in programming: a rationale for attention investment models. In *Proceedings IEEE 2002 Symposia on Human Centric Computing Languages and Environments.* https://doi.org/10.1109/HCC.2002.1046334

[2] Eric Bollens, Brett Pollack, and Rosemary A. Rocchio. 2015. Understanding Responsive Web Design in Higher Education. In *EDUCAUSE Center for Analysis and Research(ECAR).*

[3] Karen Brennan and Mitchel Resnick. New frameworks for studying and assessing the development of computational thinking. In *AERA '12.*

[4] U.S. Department of Labor Bureau of Labor Statistics. 2016. Computer and Information Technology Occupations. (2016). https://www.bls.gov/ooh/computer-and-information-technology/home.htm Accessed: 2017-08-08.

[5] Brian Dorn, Derek Babb, Dawn M. Nizzi, and Cory M. Epler. 2015. Computing on the Silicon Prairie: The State of CS in Nebraska Public Schools. In *Proceedings of the 46th ACM Technical Symposium on Computer Science Education.* 296–301. https://doi.org/10.1145/2676723.2677261

[6] Samuel Gibbs. 2016. Mobile web browsing overtakes desktop for the first time. (2016). https://www.theguardian.com/technology/2016/nov/02/mobile-web-browsing-desktop-smartphones-tablets Accessed: 2017-08-08.

[7] Thomas H. Park, Meen Chul Kim, Sukrit Chhabra, Brian Lee, and Andrea Forte. 2016. Reading Hierarchies in Code: Assessment of a Basic Computational Skill. In *Proceedings of the 2016 ACM Conference on Innovation and Technology in Computer Science Education.* https://doi.org/10.1145/2899415.2899435

Do It Again: Learning Complex Coding Through Repetition

Dr. Michael Jonas
University of New Hampshire
88 Commercial Street, Manchester, NH 03101
michael.jonas@unh.edu

ABSTRACT

Coding is an important skill set to develop in any computing discipline and can be especially challenging for Information Technology majors, many of whom shy away from the topic. Learning to program is an iterative process that takes time, requiring trial and error, but as students learn new concepts and tackle more sophisticated problems, it becomes difficult to let go of bad ideas. Instead, students try to improve a bad design when starting over may be a better approach. In an advanced programming course, we design a challenging homework assignment and add in a restart. Students first solve the problem in their own way, after which the instructor develops the solution live in a lab session while students watch without taking notes. Afterwards, students get a second attempt to solve the assignment but must not use any of their original code. The idea is to teach students to throw away code and start over as that is sometimes the best way to learn. This paper details the approach and how it impacts student learning.

CCS CONCEPTS

• Social and professional topics~Computing education • Social and professional topics~Computational thinking • Social and professional topics~Computing literacy

KEYWORDS

Second-chance learning; coding; data structures

1 INTRODUCTION

Second-chance learning is a term used in education that describes a strategy to improve student outcomes by allowing the repetition of a learning activity and can take the form of re-submitting an assignment [1][2] or re-taking an exam [3]. Although mutli-stage homework assignments can similarly

impact student learning [4], we focus on the second-chance learning approach by allowing the redo of the most challenging assignment in a programming course in order to increase the number of students that successfully complete it; something that prior to this approach was problematic.

One of the courses offered at the University of New Hampshire at Manchester (UNH Manchester) is Data Structures and Algorithms, an advanced programming course that combines portions of more traditional Computer Science (CS) courses in both the study of basic data structures and the study of algorithms and their complexity. The course was initially developed for Information Technology (IT) majors[1] to give them exposure to advanced programming techniques without delving too deep into the two specific topics. Students learn basic data structure concepts including stacks, queues, heaps and various tree topologies as well as basic searching and sorting algorithms with a rudimentary study of runtime complexities. The course builds up with a set of assignments, each a continuation of the same topic, with different data structures, and the algorithms they use, to better solve the shared task: a mobile phone style searchable contact list. The final project allows students to apply all the concepts they studied during the semester to develop a multiple key-indexed, flat-file, searchable database management system.

The course supports several majors with different levels of programming strengths. This includes IT as well as CS and Computer Engineering (CE) majors. Other work in the computing program at UNH Manchester has focused on improved methods of teaching introductory programming [6], itself a challenging task as not every student at that level has yet determined if programming is something they like and want to further pursue. This work differs in that each student not only wants to learn how to become a better programmer, but some already feel they have mastered the art only to be confronted with a challenging course and can gain further insight into their strength, weaknesses, and what is left to learn.

2 MOTIVATION

The paper focuses on the final homework assignment, whose difficulty level pushed student's skill set. With only one exam, towards the end of the semester, the final homework assignment prepared students for it as well as the final project. The homework assignments preceding this were somewhat simpler

---

[1] The IT major offers an elective programming track to improve student problem solving skills and has become popular over time. [5]

and more closely followed the trajectory of the course and what was done in lab, but it was this final homework assignment that made students think more about its solution. All assignments were somewhat open ended in that students had to develop them from the ground up. The instructor didn't want students to finish partially written code, but instead be forced to confront both object design and interaction as well as the data structures they had to represent. This was especially the case for the final project that gave students plenty of leeway in how to design the object hierarchy to implement a somewhat complex database. The one element that was kept simple was the interface, where all assignments used a simple command-shell menu-driven approach. The point was not about software engineering an elegant interface or even bulletproofing I/O, it was to focus on the specific data structures to solve problems.

2.1 Improving the Course

If one condenses data structures into its primary element, outside of studying common algorithms and structures, the main hurdle for students is to understand how complex structures, created dynamically in memory, can be chained together in different topologies to create searchable models for these sets of algorithms. In its simplest form, a linked list creates a linear topology, but with more complex forms, one can generate binary search trees, heaps, as well as hybrid structures such as b-trees that integrate both static memory (arrays) with more complex dynamic memory models.

Many of these topologies are well understood and there is plenty of material that can be found in textbooks and online that defines clearly-described solutions. This also presents a problem when trying to get students to develop their own models and build solutions from the ground up. It is, in fact, one of these instances, in a homework assignment, during the middle of the semester, when the course was first formulated, that created the challenging assignment that this paper focuses on. Students were tasked to build a searchable contact list stored in a static array and implement binary search to efficiently find each entry. At its completion, all students, even those that had struggled with elements of previous concepts, easily solved this problem, primarily because they found many examples of the algorithm online.

It was unclear whether this copying of code actually taught students anything and so the homework assignment that followed, which also happened to be the last one before the final project, was designed so that it was impossible to find any code samples online to help students solve it. The new searchable list was to be a doubly-linked list but with the addition of a mid-pointer that needed re-centering to keep the list balanced after each insertion, requiring students to insert to either side of it depending on where the new entry belonged. This would then require a double-link insertion from either direction as well as continuously balancing the list along the mid-pointer depending

on which side the insertion occurred.[2] An assignment that students found indeed challenging, even the best programmers in the class.

3 APPROACH

Solutions to this assignment tended to be long and complex as students struggled to find elegant ways to divide the problem and solve it. Students generally did well on the first three homework assignments but hit a roadblock on this challenging fourth one, as figure 1 highlights during the first three years of the course.

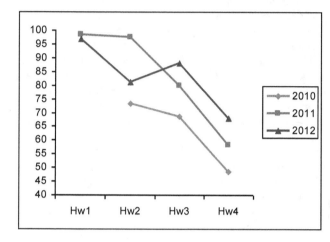

Figure 1: Student performance on homework assignments[3]

It provided the perfect forum for the instructor to step in and create many learning moments. One of these moments was to develop the entire assignment in a lab session on a whiteboard in front of students. A live-programming exercise that had the instructor start from scratch, sketch out the problem, design it and then develop the code. The instructor did not use notes, thus allowing students to see the entire process, stumbles and all. Each semester this was repeated with a slightly different solution derived. The important point was that students saw how the problem was first decomposed and then constructed.

In its fourth incarnation of the course, it was decided that students ought to not only watch this live-programming exercise but have them then redo the assignment once they've seen the process. The one caveat, they could not reuse any of their previous code and they were not allowed to take notes, take pictures, or use their laptop during the exercise. The idea was to instill in students that it was ok to throw away lengthy solutions and start from scratch. That sometimes, restarting a difficult problem enables quicker paths to better solutions. One drawback

---

[2] Having to switch a linear search from ascending to descending, depending on which side of the center an entry is, and having to flip linked list insertions from a next-to-previous order to a previous-to-next order, challenged student comprehension of how to manipulate objects (i.e. links) in memory.
[3] Table 1 gives more details on class composition.

with this approach is that after having spent several weeks on the assignment, getting students to restart can be problematic.

3.1 Refining the Assignment

The grading rubric was augmented to assist in motivating students. If presented only as extra credit, few students might pursue the additional work. There is a delicate balance in the original grading rubric with homework assignments, lab work, final project and the exam and it was important to not alter this too much. Adding too many extra-credit points could make other meaningful learning activates, such as lab-work, less pertinent. A fundamental, built-in, mechanism in the grading rubric is to not overly weigh homework assignments more than other work so that students can work with challenging problems without fear of failure unduly impacting their grade. To then successfully add an additional set of points that did not upend this balance required some trial and error.

Initially, the originally assignment was downgraded to only 75% of its value with the remaining 25% set aside to redo the work. The assignment itself represented less than 10 points of the overall grade. With so little value assigned to redoing the assignment, not all students took on the challenge. Over the course of two semesters, a little over half of the class would successfully submit a new working version that reflected what they had learned in the live-programming exercise. Another quarter attempted it with some degree of work but what they handed in lacked the kind of effort compared to their original submission.

In its third year the point value was further tweaked in an attempt to increase student participation. The assignment was given an additional 25% extra-credit point value that made the second attempt at the problem more worthwhile. The additional extra-credit now made it substantial enough to increase the number of students participating. Plus, the psychology of potentially receiving extra points that could be applied to help push up other assignment grades likely also added incentive. Additionally, the amount of time students received for the first iteration was reduced and moved to the second attempt. With a larger point total allocation and less time invested in the original solution, a majority of the class participated in submitting a substantial effort for the second iteration of the homework assignment.

3.2 Variation

The impact on allowing students a second opportunity to do a difficult assignment is in how much attention is given to them on the initial try. Would students be better off with a more guided approach on their initial attempt instead of being given the freedom to implement it in the way best suited to each individual? What if the instructor gave more starting context for an overall skeletal outline of the assignment and if so, would this improve the chances of students more easily finishing it and make moot the second try?

These questions were somewhat answered in the third installment when the instructor did exactly that, giving a more deliberate outline to students that was developed on the whiteboard. The instructor discussed the main loop, and gave an overview of how to generate the central driving body of the code. It was purposefully not done in electronic form since there is something lost in the transferal of information from whiteboard to notes to actual implementation and this was deemed a positive thing.

In the end, adding this additional step had little impact as many students still had their final solution explode into undue complexity. It seemed that many students simply ignored the outline and focused on their notion of a best solution. Those that started with the outline simply got stuck more quickly when they reached the more difficult coding sections. In fact, it seemed that having the instructor add some guidance ended up being more of a hindrance, as students no longer worked on solving the simpler elements on their own. Successfully working on the simpler parts actually helps students gain confidence, which is useful when addressing the more challenging aspects of the problem.

3.3 Applying to Introductory Course

With this method demonstrating success in the advanced programming course, it was applied more recently to an introductory programming course. The final, and most challenging homework assignment was chosen but with a variation on the approach. Because the finished assignment was to be the starting point for the final project, it was important that students understood the concepts in it thoroughly. To have students, who are just learning how to program, tackle the same assignment twice, would likely be too exhausting and could disengage some, something of greater concern in an introductory programming course. Instead, students were tasked with finishing the assignment and, after an initial submission, it was started again from scratch as a in-class group lab exercise, with the instructor's guidance. Each student would get to develop, from the beginning, the same solution, with the instructors giving incremental help along the way to insure that everyone succeeded.

With an exhaustive set of labs that followed, whose purpose is to enhance the features of that assignment as it transitions into the project, there was a good amount of learning activity already built into the course that may mute the effect of the guided restart. It seems a good supposition that a better starting point aided these labs but how much it assisted is open to interpretation. In the advanced programming course, students had to tackle a final project as well, and what was gleaned from redoing the final homework assignment, i.e. how to develop strategies to better solve complex problems, could then be applied to the project. However, the project was independent of the assignment they redid and thus easier to determine how the approach students used to design and incrementally develop that project improved over the course of the past three years, whereas that was not directly the case for the introductory programming course since the point was more about having repetition help understand the code.

4 OBSERVATIONS

After three years of applying this method in the advanced programming course, evidence suggests it has merit. Although the class makeup during this period has had a mix of talent, ranging from a few advanced students that solved the problem with relative ease, to struggling students that seemed lost, making students redo the assignment positively impacted all. The confidence that students gained from successfully completing a difficult assignment, albeit after a second try, added an important element as they transitioned to a more comprehensive final project that required not only coding but also added an object design element. What was learned from this process was not only techniques such as divide-and-conquer to decompose a problem, top-down coding to build up an assignment in stages, and incremental refinement to iteratively develop a solution, but also the idea that there is an alternative to staying with a bad design, namely to restart complex problems from the beginning to give a different perspective on potential solutions.

4.1 Analysis

Table 1 highlights student performance on the final two assignments spanning over a six year period split between pre and post-application of the approach. In the first three years, with students only getting a single attempt to do the final homework assignment, little feedback was given on how they could have improved it other than instructor comments on the grading sheet. This was then immediately followed by the final project, which they had to design from the beginning. In the final three years, the second-chance learning approach was applied. Students were given a second attempt at the assignment and many who struggled with the initial submission were successfully able to submit a solution.

Table 1: Final two assignments – impact of homework on project

Year (fall semester)	# students in course	final homework average	final project code average
final homework only done once			
2010	9	48.61%	50.35%
2011	6	58.33%	68.88%
2012	16	67.81%	59.06%
second chance on final homework			
2013	9	78.33%	73.70%
2014	14	72.31%	72.82%
2015	6	75.00%	70.53%

Although not all students were able to submit a fully workable program for the second attempt, even those that struggled had learned something from their additional submission. The number of non-compliable solutions, filled with numerous syntax errors demonstrating student frustrations as they tried solving the challenging problem, disappeared almost entirely from student submissions.

Though both the final homework assignment and project were difficult for students and are reflected in somewhat low scores, the overall impact on student's grades was minimized in two ways. Not only was the point value of the homework assignment designed not to impact students' too harshly, but the final project had an added design element that enabled students to garner a small amount of points for a slightly improved overall grade.[4] The averages listed in table 1 focus on the scores that students received on the coding portion only and demonstrate that, as the final homework assignment grades improved, so did the subsequent project grade. With the second-chance approach, final homework grades rose on average by 29.1% from the first three years to the last three years, while final project grades rose only by 21.7%. The difference is not surprising since the final project was challenging and was not a continuation of the homework so the improvement was more in technique and approach.

4.2 Evidence

Clear evidence of student transformation could be seen in the final project. The assignment, a flat-file database with key indexing, provided a robust platform that challenged students. Not only were students required to tie together complex data structures, but the project required them to design the entire object hierarchy from the ground up. In the past, students would stick to their first attempt and then patch together changes to develop a solution. It was difficult for students to throw out an idea once they had spent some time coding it and this could be detrimental to developing a solution. Once students were exposed to the idea that throwing out code may shorten their development cycle, some followed this approach and found success.

Part of the final project deliverable required a revised design document that detailed what changes were made from the initial model. Before the second-chance learning approach was applied, the revision document showed little design change in student work. On most occasions it either added or removed features but kept the object hierarchy that was given with the initial design document. Once students had the opportunity to redo the final homework assignment, a number of them also changed their object design on their final project. Though not uniform across students, some decomposed the problem further; creating additional objects to better support their design while others reworked their base objects to build a better object hierarchy that could more easily be developed into a working system in shorter time.

---

[4] In addition, an overall class curve was also applied when the majority of student scores were below expectations (i.e. 2010 for instance).

4.3 Feedback

Another measure of a course is how students evaluate the instructor at the end of the semester. In the first three years, with the initial introduction of the challenging homework assignment, student feedback was critical as to why such a difficult assignment was given to the class. Although students felt they learned from the material presented, it was noted that perhaps splitting up the final homework assignment into smaller, more manageable, parts made more sense. Though intrigued by this idea, time was too short to add additional assignments. Although the rewrite could be considered an assignment in its own right, the turnaround time was shorter since students had already attained an intimate knowledge of what the problem asked for, and having seen a solution, how to approach their second attempt. Once redoing the assignment was introduced, this particular concern vanished from student evaluations and feedback suggested this was a positive addition to the course.

5 SUMMARY

Over the span of three years, an advanced programming course, Data Structures and Algorithms, introduced the idea of redoing a challenging homework assignment. Prior to this, many students had difficulty in completing the work, simply giving up and taking the point loss. Initially, through a live-programming exercise, the instructor developed the solution in a lab session whilst students followed along, asking questions and learning the various approaches of deconstructing a problem using sound techniques. Student feedback lamented the fact that, after seeing the solution, it seemed so much simpler and wondered how the instructor could have provided this kind of guidance during the assignments. Allowing students to redo the work for credit, with a mix of extra and remaining point values, gave incentive for more students to participate.

5.1 Benefit

In its third iteration, the process has been refined to the point that students feel that the second attempt is beneficial in helping better understand the complexities of data structures. Students continue to struggle with the difficult homework assignment but the level of anxiety seems less elevated knowing they will get to redo it after seeing the instructor develop the solution. Because significant point values are still attached to the first attempt, students continue to put a good deal of effort into their initial solution, an important element of this model. If students just gave up and waited to see the solution without investing any time in it, then all the benefits would disappear and it would simple turn the assignment into an easier problem for them to solve. This is something that would be counter to what the original goal of the second-chance attempted had intended it to be.

5.2 Conclusion

Overall, results in the course have been positive with students demonstrating better aptitude on future assignments, specifically the final project, enabling them to develop more robust and complex solutions. Students demonstrated a marked difference from how they approached the two assignments, both challenging what they have learned, with the latter having them show better refinement techniques that they gleaned from both watching the instructor's live-programming example to themselves then attempting their second try. The same model was also integrated into an introductory programming course but results where somewhat mixed as it was unclear how much this aided student learning. Though it did not impede or hinder student progress, further work is needed to investigate how to optimally configure a second-chance learning assignment for beginner-level programming students.

ACKNOWLEDGMENTS

I want to thank my fellow colleagues for helping with this course. I'm extremely grateful to all my students over the past six years who struggled to grasp the difficult concepts in a hectic and challenging environment that is UNH Manchester.

REFERENCES

[1] Wormeli, R., Redos and Retakes Done Right. In Educational Leadership magazine, (November 2011) Association for Supervision and Curriculum Development, Pages 22-26.

[2] Jones, S., Instructional Strategies Motivate and Engage Students in Deeper Learning. Southern Regional Education Board (srb.org), Atlanta, GA, April 2013.

[3] Stephenson, B., The Impacts of Providing Novice Computer Science Students with a Second Chance on their Midterm Exams. *Journal of Computing Sciences in Colleges*, Volume 27 Issue 4, April 2012, Pages 122-130.

[4] Huggins, J., Kusssmaul, C., Kumar, A., and Trono, J., Multi-phase homework assignments in CS I and CS II. *Journal of Computing Sciences in Colleges*, Volume 19 Issue 2, December 2003, Pages 182-184.

[5] Jonas, M, Strengthening IT Curriculum by Improving Problem Solving Skills with Programming. in D. Slykhuis & G. Marks (Eds.), *Proceedings of Society for Information Technology & Teacher Education International Conference 2015*, Las Vegas, NV, March 2015, Pages 49-51.

[6] Jonas, M, Teaching Introductory Programming using Multiplayer Board Game Strategies in Greenfoot. in *Journal of Computing Sciences in Colleges*, Loudonville, NY, Volume 28 Issue 6, June 2013, Pages 19-25.

On the Likes and Dislikes of YouTube's Educational Videos

A Quantitative Study

Abdulhadi Shoufan
Khalifa University
P.O. Box 127788
Abu Dhabi
abdulhadi.shoufan@kustar.ac.ae

Fatma Mohamed
Khalifa University
P.O. Box 127788
Abu Dhabi
fatma.mohamed@kustar.ac.ae

ABSTRACT

As major product of information technology, YouTube is a ubiquitous source for education, also in the field of information technology. Learners, however, are facing the increasing problem of finding appropriate videos on YouTube efficiently. Users' rating in terms of Likes and Dislikes could provide a starting point. However, it is unclear what the number of Likes and Dislikes reveal about the video. This paper tries to create links between different video features and users' rating of YouTube's educational content. For this purpose, 300 educational videos were collected and analyzed and regression models were established that describe the number of Likes per view and the number of Dislikes per view as functions of different video features and production styles. Results show that the number of Likes per view can be predicted more reliably than the number of Dislikes per view. The number of Likes per view increases with higher video resolution and higher talking rate (words per second), and when the instructor or tutor speaks English as a native language. Videos using explanations on paper or whiteboard as well as videos that use more than one style attract more Likes per view. In contrast, the model that describes the number of Dislikes per view has a low adjusted R-squared and the contribution of its significant variables is rather difficult to interpret. This suggests that further research is required to understand users' behavior in terms of disliking an educational video.

CCS CONCEPTS

• **Human-centered computing** → **Social network analysis**; Youtube;

KEYWORDS

User behavior, Likes, Dislikes, video features, video production style

ACM Reference format:
Abdulhadi Shoufan and Fatma Mohamed. 2017. On the Likes and Dislikes of YouTube's Educational Videos. In *Proceedings of SIGITE'17, Rochester, NY, USA, October 4–7, 2017,* 6 pages.
https://doi.org/10.1145/3125659.3125692

1 INTRODUCTION

YouTube is becoming an indispensable source for learning and information seeking [7, 10, 12, 15]. According to a quick survey by the authors, only one out of 429 students indicated not to use YouTube for learning. Nevertheless, YouTube is still an under-researched platform compared to other social media such as Facebook [12, 18]. Snelson et al. identified and prioritized seven research categories for YouTube and video-sharing technologies [18]. Education was ranked the next highest priority category with seventeen research directions. These include among others the actual use of YouTube videos in classroom from teacher and students' perspective, the instructional design elements of effective online videos, the potential of online videos to transform education, as well as success factors of educational videos [18].

As a social platform, YouTube allows any registered user to upload videos. This has led to the situation that tens or even hundreds of videos can be found that address the same topic. This creates an increasing difficulty of finding the "correct" video efficiently. Using the provided filters and sorting criteria does not seem to be very helpful. For example, when a user sorts videos according to the provided rating, a video with one Like and zero Dislikes is listed before a video with 100 Likes and one Dislike.

This paper tries to link user's behavior in terms of rating to typical features of videos such as video length, talking rate, video and audio quality, gender and native language of the speaker, as well as video production style. For this purpose, 300 videos were collected and annotated. For each video the number of Likes per view LPV, and the number of Dislikes per view DPV were determined. In addition to some simple descriptive statistics, regression analyses were performed to establish relationships between LPV or DPV and the video features, respectively. The main findings of this research can be summarized in the following points:

(1) Users' behavior in terms of liking videos can be predicted more reliably than in the case of disliking.
(2) The number of Likes per view is affected positively by two video production styles, by the video resolution, and by the talking rate.
(3) The gender of the speaker is not significant neither for liking nor for disliking a video.
(4) Videos with instructors/tutors speaking English as a native language attract more Likes. However, this feature is insignificant for disliking a video.
(5) The video length is not significant for liking a video. Surprisingly, however, longer videos seem to cause slightly less dislikes.

The paper is organized as follows. Section 2 reviews related work. Section 3 describes the research methodology. Section 4 summarizes the results of the statistical tests. Section 5 discusses the paper findings and Section 6 concludes the paper.

2 RELATED WORK

Many authors have investigated Youtube as a source for learning and teaching of different topics including English, music, physics, nursing, anatomy, and performing art [1, 5, 9, 11, 14, 17]. The quality of content has concerned some researchers especially in medical fields [2, 3, 8].

According to Khan [12], the number of Likes, Dislikes, Views, Shares, Comments, and Uploads on YouTube are determined by user's motives to consume or participate. Khan investigated five types of motives: seeking information, giving information, self-status seeking, social interaction, and relaxing environment. If the user's motive is known, user's behavior, e.g., in form of liking or disliking a video could be predicted according to regression models. For example, a YouTube user seeking information is likely to engage in liking or disliking videos, as well as in giving comments rather than in sharing or uploading videos. Khan did not analyze any videos and based his study on a pilot survey of 1143 students. Earlier, Haridakis and Hanson presented a similar study, which, however, was limited to users' motives for viewing and sharing [7].

Formal quality features of educational videos such as video production style, video length, etc. were mainly investigated in the context of Massive Open Online Courses (MOOCs) [4, 20]. Such studies are relevant to our work since many MOOC videos are posted on YouTube. Guo et al. investigated some edX MOOC courses and found out that informal talking-head videos and Khan-style videos attract more engagement than PowerPoint slides, recorded classroom lectures, or code screencasts. Also, shorter videos and faster speaking were found to be more engaging [4]. Engagement was measured by the watching time and by students' attempts to answer post-video assessment problems. YouTube does not support post-video assessment and the watching time, which can be obtained using the YouTube API, is probably a weak indicator for engagement because many YouTube users skip a video just because it is not the right one. In contrast, MOOC attendees usually know what videos they want to watch.

Hove and van der Meij investigated factors that affect the popularity of educational videos on YouTube [19]. For this purpose, they used a metric that takes the numbers of Likes (L), Dislikes (D), Views (V), and Shares (S) into consideration. In particular, they defined what they called popularity rate as $PR = (2L_r + V + S)/4$, whereas $L_r = (L/(L + 2D) * 100)$ refers to the like ratio. By analyzing 75 videos, the authors found out that the popularity rate increases when the video has higher resolution, higher picture frequency, and higher speaking speed, and when it includes on-screen texts, subtitles, background music, and less background noise. The analyzed videos were limited to educational content providing general factual and conceptual knowledge without academic context. The definition of the popularity rate shows three issues. First, the number of Views is significantly larger than the numbers of Likes, Dislikes, and Shares. The popularity rate, therefore, is essentially determined by the number of Views. Second, the absolute number

of Views is problematic because videos published earlier are likely to have more Views. Also, the authors did not explain why the actual number of dislikers is assumed to be twice the number of viewers who hit the Dislike button.

The presented study is mostly related to the work by Guo et al. [4] and Hove and van der Meij [19] in terms of linking video features to users' behavior. Guo et al. work, however, was limited to MOOC videos and their results may not be generalized to other online videos. This –as commented by the authors– is because MOOC participants are differently motivated than YouTube users. On the other hand, Hove and van der Meij treated a different class of educational videos (video offering declarative knowledge without academic context). They did not study the effect of video production style, and combined the number of Likes, Dislikes, Views, and Shares in one formula to describe the popularity rate with associated issues as discussed above.

In this paper we try to link users' behavior in terms of liking and disliking a video to the features of the video. The novel aspects of our contribution can be summarized as follows:

(1) We build the relationship between video features and users' behavior using regression analysis. The coefficients of a regression model do not only indicate the significance of respective variables but also allow us to compare the impact of different variables. Moreover, regression models help producers of educational video to predict users' behavior depending on the features of the new video.

(2) In contrast to [19], we treat the number of Likes, Dislikes, and Views as 3 separate variables to understand the semantics of each one of them. This individual consideration is motivated by the observation that the number of Views is significantly larger than the other two values. For example, in our sample videos the Like button was hit 60 times per 10,000 views while the Dislike button was hit 3 times per 10,000 views on average.

(3) The gender and the native language of the speaker are considered.

(4) Guo et al. and Hove and van der Meij analyzed videos with a total of 9.6 and 2.5 million views, respectively. Our study shows a significantly larger scale than related work with 124.2 million views.

3 METHODOLOGY

The research methodology used in this study consists of data collection, video annotation, and statistical analysis. The following three sections explain each phase in details.

3.1 Data collection

A sample of 300 videos addressing five different academic topics were collected, see Table 1. All collected videos seem to be directed to university students or learners on a similar level. For statistical significance, only videos were selected that have a minimum number of Likes plus Dislikes, in particular $N_L + N_D \geq 30$, whereas $N_D \geq 1$. To facilitate the analysis, each video was assigned an identity number. The video title and a link to the video were added to the Excel sheet to allow a quick review of the video when necessary. The selection of 300 as sample size was essentially based on a rule

Table 1: Selected subjects and related number of analyzed videos

Topic	No. of Videos
Programming in Java, C, and Python	50
Digital logic design	105
Artificial intelligence	85
Ethical hacking and penetration testing	40
Calculus and differential equations	20
Total	**300**

of thumb specifying the minimum number of data points required for regression analysis. This rule states that at least ten data points should be available per independent variable [16]. As will be discussed below, a total of 25 independent variables were identified in this study. So, at least 250 videos should be analyzed. While taking a larger sample is beneficial for the regression analysis, it increases the overhead of video collection and annotation. That is why we restricted the sample to 300 videos. The topic selection according to Table 1 was mainly based on authors' experience in related courses and on the requirement that all topics should relate to computer science education on undergraduate or graduate levels. The number of videos in the different topics was unplanned and more or less arbitrary.

3.2 Video Annotation

Each video was annotated with two sets of data. The first set includes four basic information including the number of Likes (N_L), Dislikes (N_D), Views (N_V) and the number of days the video is being online (D). To determine (D), the video view date was subtracted from the video upload date. Based on these data, three metrics were determined to describe the users' behavior for each video. These metrics include the number of Likes per view (LPV), the number of Dislikes per view (DPV), and the number of views per day (VPD) as summarized in Table 2. LPV, DPV, and VPD are treated as dependent variables in the regression analyses.

The second set of annotation data includes different video features and production styles. A total of six features and 19 production styles were considered as summarized in Table 3. According to [6], the majority of educational videos are produced using one out of 18 production styles. However, our study showed that 42 out of the collected videos used mixed styles where the instructor/tutor changed

Table 2: Metrics treated as dependent variables in the regression analyses

Metric	Abbreviation	Value
Number of Likes per view	LPV	$LPV = N_L/N_V$
Number of Dislikes per view	DPV	$DPV = N_D/N_V$
Number of views per day	VPD	$VPD = N_V/D$

Table 3: Video features and production styles treated as independent variables in the regression analyses

Metric	Abbreviation	Estimation Method
Video length in minutes	LENGTH	Determined from the video length given by YouTube in minutes and second
Video resolution in pixels	RESOLUTION	The maximum resolution available for the video as given in the video's setting menu.
Audio quality	AUDIO	A binary variable describing our subjective perception of the audio quality. $AUDIO = 1$ when the perceived audio quality is acceptable, otherwise $AUDIO = 0$, e.g, in the case of background noise or loud music.
Talking rate in words per minute	SPEED	Automatically generated transcript was used to count words within a reasonable interval. Then the number of words was divided by the length of this interval.
Speaker gender	GENDER	A binary variable describing whether the instructor/tutor is female $GENDER = 0$ or male $GENDER = 1$.
Native language	NATIVE	A binary variable describing whether the instructor/tutor speaks English as native language $NATIVE = 1$ or not $NATIVE = 0$.
Khan style	KHAN	Binary variables that describe the used video production style. Only one of these variables can be 1 for some video.
PowerPoint slides	SLIDES	
Classroom lecture	CLASS	
Paper/ whiteboard	PAPER	
Udacity style	UDACITY	
Animation	ANIM	
Screen cast	SCREEN	
Talking head	HEAD	
Picture in picture	PIP	
Text overlay	OVERLAY	
Recorded seminar	SEMINAR	
Interview	INTERVIEW	
Conversation	CONVERS	
Live video	LIVE	
Webcam capture	WEBCAM	
Demonstration	DEMO	
On location	LOCATION	
Green screen	GREEN	
Mixed style	MIXED	

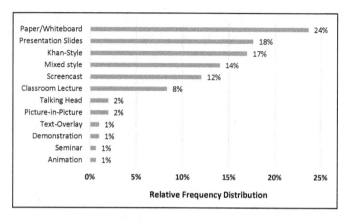

Figure 1: Relative frequency distribution of production styles

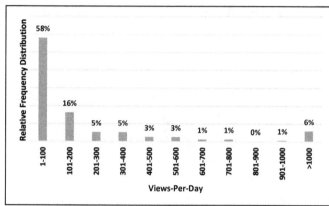

Figure 2: Relative frequency distribution of Views-Per-Day

between at least two presentation styles, e.g., screencast and PowerPoint slides. The variable *MIXED* was used to describe the style of such videos. Apart from the AUDIO and NATIVE features, the values of all other features can be determined unambiguously. The perception of audio quality and whether a speaker is native, can be subjective. In our case, the video sample was divided into two sets and each author annotated one set independently as long as the AUDIO and NATIVE features appeared to be unambiguous. Otherwise, the authors discussed unclear cases to reach an agreement. No methods for inter-rater agreement were applied.

3.3 Statistical Analysis

To have a general overview of users' behavior, some descriptive statistics, frequency distributions and histograms were generated to address the pre-defined metrics including Views per day, Likes per view, Dislikes per view.

To understand the relationship between users' behavior and video features, different regression analyses as well as analysis of variance were performed to identify the significant features and establish predictive models.

4 RESULTS

Figure 1 shows the relative frequency distribution of the different production styles used in the analyzed videos. Only 12 out of the investigated 19 styles were used in the collected sample videos. Six out these 12 styles cover 92% of the collected videos. The diagram shows that the Paper/Whiteboard, PowerPoint slides, and Khan were the dominant styles.

Figure 2 shows the relative frequency distribution of the number of Views per day *VPD* for the analyzed videos. The mean, standard deviation, maximum, and minimum values of *VPD* are given in Table 4. *VPD* seems to show an exponential distribution with the majority of the videos obtaining 100 views per day or less.

Figure 3 shows the relative frequency distribution of the number of Likes per view *LPV*. The descriptive statistics of *LPV* are given in Table 4. The distribution of *LPV* shows positive skewness with most videos deviating from the mean have more Likes per view.

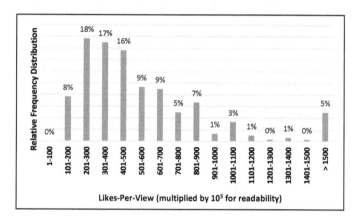

Figure 3: Relative frequency distribution of Likes-Per-View

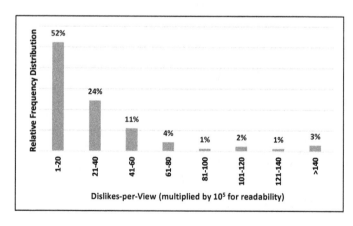

Figure 4: Relative frequency distribution of Dislikes-Per-View

Figure 4 shows the relative frequency distribution of the number of Dislikes per view *DPV* for the analyzed videos with some descriptive statistics given in Table 4. The distribution of *DPV* seems to have an exponential form with the majority of the videos obtaining 20×10^{-5} Dislikes per view or less.

Table 5 summarizes the results of three regression analyses which were performed to understand if and how the video production style as well as other video features affect the number of Likes per view, the number of Dislikes per view, and the number of Views per day. Based on these results we can conclude the following:

(1) The number of Likes per view seems to be affected by two video production styles, by the video resolution, the talking rate, and the native language. The regression model shows positive values for all related coefficients and explains 73% of the variance in the data.

(2) The number of Dislikes per view seems to be affected by the Paper/Whiteboard production styles, the video resolution and the length. Due to the negative coefficient, a longer video obtains less Dislikes per view.

(3) The number of views per day is affected by one of four production styles (Slides, Mixed-Style, Paper/Whiteboard, Khan). Recall that the production styles are encoded as one-hot binary variables, which means that one of them can be one for some video. Thus, if a video has a production style different from the four styles listed in Table 5, the VPD is only affected by the video resolution, the talking rate, and audio quality. However, the generated regression model is not strong enough since it only explains 24% of the variance in the data. Also, the negative coefficients for the audio quality variable and the video production style variables make interpretations less obvious. Nevertheless, it can be seen, for example, that a Khan-style video obtains almost 266 more views per day than a video using PowerPoint slides (769.2-502.8).

5 DISCUSSION

According to Test 1, users mostly seem to like videos that have more than one production style such as slides and screencasts followed by paper/whiteboard presentations. These results are different from what Guo et al. found out, namely that Khan-style tablet drawings are more engaging than slides and code screencasts. The positive impact of higher video resolution and higher talking rate supports the findings by Guo et al. [4] and Hove and van der Meij [19]. In contrast to Guo's finding, however, the video length is not significant. This supports what Lagerstrom et al. identified in his discussion about the "Myth of the Six Minute Rule" [13]. As probably expected, the learners on YouTube do not show any gender bias when they like or dislike a video. However, videos with persons speaking English as a native language obtain more Likes. The native speaker feature has even a higher contribution than the video production style (compare the regression coefficient 0.001579 vs. 0.001434 or 0.001273).

Table 4: Descriptive statistics for VPD, LPV, and DPV

	VPD	LPV	DPV
Mean	330	5.57×10^{-3}	3.30×10^{-4}
St. Dev.	71	2.23×10^{-4}	2.46×10^{-5}
Min	1.2	1.03×10^{-3}	3.53×10^{-5}
Max	17610	2.19×10^{-2}	2.98×10^{-3}

Test 2 revealed that the regression model for the number of Dislikes per view has a lower prediction ability than the LPV model due to lower adjusted R-squared. Also, the contributing variables and their coefficients are rather difficult to interpret. So, the model implies that the number of DPV increases with higher video resolution which is implausible. Also, the video length feature affects the number of Dislikes in an unexpected way: longer videos cause less Dislikes. The DPV model, furthermore, shows a positive coefficient for the paper/whiteboard production style. This means that this production style causes both more Likes and more Dislikes per view, indicating that there are users who like this style and others who dislike it and both is significant.

By comparing the regression models for LPV and DPV, it can be seen that the LPV model is not only more plausible with respect to contributing variables and their coefficients but also can explain clearly more variance in the data than the DPV model (73% vs. 45%). We believe that this situation is not specifically related to the quality of the collected data. Rather, other aspects should be considered. First, according to experience, most users, who do not like a video, just skip it without hitting the Dislike button. Thus the number of Dislikes does not reflect the number of actual dislikers. Another aspect is that the number of Dislikes is probably affected by other factors that were not captured in this study. This suggests that more research is required to understand the dislikers behavior.

The regression model that describes VPD is descriptive rather than inferential. Users usually don't choose a video with a specific production style and they, for example, cannot perceive the audio quality and the speaking rate before they start the video, (i.e., before a view is counted). The fact that VPD is influenced by the listed four production styles in Table 5 seems to be less surprising when Figure 2 is reviewed: Videos with high-frequency styles are viewed more frequently. The negative coefficients of the production style variables are caused mathematically by the regression algorithm.

6 CONCLUSIONS

In this paper we threw light on the behavior of YouTube users in terms of liking or disliking a video. The results showed that the liking behavior can be described more reliably than the disliking behavior. It also emphasized that the liking behavior is more related to the considered video features and production styles. The findings of this research can be used for the production of educational videos, especially for institutions/instructors for whom video production work is a featured part of their instructional delivery. Specifically, the variables significant for LPV can be considered to produce videos with corresponding features such as higher talking rate and higher video resolution. This work does not give insight into students' motivation to like or dislike an educational video. The relationships between the identified significant features and users' behaviors should be understood as association rather than causation. Further research is required to understand why students like or dislike a video considering the features identified in this work. Such research should also help in estimating the number of "passive dislikers" and "passive likers". These are users who dislike or like a video but do not hit corresponding buttons. If the numbers of passive likers and dislikers can be predicted, the general perception of educational videos can be estimated more accurately. This can

Table 5: Results of regression analysis: *VPD*, *LPV*, and *DPV* as functions of different video features

Test	Dependent Variables	Adjusted R-Square	Standard Error of Estimates	Significant Independent Variables	Regression Coefficients
1	Likes per view (*LPV*)	73%	0.003486	MIXED-STYLE*	0.001434
				PAPER**	0.001273
				RESOLUTION****	3.23×10^{-6}
				SPEED***	1.37×10^{-5}
				NATIVE**	0.001579
2	Dislikes per view (*DPV*)	45%	0.000398	PAPER*****	0.000314
				RESOLUTION*****	4.2×10^{-7}
				LENGTH*	-1.9×10^{-6}
3	Views per day (*VPD*)	24%	1107	SLIDES****	-769.2
				MIXED-STYLE**	-536.4
				PAPER**	-516.9
				KHAN*	-502.8
				RESOLUTION*****	1.228623
				SPEED**	5.605185
				AUDIO***	-966.132

*:p-value<0.05, **:p-value<0.01, ***:p-value<0.001, ****:p-value<0.0001, *****:p-value<0.00001

help establishing more reliable relationships between the features of an educational video and how students perceive it. This study addressed videos on topics related to IT education. Video formats and surface features were significant to this study while, the actual content of the collected videos was not. Such formats and features are common to educational videos on different topics. Thus, the study findings can be generalized to other academic fields.

REFERENCES

[1] Dorothy DeWitt, Norlidah Alias, Saedah Siraj, Mohd Yusaini Yaakub, Juhara Ayob, and Rosman Ishak. 2013. The potential of Youtube for teaching and learning in the performing arts. *Procedia-Social and Behavioral Sciences* 103 (2013), 1118–1126.

[2] Ian Duncan, Lee Yarwood-Ross, and Carol Haigh. 2013. YouTube as a source of clinical skills education. *Nurse education today* 33, 12 (2013), 1576–1580.

[3] Jonas Fischer, Jeroen Geurts, Victor Valderrabano, and Thomas Hügle. 2013. Educational quality of YouTube videos on knee arthrocentesis. *JCR: Journal of Clinical Rheumatology* 19, 7 (2013), 373–376.

[4] Philip J Guo, Juho Kim, and Rob Rubin. 2014. How video production affects student engagement: An empirical study of mooc videos. In *Proceedings of the first ACM conference on Learning@ scale conference*. ACM, 41–50.

[5] Peter Gustafsson. 2012. YouTube as an educational tool in physics teaching. In *IOSTE XV International Symposium, Science & Technology Education for Development, Citizenship and Social Justice, La Medina-Yasmine Hammamet*.

[6] Anna Hansch, Katherine McConachie, Philipp Schmidt, Lisa Hillers, Christopher Newman, and T Schildhauer. 2015. The Role of Video in Online Learning: Findings From the Field and Critical Reflections. (2015).

[7] Paul Haridakis and Gary Hanson. 2009. Social interaction and co-viewing with YouTube: Blending mass communication reception and social connection. *Journal of Broadcasting & Electronic Media* 53, 2 (2009), 317–335.

[8] Matthew Ho, Lynn Stothers, Darren Lazare, Brian Tsang, and Andrew Macnab. 2015. Evaluation of educational content of YouTube videos relating to neurogenic bladder and intermittent catheterization. *Canadian Urological Association Journal* 9, 9-10 (2015), 320.

[9] Akram Abood Jaffar. 2012. YouTube: An emerging tool in anatomy education. *Anatomical sciences education* 5, 3 (2012), 158–164.

[10] Insung Jung and Yekyung Lee. 2015. YouTube acceptance by university educators and students: a cross-cultural perspective. *Innovations in education and teaching international* 52, 3 (2015), 243–253.

[11] Brent Kelsen. 2009. Teaching EFL to the iGeneration: A survey of using YouTube as supplementary material with college EFL students in Taiwan. *Call-EJ Online* 10, 2 (2009), 1–18.

[12] M Laeeq Khan. 2017. Social media engagement: What motivates user participation and consumption on YouTube? *Computers in Human Behavior* 66 (2017), 236–247.

[13] Larry Lagerstrom, Petr Johanes, and Mr Umnouy Ponsukcharoen. 2015. The Myth of the Six Minute Rule: Student Engagement with Online Videos. *age* 26 (2015), 1.

[14] Katie Lai. 2013. How Are Our Undergraduates Using YouTube? A Survey on Music StudentsâĂŹ Use of YouTube and the Library's Multimedia Collection. *Music Reference Services Quarterly* 16, 4 (2013), 199–217.

[15] Wen Ying Lim, Yuin Xian Chew, Cyn Ye Chan, Shyir Khie Leow, Siti Badriyah Mohamad Rozlan, and William Junior Yong. 2016. Students' Acceptance of YouTube for Procedural Learning. *Handbook of Research on Leveraging Consumer Psychology for Effective Customer Engagement* (2016), 57.

[16] Iain Pardoe. 2012. *Applied regression modeling: a business approach*. John Wiley & Sons.

[17] Diane J Skiba. 2007. Nursing education 2.0: YouTubeâĎć. *Nursing Education Perspectives* 28, 2 (2007), 100–102.

[18] Chareen Snelson, Kerry Rice, and Constance Wyzard. 2012. Research priorities for YouTube and video-sharing technologies: A Delphi study. *British Journal of Educational Technology* 43, 1 (2012), 119–129.

[19] Petra ten Hove and Hans van der Meij. 2015. Like It or Not. What Characterizes YouTube's More Popular Instructional Videos? *Technical communication* 62, 1 (2015), 48–62.

[20] Ahmed Mohamed Fahmy Yousef, Mohamed Amine Chatti, Ulrik Schroeder, and Marold Wosnitza. 2014. What drives a successful MOOC? An empirical examination of criteria to assure design quality of MOOCs. In *Advanced Learning Technologies (ICALT), 2014 IEEE 14th International Conference on*. IEEE, 44–48.

Rebooting Information Technology Programs

Panel

Rajendra K. Raj
Rochester Institute of Technology
Rochester, New York, USA
rajendra.k.raj@rit.edu

Jim Leone
Rochester Institute of Technology
Rochester, New York, USA
jim.leone@rit.edu

Allen Parrish
United States Naval Academy
Annapolis, Maryland, USA
aparrish@usna.edu

Mihaela Sabin
University of New Hampshire
Manchester, New Hampshire, USA
mihaela.sabin@unh.edu

ABSTRACT

The continuing worldwide demand for a diverse, competent, computing workforce has had a major impact on undergraduate information technology (IT) education. New degree programs in IT have been created and existing IT programs have been recreated. The enormity of the demand for IT graduates, as well as societal pressures, require such rebooted IT programs to attract a diverse student body. The panelists will describe their experiences and present different perspectives toward rebooting IT education to handle technological changes, to ensure competent graduates via program accreditation, and to address issues of diversity and inclusion.

CCS CONCEPTS

• **Social and professional topics** → Accreditation • **Social and professional topics** → Information technology education

KEYWORDS

Information technology programs; computing programs; technological change; diversity; gender gap; program accreditation

1 INTRODUCTION

In the early days of information technology (IT) education, it was critical for the new academic discipline to demonstrate its uniqueness and establish how it was different from existing computing disciplines [3]. With an early focus on clarifying IT curriculum and degree programs, IT educators seemed to act as

if they had a "tiger by its tail" and felt IT education needed to deal with ongoing and emerging changes [10]. In the ensuing decade, significant changes in technologies, combined with a worldwide need for a computing workforce, resulted in the growth of new IT programs and modifications to existing ones.

Rapid growth in IT programs brought its set of issues. Identifying IT programs simply based on the "information technology" name was inadequate, necessitating a process to distinguish and evaluate IT degree programs [5]. Determining knowledge areas and curricular also became critical [7, 8]. The need for quality and standardization thus led to new ABET accreditation criteria for IT, as IT programs sought recognition via accreditation [1].

The continued developments in IT have not brought clarity, as to what IT programs of the future ought to be and how to get there. Fitting well into the "Enabling the Future" theme of both SIGITE and RIIT conferences, this panel focuses on how IT programs can continue to be rebooted to meet societal needs of computing. The panelists will discuss how their diverse experiences are reshaping their IT-related programs.

2 SESSION GOALS

The primary goals of this panel session are to:

1. Present different perspectives toward rebooting IT education to handle dynamic growth of technologies, and address issues of diversity and inclusion.
2. Discuss approaches needed to ensure competent IT graduates including accreditation and certifications.
3. Seek audience input on rebooting IT education.
4. Summarize the session.

The panel targets college faculty and administrators who are looking to adapt their existing programs in IT and IT-related disciplines and grow them to meet workforce needs for competent graduates with broader participation from diverse groups. Thus, the focus on rebooting information technology education is likely to be of interest to the typical SIGITE and RIIT audience.

Table 1: Panel Structure

	Description	Duration (minutes)
1.	Introductions	5
2.	Panelists' presentations	45
3.	Audience Q&A/Discussion	30
4.	Summary	10

3 PANELISTS' POSITIONS

Table 1 outlines how the panel will be structured. Ample time is provided for audience interaction. What follows next are brief bios and position statements of the panelists.

- **Rajendra K. Raj**, a professor of computer science at Rochester Institute of Technology (RIT), focuses on computing education; program assessment and accreditation; and developing well-rounded computing professionals. Prior to RIT, he worked as an IT professional for a major financial services firm as a manager, architect and software developer responsible for delivering IT solutions in global settings.

  Raj will moderate the panel, introduce the panelists, and present the panel's motivation including the critical needs to (a) ensure student competence via program accreditation and standardization, and (b) attract a larger and more diverse student population. He will facilitate the audience Q&A and discussion, and summarize the session.

- **Jim Leone** is a professor of information sciences and technologies at RIT. His career spans two primary STEM disciplines, chemistry and computing. He has always viewed himself an educator, devoting his efforts in the past three decades in supporting IT curriculum development and program accreditation.

  Leone will describe how two long-time successful RIT degrees, IT and Networking, began to experience declining enrollment at a time when the rest of RIT's computing college was experiencing significant growth. The two programs were thus in need of an urgent reboot. He will discuss the role of various factors—such as a reconstituted academic department, a dissolved department, newly launched degree programs within the college, and alphabetical program listing—in the rebooting of RIT's new IT programs titled Web and Mobile Computing (WMC), and Computer Information Technology (CIT).

- **Allen Parrish** is Professor and Chair of the department of Cyber Science at The United States Naval Academy (USNA), which offers the Cyber Operations degree. Prior to this appointment, Dr. Parrish served for 26 years on the faculty at the University of Alabama. He currently heads major efforts to revise the ABET's computing accreditation criteria and to develop new criteria for cybersecurity [4].

  Parrish will discuss the Cyber Operations program at the USNA. Combining both cyber offense and defense, the degree is a computing program that provides a foundation of computers, programming, networks, cyber-physical systems and applied cryptography. As the program favors breadth of topics over depth, it then broadens out to a view of cyber, which includes legal issues, policy, hacktivism, and social factors. Although the degree is offered in a military setting, its fundamental approach and curricular content equally applies to private sector enterprise computing.

- **Mihaela Sabin** is Chair of the IT2017 Task Group. She serves as Vice-Chair for Education on SIGITE Executive Committee. Sabin is an associate professor of computer science at the University of New Hampshire (UNH). She has been involved in curriculum development and revision of undergraduate and graduate programs in CS and IT at UNH. Her research areas include IT curricula and women in computing.

  Sabin will discuss issues relating to the gender gap in IT education and how IT programs can reclaim the talent of women and underrepresented groups [2, 6]. She will focus on the breadth of skills that require contexts where collaborative, project-based, and reflective practices happen among peers and mentors and with expertise from IT professionals, in and outside the classroom [9].

REFERENCES

[1] ABET, Criteria for Accrediting Computing Programs, 2017-2018, on the Internet at http://www.abet.org/accreditation/accreditation-criteria/criteria-for-accrediting-computing-programs-2017-2018/, accessed: August 7, 2017.

[2] Catherine Aschcroft, Brad McLain, and Elizabeth Eger. Women in Tech: The Facts. National Center for Women & Technology (NCWIT). 2016. on the Internet at https://www.ncwit.org/resources/women-tech-facts-2016-16-update, accessed: August 7, 2017.

[3] Ed Anthony. 2003. Computing education in academia: toward differentiating the disciplines. In *Proceedings of the 4th conference on Information technology curriculum* (CITC4 '03). ACM, New York, 1-8.

[4] Jean Blair, Joseph J. Ekstrom, and Mark Stockman. 2017. Breakout: Developing Accreditation Criteria for Undergraduate Cybersecurity Programs. In *21st Colloquium for Information Systems Security Education (CISSE 2017)*, Las Vegas.

[5] Andrew Hansen, Bikalpa Neupane, Barry M. Lunt, and Richard Ofori. 2012. Identifying and evaluating information technology bachelor's degree programs. In *Proceedings of the 1st Annual conference on Research in information technology* (RIIT '12). ACM, New York., 19-24.

[6] Paul Lee, Duncan Stewart, and Cornelia Calugar-Pop. 2016. Women in IT. Technology, Media, and Telecommunication Predictions 2016. Deloitte Touche Tohmatsu Limited, UK: London

[7] Barry M. Lunt, Joseph J. Ekstrom, Sandra Gorka, Gregory Hislop, Reza Kamali, Eydie Lawson, Richard LeBlanc, Jacob Miller and Han Reichgelt. 2008. Information Technology 2008: Curriculum Guidelines for Undergraduate Degree Programs in Information Technology, November 2008, on the Internet at http://www.acm.org/education/curricula/IT2008%20Curriculum.pdf, accessed: August 7, 2017.

[8] Mihaela Sabin, Svetlana Peltsverger, Cara Tang, and Barry M. Lunt. 2016. ACM/IEEE-CS Information Technology Curriculum 2017: A Status Update. In *Proceedings of the 17th Annual Conference on Information Technology Education* (SIGITE '16). ACM, New York, 102-103.

[9] Rebecca Winthrop and Eileen McGiveney. 2017. Skills for a Changing World: Advancing Quality Learning for Vibrant Societies. Center for Universal Education, Brooking Institute.

[10] Stephen J. Zilora, Daniel Bogaard and Jim Leone. 2013. The changing face of information technology. In *Proceedings of the 14th annual ACM SIGITE conference on Information technology education* (SIGITE '13). ACM, New York. 29-34.

Teaching IoT (Internet of Things) Analytics

Jai W. Kang
Rochester Institute of Technology
152 Lomb Memorial Drive
Rochester, NY 14623
585-475-5362
jai.kang@rit.edu

Qi Yu
Rochester Institute of Technology
152 Lomb Memorial Drive
Rochester, NY 14623
585-475-6929
qi.yu@rit.edu

Erik Golen
Rochester Institute of Technology
152 Lomb Memorial Drive
Rochester, NY 14623
585-475-4409
efgics@rit.edu

ABSTRACT

The rapid proliferation of Internet of Things devices around the world has led to a major increase in demand from industry for students equipped with the skills necessary to make continued advances in this area. Consequently, advanced analytical skills are in urgent need to capitalize the massive amount raw data collected by various IoT devices. To address the market demand in IoT and Analytics, the Information Sciences and Technologies department at the Rochester Institute of Technology has proposed an advanced certificate in IoT Analytics that extends across its three Master of Science degree programs. The central focus of this work is a presentation of this advanced certificate program that is designed to encompass the four pillars of IoT, namely Sensors, Communications, Computing Devices, and Analytics.

Keywords

Information sciences and technologies; big data; cloud computing; curriculum; data analytics; internet of things; network.

1. INTRODUCTION

The Information Sciences and Technologies (IST) department at Rochester Institute of Technology (RIT) strives for keeping the degree programs up to date with technology advances to prepare students for their job hunting and future professional career. We adopted one of the disruptive technologies, *Cloud Computing*, as a database course in 2009 [11] and reported its progress in 2011 [10]. In 2013, we revised our master's program as an *Analytic* centric program [14], and its success story appeared in [15]. While recommending *Security* requirements to be embedded in the courses across two master's degree programs in IST and NSA (Networking and Systems Administrations), we also considered the modern computing landscape of three key building blocks: *Internet of Things (IoT), Cloud Computing,* and *Big Data* [16]. This paper emphasized that students need to understand security requirements not only within each of the three building blocks but the interactions thereof.

SIGITE'17, October 4–7, 2017, Rochester, NY, USA
© 2017 Association for Computing Machinery.
ACM ISBN 978-1-4503-5100-3/17/10...$15.00
https://doi.org/10.1145/3125659.3125689

Gartner anticipates that there will be 26 billion Internet connected things by 2020 resulting in the generation of massively amounts of data that need to be stored and processed [18]. As IoT technology advances, the value can be realized from analyzing the data generated by the connected things. In other words, a real insight is generated by the intersection of IoT and Analytics, which is referred as *IoT Analytics* [17]. [7] refers IoT as a prominent driver to the fourth Industrial Revolution (IR) that will have impacts throughout the business and industry continuum around the world. *IoT Analytics* motivates our next curricular update in the IST department at RIT.

As part of pursuing details of IoT Analytic course topics, a number of IT related recent curricula research articles reveal many IoT course offerings: Teaching IoT Concepts [1]; IoT Design of Experiment [4]; Open Source Platform Design [5]; Course Design for IoT Using Lab of Things from Microsoft Research that includes Data Mining for future plan [13]; Active Learning in Open Elective Courses [19]; Raspberry Pi: An Effective Vehicle in Teaching the IoT [26]; Integrating IoT into STEM Undergraduate Education [9]; and Teaching the IoT [6] which is the only graduate course in these findings. None of these courses associate teaching to the interaction of IoT and Data Analytics as IoT Analytics. A few courses include their teaching approaches by Active Learning, Project-Based, and Problem & Project Based Learning.

As far as IoT Analytic course topics are concerned, we start defining the pillars of IoT with their technologies. The four pillars are Sensors, Communications, Computing Devices, and Analytics. Together, these pillars constitute the progression of IoT data from its rawest form to knowledge discovered from collected data. While raw sensor data progresses to a gateway and then to the cloud, it is important to recognize which locations we are able to apply the analytics to generate real insight: *Edge, Data Stream, and Data Lake*.

To ensure success, it is also important to determine the correct format for a curricular structure. In this paper, we provide an overview of the IST department, which justifies why we are at a unique position to teach IoT analytic related topics. We then identify a number of curricular structures to teach these topics, including a new master program, a concentration within an existing master program, and an advanced certificate focusing on IoT analytics. We discuss the major benefits of an advanced certificate to show why it provides the best option for us.

The remainder of the paper is organized as follows. We begin by introducing the four pillars of IoT and describe the basic concepts and functionalities of each in Section 2. Section 3 describes our curricular choice of teaching IoT Analytics. Section

4 discusses the curriculum of an advanced certificate consisting of four courses, which will be offered in a 2+2 format with the first two as core courses and the last two as elective courses. Section 5 discusses how the new program will be assessed before concluding the paper in Section 6.

2. Pillars of IoT

Our Advanced Certificate in IoT Analytics is structured around what we have deemed to be the pillars of IoT, which include *sensors, communications, computing devices, and analytics* as shown in Figure 1. Together, these pillars constitute the progression of IoT data from its rawest form to knowledge discovered from collected data.

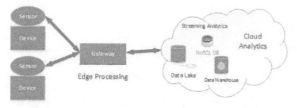

Figure 1. IoT Pillars

2.1 Sensors

With respect to IoT, sensors are miniature devices that monitor a particular phenomenon of interest [8]. For example, in a Smart Home, some typical phenomena include temperature, humidity, and motion sensing for monitoring the environment and keeping track of its inhabitants. Personalized healthcare monitoring devices like the FitBit extend beyond a static environment and accompany their users by sensing motion through accelerometers, gyroscopes, and magnetometers, depending upon their complexity. Regardless of the application, sensors convert electrical input signals to units called *counts* that are related to the sensitivity of the sensor. Using the known sensitivity of the sensor, the counts are then scaled to provide human understandable units such as degrees Celsius.

Sensor data must be periodically transmitted from the source to a sink node, or *aggregator* [2]. The responsibility of the aggregator is to collect data from various IoT devices and direct the data towards remote processing resources in the cloud and eventually, back to the IoT devices. As such, communications play an important role in moving data from the sensor that generated it to the processing resource that will perform analytics. To limit locality restrictions on IoT devices, wireless communication between IoT devices and an aggregator is standard.

2.2 Communications

In most IoT applications, the distance between an IoT device and an aggregator is short, which allows for single hop wireless communication standards such as Bluetooth Low Energy, Zigbee, and 802.11 in either infrastructure or ad-hoc mode to be used. In terms of curriculum, the amount of prerequisite networking knowledge required for students is minimal since the networking is accomplished on a point to point basis with little complexity [2]. For rare cases where large areas must be sensed, such as monitoring moisture across farmland extended tens of acres, multi-hop communication may be needed, at which point more advanced protocols are required. Regardless of the distance between IoT devices and an aggregator, once sensor data has reached aggregator, it will reach its processing resources over a wired connection on the Internet.

2.3 Computing Devices

Computing devices consist of three main types in IoT. These include data collection platforms, aggregators, and remote processing resources [8]. Data collection platforms comprise one or more sensors, resource limited processor boards, low capacity memory modules, and wireless communication devices. These platforms are constructed in a variety of ways from prototype boards, such as an Arduino or Raspberry Pi to custom micro controllers to single board computers. Common among all of these approaches is that data collection platforms have relatively finite processing resources and memory, which means that they must possess the capability to offload sensor data with sufficient frequency to support the application at hand.

As previously stated, data aggregators act as gateways for IoT device data to reach remote computing devices and for the remote computing devices to command IoT devices after processing data. Data aggregators are therefore equipped with both wireless and wired communication devices and have much higher processing capabilities and onboard memory than data collection platforms. When IoT data reaches the aggregator, it must identify which device sent the data and then determine which remote processing resources it should be routed to and vice versa. Depending upon the technological maturity of the data collection platform, an aggregator may be as simple as a Linksys access point to as complex as a customized data collector housed in a microcomputer.

Once the aggregator has directed IoT device data to the appropriate remote processing resource in the cloud, analytics can begin. Remote processing resources may range from high performance computing clusters to servers equipped with GPUs to virtualized processing containers.

The progression of raw sensor data reaching an aggregator and then its ultimate destination of the remote processing resource leads up to the final IoT pillar, analytics. Within the analytics pillar, we consider three types - *Edge Processing, Streaming Analytics,* and *Cloud Analytics* [12].

2.4 Analytics

While the raw sensor data make progresses to reach an aggregator and then to its ultimate destination of the remote processing resource, it is important to recognize at which locations we are to apply the analytics in order to generate real insight from the IoT ecosystem. There are three potential locations: *Edge, Data Stream, and Data Lake*. The types of analytics depend on factors like volumes of datasets, data types, quality of data, privacy concerns, real-time or batch processing needs.

Edge Processing: When the IoT sources generate large datasets, it increases latency and may be infeasible to transfer due to poor or underpowered network connections. A solution to these types of issues is to process and analyze data directly at or near the source – also known as *Edge Processing* [12]. For example, modern jet engines generate up to 1 TB of data per flight. Even though traditional aggregators are equipped with limited computing power, both hardware gateway vendors like Cisco and Intel, and server vendors like Dell offer smart gateways with more computing power including more storage and even analytic capabilities. The large dataset can be processed in a smart Gateway to send only average values or outliers to the cloud. Alternatively, the aggregated data can be stored locally in the smart Gateway and transferred to the cloud when the network connection is better [3].

Streaming Analytics: Forrester defines *Streaming Analytics* platform as a "software that can filter, aggregate, enrich, and analyze a high throughput of data from multiple disparate live data sources and in any data format to identify simple and complex patterns to visualize business in real-time, detect urgent situations, and automate immediate actions [23]." When data streams generated from the sensors reach the remote processing resource, the Cloud, they can be applied to either a real-time system or a batch system based on system requirements. The real-time system analyzes the streaming data to perform analytics without storing them on a data store, which is called *Streaming Analytics*. This streaming analytic includes performing statistical analysis of data in motion or applying a predictive model to find any deviations in the real-time stream data. The predictive models are built offline using machine learning algorithms based on the historical training data.

Cloud Analytics: When the sensor data reach the Cloud for batch processing, they arrive in a Data Lake, which is driven by the Hadoop platform and conceptually similar to a Data Mart or Data Warehouse. But data in a Data Lake holds its raw format until it is needed for *Cloud Analytics* or other needs like OLAP (Online Analytical Processing) cube analysis. Appling ETL (Extract, Transform and Load) processes to data in the lake, they can be updated in either a data warehouse for the OLAP queries or a NoSQL database for Natural Language Processing (NLP) as well. Data analytics techniques including statistical analysis, machine learning and visualization can be applied to the IoT datasets in the Data Lake [12].

3. ADVANCED CERTIFICATE in IoT ANALYTICS

In this section, we start by providing an overview of the IST department, which helps justify why we are at a unique position to teach IoT analytics related topics. We will then identify a number of curricular structures to teach these topics, including building a new degree program, forming a concentration within a program, and creating a new advanced certificate focusing on IoT analytics. We will discuss the major benefits of the advanced certificate to show why it provides the best option for us.

The IST department is the home of three undergraduate and three graduate programs. Since the IoT and analytics related courses are at the graduate level, we will briefly introduce the three graduate programs of the department. In particular, the M.S. in Information Sciences and Technologies (IST) puts a strong emphasis on data science with a focus on how data is analyzed, managed, and visualized in the modern computing industry. The M.S in Networking and System Administration (NSA) covers both classical theories/concepts on wired and wireless network modeling and analysis as well as emerging computing and networking technologies, such as cloud computing and Internet of Things. Finally, the M.S. Human-Computer Interaction (HCI) explores the design, evaluation, and implementation of interactive computing systems. The ability to offer these three graduate programs demonstrates that the faculty of the department has the required expertise to cover all the important components in an IoT system that includes the underlying (wired and/or wireless) network infrastructure, data acquisition techniques and UI design patterns to collect data from IoT devices, and analytical tools/models for knowledge discovery from the collected data.

The desired technical expertise from the faculty coupled with the success of running three graduate programs puts the IST department in a unique and strong position to offer IoT

analytics. To ensure success, it is also important to determine a right format for a curricular structure. There are three possible choices: a separate degree program, a concentration with a program, and an advanced certificate. A master level graduate program at RIT consists of 30 credit hours, which is roughly equivalent to 10 courses (most graduate courses in RIT are worth of 3 credits). Even though we can reuse some of the courses from department's existing graduate programs, a decent number of new courses may still need to be developed to make a complete degree program. This will be a rather time consuming process. Even after these courses are developed, new faculty members may need to be recruited to teach these courses as the department has already fully utilized its personnel to cover the existing courses. Getting additional faculty lines demands a lengthy administrative approval process. A much more efficient way is to offer IoT analytics related topics to group a number of relevant courses and make them a concentration. A concentration typically consists of 2-4 elective courses to provide enough depth of study in a given program. However, there are two major limitations with a concentration. First, it is only available to the students in one graduate program. Due to the interdisciplinary nature of the IoT analytics, it is hard to decide which of the three existing programs is the best host for this new concentration. Second, while a concentration offers a way to organize students' plan of study, it is not explicitly reflected in their transcripts or diplomas. However, students may want this important skillset to be formally recognized, which may benefit their job hunting and future professional career.

Finally, an advanced certificate is comprised of a four-course sequence that allows a student to develop expertise in a particular field. An advanced certificate offers a number of key benefits, making it our best choice to offer IoT analytics. First, it only consists of four courses, making both course development and delivery much easier than a 10-course degree program. Second, it is standalone and independent from other degree programs. But students in other degree programs (e.g., IST, NSA, and HCI) can pursue the advanced certificate simultaneously. Third, the certificate provides a formal way to recognize the skills and special training that a student receives in this field. Last, besides serving the current students, the advanced certificate also provides an effective means to attract new students into RIT and the IST department. Some students may start by joining the advanced certificate and then extend their study to a full M.S. program, such as IST, NSA, and HCI based on their interest.

4. CURRICULUM

The curriculum of the advanced certificate consists of four courses, which will be offered in a 2+2 format with the first two as the core courses and the last two as the elective courses. The two core courses aim to build the foundation in IoT analytics, which all the students are required to take. The first core course will be a newly developed IoT foundation course that focuses IoT side of the advanced certificate, covering the fundamental concepts in IoT technology. The second core course will be an existing data analytics course being offered by our MS-IST program, titled "Analytical Thinking (ISTE-600)". This course will focus on the analytics side of the certificate, covering fundamental data mining techniques, including various kinds of supervised and unsupervised data mining models, data preprocessing, and model evaluation.

The elective courses will build upon the fundamental skills that students develop through taking the core courses and further extend them through advanced training. We are currently considering the following five elective courses including two advanced analytics courses: Data-Driven Knowledge Discovery (ISTE-780) and Visual Analytics (ISTE-782), and two IoT related courses: Data Acquisition and Analysis in IoT (NSSA-yyy), Prototyping Wearable & IoT Devices (HCIN-720). Four of these courses are exiting courses currently being offered by one of our three graduate programs. Reusing existing courses not only minimizes the effort for course development and delivery, but also facilitates and motivates students in our current graduate programs to take the advanced certificate. Table 1 summarizes topics covered in the certificate by core and elective courses followed by course descriptions.

Table 1. IoT Topics vs. Courses

	Core Courses		Electives (Choose 2)			
	NSSA-xxx	ISTE-600	ISTE-780	ISTE-782	NSSA-yyy	HCIN-720
Hosting Degree Programs	NSA (new)	IST	IST	IST	NSA (new)	HCI
IoT Pillars/Topics						
1) Sensors:						
Programming sensors	x					x
API	x					x
Hardware	x					x
2) Communications:						
Wireless Communications	x				x	x
Networking Protocols & Standards	x				x	x
Info Privacy & Security	x					
3) Computing Devices:						
Data Collection Devices	x				x	x
Aggregator	x				x	
Remote Processing Resources	x				x	
4) Analytics:						
Data Mining (Supervised/Unsupervised)		x	x			
Data Collection		x	x	x	x	
Data Preprocessing		x	x	x	x	
Statistical Analysis		x	x	x	x	
Big Data (Hadoop, NoSQL)			x			
Cloud Computing	x		x			
Visualization		x		x	x	x

4.1 Core Courses

4.1.1 NSSA-xxx Foundation of IoT

This course provides students with an overview of the area of IoT and hands-on laboratory experiences to put their knowledge into practice. The overall IoT architecture is first presented with the information flow from data collection devices to aggregators to remote processing resources and back again. Throughout the remainder of the course, the underlying technologies for these architectural building blocks are discussed in detail, with laboratory exercises given on both the Raspberry Pi and Arduino Uno as exemplary platforms, culminating in a final project where students develop a prototype IoT system of their own. To motivate the data analytics side of IoT, example applications are shown throughout the semester that highlight Edge Processing, Streaming Analytics, and Cloud Analytics, and how these processing techniques and resultant feedback are integrated into the IoT architecture.

4.1.2 ISTE-600 Analytical Thinking

This core course focuses on the analytics side of the IoT Analytics certificate, covering fundamental data mining techniques, including various kinds of supervised and unsupervised data mining models, data preprocessing, model evaluation and visualization.

The Critical Thinking Community [12] defines all thinking by eight elements: "Whenever we think for a purpose within a point of view based on assumptions leading to implications and consequences. We use concepts, ideas and theories to interpret idea, facts, and experiences in order to answer questions, solve problems, and resolve issues. Thinking, then 1) generates Purposes, 2) raises Questions, 3) uses Information, 4) utilizes Concepts, 5) makes Inferences, 6) makes Assumptions, 7) generates Implications and 8) embodies a Point of View."

Students customize the above analytical thinking approaches to solve data mining problems following the Cross Industry Standard Process for Data Mining [20]: 1) business understanding, 2) data understanding, 3) data preparation, 4) modeling, 5) evaluation, and 6) deployment.

Students work in teams on a problem of their choosing that is interesting, significant and relevant to applying data mining algorithms and techniques to real-world problems like IoT. Students use the Weka [25], other data mining software, and Tableau [21] for visual analysis and presentations. Student teams construct excellent stories with interactive and dynamic dashboards for their projects with the help of these visual analytic tools.

Topics covered in Fundamental Analytics: Fundamental data mining techniques, including supervised (e.g., Decision Tree, Rule-based, Nearest-Neighbor, Naïve Bayes, Artificial Neural Network & Ensemble Models) and unsupervised (e.g., Association, Cluster Analyses & Anomaly Detection) data mining models; data preprocessing; model evaluation; and visualization.

4.2 Elective Courses

4.2.1 ISTE-780 Data Driven Knowledge Discovery

ISTE-780 is one of the advanced elective courses in the analytics domain of the MS-IST program. This course provides advanced training to students in data analytics, with a focus on statistical learning approaches in the context of the data-driven knowledge discovery process. The main objectives of this class are to

1. Model and understand complex datasets using statistical learning tools that discover useful information and knowledge from large-scale datasets by conducting both supervised and unsupervised learning.
2. Scale statistical learning algorithms with powerful, distributed, and cloud-based systems (e.g., Apache

Hadoop and Mahout) to handle large-scale datasets.

3. Learn data analytics languages (R and Python) and apply statistical packages (R and scikit-learn) to tackle real-world data analytics problems

Main topics of the course include both state-of-the art supervised and unsupervised statistical learning models. On the supervised learning side, it covers regression models, such as best subset regression, ridge regression, LASSO, and principle components regression, and classification models, such as logistic regression, linear discriminant analysis, support vector machine, and random forest. On the unsupervised learning side, it covers key clustering models, such as k-means and spectral clustering, and dimensionality reduction techniques, such as principle component analysis and latent dirichlet allocation.

4.2.2 ISTE-782 Visual Analytics

The main thrust of visual analytics is to discover patterns in data that were previously obscured prior to visualizing it [24]. Latent patterns are rarely seen when data is confined to a spreadsheet or database. From an IoT perspective, visual analytics is important in that collections of disparate sensors are likely to be analyzed and the ability for humans to make sense of multiple inputs is necessary. For example, in a smart home, a user would like to gain a complete understanding of their monitored environment whether or not they are home to allow them to make necessary adjustments to temperature, humidity, and other phenomena. Furthermore, sensor readings are space and time varying, as these are the key features in Geographical Information Systems (GIS) and remote sensing applications. This space-time visualization is also critical in visualizing IoT data since these devices may span longer distances than a single home and consist of long time spans. This course covers space-time variations in data, interaction with visualizations, human cognition of visualizations, and extends to application areas of GIS, IoT, and cyber security and how visualizations inform practitioners in those areas.

4.2.3 NSSA-yyy Data Acquisition and Analysis in IoT

To bridge the gap from IoT data generating platforms to data analytics, this course provides students with the opportunity to learn how to generate data sets of their own from existing IoT devices in order to produce meaningful results from analytics. This is in stark contrast to typical student experiences, where the student will locate a data set online that has been analyzed countless times and may not contain the data necessary to produce meaningful results. The course begins with a discussion of practical issues associated with gathering data from sensors, include sensitivity of sensing devices, power consumption, data storage and in the case of multi-sensor systems, time synchronization between devices and differing sampling rates. Fundamentals of data acquisition are then discussed with classical design of experiments presented, including hypothesis testing and data sampling, so that students understand the importance of collecting the "correct" data so that features can be constructed. During the feature construction process, students are shown that data acquisition and performing analytics is an iterative process where the analytics often informs the experimenter about whether or not the features are sufficient in number and in content.

4.2.4 HCIN-720 Prototyping Wearable and IoT Devices

This course focuses on rapidly prototyping and evaluating the utility of IoT devices, wearable or otherwise, specific. For the purposes of this course, the student will recognize an IoT device as the proliferation of hardware, software, and resultant data generated by the device. As this course is offered out of the

Human Computer Interaction MS degree program, its focus is on the user experience with the device being prototyped. This includes the physical interaction between user and prototype, such as how understandable a smart thermostat may be to the average person. Prototyping skills learned in this course range from 3D printing, laser cutting, sewing, and modeling to capacitive sensing, actuation, and electronics theory. To bring the prototypes to life, students learn event-driven programming skills required in programming an Arduino or Photon and external communication through Bluetooth Low Energy or WiFi. Data is represented in the course through visualization and web technologies for display, such as the REST web API and node.js.

5. ASSESSMENT

In this section, we identify a few program goals and student learning outcomes (see Table 2), which will be used to assess the Advanced Certificate in IoT Analytics. Assessment data will be collected and reviewed every three years. The student learning outcomes are assessed from student activities in coursework against a rubric designed for that outcome. The benchmark is that 80% of the students will achieve competence in that outcome. Two of those are assessed using coursework in the core and one from a selected elective course.

Table 2. Program Assessment

Program Goals	Student Learning Outcomes	Data Source / Measurement
1. Design IoT systems to collect, communicate, and aggregate sensor data.	Create a prototype IoT system that consists of all the major computing devices and collect data for simple analysis.	NSSA-xxx *Foundations of IoT:* Rubric used to assess the fundamental knowledge in IoT
2. Apply specialized analytical and technical skills for IoT data analysis	Preprocess and mine sensor data using different types of IoT analytics techniques	ISTE-600 *Analytical Thinking:* Rubric used to measure effectiveness of IoT data analysis
3. Design IoT information services to enhance the value of raw IoT data of various types	Demonstrate advanced data acquisition and/or analytical skills in the IoT domain	An advanced project in a student-selected elective course - Project is assessed via rubric

Besides assessing student-learning outcomes, we also plan to evaluate the attractiveness of the proposed advanced certificate by keeping track of the number of capstones that our current MS students choose to work in IoT analytics. The capstone is the culminating experience that a student must complete in order to obtain a MS degree. Choosing a capstone topic in IoT analytics demonstrates that a student has not only gained sufficient technical expertise but also developed strong interest in studying and working in this area.

6. CONCLUSION

To meet industry demand for skilled practitioners in IoT and data analytics, the IST Department at RIT has crafted a new IoT Analytics advanced certificate program that extends across its three MS programs. Students who earn this certificate are expected to carve out a valuable niche in that their skills will run the gamut of the four pillars of IoT, namely Sensors, Communications, Computing Devices, and Analytics. Through its two core courses, students will acquire the background knowledge in IoT architecture and analytics needed to delve further into their chosen interest areas that are covered by the four elective courses that span the three MS programs. Future work includes additional electives, such as an advanced networking and computing technologies course for implementing cloud analytics applications.

7. REFERENCES

[1] Ali, Farha. 2015. Teaching the Internet of Things Concepts. In *Proceedings of the WESE'15: Workshop on Embedded and Cyber-Physical Systems Education* (WESE'15), Martin Edin Grimheden (Ed.). ACM, New York, NY, USA, , Article 10 , 6 pages. DOI: http://dx.doi.org/10.1145/2832920.2832930

[2] Atzori, L., Iera, A., & Morabito, G. 2010. The Internet of Things: A Survey. *Computer Networks*, 54(15), 2787-2805.

[3] Baars, H., & Ereth, J. 2016. From Data Warehouses to Analytical Atoms–The Internet of Things as a Centrifugal Force in Business Intelligence and Analytics.

[4] Chen, G. W. 2016. The Design of Experimental Course for Internet of Things Based on ZigBee. In *Intelligent Human-Machine Systems and Cybernetics (IHMSC), 2016 8th International Conference on* (Vol. 2, pp. 341-344). IEEE.

[5] Dobrilovic, D., & Zeljko, S. 2016. Design of open-source platform for introducing Internet of Things in university curricula. In *Applied Computational Intelligence and Informatics (SACI), 2016 IEEE 11th International Symposium on* (pp. 273-276). IEEE.

[6] Förster, A., Dede, J., Könsgen, A., Udugama, A., & Zaman, I. (2017). Teaching the Internet of Things. *GetMobile: Mobile Computing and Communications*, 20(3), 24-28.

[7] Geng, H. (Ed.). 2017. *Internet of Things and Data Analytics Handbook*. John Wiley & Sons.

[8] Gubbi, J., Buyya, R., Marusic, S., & Palaniswami, M. 2013. Internet of Things (IoT): A Vision, Architectural Elements, and Future Directions. *Future generation computer systems*, 29(7), 1645-1660.

[9] He, J., Lo, D. C. T., Xie, Y., & Lartigue, J. 2016. Integrating Internet of Things (IoT) into STEM undergraduate education: Case study of a modern technology infused courseware for embedded system course. In *Frontiers in Education Conference (FIE), 2016 IEEE* (pp. 1-9). IEEE.

[10] Holden, E.P., J.W. Kang, Anderson, G.R., D.P. Bills, M. 2011. Databases in the Cloud: A status report. ACM SIGITE Conference 2011, October 20-22, 2011 West Point, NY.

[11] Holden, E.P., J.W. Kang, D.P. Bills, M. Ilyassov. 2009. Databases in the Cloud: A work in progress. ACM SIGITE Conference 2009: pp 138-143, October 22-24, 2009 Fairfax, VA.

[12] Jaokar, A. 2017, Data Science for Internet of Things: Strategies for Product Development Using Streaming, Sensor Fusion and Deep Learning.ajit.jaokar@futuretext.com

[13] Jeong, G. M., Truong, P. H., Lee, T. Y., Choi, J. W., & Lee, M. 2016. Course design for Internet of Things using Lab of Things of Microsoft Research. In *Frontiers in Education Conference (FIE), 2016 IEEE* (pp. 1-6). IEEE.

[14] Kang, J. W., Holden, E. P., & Yu, Q. 2014. Design of an analytic centric MS degree in information sciences and technologies. In *Proceedings of the 15th Annual Conference on Information technology education* (pp. 147-152). ACM.

[15] Kang, J. W., Holden, E. P., & Yu, Q. 2015. Pillars of Analytics Applied in MS Degree in Information Sciences and Technologies. In *Proceedings of the 16th Annual Conference on Information Technology Education* (pp. 83-88). ACM.

[16] Kang, J. W., Yu, Q., Holden, E. P., & Oh, T. H. 2016. Security Requirements Embedded in MS Programs in Information Sciences and Technologies. In *Proceedings of the 17th Annual Conference on Information Technology Education* (pp. 77-82). ACM.

[17] Markkanen, A., & Shey, D. 2014. The intersection of analytics and the internet of things. *IEEE Internet of Things*.

[18] Modi, C., Patel, D., Borisaniya, B., Patel, A., and Rajarajan, M. 2013. A survey on security issues and solutions at different layers of Cloud computing. *The Journal of Supercomputing*, 63(2): 561-592.

[19] Raikar, M. M., Desai, P., & Naragund, J. G. 2016. Active learning explored in Open elective course: Internet of Things (IoT). In *Technology for Education (T4E), 2016 IEEE Eighth International Conference on* (pp. 15-18). IEEE.

[20] Shearer, C. 2000. The CRISP-DM model: the new blueprint for data mining. *Journal of data warehousing*, 5(4), 13-22.

[21] Tableau: http://www.tableausoftware.com/.

[22] The Critical Community: Elements and Standards Learning Tool. Retrieved May 12, 2014, from http://www.criticalthinking.org/pages/elements-and-standards-learning-tool/783.

[23] The Forrester Wave: Big Data Streaming Analytics, Q1 2016. Retrieved June 1, 2017 from http://sqlstream.com/wp-content/uploads/2016/12/Forrester-Streaming-Analytics-Report-2016.pdf

[24] Thomas, J. J. 2005. Illuminating the Path: The research and development agenda for visual analytics. *IEEE Computer Society*.

[25] Weka: http://www.cs.waikato.ac.nz/ml/weka/.

[26] Zhong, X., & Liang, Y. 2016. Raspberry Pi: An Effective Vehicle in Teaching the Internet of Things in Computer Science and Engineering. *Electronics*, 5(3), 56.

Exploration of Text Analytic Tooling on Classwork to Support Students' Learning in Information Technology

Madhuri Jujare
San Jose State University
madhuri.jujare@sjsu.edu

Anna Baynes
IBM
ashaver@us.ibm.com

ABSTRACT

Information technology graduates reach industry and innovate for the future after completing demanding degrees. Upper division college courses require long hours of work on class projects and exams. Some students have hopes of completing their degrees, but are deterred due to many different issues. Instructors can monitor students' progress based on their assignments, projects, and exams. Judging students' understanding and potential for success becomes more difficult when handling large classes. In this paper we utilize IBM Text Analytics Web Tooling on large amounts of unstructured text data collected from past assignments, exams, and discussions to help professors make assessments faster for large classes. In particular, we focus on an Information Security course offered at San Jose State University and use its classroom-generated data to determine if the extracted information provides strong insights for professors to help struggling students. We examine these issues through exploratory analysis.

1 INTRODUCTION

Several thousand students enroll in information technology classes each year at universities around the world. They are inspired by their projects, professors, and classmates to develop their information technology experience and skills. They take these experiences to industry and workplaces in the form of developers, management, validation engineers, technical writers, and other professionals. The students who reach industry to contribute and innovate for the future, are not there by accident, but through hard work, dedication, and time in the required upper division information technology courses. There are several hundred students who had hopes of completing their information technology degrees, but due to different hardships and decisions, fell short. It is natural for courses to have a bell-curve outcome of grades and success, but given the extreme shortage in STEM degrees for the workforce [1], there is potential for improvement in information technology education within the classroom to accelerate the foundation for success in upper division computer science courses.

In particular, we consider courses at San Jose State University, which is largely a commuter school with diverse student demographics and experience levels in information technology courses.

There are students ranging from the traditional "college student" who went straight to college after high school, to students who are returning to college later in life. At San Jose State University, there is an upper division course called Information Security which covers Cryptography, Access Controls, Protocols, and Software Engineering Security Issues. Security knowledge is not isolated to a security engineer, but all information technology careers need to be aware of security principles, especially for innovation in enterprise. Each year, about 400 students take this course. This course is challenging for students, because there are several topics covered within a semester period. In a large class of 70 students, it can be a daunting feat for a professor to quickly detect students who are falling behind.

The professor usually can see a trend of how a student is progressing based on her homework, projects, participation, and exams. Our goal in this paper is to increase successful completion of upper division information technology education courses by applying information technology to the professor's toolset. We focus our analysis on the Information Security course at San Jose State University. This class has been taught for over ten years, with several hundred students a year. The class usually has ten assignments and three exams. This work accumulates thousands of assignments, exams, and not to mention, emails and class discussions generated over a year. For example, Piazza, which is a class discussion board (https://piazza.com/class/), can amass several thousands of discussions between students on completing assignments, as well as understanding difficult topics. All these resources over several years can total terabytes of unstructured text.

In this paper, we ask if it is possible to use the material generated from students in the past and current semesters to improve and encourage information technology students who are currently taking the course. Information technology has tackled analytics on large amounts of unstructured and structured text [3]. We consider IBM Text Analytic Web Tooling [6], which gains sentiments and analytics on unstructured text by employing SystemT advanced machine learning and text analytics extractors. In the enterprise industry, CEOs and business leaders use these tools to understand customer sentiment through large amounts of unstructured text data, such as those collected from Twitter. We apply the same tooling to an upper division Information Security class. With stronger analytics, the professor has faster insights on students who are struggling. For example, text analytics may show confusion on the concepts in authentication protocols. Then the professor may suggest examples for the particular weakness the students are having. Currently, in the typical large classroom, it might take some time for the professor to gauge everyone's understanding. For example, she can make this assessment based on exam scores. Our goal is to help professors

SIGITE'17, October 4–7, 2017, Rochester, NY, USA.
© 2017 ACM. ISBN 978-1-4503-5100-3/17/10...$15.00
DOI: https://doi.org/10.1145/3125659.3125677

better gauge students' understanding and support students' success before exams, and before students receive an actual final grade.

In our experiment, we used the Text Analytics Tooling based on SystemT to analyze students' understanding of Information Security concepts. We see how the tool can help the instructor compare a student's understanding of similar problems with slight modifications. Also, we see how the tool can help speed up the process of the instructor identifying where the class is struggling to understand cryptography concepts. In the following sections, we will present related work, our experimental setup, and the exploratory analysis on the results, and conclude with our thoughts for future directions of this work.

2 RELATED WORK

In the field of human-computer interaction, user experience plays a crucial role in determining areas of improvement, particularly areas of improvement in software appliances aimed at educating. Similarly, the machine learning aspect embodies this aim in the form of recurrent neural networks in automated essay scoring systems. Research by [8] demonstrates how recurrent neural networks can be used to achieve the task of automated essay scoring, specifically in determining the relation between an essay and its assigned score without any feature engineering. Recurrent neural networks prove beneficial in that they enable an automated essay scoring (AES) system to effectively encode the information required for essay evaluation. These techniques, while in line with speeding grading and evaluation, are orthogonal techniques to our usage of Text Analytic tooling to analyze classwork.

Furthermore, the importance of the design and mechanics of software tools aimed at boosting creativity in learning is spurred by user experience. For example, [7] suggest and delineate twelve different areas of improvement in the generation of software tools targeting creative learning, primarily via the experiences of everyday users. Through these experiences, the authors shed light on the potential shortcomings of tools that are too complex for the audience. These conclusions motivated us to find a tool with a high usability factor. We do not expect the professor to be an expert in text analytics and machine learning. Therefore, the tooling must be open to a wide audience.

Suspended between the nuances in human-computer interaction and machine learning, text analytics tooling acts as the halfway mark tying the two ends of the (semi)-manual and digital spectrum together. Fairly simple in regards to user manipulation with the intent to garner rapid results, [9] present text analytics as one of the more complicated fields of software development, while introducing a new technique to reducing learning barriers by way of gaining proficiency in text analytics. Though there exist software tools specially created to minimize the manual effort associated with the development of text analytics, these tools are only of use to expert developers. As text analytic tooling is the fast-growing ubiquitous option for information extraction in the software world, researchers [5] expound on the software tool, VINERy (Visual Integrated Development Environment for Information Extraction), whose development proved of significance in aiding extractor development for both expert and novice IE (information extraction) developers.

[4] identifies the benefits of developing curriculum to improve student outcomes, better manage scheduling, staffing, and operation of the IT courses, and improve alumni competitiveness in the rapidly changing IT environment. Our goals in this paper are similar, but we hope to embed analytics in the information security classes on the instructor side. In [10] innovative teaching is used to form industry-education relationships. This train of thought leads us to [2] which calls for an advanced curriculum needed in real world industry information technology to include software components, integrations, and architected software systems to contribute to effective future leadership. Information technology education must support accelerated learning in information security to enable innovative future leadership, especially in the enterprise sector.

In addition, [11] are also proposing adding analytics to the curriculum as an overarching theme. Given petabytes of data at our fingertips, extracting useful information is non-trivial. Industry recognizes the value in this process, and in this paper we apply the same tooling to information technology education.

3 PROBLEM STATEMENT

We explore the use of IBM's text analytics tool based on SystemT for extracting insights from an upper division Information Security course, which we assign the course name, "CS166." It is important that we find out if and how the tool addresses two pivotal questions:

(1) *Is the student's understanding of the material evident in her answer to the homework or exam problem?*
(2) *Does the information extracted from the tool provide a sufficient basis for professors to design assignments, exams, and classes in favor of better gauging their students?*

The first question studies the benefits of text analytics on class material for a single student, while the second question's aim is improving the class overall. We use these questions to focus our experiment and exploration.

4 EXPLORATORY TASK ANALYSIS USING TEXT ANALYTICS TOOLING

The IBM's text analytics tool, based on SystemT, was used as a way of extracting selective information from homework assignments, exams, student emails, and student doubts on the popular academic forum, Piazza, to gauge said student's performance in the upper-division computer science course elective, Information Security at San Jose State University. We access the tool for free after completing a course on IBM BigData University (https://bigdatauniversity.com/learn/text_analytics/).

4.1 Data Set

In our preliminary experimentations, we incorporate selected classwork from two different offerings of the same course; student information was gathered in the form of homework and exam answers, email questions, and forum comments including doubts and clarifications.

4.1.1 Tool Activation. To activate SystemT, the user should first upload input in the form of a text document. Once the desired documents are uploaded in text format, it is then up to the user to manipulate the tool. One method of achieving this is to use the

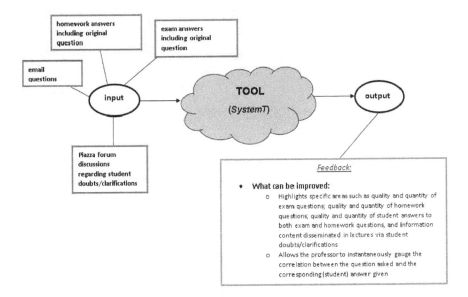

Figure 1: The flow chart above shows the overall simulation of the Text Analytic tool SystemT Process to generate insights.

Figure 2: When there are two matches between dictionaries, it is possible to view the characters in between. These characters are called tokens. In this case there are two streams of tokens, ranging from zero to twenty.

tool's features to create categories and subcategories specializing in a function, some of these categories and subcategories will be extractors. After filling up these categories with choice identifiers (i.e. commonly occurring nouns, adjectives, and/or phrases in the inputted documents) the tool can then be run.

After SystemT has finished running, the extracted information consisting of those identifiers will be displayed at the bottom in a grid-like console; this is the output. The user can then click on one of the outputted rows for that extracted line in particular to be magnified as a series of occurrences in the inputted documents on the right side of the screen. A basic simulation of this process is shown in Figure 1.

First, input in the form of homework assignments, exams, forum doubts and clarifications, and emails is injected into the tool. Second, after igniting some of the tool's features, the tool, SystemT, runs its course. Third, the result is then outputted in a table. Fourth, the user can now interpret the result as feedback regarding the state of the class, simply by gauging the content of the highlighted text. This highlighted text can include student answer choices and student questions for the professor, as well as the original problems appearing on the homework assignment or exam.

4.1.2 Detailed Task Exploration Specific to CS166. Step One: Gathering the Data

While crops of student doubts and clarifications expressed via email and Piazza were collected in a somewhat generic sense, the collection of homework assignments and exams was done while exercising a particular constraint: Information was gathered from two accompanying extremes (i.e. high-performing students and low-performing students); this tactic was employed to trigger solid variation in the results.

Step Two: Text File Conversion

Initially, the homework assignments and exam papers were all in the form of either hard copies or electronic documents such as PDFs. And so, the first task entailed the conversion of all relevant documents i.e., homework assignments, exam papers, emails, and forum comments into text files.

Step Three: Loading the Data Set

After checking that no special characters made an appearance in the titles of the documents, the newly converted text files were uploaded onto SystemT, as the input.

Step Four: Extractor Selection and Creation

First, the dictionary extractor, the term indicating a category, was created and reproduced four times in the form of Doubts, Assignments, Midterms, and Grades (transcripts). (Questions, concerns, and clarifications expressed via email and Piazza were clubbed under Doubts.) For each of the four categories, commonly occurring words (phrases, verbs, nouns, and adjectives) signifying sentence starters appropriate to the category, were inserted. For example, the following list of ten sentence-starters encapsulates a few of the commonly occurring phrases found in the questions given in two midterm exam papers: *(1) What... (2) Find and decrypt... (3) Why... (4) How many... (5) Which... (6) Give an example... (7) Assume... (8) Describe... (9) Design... and (10) Explain...* Consequently, these ten phrases were inserted into the dictionary, *Midterms*.

Similarly, such discretion was exercised for each of the remaining three categories when selecting which commonly occurring words to insert. Once the appropriate insertions for each dictionary were

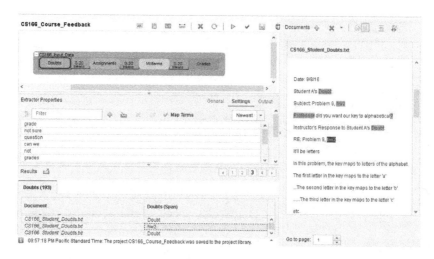

Figure 3: Selecting hw2 will show the results screen to the right, which is an email exchange discussing the assignment.

made, each of the four categories were merged together to form a sequence extractor as shown in Figure 2.

Next, the tool was run and after approximately 20 seconds, the results surfaced.

Execution of a dictionary or a sequence can be implemented in one of two ways: right clicking on the target dictionary or sequence and selecting Run, or, selecting the target dictionary or sequence and clicking on the green arrow in the toolbar labeled CS_166_Course_Feedback. Once execution has finished, a results table is displayed comprising the console at the bottom of the screen, while a window to the right shows all instances of word identifiers as initially inserted into each dictionary.

By default, all identifiers are highlighted following a fairly intricate color-coded system, but when the user clicks on a single identifier in the results table, then that highlighted identifier is again highlighted in dark blue. Figure 3 shows the results after executing the *Doubts* dictionary.

This process can be continued to display results for Assignments, Midterms, and Grades, as shown in Figure 4.

Though bearing a resemblance to the ubiquitous "ctrl f" functionality, SystemT allows the user to view multiple instances of multiple terms at once, rather than searching one term at a time and finding instances of solely that term. Therefore, if the user has any concerns regarding a certain term, then her doubts can be reassured at once instead of one instance of said term at a time. In contrast, multiple terms of data can be examined simultaneously for more exploratory insights. This interface scales for large amounts of assignments.

4.2 Analyzing the Results

Let us first take a look at the results yielded from student exams. When we added the identifier, "midterm," to the Grades and Midterms dictionaries and conducted a search, all instances of midterm showed up on the screen. In the students' transcript, we could see *Midterm 1* and *Midterm 2* and the corresponding grades for each; based on that grade, we could clarify where the student went wrong (or where the student went right), and if we scrolled

further down the displayed results, we could see the two exam documents with their respective titles highlighted *(Midterm 1, Midterm 2)*. Thus, we could scrutinize the students' answers and see the correlation between the students' grade and the quality of their answers.

As can be gathered from the results in Figure 4, this particular student's performance in the class is very high. The professor can explore the different files, for example, Miderm_1.txt or Midterm_2.txt through the tool. A high-performing student's exam results can ensure different possibilities in regards to how the professor wants to tune her focus on that student.

4.2.1 Exploring Pivotal Question: Single Student Case. First, we explore the pivotal question, *"Is the student's understanding of the material evident in her answer to the homework or exam problem?,"* by studying a common occurrence: We consider the case where a problem nearly identical to one that appeared in a homework assignment, appeared on a midterm exam. For example, if the only notable difference between the two problems was the given numbers, if any, and the student incorrectly answered one of the problems, then it is very likely that the student would want to review the problem she answered correctly, in order to see where she strayed in the problem answered incorrectly. Similarly, the professor might wish to check both the problem on the midterm and the problem in the homework assignment in order to gauge how much work was shown by the student. If, for instance, the answer to the problem on the homework assignment depicted rogue guesswork resulting in the correct answer, while the problem on the midterm exam depicted work reflecting thorough understanding of the concepts learned in class but an incorrect answer due to an arithmetic error, then she'd have a clearer discretion on where to tip more credit.

Figure 5 projects the security concept of superincreasing knapsack, a heavily calculation-oriented problem whose methods are reinforced in the earlier weeks of the Information Security course at San Jose State University. In order to use SystemT to check for discrepancies between the answer to the problem on the homework assignment and the answer to the problem on the midterm exam,

Figure 4: The Grades Results view can be helpful to directly access the students' grades.

Figure 5: Shown above is the answer to a midterm question highlighting instances of the cryptographic term, "public key" among other terms.

it is a good idea to first locate any common terms composing the wording of the problem question.

As shown in the results screen in Figure 5, one distinctive term shared between the two problems, is the appearance of the cryptographic term, "public key." Therefore, the professor can simply execute either the *Assignments* dictionary or the *Midterms* dictionary, as both dictionaries contain the keyword, "public key." The professor can then sift through the pages of the results table shown at the bottom console, until she finds "public key" adjacent to, again, in this case, either Assignment_4.txt or Midterm_1.txt. Then clicking on that instance of "public key," she will see all instances of the term, including in the desired problem.

This process of comparing the language between both instances of the similar problem benefits the student to understand which solution is exemplary. Moreover, the professor can identify new text extractors based on this problem: Pattern A, whose wording shows the student is lacking full understanding, and Pattern B, whose wording shows the student provides a perfect solution. In future classes, she can apply these new extractors on classwork to quickly assess which students are falling into Pattern B. Of course, an experienced professor can identify these patterns without text analytics tooling. But these extractors can be shared with new

professors, and can help make these improvements in large classes faster.

4.2.2 Exploring Pivotal Question: Overall Class. Next, we explore the question, *"Does the information extracted from the tool provide a sufficient basis for professors to design assignments, exams, and classes in favor of better gauging their students?"* To see how text analytics on classwork can improve how the professor gauges the overall understanding of the class, we look at an exact scenario where the professor wishes to diffuse any student confusion that may be circulating after assigning the next homework assignment. This would first entail the professor finding sources of confusion, which can be achieved by scouring Piazza. Let us say she does exactly that and locates her first source of student confusion regarding Problem 20 in the homework set she assigned.

Now that she has established which problem is the source of the first bout of student confusion, the professor simply needs to look at the particular problem to rehash the problem objective and if necessary, reinforce her understanding, before attempting to cast away any confusion. Figure 6 demonstrates how this is done with the Text Analytics Tooling.

After executing the *sequence* extractor, CS166_Input_Data, when the professor clicks on the *Question* identifier visible beneath the *Doubts* (Span) category beneath the tab, CS166_Input_Data (6), the "6" indicates that there are six categories, the results screen depicts the entire span of student doubts comprising the target input document. Cryptographic jargon such as "message" and "public key" is underlined in addition to highlighted, while words commonplace in expressing doubt such as "confusion" and "question" are only highlighted and that too, in a bolder hue. This nuance indicates that the function of the identifiers, "confusion" and "question," is to rein in the attention of the user, as the content in which they are incorporated is precisely what the professor desires to view, while the function of the identifiers, "message" and "public key," is to accentuate the key details of the problem being discussed.

Now, the professor can select the *Assignments* dictionary to locate Assignment_4.txt and one of its identifiers, "public key." Once the professor has clicked "public key" in the results table, the document in the right-hand window shifts to to Assignment_4, Problem 20. (Note: Assume that Assignment_4.txt is a proxy for the answer key. In other words, Assignment_4.txt consists of all the correct answers, including the correct answer to Problem 20.) The professor can switch between studying Problem 20 and its correct answer, and the student's question regarding Problem 20 on Piazza, before finally reaching out to the students with an appropriate answer.

The pattern established in the course of manipulating SystemT to procure rapid results, strips down to the use of word identifiers. The insertion of word identifiers in the dictionary extractors is to aid the process of viewing various sections of multiple documents at once. Simply put, these identifiers whether they are CS166 jargon such as "public key," "symmetric key," and "ciphertext," or sentence-starters such as "what," "why," and "explain," flag the user's attention, particularly at times when the user wishes to compare two or more sections of a span of documents.

Overall, this tool is especially convenient for professors to see firsthand, the areas in which their students are excelling and/or struggling. Text exploration helps pull out sentiments students have

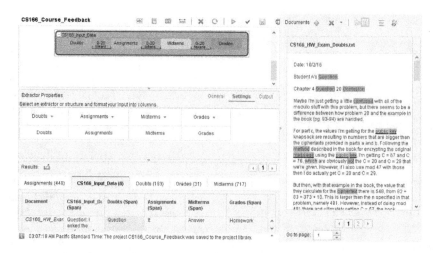

Figure 6: After clicking on Question, the results screen outputs multiple, highlighted identifiers to show an organized color scheme.

such as "confused" which can be helpful in a large class with hundreds of message board comments. Core curriculum classes would have years of message board unstructured text data, which leads to more insights, especially during a semester when the message boards are not as popular. The professor is able to understand how the students are understanding the material before the homework is due, or the exam is graded.

5 CONCLUSIONS

We see in our analysis, pivotal questions on gauging a specific student's and overall class's understanding through text analysis of classwork can be answered with SystemT tooling. We identify several benefits of the tooling, for example, quickly assessing and correlating different problems, identifying the sentiments the overall class has on homework, and defining text extractor patterns for future classes. Thus, SystemT allows for quicker meaningful correlation between professorship and student performance.

In this paper, we only consider text analysis through text output and highlighting interface of the tool. However, presenting the results as charts and tables might help assess information better. For future work, we would like to expand this exploration process to use charting tooling in conjunction with the text analytics data.

Our exploration presents evidence of using the tool to improve the Information Security class by focusing on our pivotal questions. For future work we would like to perform usability experience testing to observe how professors can incorporate this tool into their classroom. The initial stages of using the tool has learning curves, because the professor will need to design a preliminary set of text extractors to tune throughout the semester. We would like to research if we can create a library of text extractors for different Information Technology courses.

ACKNOWLEDGMENTS

The authors would like to thank Yunyao Li for her comments and suggestions on the subject.

REFERENCES

[1] Anthony P Carnevale, Nicole Smith, and Michelle Melton. 2011. STEM: Science Technology Engineering Mathematics. *Georgetown University Center on Education and the Workforce* (2011).

[2] Deborah G. Coleman and Stephen J. Zilora. 2003. Dynamic Enterprises Demand Advanced Curricula in Software Development and Management. In *Proceedings of the 4th Conference on Information Technology Curriculum (CITC4 '03)*. ACM, New York, NY, USA, 23–27. https://doi.org/10.1145/947121.947126

[3] Lipika Dey and Ishan Verma. 2013. Text-Driven Multi-structured Data Analytics for Enterprise Intelligence. In *Proceedings of the 2013 IEEE/WIC/ACM International Joint Conferences on Web Intelligence (WI) and Intelligent Agent Technologies (IAT) - Volume 03 (WI-IAT '13)*. IEEE Computer Society, Washington, DC, USA, 213–220. https://doi.org/10.1109/WI-IAT.2013.186

[4] Rich Halstead-Nussloch and Han Reichgelt. 2013. Leveraging HCI in Teaching Mobile, "Anytime and Everywhere" IT. In *Proceedings of the 14th Annual ACM SIGITE Conference on Information Technology Education (SIGITE '13)*. ACM, New York, NY, USA, 13–18. https://doi.org/10.1145/2512276.2512295

[5] Yunyao Li, Elmer Kim, Marc A. Touchette, Ramiya Venkatachalam, and Hao Wang. 2015. VINERy: A Visual IDE for Information Extraction. *Proc. VLDB Endow.* 8, 12 (Aug. 2015), 1948–1951. https://doi.org/10.14778/2824032.2824108

[6] Fatma Özcan, David Hoa, Kevin S. Beyer, Andrey Balmin, Chuan Jie Liu, and Yu Li. 2011. Emerging Trends in the Enterprise Data Analytics: Connecting Hadoop and DB2 Warehouse. In *Proceedings of the 2011 ACM SIGMOD International Conference on Management of Data (SIGMOD '11)*. ACM, New York, NY, USA, 1161–1164. https://doi.org/10.1145/1989323.1989446

[7] Mitchel Resnick and Brian Silverman. 2005. Some Reflections on Designing Construction Kits for Kids. In *Proceedings of the 2005 Conference on Interaction Design and Children (IDC '05)*. ACM, New York, NY, USA, 117–122. https://doi.org/10.1145/1109540.1109556

[8] Kaveh Taghipour and Hwee Tou Ng. 2016. A Neural Approach to Automated Essay Scoring. In *Proceedings of the 2016 Conference on Empirical Methods in Natural Language Processing (Association for Computational Linguistics)*. 1882–1891.

[9] Huahai Yang, Daina Pupons-Wickham, Laura Chiticariu, Yunyao Li, Benjamin Nguyen, and Arnaldo Carreno-Fuentes. 2013. I Can Do Text Analytics!: Designing Development Tools for Novice Developers. In *Proceedings of the SIGCHI Conference on Human Factors in Computing Systems (CHI '13)*. ACM, New York, NY, USA, 1599–1608. https://doi.org/10.1145/2470654.2466212

[10] Stephen J. Zilora. 2004. Industry-based Web Services Project As a Classroom Teaching Tool. In *Proceedings of the 5th Conference on Information Technology Education (CITC5 '04)*. ACM, New York, NY, USA, 13–18. https://doi.org/10.1145/1029533.1029537

[11] Stephen J. Zilora, Daniel S. Bogaard, and Jim Leone. 2013. The Changing Face of Information Technology. In *Proceedings of the 14th Annual ACM SIGITE Conference on Information Technology Education (SIGITE '13)*. ACM, New York, NY, USA, 29–34. https://doi.org/10.1145/2512276.2512288

Database Query Analyzer (DBQA) - A Data-Oriented SQL Clause Visualization Tool

Ryan Hardt
University of Wisconsin - Eau Claire
Eau Claire, Wisconsin
hardtr@uwec.edu

Esther Gutzmer
University of Wisconsin - Eau Claire
Eau Claire, Wisconsin
gutzmeej@uwec.edu

ABSTRACT

While SQL has a relatively simple syntax with a small set of commands, it allows for complex query construction that is deceptively challenging. SQL is often the first declarative programming language learned by students, which requires a different analysis approach than that used to understand the procedural or object-oriented programming paradigms with which students are more familiar. While some tools exist to help assess the correctness of an SQL query or address syntax errors, few tools focus on query semantics. DBQA does so by illustrating the effects that clauses and conditions have on an SQL SELECT statement using a visualized, data-oriented approach. We expect DBQA's approach to query evaluation to feel more familiar to those with experience in procedural or object-oriented programming and to help those users better understand the semantics of complex queries. DBQA includes support for SQL queries containing JOINs and subqueries, which have been shown to be among the most difficult for students to construct.

KEYWORDS

SQL; databases; computer science education; information systems education

1 MOTIVATION

Students in an introductory database course have often been exposed only to procedural or object-oriented programming paradigms. These paradigms lend themselves well to a step-by-step construction and analysis approach, in which the effects of one statement are considered before addressing the effects of any subsequent statements. SQL (Structured Query Language) is often the first declarative language learned by students. It requires a different analysis approach than that used to understand procedural paradigms. Sadiq [15] described this as a need to think in sets rather than steps. While the syntax of an SQL query is relatively straightforward, its semantics can quickly become complex, particularly when a query involves aggregate functions, JOIN statements, and subqueries. Ahadi et al. [3] showed that semantic errors in an SQL SELECT statement are much harder for students to fix than syntactic errors.

SIGITE'17, October 4–7, 2017, Rochester, NY, USA
© 2017 Association for Computing Machinery.
ACM ISBN ISBN 978-1-4503-5100-3/17/10...$15.00
https://doi.org/10.1145/3125659.3125688

When students are first learning SQL, they are typically presented with a visualized, data-oriented approach that includes:

- A single table SQL SELECT statement
- An illustration of the corresponding table and its data
- An illustration of the result set obtained when executing the query

However, as queries become more complex (particularly through use of aggregate functions, JOIN statements, and subqueries), static illustrations lose the ability to effectively convey the intermediate sets of data that are used by the database to obtain the query's final result set. As a result, students must mentally manage how these intermediate datasets are obtained and used by the database, which requires a significant cognitive leap from understanding single table SELECT statements, especially for students who are new to databases and SQL.

Our tool, Database Query Analyzer (DBQA), aims to bridge the gap between understanding simple, single table SELECT statements and those that are more complex. It does so by taking a more procedural-like approach to SQL query analysis. For a given SQL SELECT statement, DBQA repeatedly:

- highlights the currently evaluated clause or condition
- displays the associated intermediate dataset
- allows the user to move forward or backward in the query evaluation

This step-by-step approach allows users to see how a dataset is initially obtained by the FROM clause and ultimately processed and filtered by the other clauses and conditions to obtain the final result set. To the best of our knowledge, DBQA is the only such tool with support for subqueries, which have been shown to be among the most difficult types of SQL queries for students to construct [2]. Because users find difficult query construction easier when written in a procedural style vs. a declarative style [16], we anticipate that DBQA's procedural-like approach to SQL SELECT statement execution will feel more familiar to students in an introductory database course and help them to understand such queries more effectively.

2 METHODOLOGY

This section will describe how DBQA's query processing engine parses an SQL SELECT statement to allow its step-by-step query analysis. It will first, however, describe the current state of its web interface to better illustrate how users can interact with DBQA.

Figure 1: DBQA web interface - database schema

2.1 Web Interface

DBQA works with an Oracle database used by multiple courses in the computer science department at the University of Wisconsin-Eau Claire, though it could be configured to work with any relational database. Users log into DBQA using the same credentials used to access their schema in this database. DBQA can be used to analyze queries involving any tables in the user's database schema. For convenience, each user's schema is read on login and displayed on the left side of the interface, as seen in Figure 1. Users can see all tables in their schema along with their columns, primary keys, and foreign keys. This avoids the need to memorize schema information or use another tool along with DBQA to obtain this information.

The main web interface component can be seen in Figure 2. It allows users to:

- Enter and submit an SQL SELECT statement
- Step forward and backward in the query's clause and condition evaluation using the "Next" and "Previous" buttons
- View the dataset obtained by "executing" the current clause or condition
- Limit the number of results in the current dataset
- Identify all clauses and conditions evaluated thus far

The currently evaluated clause or condition is highlighted in yellow, and previously evaluated clauses and conditions are highlighted in blue (if desired). At any given point, the dataset displayed is a result of executing the current clause or condition *along with all previously executed clauses and conditions*. This allows the user to easily see which clauses and conditions the current dataset is recognizing. The ability to step forward and backward gives users a simple way to see the effects that a clause or condition has on the query by observing the differences in the generated datasets. Further details on the processing of individual clauses and conditions follow in Section 2.2.

DBQA's focus is on helping students understand the semantics of an SQL SELECT statement rather than its syntax. However, DBQA is designed for use by students who are new to SQL. Because these students struggle with SQL syntax and often abandon their efforts due to syntax errors [1], DBQA includes an error interpreter that

Figure 2: DBQA web interface - query submission (processing FROM clause)

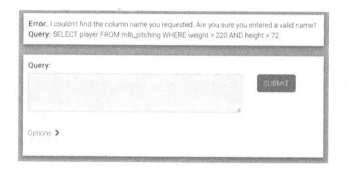

Figure 3: DBQA web interface - error interpreter

better describes the error provided by the database. Default error messages provided by the database are often confusing, especially to SQL beginners. Figure 3 illustrates DBQA's error interpreter with a query that contains an invalid column name. The database error message for this query reads "ORA-00904: 'PLAYER': invalid identifier". To novices, this error message may not be clear enough to identify the error: "player" is not a valid column in the table. DBQA instead reports the error as "I couldn't find the column name you requested. Are you sure you entered a valid name?". DBQA includes syntactic support for many different types of syntax errors including the most common syntax errors involving invalid column names and GROUP BY expressions [1].

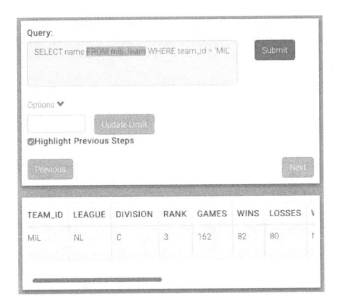

Figure 4: DBQA web interface - query submission (processing WHERE clause)

2.2 Clause Evaluation

DBQA processes a SELECT statement's clauses in the following order:

(1) FROM
(2) WHERE
(3) SELECT
(4) GROUP BY
(5) HAVING
(6) ORDER BY

This is likely the order in which a database system without query optimization would process these clauses, with the exception of the SELECT clause. Processing details for each clause are described later in this section. In practice, a database system is likely to optimize a query based on the contents of these clauses. The goal of DBQA is not to show users precisely how the database is optimizing and executing their queries but rather to more clearly illustrate the effects that each clause and condition has on the query. It does this as closely as possible to the actual clause execution order.

Some clauses may contain multiple components. For example, a FROM clause may also include JOIN clauses, which DBQA processes in separate steps. Subqueries and conditions are other examples of components that may exist within clauses. We will use the term *query fragment* to describe the condition, clause or clause component that DBQA is currently evaluating. The DBQA web interface highlights the currently evaluated query fragment in yellow as well as all previously evaluated query fragments in blue (as seen in Figure 4). When evaluating a query fragment, DBQA obtains the associated dataset by generating a new SQL SELECT statement that involves the query fragment. We call this new SQL SELECT statement the *generated query*. How a generated query is constructed also differs by clause. The remainder of this section provides more details about the identification of query fragments and construction of generated queries.

2.2.1 FROM. The first clause in an SQL SELECT statement that DBQA evaluates is the FROM clause. The FROM clause is used by the database to obtain the initial dataset that will be filtered by other clauses. The FROM clause must be present in a valid SQL SELECT statement. This clause may or may not include JOIN operations. If no JOIN operations are present, the associated query fragment is the entire FROM clause, and the corresponding generated query is constructed by appending "SELECT *" to the beginning of the query fragment. For example, in Figure 2, the query fragment is "FROM mlb_team", and the associated generated query is "SELECT * FROM mlb_team". This generated query is used to produce the associated dataset. If JOIN operations are present, each operation will have its own query fragment and generated query. This allows DBQA to treat each JOIN as a separate step. Each query fragment will include the JOIN operation and its associated ON or USING component. Each generated query will be constructed by appending the associated query fragment onto the end of the previous JOIN operation's generated query.

2.2.2 WHERE. When the FROM clause has been processed, DBQA looks for the WHERE clause. The WHERE clause is used by the database to filter out rows in the dataset. A valid SQL SELECT statement may or may not have a WHERE clause. If it does, this clause will contain one or more conditions. DBQA treats each condition as a separate step, which means that each condition will have an associated query fragment and generated query. Each query fragment will consist of the newly evaluated condition. Each generated query will consist of:

- the generated query from the FROM clause processing
- all query fragments associated with previously evaluated conditions
- the query fragment associated with the new condition

As a result, each step is likely to filter out rows in the dataset from the previous step (assuming the condition matches data present in the previous dataset). In Figure 4, the query fragment is "team_id = 'MIL'", and the associated generated query is "SELECT * FROM mlb_team WHERE team_id='MIL'". This generated query is used to produce the associated dataset.

WHERE clause conditions are not always processed in the order in which they appear in the query due to operator precedence. For example, parenthesized conditions are executed before AND conditions, which are in turn executed before OR conditions. DBQA minds this precedence, and as a result, will not always process conditions in the order present in the query.

We anticipate that DBQA's illustration of WHERE clause condition processing in particular will be helpful to students, as the majority of semantic errors have been shown to occur in this clause, especially when a large number of conditions overloads one's working memory [3].

2.2.3 SELECT. Next, DBQA processes the SELECT clause. The SELECT clause is primarily used by the database to filter out columns from the dataset. A valid SQL SELECT statement will always have a SELECT clause. DBQA's processing of the SELECT clause will always produce one query fragment unless the clause contains subqueries (subquery processing is addressed later in this section). This query

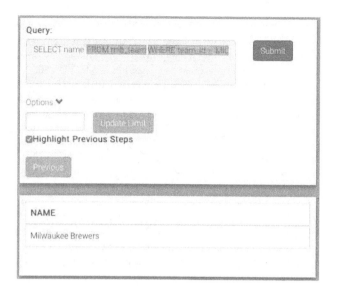

Figure 5: DBQA web interface - query submission (processing SELECT clause)

fragment will consist of the entire SELECT clause. The corresponding generated query will consist of the generated query from the WHERE clause processing with the SELECT clause from the original query. Its effect on the dataset produced in the previous step will be to filter out any columns not present in the SELECT clause. In Figure 5, the query fragment is "SELECT name", and the associated generated query is "SELECT name FROM mlb_team WHERE team_id = 'MIL'", which matches the original query and produces the final result set for the originally submitted query in this example.

The contents of the SELECT clause affect the behavior of the GROUP BY and HAVING clauses. If the HAVING clause contains an aggregate function (e.g. COUNT(), MAX(), AVG(), etc.), that function must appear in the SELECT clause. If a SELECT clause contains one or more aggregate functions, then all other columns in the SELECT clause must be present in the GROUP BY clause. However, the effects of a SELECT statement containing an aggregate function cannot be observed until the GROUP BY clause has executed (if present). In order to better illustrate the effects of the GROUP BY statement, DBQA first processes the SELECT statement with any aggregate functions temporarily replaced by the columns they operate on. For example, if a SELECT statement includes "AVG(price)" and has a GROUP BY clause, DBQA will temporarily replace "AVG(price)" with "price". The effects of the aggregate function will be seen later when the GROUP BY clause is processed.

2.2.4 GROUP BY. DBQA will look for a GROUP BY clause next. The GROUP BY clause is used by the database to group the input provided to the aggregate function(s) in the SELECT clause. It is required if the SELECT clause contains an aggregate function along with columns that aren't part of the aggregate function. DBQA will produce one query fragment containing the entire GROUP BY clause. The corresponding generated query will consist of the generated query from the SELECT clause processing with any aggregate functions now present plus the GROUP BY clause. The effects of the

GROUP BY clause will thus be illustrated by DBQA by applying the previously removed aggregate function in the SELECT clause and by reducing the number of rows in the dataset (assuming some rows were grouped).

2.2.5 HAVING. If a HAVING clause is present, it will be processed by DBQA next. The HAVING clause is used by the database to filter rows from the dataset much like the WHERE clause, but the conditions in the HAVING clause can only involve aggregate functions (which cannot be present in the WHERE clause). DBQA processes the HAVING clause just like it processes the WHERE clause. This means that it steps through each condition in the HAVING clause one-by-one, creating a query fragment and corresponding generated query for each condition. The generated query for each condition is created using a process just like that for the WHERE clause. Conditions in the HAVING clause are subject to the same operator precedence for those in the WHERE clause, so DBQA will process them in the appropriate order as well.

2.2.6 ORDER BY. Lastly, DBQA will look for the ORDER BY clause. The ORDER BY clause is used by the database to order the rows in the final result set according to values in one or more columns. DBQA will generate a single query fragment containing the entire ORDER BY clause. Because this is the last clause evaluated by DBQA, the corresponding generated query will match the originally submitted query.

2.2.7 Subqueries. DBQA looks for subqueries separately in each clause. DBQA will always evaluate query clauses in the order listed earlier, but before it processes each clause, it checks to see if it has any subqueries. If so, it recursively processes those subqueries before processing the clause that contains them. After a subquery has been processed, DBQA treats the subquery just like any other argument in the outer query.

For example, suppose the query used in the example instead read:

```
SELECT (SELECT name FROM dual) as name
FROM mlb_team
WHERE team_id = 'MIL'
```

DBQA would first process the FROM clause just as in Figure 2. It would then process the WHERE clause just as in Figure 4. When looking at the SELECT clause, however, DBQA would find the subquery "SELECT name FROM dual". As a result, it would process this subquery before processing the outer SELECT clause. So, it would process the subquery's FROM clause, then the subquery's SELECT clause. Finally, the outer query's SELECT clause would be processed, with "(SELECT name FROM dual) as name" viewed just like any other column name in a SELECT statement.

Because of its recursive handling of subqueries, DBQA supports multiple subqueries in a given clause as well as arbitrary levels of subquery nesting.

3 FUTURE WORK

We plan to run a controlled experiment to see what effect DBQA has on the ability of students in an introductory database course to write and debug various types of SQL statements. While we have yet to make any decisions on the experimental setup, we are likely to use a within-subjects design in which each student attempts to construct and debug different types of SQL SELECT queries with and without DBQA. While DBQA's engine is currently capable of supporting this experiment, its web interface needs to be updated to support the latest version of the engine.

DBQA's web interface was designed and built for an earlier version of the engine that only supported single table SELECT statements. As a result, it does not support JOINs and subqueries, which constitute some of the most difficult queries for students to write [2]. Now that the engine is complete, the web interface needs to be updated to support its latest features. Notably, the interface support for subqueries presents some challenges. For all other operations, DBQA is able to manipulate the existing dataset to illustrate the effects of the currently evaluated clause or condition. This isn't typically the case with subqueries. As a result, the interface will need to illustrate the effects of a subquery differently. When a subquery is to be executed, one possible solution is to use a popover associated with the subquery that contains the dataset manipulated by that subquery. Further additions may include animations when the datasets are updated and text describing the effects of the clause evaluated at each step.

4 RELATED WORK

Many education-focused assessment tools have been developed for learning SQL [4, 7, 8, 11–15]. These programs typically provide an English statement to be translated by a student into an SQL SELECT query. The tools use different methods to grade students on their knowledge and understanding of SQL concepts. Some of these methods include peer review, instructor review, and most commonly, comparing the dataset generated by the student's SELECT query to the desired dataset. Assessment tools like these are helpful in understanding which concepts students struggle with most.

Other systems include the ability to present alternate query representations [6, 9]. They may illustrate a given query using graphs or relational algebra. These systems often help users understand common patterns shared by SQL queries.

Much like DBQA, eSQL [10] and SAVI [5] are two systems that evaluate queries one step at a time and display visual representations of the intermediate datasets. eSQL provides a step-by-step evaluation of a given SELECT query, using English text to explain the functionality of the current clause. The current clause is highlighted and the user is able to move to the next step or the final step at any time. Using an algorithm to determine a "typical set", eSQL displays no more than twenty rows of data at a time. SAVI is a more recent system that is implemented as a web application. It is similar to eSQL but adds the ability to backtrack in the evaluation of a query and lacks the textual description of the database operation.

While DBQA is quite similar to eSQL and SAVI, DBQA's step-by-step analysis is more finely-grained. Importantly, neither eSQL nor SAVI appear to include support for subqueries, which are particularly difficult for students to implement [2]. Additionally, neither system appears to handle conditions in the WHERE or HAVING clauses separately, instead treating the entire clause as a single step. Because most semantic errors occur in the WHERE clause [3], a more fine-grained analysis is important.

5 CONCLUSION

This paper has presented DBQA, a tool to illustrate the effects that clauses and conditions have on an SQL SELECT statement using a procedural-like evaluation. It is designed for use by students in an introductory-level database course, many of who are likely to have only been exposed to procedural or object-oriented programming paradigms. DBQA allows students to execute arbitrary SQL statements using any object to which they have access in their database schema. Its web interface presents this schema to avoid the need for complementary tools. Upon query submission, DBQA will:

- highlight the currently evaluated clause or condition
- display the associated intermediate dataset
- allow the user to move forward or backward in the query evaluation

As queries become more complex, particularly through the use of JOINs and subqueries, DBQA frees users from the need to mentally manage intermediate datasets. DBQA also "translates" database-provided error codes to messages that are likely more understandable to novices.

To the best of our knowledge, DBQA is the first tool of its kind with fine-grained condition evaluation and support for subqueries, which are two of the most problematic query components encountered by students.

We plan to perform a controlled experiment to evaluate the effect that DBQA has on the ability of students in an introductory database course to write and debug various types of SQL statements.

REFERENCES

[1] Alireza Ahadi, Vahid Behbood, Arto Vihavainen, Julia Prior, and Raymond Lister. 2016. Students' Syntactic Mistakes in Writing Seven Different Types of SQL Queries and Its Application to Predicting Students' Success. In *Proceedings of the 47th ACM Technical Symposium on Computing Science Education (SIGCSE '16)*. ACM, New York, NY, USA, 401–406. https://doi.org/10.1145/2839509.2844640

[2] Alireza Ahadi, Julia Prior, Vahid Behbood, and Raymond Lister. 2015. A Quantitative Study of the Relative Difficulty for Novices of Writing Seven Different Types of SQL Queries. In *Proceedings of the 2015 ACM Conference on Innovation and Technology in Computer Science Education (ITiCSE '15)*. ACM, New York, NY, USA, 201–206. https://doi.org/10.1145/2729094.2742620

[3] Alireza Ahadi, Julia Prior, Vahid Behbood, and Raymond Lister. 2016. Students' Semantic Mistakes in Writing Seven Different Types of SQL Queries. In *Proceedings of the 2016 ACM Conference on Innovation and Technology in Computer Science Education (ITiCSE '16)*. ACM, New York, NY, USA, 272–277. https://doi.org/10.1145/2899415.2899464

[4] Peter Brusilovsky, Sergey Sosnovsky, Michael V. Yudelson, Danielle H. Lee, Vladimir Zadorozhny, and Xin Zhou. 2010. Learning SQL Programming with Interactive Tools: From Integration to Personalization. *Trans. Comput. Educ.* 9, 4, Article 19 (Jan. 2010), 15 pages. https://doi.org/10.1145/1656255.1656257

[5] Maurizio Cembalo, Alfredo De Santis, and Umberto Ferraro Petrillo. 2011. SAVI: A New System for Advanced SQL Visualization. In *Proceedings of the 2011 Conference on Information Technology Education (SIGITE '11)*. ACM, New York, NY, USA, 165–170. https://doi.org/10.1145/2047594.2047641

[6] Jonathan Danaparamita and Wolfgang Gatterbauer. 2011. QueryViz: Helping Users Understand SQL Queries and Their Patterns. In *Proceedings of the 14th International Conference on Extending Database Technology (EDBT/ICDT '11)*. ACM, New York, NY, USA, 558–561. https://doi.org/10.1145/1951365.1951440

[7] Michael de Raadt, Stijn Dekeyser, and Tien Yu Lee. 2006. Do Students SQLify? Improving Learning Outcomes with Peer Review and Enhanced Computer Assisted Assessment of Querying Skills. In *Proceedings of the 6th Baltic Sea Conference on Computing Education Research: Koli Calling 2006 (Baltic Sea '06)*. ACM, New York, NY, USA, 101–108. https://doi.org/10.1145/1315803.1315821

[8] Andreas Grillenberger and Torsten Brinda. 2012. eledSQL: A New Web-based Learning Environment for Teaching Databases and SQL at Secondary School Level. In *Proceedings of the 7th Workshop in Primary and Secondary Computing Education (WiPSCE '12)*. ACM, New York, NY, USA, 101–104. https://doi.org/10.1145/2481449.2481474

[9] Mario Guimaraes. 2003. Database Courseware: an Update. *Proceedings of 41st ACM-Southeast Conference* (2003).

[10] R. Kearns, S. Shead, and A. Fekete. 1996. A Teaching System for SQL. In *Proceedings of the 2Nd Australasian Conference on Computer Science Education (ACSE '97)*. ACM, New York, NY, USA, 224–231. https://doi.org/10.1145/299359.299391

[11] Claire Kenny and Claus Pahl. 2005. Automated Tutoring for a Database Skills Training Environment. *SIGCSE Bull.* 37, 1 (Feb. 2005), 58–62. https://doi.org/10.1145/1047124.1047377

[12] Antonija Mitrovic. 1998. Learning SQL with a Computerized Tutor. *SIGCSE Bull.* 30, 1 (March 1998), 307–311. https://doi.org/10.1145/274790.274318

[13] Antonija Mitrovic. 2003. An intelligent SQL tutor on the web. *International Journal of Artificial Intelligence in Education* 13, 2-4 (2003), 173–197.

[14] Julia R. Prior. 2014. AsseSQL: An Online, Browser-based SQL Skills Assessment Tool. In *Proceedings of the 2014 Conference on Innovation & Technology in Computer Science Education (ITiCSE '14)*. ACM, New York, NY, USA, 327–327. https://doi.org/10.1145/2591708.2602682

[15] Shazia Sadiq, Maria Orlowska, Wasim Sadiq, and Joe Lin. 2004. SQLator: An Online SQL Learning Workbench. In *Proceedings of the 9th Annual SIGCSE Conference on Innovation and Technology in Computer Science Education (ITiCSE '04)*. ACM, New York, NY, USA, 223–227. https://doi.org/10.1145/1007996.1008055

[16] Charles Welty and David W. Stemple. 1981. Human Factors Comparison of a Procedural and a Nonprocedural Query Language. *ACM Trans. Database Syst.* 6, 4 (Dec. 1981), 626–649. https://doi.org/10.1145/319628.319656

The Effect of a Computing-focused Linked-courses Learning Community on Minority and Female Students

Amber Settle
DePaul University
Chicago, Illinois
asettle@cdm.depaul.edu

James Doyle
DePaul University
Chicago, Illinois
jdoyle12@mail.depaul.edu

Theresa Steinbach
DePaul University
Chicago, Illinois
tsteinbach@cdm.depaul.edu

ABSTRACT

While enrollments in computing degrees and courses have grown rapidly in the past decade, both female and minority male students remain underrepresented in computing programs. This makes recruitment and retention of these populations a continuing concern. Affinity for a major is connected to student retention, and learning communities have proven effective for this purpose. We present an evaluation of a three-year linked-courses learning community in which we measure pre- to post-quarter changes in student attitudes and resource utilization. We find that participants in the learning community are significantly more likely to report being a part of a group of programmers and having friends interested in computing. Participants also utilize two important resources in different ways than students in the same programming classes but not enrolled in the community.

CCS CONCEPTS

• **Applied computing** → *Education*;

KEYWORDS

Attitudes, CS1, isolation, learning community, engagement, programming, Python

ACM Reference format:
Amber Settle, James Doyle, and Theresa Steinbach. 2017. The Effect of a Computing-focused Linked-courses Learning Community on Minority and Female Students. In *Proceedings of SIGITE'17, Rochester, NY, USA, October 4-7, 2017,* 6 pages.
https://doi.org/10.1145/3125659.3125679

1   INTRODUCTION

Enrollments in computing classes and programs have been rapidly rising since 2006. The Computing Research Association (CRA) recently reported that the average number of computer science majors at doctoral-granting institutions has more than tripled since 2006 and more than doubled since 2011 [1]. While the enrollment increases have resulted in an increase in the number of female and minority students in computing courses and majors, there are still

SIGITE'17, October 4-7, 2017, Rochester, NY, USA
© 2017 Association for Computing Machinery.
ACM ISBN 978-1-4503-5100-3/17/10...$15.00
https://doi.org/10.1145/3125659.3125679

areas where diversity remains problematic. For example, female student enrollments in upper-level classes remains much weaker than other student populations [1]. Minority enrollments have not seen the same increases as female enrollments, and in some cases there have been declines such as among African-American students [1]. Even in times of increasing enrollments, the recruitment and retention of underrepresented groups remains important.

For a long time computing educators have worked to understand factors that influence female and minority participation and retention in the field. One study considered factors that contribute to affinity with a computing major, which is defined to be the degree with which one perceives that the major is a good fit and enjoys the work associated with it [10]. The authors found that affinity is the most important factor in determining students' intention to leave a computing major. Among their recommendations was that computing educators work to build affinity groups as a way to improve retention [10]. Another study found that strong social support and high self-efficacy are associated with strong orientation toward careers in CIS [12]. The results differed by gender, however, as the authors found that low self-efficacy is tied to less social support for males but saw no similar tendency for females [12]. A recent and exhaustive study of comments posted to online forums found that isolation is a continuing problem for women in computing and other STEM fields[13].

An approach that has shown promise in building affinity groups and reducing isolation among students is a linked-course learning community [8]. In a linked-course learning community, students simultaneously enroll in courses from different disciplines or interdisciplines that are connected in content, purpose, and organization. In addition to simultaneous enrollment in connected courses, extracurricular activities that support the goals of the courses can be included in order to further connect students with each other and their instructors. The community is designed to provide students with a learning environment that enhances student achievement and reduces attrition rates[5]. Despite their long history, learning communities are not common in computing. A recent article discusses a living-learning community that has been in existence since 2010 at the Pennsylvania College of Technology. The authors report that the community has improved academic performance, increased student interaction, and improved retention [7].

In an effort to improve retention of female and minority students at our institution, a linked-courses learning community was created in the first term of the academic year 2014-2015 and continued in the first terms of the 2015-2016 and 2016-2017 academic years. First-year students majoring in areas that require an introductory Python programming course were also enrolled in a required general education class focused on the digital divide. The students recruited for the community were members of underrepresented groups in computing.

While the ultimate goal is improved retention, attitude changes can provide an early indication of the potential impact, or lack of impact, of the learning community. Here we present results from combining the data from the first three cohorts of the learning community and comparing with survey responses from introductory programming students taking the same programming class but not participating in the community. We find that students in the learning community are more likely to agree that they are part of a group of programmers and more likely to say that they have friends who are interested in computing. Learning community students were also significantly different from other introductory programming students in their reported utilization of the Internet and in consultation with friends or peers post-quarter, with most learning community students less likely to use the Internet and more likely to work with friends after their course experience.

2 BACKGROUND

In this section we provide background information about the courses and activities in the linked-courses community, the survey instrument used to measure student attitudes and resource use, and selected results from analysis of earlier data sets.

2.1 Courses and Activities

The learning community was created for first-quarter freshman who are either a man of color or a woman of any race in majors that require Introduction to Computer Science I (CS1), an introductory programming course taught in Python that focuses on problem solving. The included majors are computer science, math and computer science, computer game development in the gameplay and systems concentrations, and cybersecurity. Students are recruited for the community after being admitted to our institution. Participation in the community is completely voluntary.

Our college uses several interventions recommended in the literature in the introductory programming sequence for majors, including closed labs with collaborative activities, differentiated courses for novice and experienced programmers, and engaged and enthusiastic faculty[2, 4, 6, 9, 11]. It should be noted that our institution is large, with approximately 2000 undergraduates in our college. While students in any of these majors have a fixed set of classes to take during their first year including the CS1 course, there are many different sections from which to choose. For example, there are typically eight sections of the CS1 course offered during the first quarter of each academic year. One of the sections of the CS1 course is reserved for learning community students.

Every freshman at our institution is required to take a Chicago Quarter class. These classes are designed to acquaint first-year students with our institution and the metropolitan community, neighborhoods, cultures, institutions, organizations, and people of Chicago. The courses also have a "Common Hour," which addresses issues of transition for first-year students, including academic success skills and educational and career planning. Students participating in the linked-courses learning community were enrolled in a section of an Explore Chicago class focusing on the digital divide and specifically on the social issues surrounding access to information and communications technology.

To enhance the sense of community among students, the CS1 and Explore Chicago courses are scheduled in back-to-back slots. Immediately following the CS1 sessions are the Explore Chicago class sessions, and students typically walk together between the two classes. With an institution as large as ours, having the opportunity as first-year students to share classes and walk together between those classes is unique to the learning community.

In addition to these two classes, students in the learning community participated in a variety of co-curricular and extra-curricular activities, including an open house, study sessions for the midterm and final exams, a midterm gaming celebration, employer visits, and tours of specialized facilities available in our college. The open house and gaming sessions are held at the instructors' homes, with the intention of bringing the participants closer to the instructors as well as to each other. There were three cohorts of the learning community, one each during the first quarters of the 2014-2015, 2015-2016, and 2016-2017 academic years. Activities for the first cohort were for the most part optional, and activities for the second and third cohorts were either mandatory or provided extra credit for attendees. As a result, the second and third cohorts had improved participation in the co-curricular and extra-curricular activities [15]. We note that the instructor for the CS1 course and the Explore Chicago course were the same for all cohorts and that the CS1 instructor did not teach any sections outside of the learning community during the three academic years in question.

2.2 Survey Instrument

The goal of the linked-courses learning community is to engage the students in an effort to improve their feelings of belonging and confidence, improve their study habits, and ultimately, improve their retention in the courses and degree program. While improved retention is the goal measuring the potential impact of the community early is beneficial for a variety of reasons.

As an early measure of whether students experienced a change in attitudes and habits by taking part in the learning community we developed and administered a survey. Due to space limitations the survey questions are not included here. In the sections analyzing the survey responses we give the questions for each significant result, but the full survey can be found in a previous publication [15]. The survey was administered pre-quarter and post-quarter in all CS1 Python classes during the 2013-2014 academic year and during the first quarters of the 2014-2015, 2015-2016, and 2016-2017 academic years.

2.3 Selected Previous Publications

This is not our first examination of the impact of the learning community on student attitudes. In a previous publication we considered only survey responses from students in the first two cohorts (first quarter 2014 and first quarter 2015) of the learning community [15]. The analysis found that students in the second cohort (first quarter 2015) were significantly less likely post-quarter to agree that they wanted to achieve recognition for their computer science grades and to agree that they felt isolated in computer science classes than students in the first cohort (first quarter 2014).

Students in the second cohort were significantly more likely post quarter to report that they felt challenged by programming problems than students in the first cohort [15]. These results provide evidence that student participants' sense of belonging and isolation was impacted during the quarter, although the results do not allow us to distinguish whether those differences are as a result of the learning community or the Python programming class.

A second relevant article presented the first pre- to post-quarter attitude changes among participants in the learning community [14]. In considering the data from the first two cohorts (first quarter 2014 and first quarter 2015) we found a statistically significant reduction in reported isolation among learning-community students. This result was not seen in students taking the programming course during the same quarters but not participating in the learning community. We also saw a statistically-significant increase in utilization of professional organizations among learning-community students. Both of these results were correlated with participation in the learning community.

3 EVALUATION

In our continuing evaluation of the impact of the linked-courses learning community on students' attitudes about computing and utilization of resources, we compare the results of survey responses from students in the learning community with the responses from students enrolled in a section of the CS1 course but not participating in the community. The analysis includes data from the 2014-2015, 2015-2016, and 2016-2017 academic years.

3.1 Demographics

There were two basic populations considered in the study: students who took part in the learning community during the 2014-2015, 2015-2016, or 2016-2017 academic years, and students who participated in the CS1 course during the first quarter of the 2014-2015, 2015-2016, or 2016-2017 academic years but were not part of the learning community.

A total of 454 students responded to both the pre- and post-quarter surveys. Of these, 403 students took the traditional CS1 course, while 51 took part in the learning community. The 2014-2015 academic year saw responses from 198 students in the traditional group and 13 students in the learning community. In the 2015-2016 academic year, there were 98 responses from the traditional group and 23 responses from students in the learning community. Finally, the 2016-2017 academic year produced 107 responses from the traditional group and 15 responses from the learning community.

For all three academic years, each respondent's gender was recorded in the survey. Table 1 shows a breakdown of male and female students and their distribution among the traditional and learning community courses.

Starting with the 2015-2016 academic year, respondents were asked to self-report their ethnicity. Because this data was not gathered for 2014-2015, any analysis of these subpopulations is limited to the most recent two years. Table 2 shows the breakdown of students' ethnicity for these 243 responses.

Table 3 shows the number of white males enrolled in each type of CS1 program. As this classification relies on ethnicity data, only the 2015-2016 and 2016-2017 academic years were included.

Table 1: Gender for each population

Gender	LC		CS1 Non-LC		Overall	
	Ct.	%	Ct.	%	Ct.	%
Male	35	68.6%	305	75.7%	340	74.9%
Female	16	31.4%	94	23.3%	110	24.2%
No response	0	0.0%	4	1.0%	4	0.9%
Total	51		403		454	

Table 2: Ethnicity for each population (2015-2017)

Ethnicity	LC		CS1 Non-LC		Overall	
	Ct.	%	Ct.	%	Ct.	%
White	8	21.1%	118	57.6%	126	51.9%
Asian	10	26.3%	27	13.2%	37	15.2%
Latino/a	8	21.1%	36	17.6%	44	18.1%
African-American	8	21.1%	9	4.4%	17	7.0%
Multiracial	3	7.9%	12	5.9%	15	6.2%
Other	1	2.6%	3	1.5%	4	1.6%
Total	38		205		243	

Table 3: White males for each population (2015-2017)

Gender	LC		CS1 Non-LC		Overall	
	Ct.	%	Ct.	%	Ct.	%
White male	3	7.9%	94	45.9%	97	39.9%
Any other	35	92.1%	107	52.2%	142	58.4%
No response	0	0.0%	4	2.0%	4	1.6%
Total	38		205		243	

3.2 Attitude Questions

The responses to the attitude questions were analyzed using a gain-score approach, calculating the change in response provided by the same student during the quarter. Each question was analyzed separately, and the final results were adjusted for multiple comparisons using the Benjamini-Hochberg method[3].

First, the entire population was included in an analysis to determine if any gainscores were impacted by the course type alone. Next, an additional analysis was performed on data from the female students alone to determine the impact of the learning community on those students. These first two tests included data from all three academic years.

To examine the impact of the learning community on ethnic minorities, only data from the 2015-2016 and 2016-2017 academic years could be used, as ethnicity data had not been collected in 2014-2015. Due to the small number of students in each ethnicity other than white, all non-white ethnicities were combined for this analysis. Next, students who reported Asian ethnicities were combined with white students into one category while other ethnicities were grouped together in a non-Asian minority category. The responses from the non-Asian minority ethnicities were examined to see whether the learning community had an impact on ethnicities that have been historically underrepresented in CS. The final test considered the impact of the learning community on all gender and ethnic minorities by excluding only white male students from the

Table 4: Mean responses for Q25 before and after course

Q25	CS1 Pre	CS1 Post	LC Pre	LC Post
All students	2.87	2.89	3.35	3.84
Female	2.69	2.64	3.25	3.81
Non-white	3.18	3.01	3.14	3.66
Non-Asian minority	3.05	3.00	3.30	3.85
Non-white male	3.01	2.98	3.11	3.70

Table 5: Test for differences LC vs. CS1 for Q25

Q25	CS1 Gain-Score	LC Gain-Score	Test result	B-H Adj.
All students	0.01	0.49	t(442)=-2.87, p=.0043	FDR= .0455
Female	0.00	0.56	t(107)=-2.00, p=.0477	FDR= .2961
Non-white	-0.23	0.53	t(109)=-2.95, p=.0039	FDR= .0406
Non-Asian minority	-0.13	0.55	t(74)=-2.01, p=.0477	FDR= .4005
Non-white male	-0.21	0.63	t(133)=-3.69, p=.0003	FDR= .0067

Table 6: Mean responses for Q31 before and after course

Q31	CS1 Pre	CS1 Post	LC Pre	LC Post
All students	3.38	3.27	3.33	3.82
Female	2.99	2.79	2.50	3.50
Non-white	3.52	3.33	3.03	3.90
Non-Asian minority	3.46	3.29	3.10	3.75
Non-white male	3.42	3.29	3.02	3.78

Table 7: Test for differences LC vs. CS1 for Q31

Q25	CS1 Gain-Score	LC Gain-Score	Test result	B-H Adj.
All students	-0.10	0.49	t(448)=-3.33, p=.0009	FDR= .0398
Female	-0.20	1.00	t(109)=-3.64, p=.0004	FDR= .0173
Non-white	-0.15	0.83	t(113)=-3.80, p=.0002	FDR= .0098
Non-Asian minority	-0.11	0.65	t(76)=-2.24, p=.0279	FDR= .3901
Non-white male	-0.14	0.80	t(138)=-4.08, p<.0001	FDR= .0032

data to be analyzed. Since this subpopulation includes ethnicity data, only responses from the 2015-2016 and 2016-2017 academic years were included.

Due to the large number of tests, there would be a high risk of false positives (type I errors) by relying on raw p-values produced from these tests. To alleviate this risk, the results were adjusted using the linear step-up Benjamini-Hochberg method to convert the raw p-values into a false discovery rate (FDR), and only those results with FDR < .05 are discussed here.

Only two of the attitude questions produced an FDR < .05 for the entire population or any of the analyzed subpopulations. The results of Q25: "I am part of a community of programmers," and Q31: "I have a lot of friends who are interested in computing," showed a statistically significant difference between the learning community and traditional courses among the entire population. Students in the traditional course did not show a significant change in response to Q25 throughout the quarter, whereas the students in the LC did show such a gain. When limited to the female subpopulation, Q25 did not survive the Benjamini-Hochberg adjustment. The difference in gainscore remains significant when considering the subpopulation of non-white students and non-white males, but once Asian students are grouped in with the white students, the remaining minority students see no statistically significant difference between the learning community and the traditional path. Although there may well still be an impact, the number of comparisons performed in the analysis cautions against relying on the marginal p-values.

Tables 4 and 6 show the mean responses to Q25 and Q31 respectively for traditional and LC students before and after the course broken down by subpopulation. Tables 5 and 7 show the change in response (the gainscore) for each group, as well as the raw test result and adjusted false discovery rate.

In the overall population, students in both course types had similar mean responses to Q31 prior to the quarter, but the LC students showed a statistically significant gain between pre- and post-quarter responses while the students in the traditional course did not. Q31 survives with a false discovery rate under .05 for all analyzed subpopulations except non-Asian minorities.

3.3 Resource Question

The final question on the survey asked students "Outside of your classroom studies, what are your resources for learning/obtaining new computing skills?" The resources listed are: Friends/peers, Internet/web sites, professional organizations, self study, family members, tutors, faculty, and other (please specify). Students are instructed to leave a resource blank if they did not use it, so that only the resources utilized would be given a ranking. Responses

to the resource question consisted of a relative ranking of each resource ranging from 1 to 8, with 1 being the most frequently used resource. Some responses contained multiple resources ranked in a tie. To properly account for ties and resources that were left off one but not both of the pre- and post-test, all responses were analyzed by converting the ordinal ranking for each resource provided by the student into a score reflective of its position relative to other resources. For each student's response, a resource was assigned a score calculated by adding the number of lower-ranked resources to half the number of equally-ranked resources. Thus, a higher score is reflective of a more-frequently-used resource than a lower score, and all scores were between 0 and 7.

The scores for each resource were then analyzed in a similar manner to the attitude questions. A pre- to post-course gainscore was calculated for each resource, and these gainscores were analyzed

Table 8: Mean adjusted ranking for Internet/web sites

Internet/web	CS1 Pre	CS1 Post	LC Pre	LC Post
All students	5.64	5.76	5.78	4.67
Female	5.40	5.53	5.41	3.94
Non-white	5.49	5.85	5.91	4.17
Non-Asian minority	5.70	5.82	6.34	4.34
Non-white male	5.58	5.79	6.01	4.32

Table 9: Test for differences LC vs. CS1 for Internet/web sites

Internet/web	CS1 Gain-Score	LC Gain-Score	Test result	B-H Adj.
All students	0.13	-1.11	t(451)=5.17, p<.0001	FDR< .0001
Female	0.13	-1.47	t(109)=3.48, p=.0007	FDR= .0152
Non-white	0.40	-1.75	t(115)=5.91, p<.0001	FDR< .0001
Non-Asian minority	0.17	-2.00	t(78)=5.44, p<.0001	FDR< .0001
Non-white male	0.31	-1.76	t(140)=6.21, p<.0001	FDR< .0001

Table 10: Mean adjusted ranking for friends/peers

Internet/web	CS1 Pre	CS1 Post	LC Pre	LC Post
All students	4.10	4.30	3.58	4.83
Female	3.97	3.94	2.75	4.06
Non-white	3.86	4.30	3.28	5.36
Non-Asian minority	3.73	4.15	3.32	5.18
Non-white male	3.98	4.34	3.24	5.15

Table 11: Test for differences LC vs. CS1 for friends/peers

Friends/peers	CS1 Gain-Score	LC Gain-Score	Test result	B-H Adj.
All students	0.20	1.25	t(451)=-3.45, p=.0006	FDR= .0130
Female	0.02	1.31	t(109)=-2.06, p=.0418	FDR= .2961
Non-white	0.38	2.05	t(115)=-3.91, p=.0002	FDR= .0033
Non-Asian minority	0.32	1.83	t(78)=-2.74, p=.0076	FDR= .1602
Non-white male	0.53	2.00	t(140)=-3.83, p=.0002	FDR= .0027

for differences between the learning community and traditional course for the overall population, the female subpopulation, the non-white subpopulation, and the non-white male subpopulation. The test results from each resource were combined with the results from the attitude questions to calculate the overall false discovery rate using the linear step-up Benjamini-Hochberg method. All analyzed subpopulations showed a significant difference between the learning community and the traditional course in the change in reliance upon Internet/web sites as a resource from beginning to end of term. The change in reliance upon friends and peers as a resource showed a significant difference between LC and CS1 among the overall population and some subpopulations. The raw p-values for all subpopulations analyzed were less than .05, but for female students and non-Asian minority students, the adjustment for multiple comparisons drives the false discovery rate much higher. Table 10 shows the mean adjusted ranking for the use of friends and peers as a resource, while table 11 shows the test results comparing the LC against the traditional CS1 program. Tables 8 and 10 show the mean adjusted ranking for the use of Internet/web sites and Friends/peers as resources, while tables 9 and 11 show the test results comparing the LC against the traditional CS1 program.

4 DISCUSSION

The attitude changes seen in learning community participants centered on two questions, one regarding their sense of belonging to a community of programmers and the other regarding whether they have friends who are interested in computing. Among all learning community participants, there was a significant change in response to the two questions from pre- to post-quarter. Learning community students were more likely than students taking the CS1 course but

not participating in the community to agree that they belonged to a community of programmers and that they had friends who were interested in computing.

These changes were also significant for several subpopulations relevant for the learning community. All underrepresented groups (e.g. everyone but white males) and non-white students in the learning community were more likely than the equivalent CS1 populations to agree with both questions post-quarter. Unfortunately when Asian students are removed from the non-white population the results are no longer seen, but this may be because the number of non-Asian, non-white students in the learning community remain relatively small even with three cohorts of data. We hope to re-examine this when we obtain more data in the first quarter of the 2017-2018 academic year. Similarly, female participants in the learning community were more likely to agree post-quarter that they had friends who are interested in computing than women who were taking the CS1 course but not participating in the community. Unfortunately the result regarding being a part of a community of programmers was not statistically significant for female learning community participants. Our suspicion is that the female learning community data set is simply too small for a statistically significant result to emerge at this point. Like the results for non-Asian minority students we hope to re-examine this when we obtain more data later in the year.

Since a sense of belonging and the support of like-minded friends are important for retention of underrepresented groups, we are encouraged by this result. Previous work has shown that good social support is associated with strong orientation toward careers in CIS [12], and one of the goals of the community is to build that social support.

There were two significant differences pre- to post-quarter in resource utilization on the part of learning community students. All learning community students, as well as all of the subpopulations considered (female students, non-white students, Non-Asian minority students, and non-white male students) were less likely to use the Internet/web sites as resources post-quarter. All of these were significantly different from the changes seen pre- to post-quarter among the CS1 students in comparable population. It should be noted that students in the learning community were expressly forbidden from using the Internet or other online resources when completing assignments in the programming course associated with the community, primarily due to concerns about Academic Integrity violations. This is also true in many of the other sections of the CS1 class, but it appears that the learning community students were the only ones to heed the restriction.

All students as well as the non-white students and non-white male students in the learning community were more likely post-quarter to report that their consultation of friends or peers about course work had increased. The results were strongly significant. The results were not seen, however, among the female students or non-Asian minority students. This result is consistent with the experience the instructors attempted to cultivate in the community since the participants are explicitly allowed to collaborate with classmates on assignments, although they are expected to provide details about that collaboration on their submissions. Lab assignments are also highly encouraged to be completed in consultation with classmates, since there is benefit to be gained by students from working with others.

5 CONCLUSIONS AND FUTURE WORK

In analyzing survey responses from participants in three cohorts of the learning community and from students taking a CS1 course but not participating in the community, we find that students in the learning community are more likely to agree that they are part of a community of programmers and more likely to say that they have friends who are interested in computing. This result was consistent for some subpopulations (everyone but non-white males and non-white students) but not for others.

Learning community students were also significantly different from other CS1 students in their reported utilization of the Internet and in consultation with friends or peers post-quarter, with learning community students less likely to use the Internet and more likely to work with friends. Both of these results are consistent with course policies and with the goals of the community. One issue is that the data set from non-Asian minority and female students remains small, even with three cohorts. We will continue our efforts at measuring attitude and resource utilization changes when we run a fourth cohort of the learning community in the first quarter of academic year 2017-2018. It is our hope that with more data we can begin to better understand the impact that the learning community is having on certain subpopulations of participants.

We are also in the process of a qualitative analysis of the impact of the learning community. We have approval to begin an interview study in which students in the learning community and students in the CS1 courses but not in the community will be asked about their prior programming experiences, their experiences as a part of the CS1 course, and their resulting decisions and impressions of their major and career. We are recruiting students from each of the three years in which the community was offered to ensure that a variety of viewpoints and levels of maturity and experience are represented. We hope that by analyzing the interviews we can learn more about experiences in the community and in the CS1 course that may not be captured by our existing survey.

6 ACKNOWLEDGEMENTS

Our thanks go to Brian Sedlak for coding the data for the 2015 surveys.

REFERENCES

[1] Computing Research Association. 2017. Generation CS: Computer Science Undergraduate Enrollments Surge Since 2006. (2017). http://cra.org/data/Generation-CS/

[2] Lecia J. Barker, Charlie McDowell, and Kimberly Kalahar. 2009. Exploring Factors That Influence Computer Science Introductory Course Students to Persist in the Major. In *Proceedings of the 40th ACM Technical Symposium on Computer Science Education (SIGCSE '09)*. ACM, New York, NY, USA, 153–157. https://doi.org/10.1145/1508865.1508923

[3] Yoav Benjamini and Yosef Hochberg. 1995. Controlling the false discovery rate: a practical and powerful approach to multiple testing. *Journal of the royal statistical society. Series B (Methodological)* (1995), 289–300.

[4] Kristy Elizabeth Boyer, Rachael S. Dwight, Carolyn S. Miller, C. Dianne Raubenheimer, Matthias F. Stallmann, and Mladen A. Vouk. 2007. A Case for Smaller Class Size with Integrated Lab for Introductory Computer Science. In *Proceedings of the 38th SIGCSE Technical Symposium on Computer Science Education (SIGCSE '07)*. ACM, New York, NY, USA, 341–345. https://doi.org/10.1145/1227310.1227430

[5] Kima Cargill and Beth Kalikoff. 2007. Linked psychology and writing courses across the curriculum. *The Journal of General Education* 56, 2 (2007), 83–92.

[6] J McGrath Cohoon. 2002. Recruiting and retaining women in undergraduate computing majors. *ACM SIGCSE Bulletin* 34, 2 (2002), 48–52.

[7] Sandra Gorka, Matthew Helf, and Jacob Miller. 2014. Implementing a Living-learning Community in Information Technology. In *Proceedings of the 15th Annual Conference on Information Technology Education (SIGITE '14)*. ACM, New York, NY, USA, 153–158. https://doi.org/10.1145/2656450.2656470

[8] Karen Kellogg. 1999. Learning Communities. *ERIC Digest* (1999). http://eric.ed.gov/?id=ED430512

[9] Michael S. Kirkpatrick and Chris Mayfield. 2017. Evaluating an Alternative CS1 for Students with Prior Programming Experience. In *Proceedings of the 2017 ACM SIGCSE Technical Symposium on Computer Science Education (SIGCSE '17)*. ACM, New York, NY, USA, 333–338. https://doi.org/10.1145/3017680.3017759

[10] Tracy L. Lewis, Wanda J. Smith, France Bélanger, and K. Vernard Harrington. 2008. Are Technical and Soft Skills Required?: The Use of Structural Equation Modeling to Examine Factors Leading to Retention in the Cs Major. In *Proceedings of the Fourth International Workshop on Computing Education Research (ICER '08)*. ACM, New York, NY, USA, 91–100. https://doi.org/10.1145/1404520.1404530

[11] Tia Newhall, Lisa Meeden, Andrew Danner, Ameet Soni, Frances Ruiz, and Richard Wicentowski. 2014. A Support Program for Introductory CS Courses That Improves Student Performance and Retains Students from Underrepresented Groups. In *Proceedings of the 45th ACM Technical Symposium on Computer Science Education (SIGCSE '14)*. ACM, New York, NY, USA, 433–438. https://doi.org/10.1145/2538862.2538923

[12] Mary Beth Rosson, John M. Carroll, and Hansa Sinha. 2011. Orientation of Undergraduates Toward Careers in the Computer and Information Sciences: Gender, Self-Efficacy and Social Support. *Trans. Comput. Educ.* 11, 3, Article 14 (Oct. 2011), 23 pages. https://doi.org/10.1145/2037276.2037278

[13] Pooja Sankar, Jessica Gilmartin, and Melissa Sobel. 2015. An Examination of Belongingness and Confidence Among Female Computer Science Students. *SIGCAS Comput. Soc.* 45, 2 (July 2015), 7–10. https://doi.org/10.1145/2809957.2809960

[14] Amber Settle, James Doyle, and Theresa Steinbach. 2017. Participating in a Computer Science Linked-courses Learning Community Reduces Isolation. *CoRR* abs/1704.07898 (2017). http://arxiv.org/abs/1704.07898

[15] Amber Settle and Theresa Steinbach. 2016. Improving Retention and Reducing Isolation via a Linked-courses Learning Community. In *Proceedings of the 17th Annual Conference on Information Technology Education (SIGITE '16)*. ACM, New York, NY, USA, 34–39. https://doi.org/10.1145/2978192.2978212

M-CAFE 2.0: A Scalable Platform with Comparative Plots and Topic Tagging for Ongoing Course Feedback

Mo Zhou[1], Sanjay Krishnan[2], Jay Patel[2], Brandie Nonnecke[3]
Camille Crittenden[3], Ken Goldberg[1,2]

[1]UC Berkeley
IEOR Department
{mzhou, Goldberg}@berkeley.edu

[2]UC Berkeley
EECS Department
{sanjaykrishnan,
patel.jay}@berkeley.edu

[3]UC Berkeley
CITRIS Connected Communities
Initiative
{nonnecke,
ccrittenden}@berkeley.edu

ABSTRACT

M-CAFE 2.0 is an online and mobile platform that uses collaborative filtering to collect and organize student feedback each week throughout a MOOC or an on-campus course to facilitate mid-course corrections by instructors. M-CAFE 2.0 encourages students to assess course content, structure, and suggestions provided by their peers. It requires minimal extra effort from instructors and is anonymous and separate from all student records. We present results from three pilot studies from on-campus undergraduate courses with 1,211 evaluations and 5,221 peer-ratings from 169 students. Results suggest that comparative plots of past ratings, topic tags and peer-to-peer anonymous suggestion evaluations are valuable in promoting credible and diverse course evaluation. M-CAFE 2.0 is available at m-cafe.org.

Author Keywords
Course Evaluation; Student Evaluation of Teaching; Collaborative Filtering; MOOCs.

CSS Keywords
- **Human-centered computing~Collaborative filtering**
- Human-centered computing~User interface design
- Applied computing~Computer-assisted instruction
- Applied computing~E-learning

SIGITE'17, October 4–7, 2017, Rochester, NY, USA
© 2017 Association for Computing Machinery.
ACM ISBN 978-1-4503-5100-3/17/10◄$15.00
https://doi.org/10.1145/3125659.3125681

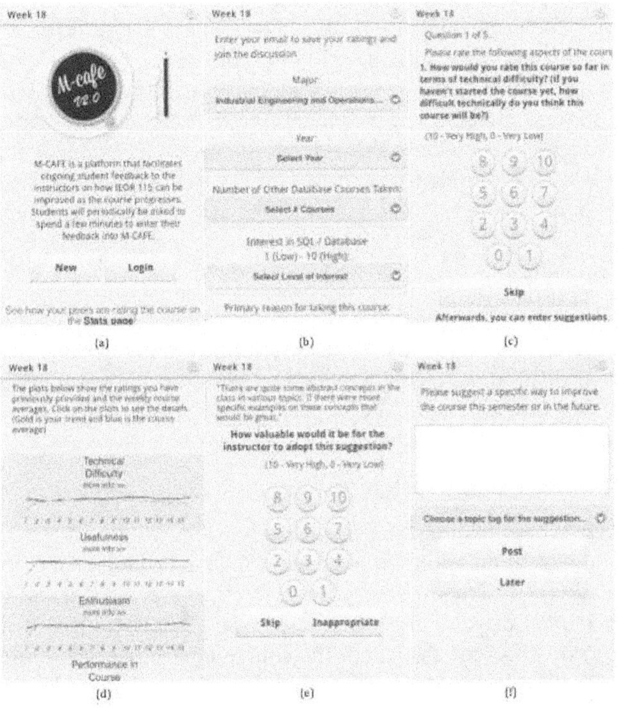

Figure 1: Screenshots of the M-CAFE 2.0 interface, compatible with desktop and mobile devices: a. the landing screen; b. new users register using their email address and provide demographics; c. users rate the course aspects (Course Difficulty, Course Usefulness, Self-Enthusiasm, Self-Performance and Homework Effectiveness); d. the comparative plots of past ratings; e. users rate the value of a peer-provided suggestion; f. users enter their own course improvement suggestions.

1. INTRODUCTION

In recent years, on-campus courses are experiencing growing class sizes, making individualized student-instructor interaction challenging. In the meantime, massive open online courses (MOOCs) have received widespread attention and excitement since 2012. But studies find that MOOCs have an extremely high dropout rate, due to limited interaction with instructors and peers, insufficient academic background and personal stress [6,

14, 20, 22, 23]. Therefore, more specific and frequent feedback from learners may help instructors identify problems in course content and provide timely responses for both MOOCs and large on-campus courses.

In 2014, we developed the MOOC Collaborative Assessment and Feedback Engine 1.0 (M-CAFE 1.0) to collect ongoing student feedback [24].

In this paper, we introduce M-CAFE 2.0, an enhanced version of M-CAFE 1.0 with comparative plots of ratings on Course Difficulty, Course Effectiveness, Self-Enthusiasm, Self-Performance and Homework Effectiveness and topic tagging for discussion suggestions centered around the question "In what specific way would you improve this course this semester or in the future?" Displaying comparative plots serves as a baseline for future ratings and enables students to quickly track their progress. By comparing self-ratings to the course average, students see where they stand among their peers. To assess the performance of M-CAFE 2.0 on traditional on-campus courses, we adopted it in two large on-campus courses at UC Berkeley in 2016 taught by Professor Ken Goldberg.

The paper is structured as follows: we first evaluate the current state of course evaluation. Then we introduce M-CAFE 2.0 and describe its features and the improvements from M-CAFE 1.0. We report results from three pilot studies with 169 students.

2. RELATED WORK

2.1 Student Evaluation of Teaching
Student evaluation of teaching (SET) is widely used to evaluate instructor's teaching effectiveness. SET usually occurs at the end of the semester when students are asked to rate different aspects of the course on a numerical scale (usually from 1 to 10 "Very Low" to "Very High"). Many studies question the validity of naively aggregating quantitative ratings from SET [1, 3, 4, 11, 13, 17]. Stark and Freishtat [18] state that "SET are ordinal categorical variables and comparing an individual instructor's average to department average is meaningless, since there's no reason to believe that the difference between 3 and 4 means the same thing as the difference between 6 and 7 and that the difference between 3 and 4 means the same thing to different students." McCullough & Radson further introduce an alternative method to analyze SET data that uses categorical proportions instead of assigning a score to each category and numerically aggregating the results to robustly evaluate teacher's performance [12]. In contrast, Khong conducted a recent study of 200 students to suggest that the SET is a valid instrument in evaluating teaching effectiveness by measures such as internal consistency and correlations [7]. Surgenor suggests that SET can be valuable to measure dedication to teaching and improvement and to promote quality learning [19]. Furthermore, he identifies the need for easily obtainable feedback on modules. M-CAFE 2.0 is a tool to help

instructors improve teaching effectiveness by encouraging and examining feedback on a weekly basis. To ensure comparable SET responses, M-CAFE 2.0 displays the average ratings for the past weeks as a benchmark for future ratings.

2.2 Collective Intelligence
Online discussion platforms such as Piazza and stackExchange are popular collective intelligence sites. Most MOOCs and large on-campus courses use one or more of these platforms to motivate interaction among peers and between students and instructors [10]. Gelman et al. investigated the emergence of interest-based subcultures in online communities and how they engage a large number of learners [5]. Sajjadi et al. adopt a peer-grading mechanism in a MOOC to explore the effective metric of aggregating peer assessments [24]. Krishnan et al. developed a self-organizing collective system called the Collective Discovery Engine (CDE) to collect insights from a diverse group on how social media can improve learning [8]. Woolley et al. quantify group performance by a collective intelligence factor and suggest that group performance exceeds individual performance [21]. Despite the various crowdsourcing applications, this approach has not been applied to student evaluations. Typical student evaluations involve anonymous individual responses to the questions where students are not allowed to discuss or view each other's response. This mechanism is inefficient because it requires extensive time from the instructors to read each of the responses, and the responses contain many repetitions. M-CAFE 2.0 aims to overcome these challenges by adopting a collaborative filtering mechanism, where students provide peer-to-peer ratings on suggestions with the interested topic and assign a reputation score to each suggestion. The set of suggestions with the highest reputation are presented to the instructors each week.

2.3 M-CAFE 2.0 INTERFACE SUMMARY AND CHANGES
After entering M-CAFE 2.0 (Figure 1a), students specify if they are new users or returning users. New users are prompted to register using their email and are encouraged to provide demographics information, such as gender, age, home country and their primary reason for taking the course (Figure 1b). Then they rate five quantitative assessment topics (QAT) on each separate page on a scale of 0 to 10: Course Difficulty, Course Usefulness, Self-enthusiasm, Self-performance and Homework Effectiveness (Figure 1c). Next, students are shown the comparative plots of their past ratings and the course average ratings on the QATs (Figure 1d). Then students enter the discussion space about the topic "In what specific way would you improve this course this semester or in the future?" (Figure 2). Students click on the tagged spheres to view the suggestions previously provided by their peers on the specific topic tag, evaluate the suggestions on a scale of 0-10 (Figure 1e) and suggest new suggestions with the appropriate topic tag (Figure 1f).

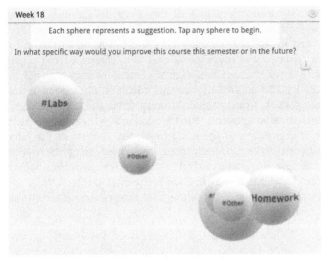

Figure 2: the space of course improvement suggestions with topic tags in M-CAFE 2.0.

Compared with M-CAFE 1.0, the new version, M-CAFE 2.0, adopts a more intuitive interface with a keypad design for ratings. In addition, M-CAFE 2.0 introduces comparative plots displaying the rating history of the current user against the course weekly average for each QAT, enabling users to track their own performance and quickly compare themselves to the course average (Figure 1d). As show in Figure 2, M-CAFE 2.0 further deploys topic tagging in the discussion phase to bring more structure to the textual suggestions. The list of tags includes Exams, Homework, Labs, Lectures, New Topic, Logistics, Projects and Other.

3. PILOT STUDIES AND ANALYSIS

We used M-CAFE 2.0 in two UC Berkeley undergraduate in-person courses to investigate its effectiveness: IEOR 115: Commercial Database Systems in Fall 2015 (F15) and IEOR 170: Industrial Design and Human Factor in Spring 2016 (S16). We compare the results of IEOR 170 in Spring 2015 (S15) with M-CAFE 1.0 usage and IEOR 115 in Fall 2016 (F16) without M-CAFE usage to illustrate that absolute comparison of numerical ratings are unreliable and adopting M-CAFE 2.0 encourages a more diverse set of course improvement suggestions. All four courses were taught by Prof. Ken Goldberg. The two IEOR 170 courses covered the same set of topics/materials on industrial design concepts with similar weekly progress. The two IEOR 115 courses were also similar in content and introduced industrial and commercial database systems. Approximately 60 students enrolled in each course and students in IEOR 170, F16 and IEOR 115, F15 were encouraged to participate anonymously in M-CAFE 2.0 at the beginning of the semesters. Participation in M-CAFE 2.0 is fully voluntary, thus the results suffer from self-selection bias. Furthermore, for IEOR 170, S15, the instructor adopted M-CAFE 1.0 and frequently discussed M-CAFE feedback in class and reminded students to continue participating on a weekly basis. However, for

IEOR 115, F15 and IEOR 170, S16, the instructor put less emphasis on M-CAFE 2.0, resulting in a lower participation rate.

Table 1: Participation statistics in different stages of M-CAFE for IEOR 115, F2015 and IEOR 170, F15 and F16, and participation of traditional mid-term evaluation in IEOR 115, F16

	IEOR 170, S15	IEOR 115, F15	IEOR 170, S16	IEOR 115, F16
M-CAFE version	1.0	2.0	2.0	Not used
Total user count	58	57	54	36
Mean weekly user count	32	32	17	N/A
QAT set rating count	474	483	254	N/A
Suggestion count	270	110	90	34
Peer-to-peer rating count	2,483	1,759	979	N/A
Date range of the course	Jan - May, 2015	Sep - Dec, 2015	Jan - May, 2016	Sep – Dec, 2016
Term length of the course	15-week	15-week	15-week	15-week

3.1 Quantitative Evaluation Consistency

Comparing M-CAFE course ratings of two IEOR 170 courses offered in S15 and S16, we find that absolute course assessment rating is not reliable. Figure 3 shows the mean weekly ratings of Course Difficulty from IEOR 170 in 2015 and 2016. Both trends increase gradually as the semester proceeds. Interestingly, there exists a gap between the two ratings from different years throughout the semester. Since the two courses were nearly identical in terms of instructor, material and schedule, there is no reason to believe that the course offered in 2016 was significantly harder than the same course offered in 2015. We suspect that the different rating scales of participating students in the two courses led to this gap, confirming that absolute course evaluation ratings can be unreliable when the population changes. For example, for some course material, one student may assign a Course Difficulty score of 6 but another student may assign a difficulty score of 8. Furthermore, displaying rating history to students provides a benchmark rating scale, which reinforces the difference between the two course ratings in later weeks. Thus we see a consistent relative change over time in average Course Difficulty ratings but a statistically significant difference in absolute ratings between the two courses. Comparing the weekly ratings from the two courses using a t-test, we see that with 5% significance level, the difference in means each week in the two years is not equal to 0, with an overall mean of 3.57 in 2015 and 5.845 in 2016. Similar gaps are found in the other 4 QATs between the two courses.

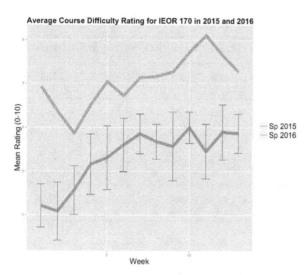

Figure 3: blue line: mean Course Difficulty ratings for 15 weeks in IEOR 170, S16; red line: mean and 2 standard errors above and below the average Course Difficulty ratings for 15 weeks in IEOR 170, S15.

3.2 Qualitative Evaluation Structure and Diversity

Two major challenges in the qualitative part of end-of-course evaluations are the analysis difficulty of unstructured data and the limitation of comment variety resulting from repetition. M-CAFE 2.0 addresses these challenges by collecting textual suggestions from students using topic tagging. For instance, after articulating a suggestion, students are required to choose the appropriate topic tag from a dropdown containing {Exams, Homework, Labs, Lectures, Logistics, New Topics, Projects, Other}. If the student chooses "Other," he/she is encouraged to suggest a new topic tag. For the following analysis, we define "Course Topic" as the topic tags associated with the suggestions, i.e., Exams, Homework, etc. and "Course Module" as the topic of the course materials, i.e., SQL, Relational Schema, etc.

M-CAFE 2.0 organizes feedback by topic tags and encourages students to evaluate the course on a weekly basis when different course modules are covered.

Initial results suggest that:

(1) Students are more likely to provide a new suggestion for topics they have not considered in the peer-rating phase.

By requiring students to provide at least two peer ratings before supplying their own, M-CAFE 2.0 aims to reduce suggestion repetition. After investigating data from the two courses that used M-CAFE 2.0, we find that in both

courses more than half of the students supplied a new suggestion with a topic different from the topics that they rated in the peer-rating phase, indicating an intention to articulate new suggestions that are different from those already in the system. Eighty percent of the students in IEOR 115 and 76% of students in IEOR 170 articulated a suggestion from a topic different from the topic of their last rated suggestion. For the students who rated at least one suggestion of the same topic, the content of the new suggestion is different from the rated suggestion. For example, a student in IEOR 115 rated 6 suggestions before providing his/her own, 3 on lectures, 1 on projects, 1 on homework and 1 on other. The suggestions on lectures he/she rated are:

1. "When drawing E-R Diagrams on the board--or any other diagrams that are complex--plan it out so that none of it has to be erased/moved to another board. It is way harder to fix diagrams on paper as we take notes."
2. "Slow down a little bit."
3. "The discussion sections could be clearer. It is difficult to see what kind of table manipulations are going on."

And the student provided the following new suggestion on lectures:

"If possible, posting an outline of every lecture will be very helpful considering the fast pace of the lecture. As a result, we can pay more attention to the explanation instead of putting too much effort in copying down everything in the notes."

Below is another example of a student who rated two suggestions on Homework and further provided a suggestion on Homework. The two suggestions he/she rated:

1. "I hope we receive plenty of feedback on what to improve from graders on our homework and exams."
2. "Re-evaluate homework length. The current homework on designing and prototyping a restraint was too much to ask for in one week -- the design and report alone took me 5 hours. Prototyping was much harder this week due to reduced Jacobs access hours, and my friends and I were not able to make a physical prototype. This homework in particular should have its point balance changed to not take a physical prototype into account."

And the suggestion he/she provided afterwards:

"The fusion360 tutorial in class is not helpful for a first time user at all, and the assignment this week is not easy for students who never use 3D graphic software before."

In case of this student, we suspect that this student is interested in the topic "Homework". Thus he/she purposefully clicked on the spheres with the Homework tag to see if any other students have already suggested the same suggestion. After finding that these two existing suggestions are different from his/hers, he/she articulated his own.

(2) Course improvement suggestions from M-CAFE 2.0 are more diverse than those from traditional mid-course evaluations.

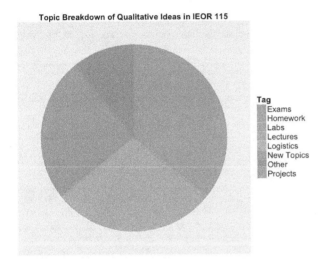

Topic Breakdown of Qualitative Ideas in IEOR 115

Tag
- Exams
- Homework
- Labs
- Lectures
- Logistics
- New Topics
- Other
- Projects

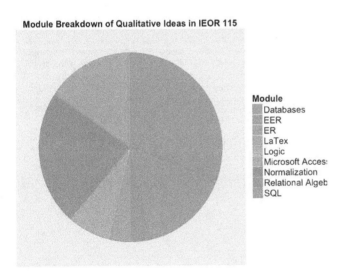

Module Breakdown of Qualitative Ideas in IEOR 115

Module
- Databases
- EER
- ER
- LaTex
- Logic
- Microsoft Access
- Normalization
- Relational Algeb
- SQL

Figure 4: (a) Pie plot of IEOR 115 in 2015 indicating the breakdown of qualitative suggestions in terms of course topics; (b) Pie plot of IEOR 115 in 2015 indicating the breakdown of qualitative suggestions in terms of course modules.

We compare two IEOR 115 courses offered in 2015 and 2016 to observe their suggestion diversity. IEOR 115, F15 used M-CAFE 2.0 and encouraged students to provide qualitative suggestions on a weekly basis, whereas the same course with the same instructor, materials and schedule offered in 2016 didn't use M-CAFE 2.0. Instead, a paper-based mid-term unofficial course evaluation was conducted in lecture on Oct. 3, 2016. We compare the

paper results to the qualitative suggestions on M-CAFE 2.0 suggested before Oct. 3, 2015. For IEOR 115, F15, M-CAFE 2.0 collected a total of 50 unique suggestions with topic distribution shown in the pie plot (Figure 4 a), with 13 on Homework, 5 on Labs, 16 on Lectures, 2 on Logistics, 4 on New Topics, 1 on Policies, 5 on Projects and 4 on Other, covering most topics of the course. Out of the 50 suggestions, 35 suggestions mention a specific course module. Figure 4b displays the proportion of suggestions on each course module and results show that most modules received improvement suggestions and the number of suggestions per module is positively correlated with the number of lectures the instructor spent on the module. The suggestions range from "I hope we receive plenty of feedback on what to improve from graders on our homework and exams." to "Despite the pace of the lecture, the examples given in the lecture so far are helpful to understand the overall concept of entity-relationship diagram. For the future, I think it would be better if the Professor can elaborate more why he does a particular step."

For IEOR 115, F16, we manually analyzed the mid-term evaluations from 36 students and summarized the textual suggestions. Out of all the suggestions, 18 are unique within the list, covering multiple course aspects such as Lectures, Homework, Labs, Logistics, etc. However, many students provided the same suggestion: for example, 5 students requested the instructor "to provide a study guide/notes for the lectures." Seventeen of the 18 suggestions are general statements that do not refer to any particular course module, thus making it impossible for the instructor to understand how the students perceive each course module.

4. CONCLUSION

M-CAFE 2.0 collects ongoing student course evaluations and effectively identifies valuable suggestions. Two pilot studies suggest that visualizing relative changes in course assessment over time and topic tagging encourages a more diverse set of course suggestions.

5. FUTURE WORK

This paper provides an evaluation of the effectiveness of M-CAFE 2.0 in regular on-campus courses. In the future, we would like to evaluate the performance of M-CAFE 2.0 in MOOCs/online courses and conduct comparative analysis between the two types of course.

ACKNOWLEDGEMENTS

This study is IRB approved by UC Berkeley under CPHS Protocol 2014-04-6297. This work is supported in part by the Blum Center for Developing Economies and the Development Impact Lab (USAID Cooperative Agreement AID-OAA-A-12- 00011) as part of the USAID Higher Education Solutions Network, UC Berkeley's Algorithms, Machines, and People (AMP) Lab, and the Connected Communities Initiative at the Center for Information Technology Research in the Interest of Society (CITRIS) and the Banatao Institute at UC Berkeley. This work is also supported in part by the Philippine Commission on Higher Education through the Philippine-California Advanced Research Institutes Project (no. IIID-2015-07). Thanks to Animesh Garg, Allen Huang, Allison Cliff and Steve McKinley. Thanks to all students who participated and colleagues and reviewers who provided feedback on earlier drafts.

REFERENCES

1. Adams, M.J. and Umbach, P.D., 2012. Nonresponse and online student evaluations of teaching: Understanding the influence of salience, fatigue, and academic environments. *Research in Higher Education, 53*(5), pp.576-591.

2. Daradoumis, T., Bassi, R., Xhafa, F. and Caballé, S., 2013, October. A review on massive e-learning (MOOC) design, delivery and assessment. In *P2P, Parallel, Grid, Cloud and Internet Computing (3PGCIC), 2013 Eighth International Conference on* (pp. 208-213). IEEE.

3. Flaherty, C. (2016). Zero Correlation Between Evaluations and Learning. Retrieved from https://www.insidehighered.com/news/2016/09/21/new-study-could-be-another-nail-coffin-validity-student-evaluations-teaching.

4. Freeman, R. and Dobbins, K., 2013. Are we serious about enhancing courses? Using the principles of assessment for learning to enhance course evaluation. *Assessment & Evaluation in Higher Education, 38*(2), pp.142-151.

5. Gelman, B.U., Beckley, C., Johri, A., Domeniconi, C. and Yang, S., 2016, April. Online Urbanism: Interest-based Subcultures as Drivers of Informal Learning in an Online Community. In *Proceedings of the Third (2016) ACM Conference on Learning@ Scale* (pp. 21-30). ACM.

6. Greene, J.A., Oswald, C.A. and Pomerantz, J., 2015. Predictors of retention and achievement in a massive open online course. *American Educational Research Journal*, p.0002831215584621.

7. Khong, T.L., 2016. The Validity and Reliability of the Student Evaluation of Teaching: A case in a Private Higher Educational Institution in Malaysia.*International Journal for Innovation Education and Research, 2*(9).

8. Krishnan, S., Patel, J., Franklin, M. and Goldberg, K., 2014. Social influence bias in recommender systems: a methodology for learning, analyzing, and mitigating bias in ratings. In *Proceedings of the 8th ACM Conference on Recommender systems* (pp. 137-144).

9. Krishnan, S., Okubo, Y., Uchino, K. and Goldberg, K., 2013. Using a social media platform to explore how social media can enhance primary and secondary learning. In *Learning International Networks Consortium (LINC) 2013 Conference*.

10. Mak, S., Williams, R., & Mackness, J. (2010). Blogs and Forums as Communication and Learning Tools in a MOOC. In *Proceedings of the 7th International Conference on Networked Learning*, ISBN 978-1-86220-225-2, p.275-284.

11. Marsh, H.W., and Roche, L.A. Making students' evaluations of teaching effectiveness effective: The critical issues of validity, bias, and utility. *American Psychologist*, 52(11). (1997)

12. McCullough, B.D. and Radson, D., 2011. Analysing student evaluations of teaching: comparing means and proportions. *Evaluation & Research in Education, 24*(3), pp.183-202.

13. Morley, D., 2014. Assessing the reliability of student evaluations of teaching: choosing the right coefficient. *Assessment & Evaluation in Higher Education,39*(2), pp.127-139.

14. Pursel, B.K., Zhang, L., Jablokow, K.W., Choi, G.W. and Velegol, D., 2016. Understanding MOOC students: motivations and behaviours indicative of MOOC completion. *Journal of Computer Assisted Learning, 32*(3), pp.202-217.

15. Sajjadi, M.S., Alamgir, M. and von Luxburg, U., 2016, April. Peer Grading in a Course on Algorithms and Data Structures: Machine Learning Algorithms do not Improve over Simple Baselines. In *Proceedings of the Third (2016) ACM Conference on Learning@ Scale* (pp. 369-378). ACM.

16. Sandeen, C., 2013. Assessment's place in the new MOOC world. *Research & practice in assessment, 8*.

17. Spooren, P., Brockx, B. and Mortelmans, D., 2013. On the validity of student evaluation of teaching the state of the art. *Review of Educational Research,83*(4), pp.598-642.

18. Stark, P.B. and Freishtat, R., 2014. An evaluation of course evaluations.*Center for Teaching and Learning, University of California, Berkley*.

19. Surgenor, P.W.G., 2013. Obstacles and opportunities: addressing the growing pains of summative student evaluation of teaching. *Assessment & Evaluation in Higher Education, 38*(3), pp.363-376.

20. Wang, Y., 2013, June. Exploring possible reasons behind low student retention rates of massive online open courses: A comparative case study from a social cognitive perspective. In *AIED 2013 Workshops Proceedings Volume* (p. 58).

21. Woolley, A.W., Chabris, C.F., Pentland, A., Hashmi, N. and Malone, T.W., 2010. Evidence for a collective intelligence factor in the performance of human groups. *science, 330*(6004), pp.686-688.

22. Xiong, Y., Li, H., Kornhaber, M.L., Suen, H.K., Pursel, B. and Goins, D.D., 2015. Examining the Relations among Student Motivation, Engagement, and Retention in a MOOC: A Structural Equation Modeling Approach. *Global Education Review, 2*(3).

23. Zheng, S., Rosson, M.B., Shih, P.C. and Carroll, J.M., 2015, February. Understanding student motivation, behaviors and perceptions in MOOCs. In*Proceedings of the 18th ACM Conference on Computer Supported Cooperative Work & Social Computing* (pp. 1882-1895). ACM.

24. Zhou, M., Cliff, A., Krishnan, S., Nonnecke, B., Crittenden, C., Uchino, K., & Goldberg, K. 2015, September. M-CAFE 1.0: Motivating and Prioritizing Ongoing Student Feedback During MOOCs and Large on-Campus Courses using Collaborative Filtering. In *Proceedings of the 16th Annual Conference on Information Technology Education* (pp. 153-158). ACM.

Exploring the Use of Synchronous Video-Based Breakout Rooms

Jeffrey S. Saltz
Syracuse University
Syracuse New York, USA
jsaltz@syr.edu

ABSTRACT

With the increasing availability of synchronous video-based breakout rooms within online courses, there is a growing need to understand how to best leverage this capability for enhanced information technology education. To help understand how to use these breakout rooms, a case study on their use is discussed. The study suggests that students often struggle to effectively use breakout rooms. Since there is no currently defined methodology to structure how students could use these breakout rooms, a key finding of this case study is the need for a methodological framework that instructors and students can leverage when using breakout rooms. One proposed approach is that the concept of paired programming could be adapted to create the structure for how to guide students within breakout rooms.

Keywords

Online Education; Synchronous Video Collaboration

1 INTRODUCTION

With the growth of online education, and the increasing ability to use video conferencing tools to share computer screens and documents, there is a growing trend to use synchronous video discussions within online learning environments. Beyond having the entire class share one instructional environment, there is also the growing ability to enable video-based online small group discussion environments, which allows for a subset of students to work together on group tasks. That is to say, one method of learning that is becoming increasingly available within a web-based online learning environment is a breakout room, where students work together in small groups. While it has been reported that breakout rooms are useful for facilitating learning and that, in some situations, 25% of instructors use breakout rooms when they are available, there has been no research on how effectively students use breakout rooms and if a well-define structure would be helpful when using breakout rooms.

SIGITE'17, October 4–7, 2017, Rochester, NY, USA
© 2017 Copyright is held by the owner/author(s).
ACM ISBN 978-1-4503-5100-3/17/10.
https://doi.org/10.1145/3125659.3125664

To address these questions, this talk reports on a case study of a class that used breakout rooms within an online data science course. The talk then proposes a plan to address the challenges observed.

2 Brief Summary

A qualitative case study examined the use of breakout rooms within an online data science course. In addition to the distance class's asynchronous activities, the course met weekly at a specific day and time. For part of the synchronous sessions, students were required to work in small groups using breakout rooms. The technologies used for the synchronous sessions, based on adobe connect, included video conferencing, chat, screen sharing and the sharing of documents. Each virtual breakout room was equipped with similar tools. In total, over two semesters, twenty-six graduate information system students participated in the study and 52 breakout sessions were monitored, half in the first semester and half in the second semester.

In analyzing faculty observations and student survey responses, two key themes were identified. First, many breakout rooms did not appear to be effective, in that students did not know what to do in the breakout room. For example, one student noted "while my partner was nice, I had no idea how to properly work with him" and instructors noted that typically there was a general sense of confusion on how to effectively collaborate with their online partner. The second theme was that instructors reported an overall increase in student engagement in the classes that used breakout rooms (ex. questions to the instructor, dialog between students) as compared to other course sections that were offered in previous semesters. This was likely due to the observed team bonding that occurred within the breakout sessions, where the social sharing of information was much greater than in a more traditional online course.

A planned next step is to define a structured approach on how to use breakout rooms, perhaps basing the structure on a modified version of paired programming. The new, more structured, approach could then be validated and refined via a case study and/or experiment. It is hoped that using this more well defined breakout room process will improve collaboration due to the structure of alternating who was is "in charge" (i.e. the person typing at the keyboard). It is also possible some tasks are better suited for a specific structure when using breakout rooms (or even the use of breakout rooms in general), so this also needs to be explored.

Improving the Pipeline: After-School Program for Preparing Information Assurance and Cyber Defense Professionals[*]

Sandra Gorka, Alicia McNett, Jacob R. Miller, Bradley M. Webb
Pennsylvania College of Technology
One College Avenue
Williamsport, Pennsylvania 17701
sgorka@pct.edu,amcnett@pct.edu,jmiller3@pct.edu,bwebb@pct.edu

ABSTRACT

Improving the Pipeline is an NSF funded grant to extend the pipeline into the high school environment offering an opportunity for high school students to explore cybersecurity careers while earning credit for an introductory cybersecurity course.

ACM Reference format:
Sandra Gorka, Alicia McNett, Jacob R. Miller, Bradley M. Webb. 2017. Improving the Pipeline: After-School Program for Preparing Information Assurance and Cyber Defense Professionals. In *Proceedings of SIGITE'17, Rochester, NY, USA, October 4–7, 2017,* 1 pages.
https://doi.org/10.1145/3125659.3125665

1 INTRODUCTION

There is currently significant growth in the information security job market [1–4]. The goal of this capacity-building NSF funded project is to increase the capacity of educational institutions to produce more Information Assurance and Cyber Defense (IA/CD) professionals by developing a high-school after-school college-credit program. The program will (1) raise awareness about cybersecurity careers, (2) generate interest in those careers, (3) prepare students to pursue the education required to succeed in cybersecurity fields. This project will develop and offer an after-school for college credit program in IA/CD for high school students as well as research the impact on students' education and career choices/paths.

2 CURRENT PROJECT STATUS

Development of the coursework is currently underway and will be complete prior to August 2017. Standalone modules for various topics including basics of computing and security, security by design, network and wireless security, encryption and hashing, protecting availability, social engineering, risk, policy, and legal issues are being developed in a consistent format.

Modules are constructed to engage students in group activities and scenarios that will lead students to identify and explain the risk associated with not implementing a security control. Activities embedded in each module will demonstrate that the risk is a real issue by illustrating how a system can be compromised if no security control has been implemented. Each module will consist of several labs that address questions like: Who needs to implement the control (including the careers)? What must be protected? How can it be protected? Etc.

Faculty have visited two participating high schools to recruit students and it is anticipated that the program will run with a full capacity of 20 - 24 students during the 2017-2018 academic year.

3 PROGRAM STRUCTURE

High school participants will visit campus weekend for 2 hours of hands-on instruction in fundamental information technology and cybersecurity skills. Lessons will be reinforced at the high school using a Raspberry Pi network-in-a-box. In addition to Penn College faculty, participating high school students will be mentored by current college students majoring in Information Assurance and Cyber Security (IA/CS) at Penn College as well as by IA/CD professionals. Prior to the beginning of the program, participating students will complete a survey to determine their current educational and career goals. Additional surveys will be conducted throughout the program to determine the impact this program has on the participants' educational and career goals.

ACKNOWLEDGMENTS

This material is based on work supported by the National Science Foundation under Grant No. 1623525. Any opinions, findings, and conclusions or recommendations expressed in this material are those of the author(s) and do not necessarily reflect the views of the National Science Foundation.

REFERENCES

[1] A Corrin. 2003. Workforce Management: Is There a Cyberseucirty Workforce Crisis? *FCW: The Business of Federal Technology* (2003). http://fcw.com/articles/2013/10/15/cybersecurity-workforce-crisis.aspx.
[2] M Loeb. 2015. Cybersecurity Talent: Worse than a Skills Shortage, It's a Critical Gap. *The Hill* (April 2015). http://thehill.com/blogs/congressblog/technology/239113-cybersecurity-talent-worse-than-a-skills-shortage-its-a.
[3] Bureau of Labor Statistics. 2015. Occupational Outlook Handbook, 2014-2015 Edition, Information Security Analysts. (2015). http://www.bls.gov/ooh/computer-andinformation-technology/information-security-analysts.htm.
[4] Burning Glass Technologies. 2015. Job Market Intelligence: Cybersecurity Jobs, 2015. (2015). http://burning-glass.com/wp-content/uploads/Cybersecurity_Jobs_Report_2015.pdf.

[*]Produces the permission block, and copyright information

Improv for Geeks

Russell McMahon

University of Cincinnati

College of Education, Criminal Justice, and Human Services

Cincinnati, OH 45221

513-556-4873

russ.mcmahon@uc.edu

Abstract

This workshop will teach participants some of the basics of improvisation and ideas on how it can be used in class. There are studies that suggest improv does help us all to become better, learners, innovators and communicators. Companies are using the improv methods as a way of creating more innovative and collaborative teams, for brain storming, and creating a work environment that says "Yes" before "No". Improv training can help students become better learners and make learning more enjoyable. Come and learn about improv and why companies such as IDEO, Google, Marriott, and Twitter have embraced this to build a culture that promotes better communication, collaboration, and team building. This workshop is an interactive workshop. Please attend and have fun learning how to be more positive, vulnerable, attentive, and playful in your daily grind.

Keywords

Improvisation; innovation; creative problem solving

1. INTRODUCTION

Last September the workshop facilitator attended a local Design Thinking meetup where improv was used as an ideation tool to augment the problem-solving process. After a 2-hour introductory course, he began working on ways to incorporate these ideas into one of his Fall Semester courses. This past January, he took a formal improv class from a local drama-improv company and has now progressed to their level 4 class.

The number of Ted Talks the past several years on improv is greater than 10 and they range from improv performances to the how and why of improv. One of the key aspects of improv is that there are rules and these rules need to be followed if a team is to be successful. Although an improv show may look unstructured and chaotic, underneath it is a very well-defined structure. In her Ted talk, Natalie Nixon uses the term, chaordic (chaos + order; coined by Dee Hock of VISA) to describe improv [1].

At the heart of this structure is the "Yes, and" premise. By affirming a teammate's statement, a conversation is allowed to move forward with the possibility of new ideas being generated. "Yes Anding" is a diverging construct that is found

in most brain storming techniques. During this time ideas should be not judged, but instead allowed to expand. In the long form of improv convergent occurs as an idea is explored in more detail which involves using an If-Then questioning technique.

The agile methodology for developing applications is a place where improv fits into very easily. Agile developers work with clients to create user-stories, they follow patterns, and they work with the user to improve the system on an ongoing fashion. Listening and being in the moment are important aspects of this process.

Embracing failure allows us to take greater risks, but it also takes courage. Failure is not only how programmers develop better systems, but with the constant flood of. new technologies, it is the norm in the IT field. Learning how to use and incorporate improv concepts into the development process is one way to overcome this challenge.

2. WORKSHOP STRUCTURE

This interactive workshop is modeled after Improv Cincinnati's Level 1 class and other resources [2-6]. This workshop is open to anyone who wants an opportunity to learn some of the basics of improv and garner ideas on how they may fit these ideas into their work and personal life.

3. STUDENT OUTCOMES

Upon completion of this course, attendees will be able to
1. Identify areas where improv can be used in their teaching.
2. Perform some basis improv components.
3. Create improv games based upon a given subject.
4. Understand how failure fits into life-long learning.
5. Exemplify the "Yes And" mentality in their classes.

4. REFERENCES

[1] 7 Rules for Improvising at Work by Natalie Nixon TEDxPhiladelphia
[2] The Upright Citizens Brigade Comedy Improvisation Manual by Ian Roberts, Matt Besser, and Matt Walsh; covers the guidelines and techniques of improv with examples
[3] Two words that can change the world, YES AND by Karen Tilstra at TEDxOrlando; co-founder and director of Florida Hospital's Innovation Lab
[4] The art of improvisation by Zack Beattie at TEDxCoMo
[5] 10 Reasons for Teachers to Use Improv in the Classroom by The Second City
[6] ImprovEncyclopedia.org, a collection of games, exercises, and resources for improvisation

Speed Up PhD Completion:
A Case Study in Curriculum Changes

Tsun Chow

Capella University

226 South 6th St. 9th Floor

Minneapolis, MN 55402

tchow@capella.edu

While the discipline has been changing at a furious pace of every 18 months, the average completion time for PhD in Information Technology remains stuck at 4-5 years. The long duration of the PhD program is a complex issue, since the underlying causes are multi-dimensional. There is no single silver bullet that would magically speed up the process.

Capella first launched the PhD IT program in 2009. The basic program structure is very similar to many traditional universities into 3 stages. In the first stage, students spend their time on course work that develops the skills and knowledge to prepare the student to do original research. In the second stage, students have to pass a comprehensive exam to demonstrate their readiness to do research. It is followed by a dissertation process, during which faculty mentors are assigned to supervise students in completing their PhD dissertation.

In this paper, we describe Capella's efforts aiming at speeding up the degree completion for PhD IT by changing its curriculum over a 7 year period.

When the program was first launched, the dissertation milestone schedule was based on the five chapter structure of the dissertation document. Often students found out that it was necessary to change the previous chapters when they worked on the issues in later chapters. The extra efforts were both frustrating to the student who had to make the changes and the faculty who had to review the revised chapters again. Not to mention that each iteration of these changes caused delays in the degree completion. To avoid these issues, the first phase of curriculum changes was implemented in 2010. The dissertation development is now broken into two stages: the preparation of a research proposal and the development of the full dissertation. Speed up is achieved by allowing rapid iteration of this lightweight proposal document to reduce uncertainties in the research design.

Encouraged by the results of phase 1, we started to explore the possibility of start the dissertation earlier in their curriculum. In the second phase, preparation for the research proposal was moved up earlier to precede the comprehensive exam by allowing students to start working on research while still completing their course work. The development work of the research proposal is now decomposed into intermediate milestones and allocated to each of the residency courses. Each of the residency courses are judicially scheduled so that the students would have the just the knowledge and skills that they need to complete the individual parts of the research proposal. Residence courses for Capella consist of both an online portion and a face-to-face portion, thus providing a perfect setting for students to develop their research proposals under close faculty supervision.

Although in theory, the students have the skills that they need for each of the residencies to develop their assigned intermediate milestones, they have found the process to be very challenging. To address this issue, in 2017 we have embarked on the third phase of the curriculum evolution: integrating research perspective into specialization courses. In the third phase, subject matter and research skills are integrated to provide students ample opportunities to hone their research skills before working on their own dissertation.

When considered individually, each of these three phases of changes in the PhD IT curriculum represents only an incremental speed up of the PhD. When taken as a whole, these curriculum changes constitute a radical shift in how we perceive what the research process should be. The conceptual ideas that drive these changes may offer further opportunities for additional improvements in the future.

CCS CONCEPTS

• **Social and professional topics** → **Professional topics** → **Computer education** → **Computer education programs** → **information technology education**

KEYWORDS

PhD IT curriculum, PhD degree completion time, PhD research, PhD dissertation

ACM Reference format:

T. Chow. 2017. SIG Proceedings Paper in word Format. In *Proceedings of ACM SIGITE conference, New York, New York USA, October 2017 (New York '17),* 5 pages. DOI: https://doi.org/10.1145/3125659.3125700

SIGITE'17, October 4-7, 2017, Rochester, NY, USA
© 2017 Copyright is held by the owner/author(s).
ACM ISBN 978-1-4503-5100-3/17/10.
DOI: https://doi.org/10.1145/3125659.3125700

DStBlocks: Visual Programming for Data Structures

Daniel F. Almanza[1], Manuel F. Del Toro[1], Ricardo A. Urrego[1],
Pedro G. Feijóo[1], Fernando De la Rosa[2]

Program of Systems Engineering[1], Systems and Computing Engineering Department[2]
Universidad El Bosque, Bogotá D.C., Colombia[1]
Universidad de los Andes, Bogotá D.C., Colombia[2]
{dalmanzac, mtoros, rurrego, pfeijoo}@unbosque.edu.co, fde@uniandes.edu.co

ABSTRACT

The Data Structures course is common in Systems Engineering and Computer Science programs, providing a fundamental basis for professional training in these disciplines. This course presents a great pedagogical challenge, due to the high complexity in the algorithms studied and the levels of abstraction that it requires. Considering that the traditional pedagogical approach is sometimes not adequate to ease understanding of the structures covered in the course, we propose the development of *DStBlocks* as a playful and visual tool for the design and programming of data structures. Through this document we emphasize the context to be intervened and the problem to be solved, indicating the progress corresponding to the project. At the end we present the work which will be held in a near future, indicating how we are going to measure learning variables according to the project's objectives.

Categories and Subject Descriptors

• Applied Computing→Interactive Learning Environments

Keywords

Data Structures; E-Learning; Visual Blocks Programming; Educational Technologies; Validated Learning;

1. INTRODUCTION

Data Structures is a general course in Systems Engineering and Computer Science curriculums, that presents fundamental topics for disciplinary lines oriented to software development [1]. Although it is generally taught after introductory courses in programming, students find problems when dealing with its topics, which include algorithms with a high level of complexity and superior management of concepts related to Object Oriented Programming [2]. This adds the complexity corresponding to the handling and management of specific programming languages, which are not always intuitive to the students.

Based on this, and using visual tools to support the learning process of data structures, we propose *DStBlocks* as a Visual Blocks Programming Web tool, to allow students to learn interactively the algorithmic corresponding to the development of a data structure, without having to face syntactic problems of

SIGITE'17, October 4–7, 2017, Rochester, NY, USA
© 2017 Copyright is held by the owner/author(s).
ACM ISBN 978-1-4503-5100-3/17/10.
https://doi.org/10.1145/3125659.3125702

a particular programming language. Throughout this project, we focus on validating *DStBlocks* pedagogically, looking forward to understand how students learn data structures' concepts, and how can an interactive and visual tool support teaching and learning processes in this type of courses.

2. PROBLEM

Due to the difficulties that some students may encounter with the syntax of a particular programming language [3], the lack of pedagogical didactics in these courses, the complexity of the proposed algorithms, and the abstract nature of data structures in general; Data Structures courses tend to be hard to achieve, taking students to scenarios of frustration and academic loss.

In order to respond to this pedagogical necessity, it is required the design and development of an innovative learning tool, looking towards to enhance pedagogical processes according to the courses' topics and their teaching.

3. SOLUTION

DStBlocks is a visual and interactive Web application, which uses Visual Blocks Programming so that students do not worry about code syntax when designing and developing data structures. For this first pilot, *DStBlocks* offers mechanisms towards design and development of basic linear and tree structures.

The solution articulates *Blockly.js* as main extension, in conjunction with *vis.js* for graphical structures representation. It was designed with *JavaScript* and *Node.js* and deployed with the Cloud Platform *Heroku*.

4. STATUS

At the moment, the first version of *DStBlocks* has been successfully prototyped. We expect in the next months to evaluate it with students of different Universities, measuring learning and User Experience (UX) variables.

The experimental methodology converges both, a quantitative and a qualitative approach. This, to ensure the software's validation for future pivotal scenarios, looking forward to understand and answer how students learn data structures' concepts, and how can an interactive tool as *DStBlocks* support teaching and learning processes in Data Structures courses.

5. REFERENCES

[1] Begy, V. and Schikuta, E. (2016). A lightweight e-learning system for algorithms and data structures. In Proc. 18th Int. Conf. on Information Integration and Web-Based Applications and Services, Singapore, 199-208.

[2] Lai, A. and Wu, P. (2015). The development of simulation-based learning system for binary tree of data structures. In Proc. 15th Int. Conf. on Advanced Learning Technologies, Taiwan, 296-298.

[3] Feijóo García, P., and De la Rosa, F. (2016). RoBlock – Web App for Programming Learning. International Journal of Emerging Technologies in Learning (IJET), 11(12), 45-53. doi> http://doi.org/10.3991/ijet.v11i12.6004

BOCHICA: Educational Technologies for Water Care

Nestor I. Bernal[1], Luis F. Castillo[1], Jesús A. Henríquez[1], Pedro G. Feijóo[1],
Maria C. Ramírez[2], Edier E. Espinosa[2]

Program of Systems Engineering[1], Department of Industrial Engineering[2]
Universidad El Bosque, Bogotá D.C., Colombia[1]
Universidad de los Andes, Bogotá D.C., Colombia[2]
nbernalm, lcastilloz, jhenriquez, pfeijoo (@unbosque.edu.co); mariaram, ee.espinosa10 (@uniandes.edu.co)

ABSTRACT

This research project presents how the use of information technologies (IT) enhance learning variables for water care purposes in the province of Tequendama, Colombia. To achieve this goal, as part of *Ingenieros Sin Fronteras* (Colombia), we propose and develop two interactive technology solutions for the community, deploying them through the *Casa Museo Tequendama* (Tequendama, Colombia) foundation: a web video game and an augmented reality (AR) guided tour. Through this document, we present the context and problem to be solved, share the project's progress, what has been done and what is expected to be done in a near future.

Categories and Subject Descriptors

• Applied Computing→Interactive Learning Environments

Keywords

Water care; E-Learning; Augmented Reality (AR);

1. CONTEXT

This research addresses the main aspects related to the current environmental situation in the province of Tequendama, Colombia [1]. This province is an area with about 160.000 inhabitants, that borders Colombia's capital city, Bogotá D.C., with an economy mainly based on tourism and agriculture [2]. For the purposes of this study, we propose the development of a set of technological solutions, in order to answer the following research question: *Is it possible that the whole between a Web videogame, and a playful guided tour with augmented reality (AR), at Casa Museo Tequendama, promote children's learning towards water care and residues management?*

The province of Tequendama, Colombia, is a destination with high tourist flow and agricultural production. However, because of the contamination of the Bogotá river, where the waters discharged from the municipalities bordering the middle basin do not have the minimum residues treatment, nearby communities are highly affected in health and welfare issues, damaging the province's reputation and development [3]. The practice of informal agriculture, the presence of industries and the mismanagement of residues, have resulted in high rates of pollution from chemicals and heavy metals. According to the *Corporación Autónoma Regional* (CAR) [4], the middle basin (Bogotá - Facatativá) and the low basin (San Antonio del Tequendama - Apulo), present high chemical concentrations caused by the presence of industries and farmers.

From interviewing community's stakeholders, *Ingenieros Sin Fronteras* researchers, and the directives of *Casa Museo Tequendama*, a common consideration is that the bad practices and the lack of awareness of the residents and inhabitants has made the *Bogotá River* one of the most contaminated rivers in Colombia [4]. Consideration that takes this study to focus on a pedagogical approach, towards the generation of citizens' conscience in terms of water care [5] and residues management.

2. PROPOSED SOLUTION

The solutions designed and developed for this project, combines two technological approaches that are planned to be incorporated at *Casa Museo Tequendama*. In a first place, we elaborated a Web videogame, looking to help the foundation to achieve a pedagogical approach with elementary schools of the Tequendama province and the city of Bogotá. In compliment, we made a second technological solution, which articulates augmented reality (AR) to enhance the guided tour that is done in place at the *Casa Museo Tequendama*. This, considering the main add-on of augmented reality (AR), when it comes to providing major information within a space, using mobile and pervasive technologies for this purpose.

At the moment, both technological solutions have been successfully prototyped. It is expected for the following months, to deploy them and measure the solutions' pedagogical impact, studying the community's interaction and measuring how much people can learn after using them.

The experimental approach will consider a mixed methodology, quantitatively measuring a learning variable, in compliment of a qualitative approach towards User Experience (UX).

3. REFERENCES

[1] Casa Museo Tequendama. (n.d.). Retrieved May 01, 2017, from http://www.casamuseotequendama.org/

[2] Ingenieros Sin Fronteras Colombia. (n.d.). Retrieved May 01, 2017, from https://isfcolombia.uniandes.edu.co/

[3] Contraloría General de la República, & Ministerio de Ambiente y Desarrollo Sostenible. (2015). Auditoría especial a la gestión sobre el río bogotá – intersectorial y articulada. Bogotá-Colombia: Contraloría General de la República.

[4] CAR. (2007). Evaluación ambiental para la adecuación y recuperación hídrica del río bogotá. Bogotá, Colombia: CAR.

[5] Feijóo García, P., Medina Cortés, D., Ramírez Cajiao, M., & Espinosa Díaz, E. (2017). Cooperative Learning Web Application for Water Care in Colombia – Manglar: Actor-Network Theory Software Solution. International Journal Of Emerging Technologies In Learning (IJET), 12(04), pp. 208-216. doi:http://dx.doi.org/10.3991/ijet.v12i04.673

Computer-Related Cartoons and Humor and Its Historical Transition

Russell McMahon
University of Cincinnati
College of Education, Criminal Justice, and Human Services
Cincinnati, OH 45206
513-556-4873
russ.mcmahon@uc.edu

ABSTRACT

Humor involving computers has been around since the first computer, but really took off in the 1980s when microcomputers became part of everyone's lives This poster will examine some of the witty and satirical amusements found in pictures, comics, , and words that the author has found over the years with an examination of how some of the humor has evolved over time or may have been a predictor of things to come.

1. Introduction

Everybody is probably familiar with the quote "on the Internet nobody knows you're a dog". This cartoon was captioned by Peter Steiner and published by The New Yorker on July 5, 1993 as the Internet was becoming more mainstream. Today, Dilbert epitomizes the woos of computing and the frustrations of software engineers. But what was the computer-related humor like before those days.

Most of the cartoons featured in this poster were collected in the late 1970s and early 1980s from some of the popular magazines of the time such as Creative Computing and Interface Age or found in a book that was edited by David Ahl [1]. It will also include some humorous stories. Humor reflects what was going on during a specific time period and in this case specifically the emergence of the personal computer (PC) and the downfall of the mainframe and IBM. During this period two titans rose: Microsoft and Apple. Each had different strategy and each has revolutionized the computer industry and continue to do so.

2. Resources

In a 1962 Datamation article, Jackson Granholm and others introduced the Kludge Komputers Korporation which was a tongue-in-cheek series of articles about a fictitious and uselss computer company [2]. Twenty some years later where a group of intrepid and creative programmers at the University of Cincinnati wrote about a fictitious computer company called Piranha Corp whose motto was "Real programmers don't need menus" plus a few others. From 1985 to 1991 a series of articles related to this company ran in the university's computer journal [3]. Piranha's motto could have been played off a 1983 letter to the editor of Datamation which stated that "Real programmers don't use Pascal." [4] Datamation would run a series of

humorous articles in its April issues (possibility because of April Fools). Another magazine, InfoWorld, has very good sprinkling of small cartoons throughout its editions. Some humor is a bit more subtle such the computer HAL (IBM) in the movie "2001: A Space Odyssey."

Walter Bauer, a founder of Informatics, recalled several humorous stories about his work with some of the early computers. One of this is about a cartoon that said, "Programmers are warned not to divide by zero on the IBM 701." [5] Computers and the problems we have with them have inspired cartoonist such as Rich Tennant (5th Wave), Cathy Guisewite (Cathy), and Scott Adams (Dilbert) to show just how the computer has become a part of our daily lives whether we are a technology geek or not. Tennant gave a talk for the Computer History Museum entitled "A Cartoonist's View of Computer History" in 2000.

The book PC Roadkill by Michael Hyman chronicles a lot of the early PC history with an eye on the somewhat humorous and sometime ironical side of computer. It follows in the footstep of Robert X. Cringely (Mark Stephens – cringley.com) articles that first appeared in InfoWorld as "Notes from the Field" and the PBS documentary "Triumph of the Nerds."

A paper written by Linda Friedman and Hershey Friedman more closely examines computer humor and breaks it down into distinct categories and sub-categories [6]. The 3 main categories are: culture-specific humor, in-group humor, and I-get-it humor which embodies elements from the first two.

3. REFERENCES

[1] Colossal Computer Cartoon Book, edited by David Ahl, Creative Computing Press, 1977
[2] How to Design a Kludge by Jackson Granholm, Datamation, Feb 1962
[3] Connect, The Journal of the Deparmtental Computing at the University of Cincinnati
[4] Real Programmers Don't Use Pascal, Ed Post, Datamation, July 1983
[5] Computer Recollections: Events, Humor, and Happenings; Walter Bauer, IEEE Annals of the History of Computing, Jan-March 2007
[6] Computer-Oriented Humor (COHUM): "I Get It.", Linda Weiser Friedman, Hershey H. Friedman, CIS Working Paper Series, Zicklin School of Business Aug 2002

The Evolution of the Master of Science in Information Technology Curriculum

Svetlana Peltsverger
Kennesaw State University
Marietta, GA 30060
speltsve@kennesaw.edu

Lei Li
Kennesaw State University
Marietta, GA 30060
lli@kennesaw.edu

Rebecca Rutherfoord
Kennesaw State University
Marietta, GA 30060
brutherf@kennesaw.edu

ABSTRACT

This paper describes an ongoing process of assessment that lays the foundation for the success of the Master of Science in Information Technology degree (MSIT). It also presents a plan for a complete revision of the MSIT program using a proposed methodology - a data-driven 360 Degree Review. This methodology provides resources for those interested in program improvement.

General Terms

Documentation, Design, Standardization

Keywords

Information Technology Education; Computing Curricula; Curriculum, Graduate Program

1. INTRODUCTION

The Master of Science in Information Technology (MSIT) program at Kennesaw State University was created in 1999. The program resides in the Information Technology Department in the College of Computing & Software Engineering. The program was revised in 2007 – 2008 academic year, and started in its current version fall of 2008. With more than 200 students it is currently the largest master's degree at the university. One of the unique aspects of the MSIT degree is that a student can be conditionally admitted into the program without having a computing undergraduate degree.

The program does not have tracks or concentration, the area of focus can be defined by taking a built-in graduate certificate: Health IT, IT Security or Data Management and Analytics.

The MSIT program has also been extremely successful with the ability of students with various backgrounds to succeed in a technical master's degree, receive competitive job offers upon graduation and have successful careers in IT. Since it's been over 9 years since the MSIT program went through major revision, the department chair and faculty have begun a complete review of the MSIT program using a Data-driven 360 Degree Review model.

2. A DATA-DRIVEN 360 DEGREE REVIEW MODEL

It is critical that the MSIT program can continuously produce graduates who will succeed in the fast-changing technology field in either a managerial or a technical role.

SIGITE'17, October 4–7, 2017, Rochester, NY, USA
© 2017 Copyright is held by the owner/author(s).
ACM ISBN 978-1-4503-5100-3/17/10.
https://doi.org/10.1145/3125659.3125706

Different disciplines have different approaches to program revisions. For example, medical education uses a six step approach [1]. Curriculum 2010 initiative from Curtin University of Technology suggests that to have 360-degree perspective of the "health", you have to include [2] people layer.

Based on the best practices we present a three-layered model for reviewing the MSIT program: a systematic, 360-degree and data-driven approach. The review model consists of three layers:

1. Program Layer: admission standards, program mission and vision, student job placement, program outcomes, curriculum, and technology infrastructure.

2. People Layer: prospective students, current students, alumni, faculty and staff, industry advisory board, hiring managers, and institutional support personal.

3. a) Data Layer (internal): applicant profile, course assesment, exit survey, and student course eveluation.

   b) Data Layer (external): job market analysis, alumni job information, and comparable program evaluation.

A change in any of the components of the proposed model should trigger a review of all components of each layer.

The faculty is the center of the proposed review model. They initiate and manage the review process; interact with entities in the people layer, program and data layer; implement change and follow up on the change made. The main characteristics of the review model 1) a systematic review process; 2) a 360 degree (comprehensive) review; 3) data driven approach.

3. EXEMPLAR REVIEW PROCESSES

We tested the effectiveness of our approach for serval reviews: 1) the admission standard review as on a predefined review process that is part of the three-year review. 2) the job market analysis as on an example of using external data to determine which technical skills are desired by the job market. 3) the revision of foundation courses assigned for students with non-computing background as on an example of end of semester review.

4. RESOURCES

[1]   Oliver, B. 2008. 360-degree Feedback on Courses: Needs Analysis for Comprehensive Course Review. *Proceedings of the Australian Universities Quality Forum 2008* (2008), 55–60.

[2]   Thomas P. A., Kern, D. E., Hughes, M. T., Chen B. Y. 2015. Curriculum Development for Medical Education a Six-Step Approach. *The John Hopkins University Press*. (2015).

Motivating Students through Peer-Formulated Assignments in CS Experimental Courses

Xin Zhang, Jinfeng Huang, Libo Huang, Zhiying Wang

School of Computer, National University of Defense Technology, Changsha 410073, China

xinzhang_pst@163.com

ABSTRACT

We describe a study that uses the peer-formulated assignment method to motivate undergraduate students in computer science (CS) experimental courses. This method requires each student or group to create a problem and then to pick another problem from other students to complete. Such problem and solution exchange helps motivate the students and lead to their happy learning. Under the guidance of an instructor, students can become motivated with great interests, enhance their practical abilities, and cultivate themselves with spirits of innovation.

KEYWORDS

experimental course; peer-formulated assignment; undergraduate; computer science

1 BACKGROUND

As a crucial issue especially for computer science (CS) experimental courses, assignments give students an opportunity to put their knowledge into practice and inspire their exploratory spirit. Conventional assignments are often provided by instructors or textbooks, but students usually have varied academic interests and ambitions. The game-based learning or free choice of course assignments can attract the attention of students to a certain extent [1, 2]. However, given the dominant role of instructors in these assignments, these tasks may not match the interests of students.

2 METHODOLOGY

To address the limitations mentioned above, we introduce the peer-formulated assignment method for CS experimental courses where students engage in a problem and solution exchange. When the course enters a certain stage, each student or group must propose a problem based on their knowledge. They must provide a complete and detailed description of the problem, including the expected results and schedule.

This work was supported by the NSFC (No. 61472435).

To avoid students from having a difficult time in answering trivial problems, their instructor can provide them with some examples and motivating instructions.

For problem selection, students are not recommended to choose their own problems because of three reasons. First, some students tend to be lazy. If they are able to choose their own problems, then they are likely to choose those problems with the least difficulty of solving. Second, problem proposers easily fall into their inherent ways of thinking, thereby limiting them from producing meaningful solutions. Third, selecting the problems of others will help these students further understand the needs of users.

In the peer-formulated assignment method, the role of instructors is not weakened. Instead, these instructors continue to serve an important role in the assessment. After proposing the problems, the students are scored by their instructors to encourage them to propose high-quality problems. After completing the assignment, the instructor collects the problems and calls those students who have proposed and answered such problems, thereby stimulating their sense of accomplishment. For those problems with an additional exploitation value, extracurricular activities are encouraged.

3 EXPERIMENTS

We have applied the proposed method in two comprehensive CS experimental courses, namely, software engineering (SE) and digital system design (DSD). We evaluate the performance of different assignment methods in terms of passing rates. Each SE and DSD course is taught by the same instructor that uses different assignment methods in academic years 2014 to 2016. Approximately 89.2% and 70.3% of the students passed the SE course with peer-formulated assignment (SE-2015) and instructor-assignment (SE-2014), respectively, while approximately 94.2% and 78.4% of the students passed the DSD course with peer-formulated assignment (DSD-2016) and instructor-assignment (DSD-2015), respectively. The completion rates have obviously improved significantly, thereby indicating that stimulating the interests of students by using peer-formulated assignment will also improve their performance results.

REFERENCES

[1] Daniel C. Cliburn and Susan Miller. 2008. Games, Stories, or Something More Traditional: The Types of Assignments College Students Prefer *(SIGCSE '08)*. ACM, USA, 138–142. https://doi.org/10.1145/1352135.1352184
[2] Eow Yee Leng, Zah Bte Wan Ali Wan, Rosnaini Bt. Mahmud, and Roselan Baki. 2010. Computer Games Development Experience and Appreciative Learning Approach for Creative Process Enhancement. *Computers & Education* 55, 3 (2010), 1131–1144.

Improving the Pipeline: Modules for an After-School Program for Preparing Information Assurance and Cyber Defense Professionals*

Sandra Gorka, Alicia McNett, Jacob R. Miller, Bradley M. Webb
Pennsylvania College of Technology
One College Avenue
Williamsport, Pennsylvania 17701
sgorka@pct.edu,amcnett@pct.edu,jmiller3@pct.edu,bwebb@pct.edu

ABSTRACT

There is currently significant demand for information security professionals. Preparing students to enter the workforce in an information security career often begins in college. This poster provides an overview of the educational modules used in an after-high school for college credit program to push the pipeline into high schools.

ACM Reference format:
Sandra Gorka, Alicia McNett, Jacob R. Miller, Bradley M. Webb. 2017. Improving the Pipeline: Modules for an After-School Program for Preparing Information Assurance and Cyber Defense Professionals. In *Proceedings of SIGITE'17, Rochester, NY, USA, October 4–7, 2017*, 1 pages.
https://doi.org/10.1145/3125659.3125715

1 INTRODUCTION

Burning Glass [7] reports that cybersecurity job postings have grown 91% from 2010 to 2014. The increased demand has created a severe shortage of well-qualified IA/CD professionals [1, 3] as well as a skills shortage [2, 4]. The Bureau of Labor Statistics [5, 6] predicts that this trend will continue, projecting a 37% increase in security analyst jobs from 2012 to 2022. This equates to an estimated 27,400 new jobs and shows a growth rate that is significantly higher than the 11% average increase for all occupations. The goal of this capacity-building NSF funded project is to increase the capacity of educational institutions to produce more Information Assurance and Cyber Defense (IA/CD) professionals by developing a high-school after-school college-credit program that will (1) raise awareness about cybersecurity careers, (2) generate interest in those careers, (3) prepare students to pursue the education required to succeed in cybersecurity fields. This poster summarizes the educational modules offered in the program.

2 THE LEARNING MODULES

This program is modeled around Penn College's CIT230 Fundamentals of Information Security course. The CIT230 course has two prerequisite courses: one each in programming and networking.

*Produces the permission block, and copyright information

The after-school program covers the same basic content as CIT230; however, the prerequisite knowledge is addressed as needed. The learning modules are as follows:

(1) Basics of Security
(2) Basics of Computing
(3) Programming Concepts
(4) Security by Design
(5) Network Concepts
(6) Network Security
(7) Wireless Security
(8) Encryption: Protecting Confidentiality
(9) Hashing: Protecting Integrity
(10) Protecting Availability: Preventing Denial of Service
(11) Social Engineering
(12) Risk
(13) Policy, Legal Issues, Professionalism
(14) What happens when security measures fail?

ACKNOWLEDGMENTS

This material is based on work supported by the National Science Foundation under Grant No. 1623525. Any opinions, findings, and conclusions or recommendations expressed in this material are those of the author(s) and do not necessarily reflect the views of the National Science Foundation.

REFERENCES

[1] A Corrin. 2003. Workforce Management: Is There a Cyberseucirty Workforce Crisis? *FCW: The Business of Federal Technology* (2003). http://fcw.com/articles/2013/10/15/cybersecurity-workforce-crisis.aspx.
[2] K Evans and F Reeder. 2010. A Human Capital Crisis in Cybersecurity: Technical Proficiency Matters. A Report of the CSIS Commission on Cybersecurity for the 44th Presidency. *Center for Strategic and International Studies* (2010). http://csis.org/files/publication/101111_Evans_HumanCapital_Web.pdf.
[3] H Golden. 2015. Shortage of IT Security Professionals not Unique to Government. *Government Executive Media Group* (April 2015). http://www.nextgov.com/ciobriefing/wired-workplace/2015/04/calling-all-information-security-professionals-world-needsyou/110338/.
[4] M Loeb. 2015. Cybersecurity Talent: Worse than a Skills Shortage, It's a Critical Gap. *The Hill* (April 2015). http://thehill.com/blogs/congressblog/technology/239113-cybersecurity-talent-worse-than-a-skills-shortage-its-a.
[5] Bureau of Labor Statistics. 2012. Fastest growing occupations. (2012). http://www.bls.gov/emp/ep_table_103.htm.
[6] Bureau of Labor Statistics. 2015. Occupational Outlook Handbook, 2014-2015 Edition, Information Security Analysts. (2015). http://www.bls.gov/ooh/computer-andinformation-technology/information-security-analysts.htm.
[7] Burning Glass Technologies. 2015. Job Market Intelligence: Cybersecurity Jobs, 2015. (2015). http://burning-glass.com/wp-content/uploads/Cybersecurity_Jobs_Report_2015.pdf.

Digital Humanities: Practicum for the Future

Diane Shichtman
SUNY Empire State College
Diane.Shichtman@esc.edu

Cindy Conaway
SUNY Empire State College
Cindy.Conaway@esc.edu

ABSTRACT

This poster will address the authors' plans for student involvement in a digital humanities project. Through involvement in this project, omputing-related students will be prepared to move outside of STEM, while humanities students will be exposed to analytic techniques and tools used in the computing fields. Both groups will learn to work with multidisciplinary methodologies and data

CCS Concepts

• Applied computing~Arts and humanities   • Information systems~Data management systems   • Social and professional topics~Computing education

Keywords

Digital Humanities; Teaching; Data; Databases; Statistics

ACM Reference format:

Diane Shichtman and Cindy Conaway 2017. Digital Humanities: Practicum for the Future. In *Proceedings of 18th Annual Conference on Information Technology Education, Rochester, NY, USA, October 2017 (SIGITE'17), 1 page.* DOI: 10.1145/3125659.3125708

1. INTRODUCTION

Digital Humanities is an opportunity for students to do multidisciplinary work. A relatively new and still coalescing interdisciplinary approach to humanities questions, Digital Humanities uses formal methodologies common to social sciences and structured data gathering and analysis. It is both a form of research and a form of communication. While Digital Humanities is not the sole path for humanities, it is one of the futures, enabled by the ubiquity of technology and accessible data. For students, Digital Humanities is an opportunity to explore disciplines not normally focused on in their studies.

2. PRACTICUM

2.1 The project

The research project combines humanities questions, social science methodologies, and information management to create a Digital Humanities project. The goal is to create a database and perform analysis to explore the reach of the TV show *Seinfeld* and represent this numerically/graphically. While much of the data is available in IMDb, IMDb is a wiki and contains unorganized, missing, misleading, and incorrect data. We have had to develop category schemes, including one for genre that has become quite extensive, and we've had to fill in missing information, such as birthdate, race/ethnicity, and gender.

The focus of the project is reach, but as we have been preparing the data, we've done preliminary exploration of questions about gender participation over time, as well as participation within specified genres, and we expect to expand on these avenues. Students will be encouraged to find other avenues.

2.2 The students

We will be offering an independent study/small group study in which the students will read about Digital Humanities and perform some of our coding or tagging, potentially also doing a small project of their own, and writing a final reaction paper. Humanities students are likely to focus on data classification and review while IT students will be likely to focus on the technical data review, statistical analysis, and presentation of the data.

2.3 Learning expectations

While we will shape the independent studies once the students have signed up, we have several learning goals that we are going to suggest:

- Prepare real-world data for analysis, including cleaning and categorizing
- Develop research questions, including bounding potentially open-ended problem
- Use statistical tests, particularly for comparing groups

Of course, for humanities students, the experience of working with a database will be important, while for computing students, the experience of working with humanities questions and data will be part of the learning experience.

3. CONCLUSION

The independent studies we design could become a model for a multidisciplinary course for future students.

ACKNOWLEDGEMENTS

This student participation in this project will be partially supported by an Empire PILLARS grant.

Analysis and Impact of IoT Malware

Joel Margolis
Department of Computing Security
Rochester Institute of Technology
Rochester, New York 14623
jxm6968@rit.edu

Tae (Tom) Oh
Department of Information Sciences
and Technologies
Rochester Institute of Technology
Rochester, New York 14623
tom.oh@rit.edu

Suyash Jadhav
Department of Computing Security
Rochester Institute of Technology
Rochester, New York 14623
ssj8127@rit.edu

Jaehoon (Paul) Jeong
Department of Interaction Science
Sungkyunkwan University
Suwon, Republic of Korea
pauljeong@skku.edu

Young Ho Kim
Jeong Neyo Kim
Cyber Security Research Division
Electronics and Telecommunications
Research Institute
Daejeon, Republic of Korea
wtowto@etri.re.kr, jnkim@etri.re.kr

ABSTRACT

As Internet of Things (IoT) devices become more and more prevalent, it is important for research to be done around the security and intergrity of them. By doing so, consumers are able to make well-informed choices about the smart devices that they purchase. This poster presents information about how three different IoT-specific malware variants operate and impact newly connected devices.

KEYWORDS

Malware Analysis, Internet of Things, Mirai, TheMoon, Imeij

1 INTRODUCTION

Internet of Things (IoT) is a term used to denote various appliances, low-level devices, and machines that have been connected to the Internet. This allows for manageability, remote monitoring, and unique features that set these devices above others. As with anything that is connected to the Internet, however, these devices are filled with a myriad of vulnerabilities, security risks, and software issues that make them potentially dangerous in the hands of hackers. The analysis and protection of these devices is crucial in order to allow for them to be safely put into our homes, offices, and other buildings without welcoming in an innate security risk. In this research, three different IoT malware samples — Mirai, Imeij, and TheMoon — were statically analyzed to be able to better understand them and devise methods of mitigation for them.

2 OVERVIEW

The three malware samples that were analyzed during this research were Mirai, TheMoon, and Imeij. Each of these malware samples was specifically targeted towards the infection and utilization of improperly secured IoT devices.

Abstractly, the Mirai botnet runs a Command and Control (C2) server that is connected to by infected devices. These devices then scan for other devices and tests them for weak credentials over SSH and telnet. If able to successfully login, the credentials used are sent to a separate server which then uses them to download the malware onto said device. This device then connects to the C2 server to wait for things such as DDoS attack commands to be sent to it. This infection process is then repeated from the newly-connected device, which is why Mirai is able to grow so rapidly in comparison to similar botnets.

Next, Imeij was written to specifically infect AVTech devices by exploiting a known vulnerability in the firmware that allows for remote code execution to take place. Using this, the malware is downloaded onto vulnerable devices and used to setup persistence within the system. This is accomplished by creating a systemd service to launch the malware binary, and configuring it to launch when the system starts up. Once running on the device, the device is used to send DDoS attacks which controlled by a C2. This is similar to how Mirai operates.

Lastly, TheMoon was a malware family specifically targeting ASUS routers running a specific version of firmware. Similar to Imeij, this malware exploits an unauthenticated command execution vulnerability in the firmware to download the malware onto the device. Once on the device, the router is converted into a proxy server that allows specific IP addresses to connect to it. This malware is different from others in that it is used to infiltrate home routers to be used as recyclable and reliable IP addresses. These then may be sold on the darknet, allowing for attackers to circumvent defensive measures such as IP bans.

3 ACKNOWLEDGEMENT

This work was supported by Institute for Information & communications Technology Promotion (IITP) grant funded by the Korea government (MSIP) (B0190-16-2032, Development of Operating System Security Core Technology for the Smart Lightweight IoT Devices)

Impact of Peer Instruction and Instructional Scaffolding on a Programming Course

Debzani Deb
Winston-Salem State University
Winston-Salem, NC, USA
debd@wssu.edu

ABSTRACT

Peer instruction and instructional scaffolding were utilized in the first programming course attempted by the IT majors at Winston-Salem State University (WSSU) with the expectations of enhancing student learning and improving retention. This poster details our pedagogical approach along with example quiz and programming exercise artifacts, initial student performance and survey results during Spring 2017 (S17) deployment.

KEYWORDS

Peer Instruction; Instructional Scaffolding.

1 INTRODUCTION

In the CS department at WSSU, a bachelor in Information Technology (IT) degree provides applications-oriented undergraduate education in computer information technology to the students. The diversity among the IT majors is significant and the typical student population includes traditional, nontraditional, transfer, working, and veteran students and many of them are first generation college students. CIT 1308 (Introduction to visual basic programming) is the first computer programming course that all IT majors are required to take and lately the course has been experiencing a significant D/F/W rates. Majority of the students causing this attrition find the expected level of commitment and persistency required for a computer programming course to be much more intense than their anticipation, which causes frustration, loss of interest, and low self-efficacy and ultimately impede their successful course completion and their chance of continuing as an IT major. Our approach utilizes peer instruction [1] and instructional scaffolding [2] in order to create a supportive and engaged classroom for this diverse group of students where they want to be active, engaged and eventually successful in their first programming course as an IT major. This poster details our pedagogical approach along with example quiz and programming exercise artifacts, initial student performance and survey results during Spring 2017 (S17) deployment.

2 THE APPROACH

We utilized a variant of peer instruction where students took a graded in-class quiz, first individually, and then by pairing with another student. During S17, eight such quizzes (each with two back to back rounds) were deployed and each of them contained five multiple-choice questions that tested students' critical thinking and analytical skill based on the different computer programming related topics. On average, during their individual efforts, students scored 3.43 (Median 4:58, SD 3.30) out of 10, whereas their peer grade improved to 5.73 (Median 5.92, SD 3.18), which shows 23% improvement. It should be noted that, students were not allowed to view their individual score before they complete their peer effort. Another important pedagogical approach that was incorporated is the support for Instructional Scaffolding. In our context, scaffolding is embedded into the learning material, more specifically into the in-class programming exercises, where small programs related to the newly introduced topics were first demonstrated by the instructor while involving students in an interactive way. The demonstrations were immediately followed by a series of in-class programming exercises while progressing to larger and higher order problems. During these sessions, students are allowed to receive help from both the instructor and their peers, which in a sense promotes student learning while participating in teaching. The approach was relatively successful where the average score attained by the students are 77% (Median 90%) considering twelve such lab sessions. An end-of-class survey was conducted that showed student positive perception toward the friendly, inspiring and active classrooms. Although the intervention marginally improved D/F/W rates compared to previous offerings, there are still opportunities for improvements that may lead to the expected enhancement of the retention rate. The author expects to receive valuable feedbacks during the poster session that may enhance the quality of future intervention.

3 ACKNOWLEDGEMENTS

The work is supported by WSSU Office of Science Initiatives (OSI) Teaching Grant Program.

4 REFERENCES

1. L. Porter, C. Bailey-lee, B. Simon, Q. Cutts, D. Zingaro, "Experience report: A multi-classroom report on the value of peer instruction" In Proceedings of the 16th Annual Conference on Innovation and Technology in Computer Science Education, 2011.
2. D. Meyer and J. Turner. Using instructional discourse analysis to study the scaffolding of student self-regulation. Educ. Psychologist, 37(1):17–25, 2002.

Author Index

www.ingramcontent.com/pod-product-compliance
Lightning Source LLC
LaVergne TN
LVHW060140070326
832902LV00018B/2877